Information Multiplicity

Information Multiplicity

American
Fiction
in the
Age of
Media
Saturation

John Johnston

The Johns Hopkins
University Press

Baltimore
and London

© 1998 The Johns Hopkins University Press

All rights reserved. Published 1998
Printed in the United States of America
    on acid-free paper
07 06 05 04 03 02 01 00 99 98   5 4 3 2 1

The Johns Hopkins University Press
2715 North Charles Street
Baltimore, Maryland 21218-4319
The Johns Hopkins Press Ltd., London

Library of Congress Cataloging-in-Publication Data
    will be found at the end of this book.
A catalog record for this book is available
    from the British Library.

ISBN 0-8018-5704-X
ISBN 0-8018-5705-8 (pbk.)

To my son, Evan Bruce Johnston

Contents

■ ■

Acknowledgments

. . . .

T his book, concerned with a series of literary assemblages, is itself an assemblage, the result of many chains of connection and relayed effects. It thus owes many debts and signs of gratitude, to other writers and readers, institutional powers and bodies of discourse, but also to countless acts of kindness, generosity, and even drudgery that nourished or in some way enabled its writing.

Intellectually but also personally, Gilles Deleuze and Félix Guattari spurred me to think about American fiction in ways I would never have discovered on my own; their interest in my work, reconfirmed over a period of years and many visits to Paris, inspired me more than any other single source. Closer to home, several American literary critics and personal friends have also made inestimable differences. Without precursor studies like David Porush's *The Soft Machine: Cybernetic Fiction* and Tom LeClair's *The Art of Excess,* this book would no doubt look very different. Among the readers who generously offered detailed comments on parts of the manuscript in progress I would like to single out for special thanks Jeremy Gilbert-Rolfe, Alan Nadel, Heidi Nordberg, Patrick O'Donnell, and Gregory Rukavina. I would also like to thank Tom LeClair, Patrick O'Donnell, and N. Katherine Hayles for their continuing interest in and support of my work, and Paula Peatross Johnston for helping to make available the time I needed to write during the early stages of the book's development.

No one today can function without institutional support. The University Research Committee at Emory University made possible a one-semester release-time grant for which I am grateful. I would also like to thank my editors at the Johns Hopkins University Press, Douglas Armato and Julie McCarthy, as well as my copy editor, Irma Garlick. Earlier and shorter versions of Chapters 3, 4, and 6 appeared in the *Arizona Quarterly,* the *Review of Contemporary Fiction,* and *Modern Fiction Studies,* respectively, and I wish to thank them for permission to republish some of this material.

Finally, I would like to thank Heidi Nordberg, whose unwavering devotion during a difficult period enabled me to bring this project to fruition.

Information Multiplicity

I didn't need hands-on experience of whatever personal computing was like in 1981 to sense that we were, all of us, rushing headlong toward some unthinkable degree of interactivity, of connectivity, of the speed and breadth and depth of information.

■ William Gibson

■ ■ ■ ■ ■ ■ ■ ■ ■ ■ ■ ■

Introduction

With the birth of information theory and cybernetics in the late 1940s and early 1950s, a decisive step was taken toward the immense techno-scientific transformation of the world into coded bits of "information" and "machinic" assemblages. Following the military's development of new technologies, an entire communications industry, life sciences such as neurobiology and genetics, and a large number of corporations participated in the effort to translate all processes and exchanges into information which, when coded by automated mechanisms, would serve as the basis for a new lingua franca of control.[1] In both private and state-sponsored sectors of the economy, enormous funds of energy and capital were invested in research and development projects whose ultimate

1

unifying aim was to discover a common language, or code, in which all resistance to instrumental control would disappear and all heterogeneity would be reduced to new assemblages in which elements could be disassembled, reassembled, invested, and exchanged.[2] These elements assume the status of what is now called information, which is neither a language nor a medium.

From the outset, however, the definitions of *information* proposed by Claude Shannon and Norbert Wiener contained fruitful ambiguities and contradictions that later led theorists beyond these instrumentalist applications toward new visions of complexity, as in the study of self-organizing, or emergent, systems and chaos theory. Thus, though useful and certainly not to be ignored, the different critiques of instrumentalism, from Heidegger and Marcuse to Debord and Baudrillard, cannot render the full semantic richness of the concept of information or indicate the full range of consequences for human experience—perhaps even aspects of its impossibility—in the high-tech environment that information brings about. Even in the currency of ordinary language, the term *information* refers to multiple orders of events, from the often highly contestable "content" we glean from books, newspapers, films, television, and so on, to the nomological content of communications and exchanges in the natural world (nomological because these exchanges have an existence independent of any interpretive activity on our part).[3] Instead of ordering and giving unity to these different levels of events, the concept of information reveals the limits of traditional notions of order and unity.

Whether or not different orders of information envelop and transcend all human activities, what most distinguishes information at the human level is its viral power, its tendency to proliferate. In the nineteenth century, theorists of thermodynamics spoke of "unusable energy," energy that escaped from their imperfect machines. Today, information systems constantly produce apparently unusable information, which, instead of dissipating, often ramifies or mutates into forms that are stored elsewhere and may eventually prove useful at other sites or for other systems. This viral proliferation of information always brings about uncertainty, even making uncertainty itself a structural feature of the systems defining our world. Irradiated with information, modern social structures are thus said to "implode."[4] But information theory and cybernetics have also made possible new ways of thinking about basic concepts such as control, organization, machines, and life itself. Thus, while information has led to a new medium of control, it has also generated something that always exceeds control.[5]

I call this new state information multiplicity. Information multiplicities are profoundly corrosive of older cultural forms and identities, dissolving subjects and objects alike into systems, processes, and nodes in the circuits and flow of information exchange. But they also bring about new kinds of energy and even strange new forms of "artificial life."[6] Indeed, the information rush enveloping contemporary culture can be likened to a sudden onset of "meme" infestation, taking *meme* as what Richard Dawkins calls a "new kind of replicator"—of cultural ideas, practices, catch phrases, and tunes.[7] Dawkins's meme is simply the smallest identifiable cultural unit that can be replicated and reliably transmitted. Depending on the context, memes either thrive or perish, mutate or are parasitized by other memes. But as Daniel Dennett points out in *Consciousness Explained,* the "human mind is itself an artifact created when memes restructure a human brain in order to make it a better habitat for memes."[8] Contemporary culture—or more specifically, what is called postmodern techno- or cyberculture—is a restructuring process that can be similarly described: as an artifactual space created when information restructures modern or traditional culture in order to make it a better habitat for information.

The viral power of information and consequently this new state of information multiplicity are the informing principles of and central interest in a series of American novels published between 1973 and 1991. Taking information and the new technological communications assemblages as their primary concern, these novels of information multiplicity, as I call them, engage us with various kinds of multiplicity, both by registering the world as a multiplicity and by articulating new multiplicities through novel orderings and narrativizations of heterogeneous kinds of information. In so doing, they demonstrate the necessity of discovering alternatives to mimetic and expressive models in a culture of noise and entropic dissemination, in which information constantly proliferates and representations insidiously replicate and in which human agency finds itself enmeshed in viral, bureaucratic forms and transhuman networks.

The most exemplary narrative prose fictions in this regard are those by Thomas Pynchon, Joseph McElroy, William Gaddis, Don DeLillo, and William Gibson. In *Gravity's Rainbow* (Pynchon), *Lookout Cartridge* (McElroy), and *JR* (Gaddis), the delirious proliferation of characters, events, and bodies of knowledge is barely contained by an overarching narrative. As expansive literary "assemblages" (a term I take from Gilles Deleuze and Félix Guattari), these information multiplicities accommodate mixed regimes of signs and discourses, wide diversity in tone and subject matter, and rapid shifts of reference. In contrast, DeLillo's ten novels operate on the margins of various popular subgenres (science fiction, the detective novel, the espionage thriller); they evince a similar interest in multiplicity and heterogeneity but as diffracted throughout an entire fictional *oeuvre*. For Gibson, writing in relation to a global communications network, the space of communications itself becomes the site of a new kind of multiplicity.

This book will show how each of these writers engages with a different aspect of the information technologies and the corresponding new contents of our environment, above all mapping the new diagrammatic forms of subjectivity which emerge there: Pynchon investigates its historical foundations in the "rocket-state" that rises up in the aftermath of World War II; McElroy, the limits of the individual's search for meaning within "collaborative networks" by means of a ruminating "machinic consciousness"; Gaddis, the potential for chaos and entropy amid capitalism's cascading paper empires; and DeLillo and Gibson, the new behaviors and affective responses that this environment provokes as information becomes completely assimilated in a vast network of media assemblages. In each case, the world is presented as a multiplicity, glimpsed through the fictional multiplicity each writer invents. In each case, this multiplicity is effectuated by a different kind of "writing machine" or strategy of "writing with" contemporary information technologies. The extent to which these writing strategies are realized in relation to either modernist technical media (film, sound recording, typewriter) or more contemporary media (television and computer) points to an evolution within this literary form and a historically significant shift in emphasis.

Whereas *Gravity's Rainbow, Lookout Cartridge,* and *JR* assume the separation (and separability) of media even while straining to go beyond their limits, DeLillo's novels as well as Pynchon's *Vineland* explicitly register a shift in the conditions of mediality, from a condition of separable media to one of partially connected media systems.[9] This change in mediality is registered by a somewhat different kind of novel, one I call the novel of media assemblages. Whereas the novel of information multiplicity defines and even constitutes an always excessive and polysemic information field in which the uncertainty and ambiguity of information are both problem and solution, truth and method, the novel of media assemblages evolves from the former when information becomes fully quantified and digitalized (or is assumed to be so) and no longer carries its former viral and semantic potential. Instead of causing information to proliferate, the novel of media assemblages takes for granted a new level of information control, evident in the digitalization of media and the totalizing effects of electronic communications more generally. Instead of the separability of media, we now find a generalized "culture medium," as Don DeLillo refers to it.[10] Indeed, DeLillo's novels function as offshoots of a new mass-media assemblage, the reproduced effects of which are reconfigured in *Libra* in a new understanding of the "event." Also concerned with new kinds of events, Pynchon's *Vineland* and William Gibson's *Neuromancer* deal more explicitly with the machinery of this new media assemblage, the former engaging with the consequences of a partially connected media system and the latter with machinic intelligence, or AI, in a (not too) futuristic fully integrated communications system.

In different ways, these novels extend to new languages and levels of expression the forms of subjectivity produced by new regimes of information production, storage, and communication. In one sense, these information multiplicities and the writing machines by which they are engendered can be viewed as contemporary instantiations of what Michel Carrouges called "bachelor machines," insofar as they are all assemblages produced by male authors "hooking up" with different aspects of contemporary technology.[11] In fact, while there have been a number of distinguished women authors of science fiction (such as Octavia Butler, Ursula LeGuin, and Joanna Russ), until very recently fiction directly concerned with technology has been an almost exclusively male endeavor. Pat Cadigan's cyberpunk novel *Synners* proves to be both the exception to the rule and the herald of a new feminist sensibility challenged by these information assemblages. By engaging with music and video in the spaces redefined by the claims of the desiring body as it encounters virtual reality and a new communications assemblage, *Synners* gives a powerful inflection to the novel of media assemblages. It stands, therefore, as the appropriate end point for the trajectory sketched in this study.

That trajectory begins with William Burroughs's machinic alternative to writing conceived as representation or expression. As we shall see in the first chapter, by substituting a controller-controlled problematic for notions of authorial agency or romantic creativity, Burroughs was able to engage with the issue of language and image as viral forms at the level of writing itself. Novelists of information multiplicity and media assemblages do something similar with information. As one consequence, forms of subjectivity as usually understood are displaced and redistributed throughout the entire machinic activity that writing and reading these novels entails. While not exactly ignoring conventional forms of subjectivity, these writers are most directly and acutely concerned with the awesome power of contemporary technology and social organization to elicit, or call up, and reproduce new forms of individuation in the zones of intensity produced by "missing" information or its excess. More specifically, they are concerned with what may be called the conditions of a contemporary psychic apparatus and with problems stemming from the textualization of memory and perception. Indeed, that these novels *are* multiplicities and articulate information assemblages means that they are necessarily engaged in something other than the nuanced and realistic representation of human beings. In *Gravity's Rainbow*, for instance, Pynchon traces the construction of the paranoid/schizoid (or nomadic) subject produced by communications systems and modern bureaucracy, whose only meaningful choice is disappearance or accommodation. DeLillo pushes the construction of the paranoid subject in other directions, including both suicide and "de-multiplication." In *White Noise* and *Vineland,* however, these authors tentatively explore possibilities that fractalization by the new media may bring about.

Whereas the paranoid subject assumes a position outside socially certified channels of knowledge, the subjects of both McElroy's and Gaddis's novels are themselves nodes of connection within multiple de-centered networks and system relays. But where McElroy's subject attempts to overcome paranoia through sheer force of subjectivity, with delirium being the clear risk, Gaddis's subject exhibits a new subjectivity of force, specifically the force that capitalism impells along communication lines; it is thus a subjectivity of deterritorialization and verbal flight in which delirium becomes inevitable. With the advent of cyberpunk fiction, however, these diagrammatic forms of subjectivity are reconfigured as the paranoid/schizoid opposition gives way to a continuum extending from what we can call the "exorbital self" to "hive mind." [12] This reconfiguration becomes clearly visible in *Neuromancer* and *Synners*.

In the eyes of many readers, the energies and themes represented by the novels of information multiplicity may appear to have found a new focus in cyberpunk fiction, particularly as it is epitomized in novels by William Gibson, Pat Cadigan, Bruce Sterling, Rudy Rucker, and Greg Bear, and more recently taken to a new complexity by Neal Stephenson in *Snowcrash* and *The Diamond Age.* [13] Whatever the value and interest of cyberpunk fiction, however, it is clearly not a fiction of information multiplicity; in its attempts to deal with a "postcontemporary" high-tech milieu, it all too often returns to rather conventional narrative orderings. At the same time, novels such as *Neuromancer* and *Synners* augur a different kind of communications assemblage looming on the technological horizon, one that not only assumes a totalized information economy but one in which familiar media—and the differences that separate media make—disappear or assume completely new forms. Consequently, for these novels cyberspace, virtual reality, and artificial intelligence establish the new terms of experience. Appropriately, therefore, this study finds its *terminus ad quem* in an analysis of how cyberpunk fiction represents what this new communications assemblage is likely to bring about.

Thomas Pynchon's *Crying of Lot 49,* published in 1966, is the first novel about information in the contemporary sense of the word. For the first time in American fiction, the idea of information is not only treated thematically but is also deployed to generate a fictional story rich in multivalent meanings, the historical implications of which Pynchon investigates more fully in his next novel, *Gravity's Rainbow.* While the latter's characters search for information in the aftermath of World War II, the text makes it clear to what extent "war" takes place no longer between people or nation states but between different media, communications technologies, and data flows. *Lookout Cartridge* is similarly concerned with information, but always as it proliferates and ramifies within what McElroy calls "an impinging information field." Within this field, whether defined historically, as in Pynchon, or phenomenologically, as in McElroy, information acquires multiple senses, for it is never certain a priori what may or may not be significant for a ruminating consciousness constantly re-viewing its first registrations. In both novels, the reader is presented with more information than he or she can possibly absorb and make sense of and, of necessity, must adopt something like Salvador Dali's "paranoid-critical method" as a reading strategy.[14] By putting not only the status and value but the entire semantic range of the concept of information into play, these novels of information multiplicity offer a complex response to the condition referred to colloquially in the 1970s as information overload. Indeed, in *JR,* information becomes synonymous with chaos, as the excessive flows of information and capital become indistinguishable in an overflowing of cybernetic circuits.

In the 1980s, information increasingly entered the discourse at both colloquial and critical levels, but with a more restricted meaning. At the colloquial level, its usage became associated with and therefore indexed a suddenly increased public awareness of a new high-tech environment, evidenced directly by the rising number of personal computers, fax machines, and global telecommunications networks to which (some of) the public gained access. For the first time in history, more or less invisible expert systems (i.e., intelligent machines) could read and write texts. By the end of the decade, *smart bombs* and *virtual reality* had become household expressions. Not surprisingly, the characters in DeLillo's *White Noise,* Pynchon's *Vineland,* and Gibson's and Cadigan's cyberpunk fiction reflect this new sophistication in technological awareness. Assuming a totalized information economy, "waves and radiation, signals going back and forth," as a character in DeLillo's *White Noise* succinctly puts it, their primary concern is how to live within it.

That information and the multiple ways it is coded have come to define and shape an entire culture may well turn out to be what distinguishes our end of the twentieth century from its prehistory. The same forces ushering in this historical transformation have also set the terms for the emergence of the novel of information multiplicity and its successor, the novel of media assemblages, which both resist this transformation and attempt to delineate its most profound consequences. If one feature of complex and ambitious art is that it often wants to dream both its past and its future, and the two simultaneously, these two types of contemporary fiction do something like this by looking back to a world in which there are media and languages and forward to one in which there is only information. Their value, therefore, would seem to lie in the fullness with which they bring to awareness and propagate the complexity of this cultural moment. They do this, as I try to show, by transforming the novel into various "writing-down systems" that articulate and render visible a postmodern discourse network defined first by the formulations of information theory and cybernetics, and only secondarily by textuality and simulacra.[15] At the same time, inasmuch as they remain novels, they model and reflect new forms of postmodern subjectivity. They do this most fully by serving as exemplary instantiations of a contemporary psychic apparatus, registering material and semiotic processes that are not yet entirely assimilable but which continue to shape—or to make impossible—what we still call human experience.

part I

Writing (in) the Machinic Universe

Writing has a double function: to translate everything into assemblages and to dismantle the assemblages. The two are the same thing.

- Gilles Deleuze and
  Félix Guattari

■ 1

The Literary Assemblage

Writing Machines and Late Capitalism

I. As a literary form or, more precisely, a literary assemblage, the novel of information multiplicity works both within and against the whole apparatus of information proliferation and control which, since the 1970s, has come to typify "late-capitalist" American culture.[1] Increasingly defined by sophisticated information technologies and communication networks and by a vast expansion of entertainment and service industries, this culture turns out to be only marginally more receptive to literary excess and complexity than was American or European culture to high modernist writers such as Proust, Joyce, Musil, and Dos Passos, whose own colossal prose fictions anticipate many of the features of the novel of information multiplicity.

As we might expect, the features that set off the contemporary novel of information multiplicity from its illustrious precursors reflect certain changes in the culture at large, above all those brought about by new extensions of the mass media (especially television) and the immense growth and consolidation of new information technologies. These technologies, which include all those of whatever power source which "record, transmit, process and distribute information," were secondary industries before World War II.[2] The war, however, constituted a watershed event both in the development of new technologies and in the way research and development were carried out, as government-sponsored research became seamlessly integrated into and extended by new corporate investments in electronics, computing, and telecommunications.[3]

The novel of information multiplicity emerges precisely in the information environment created by these technologies and their industrialization. Culturally, it is a context in which realism has devolved to a problematically fluid status, at once highly conventionalized and multiply diverse, as a result of the culture's saturation with information and the corrosive effects of various competing representations in the mass media. More specifically, in a culture in which events are created or usurped in advance by their mass-media simulations, contemporary writers can no longer rely upon strategies defined by a stable opposition between the fictional and the real.[4] Furthermore, the wholly probabilistic (as opposed to veridical) character of both information and mass-media simulations renders the reality of social structures highly uncertain and the experience of the individual consciousness not only transient and arbitrary but also fragmentary and incomplete. With both objective and subjective structures no longer providing stable boundaries, writers had to find new ways to make their writing connect with what is most innovative and vital in contemporary life.

Novelists of information multiplicity do this by making the uncertainty of information itself the most important issue. By both "writing with" and in relation to new information technologies, these novelists inaugurate a writing practice fully cognizant of their own machinic relationship to these technologies and the fictions they produce within a larger information field. As a consequence, the novel of information multiplicity cannot be adequately accounted for in the terms provided by either expressive or representational models. While exhibiting many of the generic features and affiliations often attributed to the modernist encyclopedic novel, the prose fiction anatomy, the satire-collage, and the novel of delirium, the novel of information multiplicity differs distinctively from these earlier literary forms in its modes of articulation and, less obviously, in the status of its fictional discourse.[5] As we shall see, it is best described as a fictional assemblage produced by a writing machine.

This change in the mode and status of novelistic discourse—or, more simply, in the terms in which the novel of information multiplicity is elaborated and achieves coherence—responds to the new cultural and technological context in two interrelated ways: first, through writing strategies that not only register information in all its contradictory semantic aspects but reenact the logic of its proliferation; and second, through a fundamental interest in how that information is received, recorded, and disseminated in relation to new information technologies, on the one hand, and new subjects, on the other. Whereas the modernist novel arises in a context defined by the appearance of new recording and storage media (film, phonograph, typewriter), the novels under study here register the effects of these media more directly, even as their own context is being transformed by the mass media, global telecommunications networks, and computer technologies.[6] This change in the conditions of mediality, that is, from separate media to partially connected media systems, is reflected in a shift from the novelistic depiction of the movements of a complex consciousness to an investigation of the interactions among scriptive systems, various media (both analogue and digital), and information technologies.[7] In this shift, information and mediality acquire a new and central importance.

In accord with these shifts in focus and writing strategy, the novel of information multiplicity assumes a set of functions somewhat different from those of the modernist novel. In modern literary *forms,* dramas of a self-reflective consciousness are enacted and brought to fruition in language as a newly autonomized medium; in the novel of information multiplicity, however, information proliferates in excess of consciousness, and attention shifts to a new *space* of networks and connections in which uncertainties are structural rather than dramatic. Within this new discursive or informational *space,* the novel of information multiplicity instantiates an *Aufschreibesystem* [writing-down system], thereby providing a site where the culture's capabilities for inscribing, storing, retrieving, and transmitting information become a possible object of critical scrutiny.[8] In these terms, the novel of information multiplicity can be said to inquire into the nature and limits of the culture's instruments of data processing, that is, into what kinds of information are produced, how this information is addressed and stored, through what circuits it is routed, and what effects it has on the subjects it also produces.

A peculiarity of information is that it always leads to more information; it is by nature viral and can never be isolated from a mechanism of proliferation. Only a literary form that is machinic, therefore, and which takes the form of an assemblage, can fully register how various information systems, including the mass media, function as part of a larger apparatus of information production and control, while at the same time participating in processes that always exceed them. It is this aspect of information that makes it necessary to consider the novel of information multiplicity as an assemblage produced by a writing machine. As we shall see, it took several stages for such a literary assemblage to be fully realized. In this chapter, I focus on the conditions of its emergence, as reflected in William Burroughs's fiction. In chapter 2, I shall consider the assemblage as a writing-down system that registers not only material and semiotic flows but also the effects of media on the perceptual consciousness and memory of a human subject; at that point, the assemblage can be said to function as—or model the conditions for—a contemporary version of what Freud called the "psychic apparatus."

II. But what exactly is an assemblage? In *A Thousand Plateaus,* Gilles Deleuze and Félix Guattari not only propose a theory of assemblages but make their book a rhizomatic assemblage of theoretical writing(s).[9] For them an assemblage *[agencement]* is precisely a multiplicity made up of heterogeneous terms and functions that work together in a symbiosis, or sympathy. In contrast to a structure, which defines relations among homogeneous terms and functions, an assemblage is composed of relations, liaisons, and affiliations among and across an array of elements and processes that are completely different in kind. An assemblage, therefore, constitutes not a structural unity or totality but only a functional consistency or "jelling together" of diverse parts and processes. In short, it is nothing more than a functional arrangement of material and semiotic flows, and it has no other meaning than that "it works."

In Deleuze and Guattari's theory, the assemblage encompasses and conjoins two realms: the machinic assemblage of desire and the collective assemblage of enunciation. In *Dialogues* (coauthored with Claire Parnet), Deleuze concisely describes their component elements: "there are *states of things,* states of bodies (bodies interpenetrate, mix together, transmit affects to one another); but also *statements,* regimes of utterances where signs are organized in a new way, new formulations appear, a new style for new gestures."[10] To illustrate, Deleuze considers the feudal assemblage composed of man-horse-stirrup, on the one hand, and declarations of love and oaths of allegiance, on the other. What is essential is that the two sides of the assemblage constitute a reciprocally determinant arrangement of bodies and words.

For Deleuze and Guattari, then, writing always functions as part of a larger assemblage; it is not expressive but "rhizomatic," or, as Deleuze puts it, "one flow among others; it enjoys no special privilege and enters into relationships of current and countercurrent, of back-wash with other flows—the flows of shit, sperm, speech, action, eroticism, money, politics, etc."[11] But if Deleuze says that writing is only "one flow among others," it is precisely to stress that it occurs in a necessary relation with something exterior to it. In other words, writing is always a writing with: it happens as part of a conjunction and circulation of effects, specifically in relation to a machinic assemblage or particular configuration of bodies making or enabling desire to flow. Thus words flow in relation to (and as part of) the circulation of desire in the social field, and they always imply not just a personal desire to write but a "collective assemblage of enunciation." In this sense, writing can also be said to map the flows of desire, but desire conceived as a positive flow (or the production of flows) structuring the social field rather than a personalized structure of lack, as psychoanalysis postulates. Writing thus articulates the conjunction between historically new forms of expression (not only words but different semiotic regimes) and new forms of content (or interactions among bodies and other corporal forms); it makes visible new lines of connection.

Although not especially concerned with the novel as a literary form, the work of Deleuze and Guattari nonetheless suggests how it can be conceived as a multiplicity. In one sense, every novel articulates a potential multiplicity, since every novel concatenates diverse facts (real or imagined) drawn from different orders of events. However, the conventions of representation (especially genre, authorship, literary discourse or style) demand that certain kinds of unities and hierarchies that prevent the novel from *becoming* a multiplicity be respected. Underlying these restrictions and the hierarchy they imply is a dualistic logic that structures and codes the discursive field in such a way as to prevent the formation of an actual multiplicity. Thus, according to the assumptions underlying the production and reception of literature, every literary work is considered to be the creation of an author, a creation that somehow represents or reflects some aspect of the world (this yields the first dichotomy: world/representation).[12] At the same time, it is assumed that the author created his or her work by copying or modifying certain models available within an artistic tradition (this yields another dichotomy: model/copy). Modifications imposed on these models are usually explained by appeals to the author's worldview or to his or her desire to attain greater degrees of originality, fullness, realism, expressivity, and so on. Finally, since the author's representation neither repeats exactly a particular model nor objectively represents his or her world, the created representation is considered to be an expression of his or her subjectivity (hence a summary dichotomy: objective world/subjective representation). Taken together, these reciprocally supporting dualities constitute a tripartite structure comprised of world, representation, and subjectivity.

When a novel attains the status of a multiplicity (as in the case of an information assemblage), these dualities are short-circuited or exceeded such that the novel no longer makes sense and its effects are no longer accountable in the terms of this tripartite division. Negatively defined, a novel can thus be said to become a multiplicity when its fundamental coherence derives from neither a subjective nor an objective unity; that is, when it cannot be adequately described as the expression of an authorial subject or the totalizing representation of an objective reality. For the novel-as-multiplicity, attributions of unity, whether at the level of authorial intention or expression or at the level of subject matter or reference, cannot do justice to the novel's multiple effects but only reduce its multidimensional working to the parameters of a mimetic or expressive model.

Mikhail Bakhtin was probably the first literary theoretician to grasp this multidimensional potentiality latent within the novel as a literary form. Unlike classical literary genres, Bakhtin argued, the novel is composed of ever new combinations of different languages and speech forms in a state of becoming; its form, therefore, is never "finalizable." Bakhtin comes closest to a genuine theory of the novel-as-multiplicity, however, only with his notion of the polyphonic novel, in which language and speech [slovo] are fully "dialogized" and there is no longer any subordination of a represented or implied consciousness or point of view to an authorial or ideological hierarchy.[13] In such a novel, all languages, speech acts, and points of view coexist in immanent dialogue. Yet, in his reliance upon notions of speech, ideology, and above all consciousness, Bakhtin remains a modernist, his theory circumscribed within historical and theoretical limits often exceeded by contemporary novels.

A more promising route to understanding how the contemporary novel-as-multiplicity achieves its own consistency can be extrapolated from what Deleuze and Guattari call "the writing machine," or the assemblage that certain writers have invented in order to make a multiplicity "outside" pass into writing. In this translation/instantiation of a multiplicity, the writing effectuates a *becoming* through a proliferation of information, a conjugation, chain reaction, and relaying of connections and effects that often produce delirium and always exceed the terms of any dichotomizing, bipolar logic. In Deleuzian terms, the novel begins to work not only within an assemblage but also as an assemblage, one that reveals how lines of force are coded and connected in structures of language, even as the latter are sometimes decoded—dismantled or abstracted (deterritorialized) into "asignifying particles"—in the very process of their inscription.

Apart from certain anticipations such as Deleuze's book on Proust's "anti-logos literary machine," the only extended analysis of the novel in these terms is to be found in Deleuze and Guattari's *Kafka: Towards a Minor Literature,* where they analyze Kafka's fiction as a mapping of various assemblages or multiplicities.[14] Specifically, they show how two distinguishable assemblages are conjoined and articulated as complementary sides of the same assemblage in *Amerika, The Trial,* and *The Castle.* On one side there are various "machinic arrangements" in which the characters function as parts of a large social machine: the boat-machine, the hotel-machine, the circus-machine, the trial-machine, and the castle-machine. These assemblages, composed of various heterogeneous parts, human and nonhuman, produce a specific distribution of desire: "not because desire is desire of the machine but because desire never stops making a machine in the machine and creates a new gear alongside the preceding gear indefinitely" (82). In other words, desire itself is machinic, produced by and productive of connections among bodies. Hence Deleuze and Guattari call these connections "machinic arrangements of desire." On the other side, operating in conjunction with the latter, are verbal or language machines, forms of speech and expression that together compose "a collective assemblage of enunciation." In Kafka's writing, this assemblage is recognized by the production of an almost juridical formalization of statements: questions and answers, objections, pleas, reasons for a judgment, presentation of conclusions, verdicts, and so on. Indeed, *The Trial* is a veritable anatomy of such statements. These two distinguishable assemblages—one composed of bodies, the other of statements—are brought into contact and communicate through what Deleuze and Guattari call the "K-function," the letter suggesting that K is not so much a character as a collective subject through which the individual in his solitude responds to "diabolic powers knocking at the door," as

Kafka himself put it in a letter to Max Brod. It is through the K-function that Kafka brings together and articulates machines and bodies, statements and desires as parts of the same functional assemblage.

The K-function thus also designates Kafka the author's relation to the specific writing machine that he both invents and forms part of. Deleuze and Guattari trace the formative stages of this writing machine as it develops from Kafka's letters to the animal stories to the novels. They show how it functions as the offshoot of Kafka's employment in an insurance company, which constitutes a vast bureaucratic machine not only because of its adjacent offices and corridors, its bosses and secretaries, its administrative, political, and erotic distributions, but also because of the various technical devices and machines both utilized there and with which Kafka had to contend in his various capacities as an insurance adjuster. The specific object of Kafka's writing machine is not simply to represent this machine or to give its secret powers symbolic expression but to translate it into assemblages that map the movements of desire.

At the same time, Kafka's fiction also shows how desire always exceeds its coded channelings, its movements sometimes forming what Deleuze and Guattari call "lines of flight" which extend from cracks and fissures in the social structure and tend to dismantle the assemblages on which the latter depends. This decoding, or deterritorialization, works in strictly literary terms as well. As part of a larger collective assemblage of enunciation embedded within the German Jewish Prague community circa 1910 and articulating many of its cultural and geopolitical anomalies, Kafka's writing constitutes what Deleuze and Guattari call a "minority literature." Relying on neither the literary codes of the national German literary tradition nor the Prague school of Gustav Meyrink, Max Brod, and others, Kafka's writing pushes further along lines of deterritorialization already at work within the culturally and linguistically impoverished German language of this milieu. Drawn toward the limits of representation in an "asignifying intensive use of language," Kafka breaks not simply with competing styles but with the very category of style conceived as a unique extension or expression of self. The result is a diagrammatic writing that traces new circuits of desire produced by and within twentieth-century bureaucratic organizations.

The contemporary American novel of information multiplicity also emerges through a set of strategies for writing with the historical and technological assemblages contemporary with it. Compared with Kafka's novels, however, those of Pynchon, McElroy, Gaddis, DeLillo, Gibson, and

Cadigan reflect more directly the presence of current technologies of communication and mass-media reproduction, both through the awareness and behavior of the characters and through fictional appropriations of the scientific concepts and procedures that underlie these technologies. Thus, whereas Kafka's writing machine involves a particular setup between typewriter and bureaucracy, two essential components of the agency, or *agencement,* through which the night thoughts of a solitary individual are routed, American writing machines function within a configuration that includes a much wider range of storage and transmission media, not only typewriter, film, and sound recording but also television, computer, and the global communications aggregate usually referred to as the Net or the Web. Necessarily, then, the writing machines that produce American fiction of information multiplicity are concerned not simply with other media but with their own mediality.

In American fiction, moreover, the shaping of the social and corporate imaginary appears as only the most visible side of the largely unconscious (and insomniac) working of a technological rationality whose operational imperative is a society of control.[15] As a consequence, the importance of specific, separable bureaucracies as primary sites for the production and distribution of desire and its structuring of the social field is greatly reduced. Contemporary desire, in the new society of control, no longer passes from one enclosed space to another along partitions and corridors in an arrangement whose architectural geometry repeats the same analogical structure of surveillance. It no longer moves within a structure—whether the enclosure be one of office, factory, prison, school, or hospital—defined by the instrumentalities that constitute a disciplinary regime.[16] Instead, desire is dispersed throughout a corporate space of continuous modulation and variation without interruption and within which access to information (even simple cash machines) requires the insertion of special codes into global communications networks that are nowhere fully materialized.[17]

In these terms, the fiction of William Burroughs assumes an essential importance. Burroughs was perhaps the first writer—certainly the first American writer—to respond to this new society of control, as he himself called it. Indeed, for Burroughs, writing in the late 1950s and early 1960s meant the exploration of how words and images function in an increasingly technological environment of control. Hence his writing techniques, particularly his "cut-up-fold-in" method of textual manipulation and experimentation with diary-collage, tape recordings, film scripts and film-texts, not to mention his collaboration on specific films, must be seen not as some species of avant-garde or mixed-media expressionism but as a sustained attempt to understand language as a medium of, and the mass media as a new apparatus for, the dissemination and control of information.[18]

From the outset, Burroughs thought of words and images in this new environment not as media carrying messages but as viral forms capable of replication. Understood as a virus, a word or image is significant not because it bears a meaning but because it can perpetuate itself by activating an inscribed code, a code that ultimately proscribes one form of being rather than another, one set of responses rather than another. In Burroughs's fiction, therefore, the word or image virus is an agent—a secret agent—operating as a nearly invisible force in a control network. In some instances, Burroughs ascribes historical specificity to this control, as when he speaks of the *Time-Life* "word and image banks" or the role of newspapers in creating fear and envy in the population; in others he speaks more cosmically or mythically of "human being" as the product of a language virus. Historically, Burroughs's merging of biology and communications technology in a theory of language and image as viral forms marks the first attempt to represent in prose fiction the new techno-scientific assemblage then looming on the horizon and of which the mass media was only the most visible part. But what once could be dismissed as a paranoid, drug-induced science fiction fantasy now resounds with prophetic precision.

Ostensibly concerned with drug addiction, Burroughs's *Naked Lunch* (1959) offers itself as a demonstration of how writing must not function as an instrument of control but somehow must provide a release from it. In Burroughs's own words, it must constitute a "How-to Book" that opens doors.[19] Such a book would operate as a counteragent to language as a control mechanism. *Naked Lunch* realizes this objective primarily through Burroughs's refusal to integrate the book's diverse parts into any kind of organic whole or to impose any unity of narrative or point of view onto the diverse writings that make up the published text. Beginning with a first-person narrative of flight from the police ("I can feel the heat closing in, feel them out there making their moves"), it soon fragments wildly into a carnivalesque medley of satiric and pornographic "routines" punctuated by more objectively toned passages, the latter often foregrounding the writing's self-referenced status as a "report." The fictional main body concludes with an extraordinary "Atrophied Preface," a fragmented and discontinuous sequence that often refers to the writing in and of *Naked Lunch*.

This textual heterogeneity is continued in the writing that frames "Naked Lunch": a section that includes excerpts from the obscenity trial provoked by the book's publication, as well as an introduction called "Deposition: A Testimony Concerning a Sickness" by Burroughs himself. Furthermore, an appendix adds a letter and essay (both by Burroughs) purportedly published in the *British Journal of Addiction*. These miscellaneous writings establish the book's documentary dimension, while also reinforcing the "factualist" attitude extolled in various of its fictional scenes—contra both the "liquefactionists" who want to dissolve all differences, and the "senders" who are control addicts. At the level of genre, the legal and scholarly apparatus links *Naked Lunch* to prose anatomy and encyclopedic fictional forms; but more immediately, they link it to institutions of control, both legal and medical.[20] Thus, by framing his own putative fiction explicitly in relation to institutional and discursive mechanisms of control, Burroughs insists all the more radically on the abrasive instability of his own text.

In the "Atrophied Preface," the narrator, who at times identifies himself as William Lee and at others as William Seward—both being written versions of the writing I/eye—proclaims his status as a mere recording instrument and his refusal to establish control over the text: "I am a recording instrument. . . . I do not presume to impose 'story' 'plot' 'continuity.' . . . In sofaras I succeed in *Direct* recording of certain areas of psychic process I may have limited function. . . . I am not an entertainer" (221). This passage is followed immediately by a statement of the narrator's sense of his own bodily dislocation:

> "Possession" they call it. . . . Sometimes an entity jumps in the body—outlines waver in yellow orange jelly—and hands move to disembowel the passing whore or strangle the nabor child in hope of alleviating a chronic housing shortage. As if I was usually there but subject to goof now and again. . . . *Wrong! I am never here.* . . . Never that is *fully* in possession, but somehow in a position to forestall ill-advised moves. . . . Patrolling is, in fact, my principle occupation. . . . No matter how tight Security, I am always somewhere *Outside* giving orders and *Inside* this straight jacket of jelly that gives and stretches but always reforms ahead of every movement, thought, impulse, stamped with the seal of alien inspection.   (221)

Both building on and subverting a series of schizoid oppositions (direct/not fully present, inside/outside, patrolling/security), the statements follow one another according to a logic of juxtaposition, truncation, and disruption—such is Burroughs's primary compositional method. But even while the writing claims to be a direct recording (*Naked Lunch* often refers to itself as a report), it is always entwined with and permeated by other forms of writing.

Similarly, the narrator's bodily possession by alien forces echoes the stream of examples in which humans are taken over by other forms or devolve into lower forms. In both instances, what is at stake is the menace of a textual and/or bodily parasitism and thus a loss of integrity and boundary definition.

At all levels of the writing, then, body and word are not only subject to material forces, particularly those that deform, but *are* material forces and would replicate according to a viral impulsion—such, indeed, is the logic of Burroughs's text—if not continually cut up or disrupted.[21] Furthermore, it is evident (particularly in the trilogy that follows *Naked Lunch*) that for Burroughs the conjunction body/text is to be parsed in multiple ways. The body is a certain kind of text, written by genetic and biologic codes, and the text is also formed of bodies (or words as viral bodies), as becomes explicit when the narrator states that "prefaces . . . atrophy and amputate like the little toe amputates in a West African disease" (224). In this double sense, *Naked Lunch* forms and de-forms as a body/text that permutates and atrophies; it thereby becomes a rhizomatic book "you can cut into . . . at any intersection" (224) and that "spill[s] off the page in all directions, kaleidoscope of vistas, medley of street tunes and street noises" (229).

In Burroughs's hands, moreover, the English language undergoes an extraordinary deterritorialization. Already deterritorialized in relation to Standard English, American idioms are syntactically clipped and fast, marked by frequent omission of any direct reference to the speaking subject and active but uninflected verb forms. Burroughs takes advantage of this tendency toward speed and concision within American speech and intensifies its effect through wide use of the underworld slang of drug addicts and "carny" types. He also relishes and makes ample use of linguistic and grammatical deformations that characterize the speech of non-native speakers, as when third-person singular verb endings are dropped or entire words mispronounced ("No glot . . . C'lom Fliday"). But the most obvious trait of Burroughs's language is the vivid stream of hallucinatory images, with their multiple appeals to the senses, particularly vision and smell. These verbal and linguistic strategies produce a highly deterritorialized linguistic "interzone" or language within a language in which Standard English undergoes a "becoming minor."[22]

An assemblage of parts with multiple connections but without any organic or hierarchical principle of order, a writing that theorizes its overt interest in words as units ordered in multiple ways like "an innaresting sex arrangement" (229), a schizophrenic or absolute deterritorialization not only of the signifier but of desire itself, *Naked Lunch* begins to sketch the essentials of a prototypical assemblage and machinic novel. In *The Ticket That Exploded* (1962), which, together with *The Soft Machine* (1961) and *Nova Express* (1964), forms a trilogy written immediately after *Naked Lunch,* Burroughs explicitly introduces the notion of a writing machine:

> A writing machine that shifts one half one text and half the other through a page frame on conveyor belts—(The proportion of half one text half the other is important corresponding as it does to the two halves of the human organism) Shakespeare, Rimbaud, etc. permutating through page frames in constantly changing juxtaposition the machine spits out books and plays and poems—The spectators are invited to feed into the machine any pages of their own text in fifty-fifty juxtaposition with any author of their choice any pages of their choice and provided with the result in a few minutes.[23]

Earlier passages indicate that this parodic version of Burroughs's own writing machine provides one effective way to break the "air line of words" by which a viral organism—"the Other Half"—attaches itself "to your nervous system" (49). As one means to effectuate "operation rewrite," the writing machine combats the social control network, itself "a vast control machine" (31) that functions by defining "the whole structure of reality" (31). Later in the trilogy, Burroughs will refer to this control machine as the "Reality Studio," thereby suggesting that what is accepted as modern reality is essentially a cinematic production.[24] Furthermore, the human body itself is included in this proliferation of machines. In fact, in the English edition of *The Soft Machine,* Burroughs attached an explanatory appendix on the human body as a "soft machine" (soft because prey to a host of parasites). Yet even though these machines are connected in various ways, their functional articulation remains only implicit.

It may be that Burroughs's negative conception of language as a viral agent of infection prevents—or makes undesirable—the explicit, systematic articulation of these three types of machines (body/text/control apparatus) in a fictional assemblage. What is certain is that throughout this period, Burroughs's writing remains unstable and never achieves fixed form, as the trilogy undergoes constant revision and rewriting.[25] Burroughs himself clearly understood these revisions as strategic. Like his experiments with direct sound recording and playback effects, what he calls "operation rewrite" in *The Ticket That Exploded* is deemed a necessity of textual production in a society of control.[26] For the most part, the trilogy is held together by Burroughs's fragmented but overarching "nova conspiracy" and cut-up-fold-in technique, which provide consistencies of both plot and method. But by continually submitting diverse material (some dating back to the writing of *Naked Lunch*) to the highly contingent compositional procedures of the cut-up method as well as to extensive revision even as the individual books were being (re)published, Burroughs produces a series of texts that effectively short circuit not only conventional literary unities but also the boundaries and unity of the book itself. The results are perhaps best described by what one commentator calls a "false trilogy": "The machine that exploded–the nova ticket–the soft express/the nova machine–the soft ticket–the express that exploded/etc.: we are dealing with a false trilogy, and the three books actually form a whole. Not a single book repeating itself, but rather a book that completes itself in the form of three versions, each envisaging a certain number of problems under a different angle."[27]

Although Burroughs himself has declared that "all my books are one book," it has been increasingly apparent since *Naked Lunch* that his writing inscribes a space of multiplicity. Irreducible to the expansive coherencies of an authorial self or even the looser harmonies of an episodic narrative, the writing is never identical with itself or governed by a preexistent reality to which it remains true or bound as a structure of references. In a certain sense, then, the cut-up method simply provides a formal principle for a recurrent feature more or less always active in Burroughs's writing: the impulse to disrupt every discursive and representational norm. Unfolding as a repeated disruption, truncation, or displacement of words, sentences, and scenes (or what he calls routines), Burroughs's prose fiction has the tonic effect of a powerful hallucination or vivid dream whose relation to reality is complex and multifaceted.

In his most recent trilogy, *Cities of the Red Night* (1981), *The Place of Dead Roads* (1983), and *The Western Lands* (1987), Burroughs relies on more conventional narrative orderings and maintains continuities of time, place, and character for considerably longer textual segments. Here the objective is not to disrupt but to contaminate representation. In fact, *Cities of the Red Night* is not only about a specific virus but is constituted of narratives that proceed from a state of viral infection. As always, Burroughs's specific purpose is to investigate possibilities of escape: from current cultural definitions of reality, human mortality, and the limits of human being. In this last trilogy, these attempts at escape are made explicit and given narrative form, even though the narrative lines constantly cross and mutate into one another. These narrative cut-ups or mutations produce a multiplicity of narrative relations and consequently a new state of viral immanence.

However, in *A Thousand Plateaus,* Deleuze and Guattari suggest that Burroughs's cut-up method fails to produce a genuine rhizomatic writing or multiplicity because the textual folding occurs only in one dimension, thus implying "a supplementary dimension to that of the texts under consideration" (6). In other words, it allows a "spiritual unity" to be reimposed on another level. Although in the last trilogy viral effects undercut this supposed unity, perhaps it would be more accurate to say that Burroughs's writing is unable to treat viral forms in their full positivity and immanence. This would account for the evident fact that while anticipating the viral nature of information, Burroughs's writing machine does not mobilize any principle of information proliferation such as those found at work in the writing of Pynchon, McElroy, Gaddis, and DeLillo. While Burroughs's writing *is* rhizomatic because it refuses the unities of the book and works by cut-up and collage rather than by proliferation, it lacks any equivalent of the K-function, or means by which its various component machines are brought together in a functional or working unity. At the same time, by substituting a controller-controlled problematic for conventional notions of authorial agency, Burroughs engages directly with information control and the technologies of the mass media at the level of writing itself. In this way his writing does not simply anticipate the development of the machinic novel and of writing as assemblage but in fact makes it possible by opening an approach to writing—writing with technology rather than out of the self— that Pynchon, McElroy, Gaddis, DeLillo, and Gibson will soon follow.[28]

III. Of course, the mass media are only the most visible result of a larger transformation that increasingly impinges on almost every aspect of postindustrial, late-capitalist society. What is being transformed is both the form and material, and therefore the distribution and communication networks, of the exchange processes that define contemporary social and economic organizations. What is specifically new is the emergence of an electronic communications industry and the commodification of information as a new kind of raw material. More generally, this transformation forms an intrinsic part of a larger reconfiguration and expansion of contemporary capitalism into a fully global system of domination and exchange. To define more precisely the new form of domination this system imposes, and therefore the historical conditions in which the novel of information multiplicity emerges, we turn to Deleuze and Guattari's analysis of capitalism.

In *A Thousand Plateaus,* they distinguish between "machinic enslavement" and "social subjection" (456) in relation to three types of machine, which in turn correspond to three historically distinct epochs. Under conditions of machinic enslavement, human beings themselves are constituent parts of a larger machine, which operates under the direction and control of a higher unity, as in the case of archaic empires such as those Lewis Mumford describes as "mega-machines."[29]

Under conditions of social subjection, the human being is no longer a component of the machine but a worker or user: "he or she is subjected *to* the machine and no longer enslaved *by* it" (457). This second epoch is the era of technical machines properly speaking, which are definable extrinsically and which capitalism produces in a steady acceleration. In fact, as Deleuze and Guattari observe, it is through technological development that "the modern state . . . has substituted an increasingly powerful social subjection for machinic enslavement" (457). This substitution both relies upon and furthers capitalism's perverse capacity to produce an apparently liberated new subject through the wage regime:

> Capital acts as the point of subjectification that constitutes all human beings as subjects; but some, the "capitalists," are subjects of enunciation that form the private subjectivity of capital, while the others, the "proletarians," are subjects of the statement, subjected to the technical machines in which constant capital is effectuated. The wage regime can therefore take the subjection of human beings to an unprecedented point, and exhibit a singular cruelty, yet still be justified in its humanist cry: No, human beings are not machines, we don't treat them like machines, we certainly don't confuse variable capital and constant capital.   (457)

However, in what Deleuze and Guattari call a third epoch of "cybernetic and informational machines," human beings once again become constitutent parts of a machine while at the same time participating in a "generalized regime of subjection" (458). In this regime defined by the dominance of "humans-machines systems," the relation between human and machine is based on "internal, mutual communication, and no longer on usage or action" (458). From this change, other significant changes follow: the restructuring of business and factory by automation, changes in the work regime, the extension of capital in machinic forms that permeate all of society, and a new form of power operating neither by repression nor by ideology but by "processes of normalization, modulation, modeling and information that bear on language, perception, desire, movement, etc., and which proceed by way of micro-assemblages" (458). In sum, by including "both subjection and enslavement taken to extremes, as two simultaneous parts that constantly reinforce and nourish each other" (458), this cybernetic regime produces a subject in every way befitting the new society of control.

Deleuze and Guattari offer television as an example of this third type of machinic setup:

> One is subjected to TV insofar as one uses and consumes it, in the very particular situation of a subject of the statement that more or less mistakes itself for a subject of enunciation ("you, dear television viewers, who make television what it is . . ."); the technical machine is the medium between two subjects. But one is enslaved by TV as a human machine insofar as the television viewers are no longer consumers or users, nor even subjects who supposedly "make" it, but intrinsic component pieces, "input" and "output," feedback or recurrences that are no longer connected to the machine in such a way as to produce or use it. In machinic enslavement, there is nothing but transformations and exchanges of information, some of which are mechanical, others human.   (458)

Although they do not specify further how this doubly subjected/enslaved subject functions within the current cybernetic regime (that will become evident in the analyses of the novels in this study), Deleuze and Guattari do go beyond the terms of a strictly Marxist analysis of television, which can comprehend the contemporary viewer as both consumer and commodity but, because of a commitment to ideological critique, then runs into problems when it attempts to explain how a "critical subject" emerges through the alternative readings made possible by "overriding contradictions in contemporary social practice in general and television in particular." [30] On the one hand (according to one such Marxist analysis), the viewer as consumer is abstracted "into an object of exchange value that the network or station offers to a commercial sponsor" through the rating systems, which are used to determine network and local advertizing rates; on the other hand, the variety of programming practices allows the viewer multiple ideological positions, which nonetheless "express specific social, material, and class interests." However, the work of Deleuze and Guattari suggests that the contradiction(s) indicated by the splintering of the subject into multiple functions and positions cannot be understood from the point of view of the subject. What must be analyzed therefore are the processes in and through which the subject emerges. Simply stated, the new subject(s) produced by microassemblages in the current age of cybernetic and informational machines demands a different model for understanding capitalism itself.

Arising from a conjunction of two decoded flows, the abstract flow of labor (deterritorialized workers) and the abstract flows of capital (deterritorialized wealth or money), capitalism brings about a constant decoding and necessary recoding of the processes of exchange. Thus, Deleuze and Guattari say, capitalism forms "a general axiomatic of decoded flows" (453). In tracing the complexly evolving relationship between capitalism and the state (or state apparatus), they observe how the many subjectifications, conjunctions, and appropriations that capital necessarily requires for its operations do not prevent the decoded flows from continuing to flow, but instead they ceaselessly engender new flows that escape. Indeed, they argue that capitalism can function only because it is constantly exceeding itself and producing more flow than it can possibly reclaim and recode, or recontain through the imposition of new codes. Thus, whereas Marxism and critical theory view capitalism as a dynamic system regularly bringing about its own crisis through unresolvable internal contradictions, Deleuze and Guattari understand this dynamicism even more dynamically, so to speak, in terms of a conjugation of flows, thresholds of deterritorialization, and recodings at higher and more abstract levels.

If capitalism begins when the flow of unqualified wealth joins with the flow of unqualified labor, it is also this conjugation, always (re)implemented through an abstracting, deterritorializing axiomatic, that enables capitalism to produce excess and to expand rapidly beyond any control, including that of the state apparatus. In explaining how capitalism is (or constitutes itself through) an "axiomatic" of decoded flows, Deleuze and Guattari distinguish between the axiomatic itself and the processes of coding, decoding, and recoding: "the axiomatic deals directly with purely functional elements and relations whose nature is not specified, and which are immediately realized in highly varied domains simultaneously; codes, on the other hand, are relative to those domains and express specific relations between qualified elements that cannot be subsumed by a higher formal unity (overcoding) except by transcendence and in an indirect fashion. The *immanent axiomatic* finds in the domain it moves through so many models, termed *models of realization*" (454, Deleuze and Guattari's emphases).

Whereas social codes establish indirect, limited relationships between entities based on qualitative, noneconomic differences, the capitalist axiomatic establishes direct relationships between entities based on abstract qualities. This power of abstraction enables capitalism both to expand and speed up the exchange process and to displace or defer constantly any inherent limit that may impose itself. Thus not only does money breed more money, materialized labor power accumulate and transmute into ever new forms, and commodities proliferate and increase the demand for new commodities, but there is no end or limit to the process: what confronts capitalism from the outside is quickly converted into yet another model of realization. As its own ever shifting limit approaches, the capitalist machine simply and perpetually adds new axioms. The state is the example *par excellence*. Since the state is founded upon (and founds) other social finalities, it might be expected to establish limits to the movements of capital; instead, it becomes yet another "model of realization" for capitalism's expansion. Instead of disappearing or being canceled out by modern capital, the state is transformed by a worldwide axiomatic that everywhere exceeds it.

The terms and dynamic of Deleuze and Guattari's analysis of capitalism can be extended to an analysis of information, which functions in a manner similar to the capitalist axiomatic. The advantage of this model is that it allows the concept of information to retain its inherent complexity, in contrast to the more common understanding of *information* which remains bound by its association with engineering attempts to reduce noise in a communication circuit. Donna Haraway, in her well known "Manifesto for Cyborgs," incisively conveys this reductive and negative sense when she notes that "communications sciences and modern biologies are constructed by a similar move—the translation of the world into a problem of coding, a search for a common language in which all resistance to instrumental control disappears and all heterogeneity can be submitted to disassembly, reassembly, investment, and exchange."[31] For Haraway, the implications of this transformation in communications and biology are best summarized by C^3I, the military's symbol for its own operational complex of command-control-communication-intelligence:

In communications sciences, the translation of the world into a problem in coding can be illustrated by looking at cybernetic (feedback controlled) systems theories applied to telephone technology, computer design, weapons deployment, or data-base construction and maintenance. In each case, solution to the key questions rests on a theory of language and control; the key operation is determining the rates, directions, and probabilities of flow of a quantity called information. The world is subdivided by boundaries differentially permeable to information. Information is just that kind of quantifiable element (unit, basis of unity) which allows universal translation and so unhindered instrumental power (called effective communication). (206)

Harraway's understanding of *information* (and its inherent relation to coding) is useful and correct—as far as it goes. What she fails to consider, however, is the fundamental dynamism of information: that the process of abstraction/production/circulation of information within a capitalist economy necessarily and at the same time releases more information in a generalized decoding of flows. Indeed, from the outset of the "information age," *information* refers to two things at once: both the raw material of electronic and biological industrialization and what overflows and exceeds that process. This dynamism of "information"—its enlivening, viral power—partly accounts for the word's inherent ambiguity and multivalent status.

While it may be obvious that the novel of information multiplicity emerges precisely at the moment when information is commodified, what is less obvious are the multiple ways it registers the complexities of the dynamic unleashed by information. As we shall see, the writing machines that generate the novel of information multiplicity define and are defined by the double movement of the information axiomatic: a machinic inscription of information, but one that in turn yields a multiplicity since the inscription itself causes more information to proliferate and brings the various senses of information into play, and both at once. In short, the novel of information multiplicity is constantly staging the processes by which information is coded, decoded, and recoded, in flows that always exceed it.

. . . . 2

Information and Mediality

The Novel as Psychic Apparatus

I. In the late twentieth century, consciousness fractalizes across a new, technologically produced sensorium. Long banished from
the philosophical discourse of modernity, it reappears in a new conceptual universe, evident in
such books as Daniel Dennett's *Consciousness
Explained.* There Dennett argues against the
modern, Bergsonian stream of consciousness
and offers in its place a machinic theory of "multiple drafts":

> There is no single, definitive "stream of
> consciousness," because there is no central
> headquarters, no Cartesian Theater where "it
> all comes together" for the perusal of a Cen-
> tral Meaner. Instead of such a single stream
> (however wide), there are multiple channels in

31

which specialist circuits try, in parallel pandemoniums, to do their various things, creating Multiple Drafts as they go. Most of these fragmentary drafts of "narrative" play short-lived roles in the modulation of current activity but some get promoted to further functional roles, in swift succession, by the activity of a virtual machine in the brain. The seriality of this machine (its "von Neumannesque" character) is not a "hardwired" design feature, but rather the upshot of a succession of coalitions of these specialists.[1]

To develop this de-centered view of consciousness, Dennett draws extensively upon contemporary research in neuroscience and artificial intelligence, but what is most essential to his formulation is Alan Turing's work on Universal machines and von Neumann's work on the modern computer, and hence the revolution in thinking brought about by cybernetics and information theory.

From the outset, both information theory and cybernetics were formulated in machinic terms. Claude Shannon's *Mathematical Theory of Communication,* first published in 1948, defines *information* quantitatively as the probability of an encoded message in a communication channel and excludes all reference to meaning or signification; Norbert Wiener's *Cybernetics: or Control and Communication in the Animal and the Machine,* published in the same year, refers to *information* as "a name for the content of what is exchanged with the outer world" through feedback effects and autoregulatory mechanisms.[2] In neither formulation does consciousness play any essential role. However, as Raymond Ruyer points out in *La Cybernétique et l'origine de l'information* (1954), although information—unlike knowledge—does not necessarily imply a consciousness, it does require a framing activity not unlike the problems of cinematic framing.[3]

Surely one of the central (and largely untold) histories of our modernity is how the cinema—or the cinematic apparatus—so transformed the collective sensorium that *cinema* and *consciousness* could soon appear to be synonymous over a whole range of experiences. No doubt a crucial text for such a history of modern conceptions of consciousness will be Gilles Deleuze's two-volume study of cinema, which begins by showing how Bergson's theory of image and movement already contains a conception of the universe itself as cinematic.[4] In Bergsonian/Deleuzian terms, cinema renders *natural perception* a euphemism in the creation of a new machinic sensorium. Deleuze, less concerned with consciousness as a philosophical problem, simply identifies it with the camera lens. In a similar vein (although following

Jacques Lacan), Friedrich Kittler will refer to consciousness as the interiorized reflection of the current standards of technical media.[5]

If the early twentieth century saw that consciousness had to be redefined in relation to cinema, which already had transformed it, today that insight must be expanded to include all technical media. As we shall see, this reorientation underlies current conceptions of writing as well. Thus, whereas consciousness provides the site and medium of an immanent multiplicity in the great modern novels of Joyce, Faulkner, Dos Passos, Lowry, and others, in the postmodern novels of information multiplicity the site shifts to a de-centered information field conceivable only in relation to contemporary media and information technologies.[6] The latter's daily blitz, we tend to forget, is the inevitable outcome of a conceptual and scientific revolution sparked by information theory and cybernetics in the 1940s and early 1950s. Here we shall approach this field—and the revolution it entailed—only indirectly, since our central concern will be the changing cultural context in which the concept of information is embedded. Although available to modernist discourse, that concept could exceed its limited significance only with this revolution. At we shall see, what matters is not so much the scientific definition of information as the necessary relationship of information to a whole new culture based on technical media. By showing how this relationship is inscribed in the lives of its characters, the novel of information multiplicity models the dynamics of a contemporary psychic apparatus.

II. Modernist fiction generally can be said to have discovered and explored the multiplicities of human interaction in and through consciousness—or rather, its inscription and articulation in language. And for modern novelists such as Proust, Joyce, Woolf, and Faulkner, a heightened sense of consciousness-as-multiplicity is traceable to the influence—both direct and indirect—of Henri Bergson.[7] In *Essai sur les données immédiates de la conscience* (1897), Bergson describes consciousness as a continuum of interpenetrating states—a qualitative multiplicity, or *durée,* as he called it—which cannot be analyzed except as a continuous, uninterrupted flow or succession of heterogeneous elements such that there can be no repetition of former states.[8] This description provided a philosophical basis and the impetus to develop fictional techniques such as stream of consciousness and interior monologue, techniques that would enable modern novelists to register more directly than previous writing could the raw data of experience as it impinges directly upon the consciousness of a character, where it becomes part of a variegated flow, shifting and dropping in level according to the dynamics of sensation, memory, and psychological association. Bergson's definition of consciousness as a qualitative multiplicity in turn formed part of a larger effort, evident in the work of William James, Edmund Husserl, and Sigmund Freud, to cite only the most obvious major figures, to arrive at a new understanding or model of consciousness.

In relation to writers of the stream-of-consciousness novel, this model was both an enabling condition and their own achieved result, and it was quickly recognized as a monumental achievement of modernist culture. In the perspective of contemporary theory, however, the "complex consciousness" at the heart of these modern novels can be understood in somewhat different terms: less as an expression or representation of this model of consciousness-as-multiplicity than as a different kind of medium or discursive assemblage in and through which (or by means of which) new kinds of connections between things in the world could be articulated in distinctively innovative fictional modes and styles.[9] For the postmodern reader, in short, modern consciousness no longer conveys the idea of a necessarily prior state of which writing would be the expression but rather of a conglomerate of effects (sensation, memory, fugue states, etc.,) produced by new machinic assemblages specific to a modern urban/industrial milieu. Within these assemblages, discursive forms were extended, modified, and newly created, to be relayed and intensified in turn through the particular strategies of modern writing. Modern expressions of alienated subjectivity registered the effects of machinic transformations and cannot be understood apart from them.

To isolate these modern discursive assemblages according to both their semiotic functioning and historical determinations, however, requires a critical and historical distancing from the "aesthetic" tendency that dominates earlier accounts of literary modernism. The problem with this tendency, which is often congruent with the novelists' own self-understanding, is that it can only confirm those historical accounts that understand the processes of modernization exclusively as the fragmentation of experience, a fragmentation that makes reintegrations at the aesthetic or symbolic level possible, often through some overt appeal to myth. (It is of course now commonplace to observe that literature generally designated as postmodern eschews any nonironic reference to such mythic or symbolic structures.) What is missing from such historical accounts is a view of modernism as the emergence of forms of immanence and multiplicity which cannot be explained by appeals to the lost unities of earlier cultural forms.[10] The emergence of information multiplicities offers one instructive case in point.

▪ ▪ ▪ ▪ ▪

In a series of essays published between 1936 and 1939, Walter Benjamin attempts to correlate the fragmentation of experience and the evolution of certain literary forms.[11] These essays are governed precisely by the new importance in modern life Benjamin attributes to the dissemination of information. This dissemination, in Benjamin's view, leads to the decay of individual experience and gradually even comes to function as its substitute. While Benjamin's definitions of *experience* and *information* are obviously important, what will be of primary interest here is the thoroughly historical and historicizing sense that he gives to both these terms.

By *information* Benjamin usually means the content and mode of presentation characteristic of the newspapers. In fact, the basic nature of information for Benjamin is captured in a quip attributed to Hippolyte de Villemessant, the founder of *Le Figaro*: "To my readers, a fire in the Latin quarter is more important than a revolution in Madrid" (quoted by Benjamin, 88–89). Information thus supplies a handle for what is most immediate, promptly verifiable, and "understandable in itself" (89). The immediacy and verifiability of information distinguish it from news from afar, the credibility of which requires the support of some external authority. As a public proclamation of the actual, information needs no further grounding, since its intelligibility is given or assumed in its very presentation. Paradoxically, this very accessibility means that information cannot be assimilated and will never become part of the reader's experience, for the very presentational format of journalistic information—above all the lack of connection between the individual news items—"isolates what happens from the realm in which it could affect the experience of the reader," thereby prohibiting its assimilation (158). Benjamin encapsulates this paradox by noting that "every morning brings us the news of the globe, and yet we are poor in noteworthy stories" (89).

Benjamin conceives of experience in very narrow terms: "Where there is experience *[Erfahrung]* in the strict sense of the word, certain contents of the individual past combine with material of the collective past" (159). Storytelling, which, by its very form and contextual structure as oral narration, allows the listener to assimilate singular events within his or her socially acquired knowledge, thus enjoys an essential importance. In relation to experience, it assumes a function similar to occasions such as social rituals, ceremonies, and festivals, which also serve to integrate or harmonize the individual and the collective through social acts of commemoration. Though Benjamin does not say so directly, his account leaves little doubt that a traditional collective memory is a necessary condition of possibility for experience per se.

Now it is precisely this condition or this structure, which Benjamin generally associates with *Gedächtnis,* the German word for remembrance, that the fragmentation and anonymity of modern urban life have destroyed. As a result, Benjamin argues, the traditional structure of human experience has broken down. For above all, what characterizes modern urban experience, or rather, makes it impossible, is the "shock effect," at once a traumatic response to the disruptive rhythms of life in the modern city and a signal that the traditional structures formerly insuring the absorption of new experience are no longer operative. (Benjamin draws no sharp distinction between individual consciousness and the collective unconscious, since experience is primarily a matter of continuity and repetition.) With the breakdown of structures of commemoration *[Gedächtnis],* moreover, the nature of consciousness itself appears to change: as the site of a division and fundamental incompatibility, it now functions as a filter or screen. To develop this point, Benjamin draws on both Freud's model of the psychic apparatus and Proust's distinction between conscious and involuntary memory:

> The basic formula of [Freud's] hypothesis is that "becoming conscious and leaving behind a memory trace are processes incompatible with each other within one and the same system." Rather, memory fragments are "often most powerful and most enduring when the incident which left them behind was one that never entered consciousness." Put in Proustian terms, this means that only what has not been experienced explicitly and consciously, what has not happened to the subject as an experience, can become a component of *mémoire involontaire.* According to Freud, the attribution of "permanent traces as the basis of memory" to processes of stimulation is reserved for "other systems," which must be thought of as different from consciousness. In Freud's view, consciousness as such receives no memory traces whatever, but has another important function: protection against stimuli. (160–161)

Benjamin reads both Baudelaire's poetry and Proust's novel *A la recherche du temps perdu* in relation to a modern psychic apparatus that functions in these terms. Specifically, the modern psychic apparatus encompasses—yet is also constituted by—an unbridgeable rift between transient conscious perception on the one hand and the unconscious as site of a more durable and detailed inscription on the other. In both Baudelaire and Proust, it is via the unconscious that one attains access to a pure, authentic past, or the past in itself. Moreover, both invent a way of writing that registers the breakdown of the traditional structure of experience and at the same time provides something like a substitute for this loss.

More specifically, Baudelaire's poetic notion of *correspondances* provides access to the prehistoric data of *Gedächtnis* in a "crisis-proof form" (182), thereby making available an experience immune to the psychic and historical destruction physically communicated by the shock effects of daily life. In this sense, Baudelaire's poetry can be defined by the strategies it invents for giving the weight of an experience *[Erfahrung]* to something that had merely been lived through *[Erlebnis]*, specifically, the jostling, fragmentary, and above all fleeting life of urban Paris. For Proust, coming after Baudelaire and very much aware of the latter's achievement in these terms, *mémoire involontaire* will serve a function analogous to Baudelaire's *correspondances*, except that remembrance will operate primarily in relation to the individual's past life rather than to a collective past or cultural memory. However, given the increased importance of journalism and the newspapers in Proust's time, this is no less significant an achievement. As Benjamin puts it, a novel like *A la recherche du temps perdu* must be seen as an attempt to "produce experience synthetically . . . under today's conditions, for there is less and less hope that it will come into being naturally" (157).

Kafka's writing presents an even more exacerbated consequence of the incommensurability between the experience of tradition and the experience of the modern urban dweller. Indeed, Benjamin goes so far as to say that Kafka's fiction makes apparent the extent to which modern "reality can virtually no longer be experienced by an *individual*" (143). Such statements anticipate much of late-twentieth-century fiction and theory, which seek to reconceptualize (and thereby move beyond) the splitting and fragmentation of the modern subject rather than bemoan its "loss of experience." For Benjamin, Kafka's writing *à la limite* makes perplexingly evident what the literary modernism of Baudelaire, Proust, and the Surrealists already conveys in a more comprehensible form: the fundamental incompatibility between experience and information.

However, there is one vehicle of information that counters the shock effect by establishing it as a formal principle: film. In contrast to the "sacrosanct arts," which derive their relative autonomy from their origins in ritual, film makes distraction, rather than contemplation, an esthetic mode of reception. Film, moreover, intervenes into reality through the whole machinery of its production and reception. As the actor plays before the camera, rather than an audience, his or her reflected image becomes separable and transportable (i.e., deterritorialized). For the viewer, in turn, a whole new world of perceptions, heretofore imperceptible, opens up like the human body to the surgeon's scalpel, as Benjamin puts it in a striking image. With film, "the equipment-free aspect of reality [becomes] the height of artifice; the sight of immediate reality [becomes] an orchid in the land of technology" (235).

For Benjamin, in sum, the manner in which human sense perception is organized and the medium in which it is accomplished are no longer determined only by nature but also by history and technology. But if the incompatibility between experience and information is determined by the new media of newspapers and cinema and the shock effects of the modern city, so are Benjamin's formulations. Just as changes in historical conditions have brought about this incompatibility, so this incompatibility can no longer be assumed but must also be redefined as historically new technologies and modes of communication emerge (and Benjamin's analysis implicitly assumes this historicity). In short, the relationship between experience and information is a historically contingent one. Since the novels that will concern us here register the effects of what may well augur another historical transformation, let us begin to explore its terms by shifting the scene from Benjamin's Europe in the 1930s to Thomas Pynchon's California in the early 1960s.

III. The opening pages of *The Crying of Lot 49* assume a world interconnected—indeed, saturated—by mass communications media: the postal system, television, cinema, radio, magazines, Muzak, shopping malls, freeways, and automobiles.[12] The references are casual but ubiquitous. What brings them together is simply the awareness of the central character, Oedipa Maas. Oedipa functions not only as a recorder of perceptions and feelings, and therefore as a representation of a reflective consciousness, but also as a site where certain things cannot be registered, as if she were a blank or blind spot in a psychic apparatus.

Through the literary device of limited third-person narration, the novel focuses exclusively on Oedipa's activities immediately after she becomes the executrix of the will of her former lover, a California real estate mogul named Pierce Inverarity. In her quest to gather and make sense of information pertaining to Inverarity's vast real estate holdings, Oedipa gradually becomes the subject of a certain kind of "experience." Simply put, that experience is one of radical uncertainty about how to process the information that she has acquired. With Inverarity's death and the entropic dissolution of his vast complex of holdings (in the novel roughly emblematic of corporate America), Oedipa experiences a enlivening rush of new information. But as she discovers, this information is always uncertain. The more information she acquires, the more new information becomes available, but without ever yielding any definitive conclusions: "These follow-ups were no more disquieting than other revelations which now seemed to come crowding in exponentially, as if the more she collected the more would come to her" (81). Oedipa then wonders if her duty is to be "the dark machine in the centre of the planetarium, to bring [Inverarity's] estate into pulsing stelliferous Meaning, all in a soaring Dome around her" (82). But as Oedipa (the "dark machine") seeks pattern recognition, the text merely proliferates new information; even as her efforts to arrive at a single overriding interpretation founder, multiple signs of other worlds and other modes of meaning insistently repeat themselves.

But even pattern recognition must answer to logical possibility. At the end of the novel, Oedipa finds herself facing an undecidable array: (1) either she has discovered an underground mail system (called the Tristero) by means of which alienated and disenfranchised Americans are communicating; or (2) she is hallucinating such a discovery and projecting a pattern of coherence onto information that is only randomly or accidentally connected; or (3) she is the victim of an elaborate plot or hoax possibly perpetrated by Inverarity; or (4) she is hallucinating such a plot. These four possibilities resolve further into an unanswerable either-or question: either the information reveals (in the strong sense of revelation) or it implies Oedipa's own projection of patterns that are only subjective. In either case, information constitutes the fabric of her world, and her experience is almost completely a matter of reading and questioning a whole skein of heterogeneous signs. These signs, as they proliferate through the course of her quest, eventually put into doubt not only the unity of Oedipa's previously supposed world but also the very coherence of her identity within it.

Thus, however else information might be construed in *The Crying of Lot 49*, it obviously does not exhibit the features that Benjamin ascribes to it. In Pynchon's novel, information is neither immediate, nor verifiable, nor plausible, nor "understandable in itself." Whereas for Benjamin the contingent absorption or screening out of information by the psychic apparatus defines the possibility of experience in relation to a stable past stored in a collective cultural memory, in *The Crying of Lot 49* new information makes the past itself uncertain by pointing to alternative versions, as in the novel's microhistory of the postal system, traced from the Thurn and Taxis couriers in the European Renaissance to the pony express riders in America. That this history concerns a communications system is entirely consistent with the novel's fictional mode, as we shall see in a moment. But what exactly *is* information in Pynchon's novel?

References to entropy and information theory point in the direction of a scientific conception.[13] These references cluster most conspicuously around Oedipa's encounter with John Nefastis, the inventor of the "Nefastis machine." Oedipa visits him at his Berkeley apartment, hoping that he may be able to shed light on the Tristero system, since he seems to be a user. Instead, she finds herself drawn into an attempt to communicate with Maxwell's Demon through Nefastis's machine, an updated version of James Clerk Maxwell's speculative thought experiment about heat energy machines. Maxwell postulated that if an intelligence (the Demon, he called it) could somehow sort hot and cold molecules into opposing chambers, the resulting heat differential could be used as an energy source. However, what Maxwell didn't know at the time was that the energy required for the sorting would more than offset the energy gained by the machine.[14] In Nefastis's machine this loss is to be made up by an outside observer (the so-called sensitive) who supplies energy in the form of information that he or she communicates to the demon by concentrating on a photograph of Clerk Maxwell. That this information can somehow make up for the system's heat loss is assumed because the equations for thermodynamic entropy (or energy loss) and entropy in information theory (the measure of uncertainty in a system) turn out to be the same. Nefastis's machine is thus based on a spiritualist—Nefastis himself calls it metaphorical—application of the historical coincidence of two scientific laws. Aside from hinting that Nefastis's machine is a delirious and unworkable model of the psychic apparatus, this emblematic scene suggests that the history of information theory may hold more than merely passing significance for the novel.

In 1948, while working as an engineer at Bell Laboratories, Claude E. Shannon published a ground-breaking paper entitled "A Mathematical Theory of Information" in which he defines information quantitatively as a function of the probability of a message selected for transmission by a communication system comprised of five elements: an information source, a transmitter, a channel, a receiver, and a destination.[15] The messages transmitted in such a communication system may or may not have a meaning. As Shannon himself puts it: "These semantic aspects of communication are irrelevant to the engineering problem. The significant aspect is that the actual message is one *selected from a set* of possible messages" (3, Shannon's emphasis). Shannon's peremptory dismissal of the semantic dimension of communication was both necessary and scandalous. However, since information in Shannon's mathematical sense concerns only the probability of signs, it must not be confused with meaning or the content of the message. As Warren Weaver puts it, information "relates not so much to what you *do* say as to what you *could* say" (100, Weaver's emphasis), and it is the probability of the selected message's occurrence that determines its information content. Thus, in a message composed in contemporary English, the probability of the word *the* is relatively high, and its information content correspondingly low; in contrast, the word *Thee* has a much lower probability of occurrence, with the result that its information value is much higher.

Clearly, high information content reflects a large number of choices available in the selection of the message. It follows, as Weaver also points out, that "the greater this freedom of choice, and hence the greater the information, the greater is the uncertainty that the message actually selected is some particular one" (109). Furthermore, this uncertainty only increases in the transmission of the message because of noise in the channel. Thus, because noise increases uncertainty, the message received will always have higher information content than the message sent. Of course, the information entropy introduced by noise can always be counteracted by increasing the redundancy of the encoding process. Shannon notes, for example, that English prose is about 50 percent redundant, with Basic English and James Joyce's *Finnegans Wake* representing the two extremes. However, increasing redundancy in the encoding process also reduces the message's potential information value. For the total communication circuit, therefore, Shannon introduces the notion of "relative entropies" that allow one to calculate optimal signal/noise ratios for the transmission of maximum information.

The most striking feature of Shannon's theory, which Shannon himself acknowledges, is that his equation for the measure *(H)* of information in a communication system exactly mirrors the amount of entropy in a thermodynamic system ("H is then, for example, the H in Boltzmann's famous H theorem" [20]). Thus Shannon's choice of the term *entropy* soon embroiled him (or his theory) in a scientific controversy about the relationship between entropy in thermodynamic theory and entropy (or information) in information theory.[16] In 1951, for example, Leon Brillouin, following Norbert Wiener, argued that information and thermodynamic entropy are negatively related, that is, that an increase in a system's thermodynamic entropy (an increase in the measure of the system's disorder) should mean a decrease in its information, since a decrease in a system's order should mean that it contains less communicable information.[17] Shannon, contrarily, along with John von Neumann, argued not simply the opposite but a more daring hypothesis: that entropy and information are the same thing! As a system breaks down (becomes more disordered) information becomes increasingly uncertain or improbable. But this means that as a system becomes more disordered, *more* information becomes available. From this point of view, chaos is simply maximum information (and therefore a highly improbable state).

Even without this debate about information and entropy in the background, it is obvious that *The Crying of Lot 49* allegorizes the complexities of information processing. What is not so obvious is how Pynchon incorporates into the fabric of his fiction the new scientific principle underlying information theory, that is, the application of probability functions to the determination of states in a physical system. In his preface to *The Human Use of Human Beings: Cybernetics and Society,* Norbert Wiener cites Willard Gibbs's application of probability functions as "the first great revolution of twentieth century physics" precisely because it ruins the basis of the Newtonian model of the universe.[18] Wiener explains: "in a probabilistic world we no longer deal with . . . a specific, real universe as a whole [as in the Newtonian model] but ask instead questions which may find their answers in a large number of similar universes" (18–19). Thus, Wiener continues, "Gibbs' innovation was to consider not one world, but all the worlds which are possible answers to a limited set of questions concerning our environment. His central notion concerned the extent to which answers that we may give to questions about one set of worlds are probable among a larger set of worlds" (20). In these terms, the novel's interpenetration of sub rosa worlds with the common or ordinary one (the results of which Oedipa's friend Jesus Arrabal calls "an anarchist miracle") is not simply thematic but has a foundation in modern scientific theory. More specifically, in *The Crying of Lot 49,* Pynchon transposes Gibbs's innovation in physics into novelistic terms, producing a shift in the novel's fictional mode. This shift can be illustrated more concretely by contrasting two possible readings of Oedipa's dilemma.

Read in a modernist fictional mode, Oedipa's dilemma sets the terms for and brings to a crisis a drama of self-consciousness. Since the four possibilities she faces are logically exclusive of one another, the dilemma is epistemological: how can she know which one represents the way things truly are? There are four possibilities, but only one corresponds to reality. Like Borges's story "The Approach to Al Mutasim," perhaps Pynchon's implicit literary model, *The Crying of Lot 49* concludes on *this* side of the threshold of revelation, leaving Oedipa (like the reader), in a state of uncertain expectation. From a strictly modernist point of view, this state represents an extreme and schematic exacerbation of a modernist consciousness, self-reflectively open to and somehow containing dramatically conflicting possibilities.

From the same modernist point of view, however, these possibilities seem dramatically improbable, given the almost complete absence of paranoia from modernist narratives. For a brief but revealing comparison, we have only to turn to Henry James's *Turn of the Screw,* where a possibly neurotic governess thinks she perceives signs of an evil intrusion into the world of the children whose care she has been entrusted with by a handsome but distant and aloof uncle. Whereas the governess remains unaware of the possibility that this evil world may be her own projection—thus the drama is played out between an unself-conscious protagonist and a suspicious reader—Pynchon's Oedipa self-reflexively never loses sight of the possibility that she may be sick or, as she puts it, "in the orbiting ecstasy of true paranoia" (182).

Yet Oedipa's paranoia is hardly clinical or even psychological; it appears, rather, to be a systemic feature of her experience, indeed of her world. In this light, and according to the assumptions of what Brian McHale calls an ontological or postmodernist fictional mode, the four possibilities Oedipa confronts at the novel's conclusion should be read as probability functions.[19] In Willard Gibbs's terms, Oedipa is brought to the brink of considering "not one world, but all the worlds which are possible answers to a limited set of questions concerning our environment." Instead of a single revealed truth or simple ascertainable state, she faces an array of four possibilities, each with its own implicit probability. Or, to put it in yet another way, each of the four possibilities represents a virtual state of the same underlying semiotic structure.[20] One of these virtualities may or may not be actualized, but the others are no less real. Actualization will be a process of differentiation, but the outcome cannot be anticipated by concepts. In Bergsonian terms, the novel stages a "virtual multiplicity."[21]

Again a Borges story provides the literary model. In "The Garden of Forking Paths," the narrator, who is spying for the Germans while living in

England during World War I, finds himself in a desperate dilemma: he must get a message to his superior in Berlin before he is arrested. His solution is to murder a man with a certain name; his message will simply be the newspaper report, the significance of which his superior will grasp. By chance, it seems, the name he picks out of the telephone book, Stephen Albert, turns out to be a scholar engaged in deciphering the labyrinth of the narrator's own Chinese ancestor. Albert thinks this labyrinth may in fact be a novel written on the theme of time and embracing all of its possibilities. He illustrates it this way: "Fang, for example, has a secret; a stranger calls at his door . . . Fang can kill the intruder, the intruder can kill Fang, they can both escape, they can both die, and so forth . . . you arrive at this house, but in one of the possible pasts you are my enemy, in another, my friend." [22] Albert's research convinces the narrator that his ancestor's labyrinth is a temporal one and that his own murderous strategem has led him into it. This labyrinth articulates a number of virtual bifurcation points at which narrator and adversary may intersect within the history in which both participate. These bifurcation points pass through "incompossible" presents in a forking labyrinth of time, thus complicating in a modern twist Liebniz's model of the universe.

In *The Crying of Lot 49,* Pynchon makes the California landscape itself the labyrinth within which Oedipa's quest leads her to a similar point of bifurcation, one that is differentiated along four altogether different paths, incompossible while being simultaneously real or true. In Pynchon's novel, however, the simultaneous copresence of incompossible worlds arises from something inherent in the historically specific environment of California in the 1960s: the omnipresence of communications media. In other words, what might otherwise appear to be a metaphysical fable actually describes the effects produced by this environment on a sensitive individual. Relevant, then, is Fredric Jameson's observation that Pynchon's fictional strategy is to make scene serve as agency (in Kenneth Burke's dramatistic terms), as we see in the scene in which Oedipa first drives into southern California:

> She looked down a slope, needing to squint for the sunlight, onto a vast sprawl of houses which had grown up all together, like a well-tended crop, from the dull brown earth; and she thought of the time she'd opened a transistor radio to replace a battery and seen her first printed circuit. The ordered swirl of houses and streets, from this high angle, sprang at her now with the same unexpected, astonishing clarity as the circuit card had. Though she knew even less about radios than about Southern Californians,

there were to both outward patterns a hieroglyphic sense of concealed meaning, of an intent to communicate. There'd seemed no limit to what the printed circuit could have told her (if she had tried to find out); so in her first minute of San Narciso, a revelation also trembled just past the threshold of her understanding. Smog hung all round the horizon, the sun on the bright beige countryside was painful; she and the Chevy seemed parked at the centre of an odd, religious instant. As if, on some other frequency, or out of the eye of some whirlwind rotating too slow for her heated skin even to feel the centripedal coolness of, words were being spoken. (24–25)

Jameson suggests that here the California landscape "resonates with some well-nigh runic message" because the conspiracy of real estate development has been identified with the conspiracy of the media.[23] But what this Marxist interpretation neglects is the singular uncanniness of this and other similar moments in Oedipa's experience, where a present perception immediately evokes a memory mediated by or narrativized in relation to some piece of telecommunications hardware, whether a radio's printed circuit board (as in the passage above), or an old movie on television, telephone calls that come in the middle of the night, or the twinning matrices of a digital computer. It is not simply that the entire landscape, and Oedipa's affective relationship to it, is always mediated by communications technology, although that is certainly true. Rather, it is as if the spaces across which these communications transpire were haunted by invisible presences or powers that the novel as psychic apparatus can register but which cannot be integrated into an individual character's meaningful "experience."

It is precisely the Tristero as an alternative communications system that comes to figure this gap between what Oedipa knows or sees and yet feels haunted by, as a form of otherness that assumes many guises and valencies—political and religious, human and inhuman—in the course of her quest. What remains constant is how the existence of the Tristero, whether actual or only virtual, signals (in every sense) both an "other" form of communication and "the other" of presently conventionalized forms. Thus, while the reality of capitalism is undeniably important, it is the proximity and omnipresence of communications systems whose effects exceed those of capitalist enterprise that appear to condition the uncanny otherness in Oedipa's experience. For in some new sense Oedipa herself is struggling to apprehend, her identity has become inseparable from the communications systems in which she participates: her acts of communication, differentiated through different feedback loops, now define who she is.

That Oedipa completes or can complete any number of communications circuits—each one entailing a different sense of self—suggests another intertextual link with Claude Shannon's work, specifically his master's thesis, entitled "A Symbolic Analysis of Relay and Switching Circuits."[24] There Shannon showed that electric relay and switching circuits could be used to express the truth-logic operations of Boolean algebra. Not only could a true-false system be emulated by on-off switches or closed and open states of a circuit, but any operations that could be described in finite mathematical steps could be carried out by such switching relays. In *The Crying of Lot 49,* recurrent either/or grammatical structures (see pp. 22, 31, 45, 49, 109, 162, 170, 179, 181, 182) suggest a modeling of Oedipa's life as a series of potential circuits among a logical array of possibilities. There is always a choice, a decision, a judgment: "God or a digital machine" (37); "either . . . transcendent meaning, or only the earth" (181). At the novel's end, Oedipa is still left "waiting for a symmetry of choices to break down, to go skew. . . . For it was now like walking among matrices of a great digital computer, the zeros and ones twinned above, hanging like balanced mobiles right and left, ahead, thick, maybe endless" (181). With modern computer technology, transcendence comes to an end in the "halting problem."[25]

Within the interstices of multiple communicational systems, then, no transcendent or dialectical subject position from which Oedipa could view her "self" objectively ever becomes available; each self that she might affirm is only a patterned response or feedback effect in a cybernetic system. Even the sexual act becomes one connection in a more elaborate circuitry. Pulling into the Echo Courts motel because the nymph's face on its gaudy advertising sign resembles her own, Oedipa is soon visited by Metzger, the narcissistic actor-lawyer. A TV movie starring Metzger as child actor motivates a guessing game of "Strip Botticelli," during which a wildly caroming hair spray can shatters the bathroom mirror. Confronted with her absence of image, Oedipa experiences a moment of "nearly pure terror" (41). Not long after: "She awoke . . . to find herself getting laid; she'd come in on a sexual crescendo in progress, like a cut to a scene where the camera's already moving. Outside a fugue of guitars had begun, and she counted each electronic voice as it came in, till she reached six or so and recalled only three of the Paranoids played guitars; so others must be plugging in. . . . Her climax and Metzger's, when it came, coincided with every light in the place, including the TV tube, suddenly going out, dead, black. It was a curious experience" (42).

Curious indeed. If Oedipa's seduction by Metzger is a first and partial peeling away of the "insulation" that had kept her life "just perceptibly out of focus" (20), her (machinic) sex with him amid a full panoply of communications media is not simply for comedic effect. For Metzger is only the first in a whole series of men who will appear bearing signs that point ambiguously toward less verifiable, sub rosa circuits of connection, only to recede or become unavailable. As Oedipa herself realizes, pursuit of her quest strangely entails the poignant "stripping away of her lovers." But if her "de-buffering" also figures the loss of her former identity, as the novel often suggests, it is paradoxical that her increasing isolation occurs amid various and sundry groups who may be communicating through alternative communication networks. In this sense as well, Oedipa is less the site of an experience than the site where multiple connections become uncertain.

IV. In many respects, Oedipa's identity crisis models in an affective, individualized register the experience of modern society as characterized by Niklas Luhmann. In Luhmann's functionalist version of systems theory, the "subject" devolves into distinguishable systems. As Jürgen Habermas succinctly notes, Luhmann's theory "simply presupposes that the structures of intersubjectivity have collapsed and that individuals have become disengaged from their lifeworlds—that personal and social systems form environments for each other." [26] In Luhmann's theory, the modern social system (or society, in the largest sense) is highly differentiated into a number of functional subsystems—economic, political, scientific, educational, and so on. Each subsystem defines itself as a self-referential communicational system against the background of all the others, which thereby constitute the "environment." However, there is no overriding mechanism for social integration; indeed, according to the terms in which systems theory describes modern society, there is no need for integration. Luhmann acknowledges that his concept of society

> does not presuppose any kind of pooled identity or pooled self-esteem (like the nation-state). Modern society in particular is compatible with any degree of inequality of living conditions, as long as this does not interrupt communication. A self-referential system defines itself by the way in which it constitutes its elements and thereby maintains its boundaries. In systems theory, the *distinction* between system and environment replaces the traditional emphasis on the *identity* of guiding principles or values. Differences,

not identities, provide the possibility of perceiving and processing information. The sharpness of the difference between system and environment may
be more important than the degree of system integration (whatever this
means), because morphogenetic processes use differences, not goals, values, or identities, to build up emergent structures.[27]

As Luhmann stresses, these subsystems are self-regulating in relation to the
environment. For structural reasons, therefore, a high degree of social integration or totalization would prohibit the functioning of the subsystems and
reduce the complexity of modern society. Luhmann thus envisions society
not as a transcendentally grounded world but as a multiplicity of system-
relative environments.

In *The Crying of Lot 49*, the sub rosa worlds that become visible within
the interstices and beyond the edges of America's corporate grid are structurally analogous to the subsystems Luhmann describes. What makes them
different, of course, is that at this point in American history, they were un-
recognized by official culture and maintained with it a relationship of exteriority or otherness. As Oedipa herself comes to realize, America's excluded
others—especially the poor—suggest a bifurcation in America's history, a
swerve away from variety and difference toward social homogenization.
From Luhmann's point of view, however, these excluded groups would simply represent social subsystems in a state of emergent or potential evolution.
Luhmann's systems theory thus points to a limit in the way the novel's internal boundaries are thematized, as a result of which the Tristero seems both
more and less than a metaphor. Put another way, in Oedipa's experience the
novel mixes two incompatible perspectives or modes—roughly, a subjec-
t(ive) versus a systems view—in its articulation of meaning. In Oedipa's
experience the Tristero comes to designate an underground of dropouts,
"isolatoes," and poor people, in sum all the various groups marginalized by
mainstream American society, but it also designates something like a condition for her to have any experience at all.

The problem, simply put, is that the Tristero, as a symbolic operator, is
both too much and not enough. Does it signify only those groups marginalized or repressed by white middle-class heterosexual America or all social
"remainders" not assimilated into the system? But the larger question is not
sociological at all, though it may well be structural: if the uncanny moments
in Oedipa's experience are triggered by her recurrent failures to integrate
perception and memory—such failures always occurring in spaces mediated
by technological devices—why are they figured specifically by an under-

ground postal system, and one that may even appear archaic in contrast to the technical media of the contemporary world?

The work of Jacques Derrida, especially *The Post Card,* where Derrida announces his desire to write a history of the post, certainly seems relevant here.[28] But whereas Derrida understands the post as a system of networks and relays, and necessarily as a structure of deferral and delay, at all levels Pynchon's text insists on its effects of buffering, blockage, noise, or counterfeiting and disguise—in short, all the ways in which communication diverts Oedipa's direct accessibility to the Word as *logos* and thereby delimits her experience. Reflecting on the nature of metaphor, Oedipa muses that the saint, the clairvoyant, the true paranoid, and the dreamer "whose puns probe ancient fetid shafts and tunnels of truth all act in the same special relevance to the word, or whatever it is the word is there, buffering, to protect us from" (128–129). Moreover, specific puns in the novel, such as Oedipa's musing on the double meaning of *dts,* often turn out to be technoscientific; for Oedipa, the truth, or Word, of (tele)phonocentric communication is always already mediated and lost. Thinking back to Inverarity's last call, she remembers the telephone voices "searching ceaselessly among the dial's ten million possibilities for that magical Other who would reveal herself out of the roar of relays, monotone litanies of insult, filth, fantasy, love whose brute repetition must someday call into being the trigger of the unnamable act, the recognition, the Word" (180). Earlier, Oedipa wonders whether, "at the end of this (if it were supposed to end)," like an epileptic after a seizure, "she too might not be left with only compiled memories of clues, announcements, intimations, but never the central truth itself, which must somehow each time be too bright for her memory to hold; which must always blaze out, destroying its own message irreversibly, leaving an overexposed blank when the ordinary world came back" (95).

In these and other passages, *The Crying of Lot 49* adumbrates more connections and relationships than it can adequately sustain. Repeatedly, uncanny moments hint at connections that can be suggested only through the agency of metaphor and figurative language, as the text itself openly declares on several occasions.[29] But this seemingly unavoidable recourse to figurative devices at sensitive points in the text can also be understood symptomatically, as evidence of the novel's incapacity to realize fully its own textual logic. In this sense it can be said that *The Crying of Lot 49* fails to attain the status of a substantive multiplicity, where a burgeoning excess of information and proliferating connections among parts would exceed any schematic diagram of plots and relations, whether virtual or imagined, projected or real, and thus the limits of any single individual's experience. Put another way, the multiplicity in *The Crying of Lot 49* remains only virtual.

As Oedipa herself realizes, the efficacy of metaphor depends on an inside and an outside (129), that is, on the position of an observer within a specific system, and much of the novel's force depends on Oedipa's own uncertain positioning. But whereas *The Crying of Lot 49* plays out this implicit textual contradiction between subject and system, it is resolved in *Gravity's Rainbow,* as we shall see in chapter 3, through the multiplication of semiotic regimes, with each regime both producing a distinct mode of subjectivity and functioning interactively with other regimes or subsystems within a larger, nontotalized textual system. This assemblage of semiotic regimes allows for a fuller integration of connections within a structure of proliferating information, yet without any necessary recourse to metaphor.

In the terms of information theory, the difference between Pynchon's two novels can be correlated with Henri Atlan's effort to apply Shannon's theory to the analysis of organized systems (particularly in biology).[30] Atlan notes that in Shannon's theory, which concerns only the transmission of messages in a communication channel, noise can only have a negative value. However, if we consider the transmission of information among subsystems in a larger system, noise can assume two possible values. (Atlan refers to the negative possibility as "destructive ambiguity" and the positive one as "autonomy-ambiguity".)[31] In the positive instance, a faulty transmission of information from one subsystem to another leads to an increase in the total amount of information available in a system and thus to the system's complexity. Furthermore, what is noise on one level can lead to a "self-organization" of elements on a higher level. Atlan calls this "noise as a principle of self-organization," and he shows that it works through a diminution of redundancy.

While these biological mechanisms may not be strictly applicable to literary texts, something analogous obviously takes place at sites where there are multiple discourses. Thus what is noise, detritus, or waste on one discursive channel may be meaningful—or made meaningful, by rewriting, translating, or recoding—on another. In fact, writers often discover means of recoding and integrating different or conflicting discourses. But in Pynchon's fiction these obvious strategies become thematically significant. Whereas in *The Crying of Lot 49* Oedipa cannot decide whether the signs emanating from the Tristero are noise or evidence of an "other" system of communication, in *Gravity's Rainbow* the presence of multiple subsystems of communication is recognized by the characters themselves, and there is little doubt on the reader's part that these interacting subsystems contribute to the overall text's more complex organization. However, there is one kind of rewriting that is continuous from one novel to the other: the way in which each novel constitutes itself as a text precisely through a repeated reading/rewriting of the effects of other media. Since no account of either novel can ignore this essential feature, let us briefly examine how *The Crying of Lot 49* works in these terms.

The novel begins with Oedipa's reception of a letter, and it ends with the imminent auctioning of Pierce Inverarity's last effects, which is to say, the final gathering and dispersal of Inverarity's identity in a performative speech act. Bracketed by these two events, the text reads/rewrites the contents and effects of various media; whether it be a painting by Remedios Varo, the television news, several telephone calls, a Hollywood movie shown on TV, a seventeenth-century Jacobean revenge play and scholarly commentary on texual variants, a narrative history of the postal service, or pop songs sung live or played on the radio, in each case the text transposes them into the codes of its own novelistic language and produces a certain reading effect. Even as Oedipa Maas, "a whiz at reading texts" as she says, enacts the novel's staging of a hermeneutic quest, she too is the product of a certain reading effect.

The Crying of Lot 49 thus assumes that, in order for any hermeneutic questions to be posed, there must first be an agency or mechanism by which certain signs materialize in a text, a text that processes, recodes, and redistributes information, establishing both a general logic of the data's organization and a system of addresses. In so doing, the text reads and writes itself as a miniature *Aufschreibesystem,* or writing-down system, in which the culture's systems of data processing and transmission as well as their delirious effects on a sensitive subject are anatomized. In this double function, or rather, in the gap between the two—Oedipa as reader and textual effect— the novel models a psychic apparatus.

This means, first, that the text-as-machine provides the condition of possibility for any and all interpretation. As Oedipa herself discovers, questions about meaning can only follow what is written and read. Thus questions about the meaning of Pierce Inverarity and his final estate—his sending or destining in the Heideggerian sense—are inseparable from (because they presuppose) his posting in the Derridean sense.[32] Whereas Oedipa can only wonder, at the end of the novel, whether Pierce's testament actually encodes the legacy of America in binary form ("either a transcendent meaning, or only the earth" [181]), the reader must confront uncertainty as the condition of every communication, and the difference that makes. As a consequence, and in keeping with the novel's fundamental concern with the transmission of messages through a multiplicity of channels, any hermeneutic reading of the final "crying" of Inverarity's "effects" (in every sense)—that it heralds a Pentecostal descent of the spirit and a consequent speaking in tongues, for example—must yield priority to the novel's functioning as a machine that reads/rewrites media effects and which therefore makes sense only in relation to new conditions of mediality.[33]

Second, this means that the text is also constituted by its gaps and blank spaces, which register not only its conditions but also the limits of the individual subject's experience in a kind of blank or invisible figuration. Most strikingly, Oedipa's hermeneutic quest ends but does not conclude with (on) a blank page, with the dispersion of Inverarity as a name designating a putative unity of referents and effects into channels irretrievably de-differentiated by noise and the blurring of social systems as discrete communicational environments. At this precise point the *text,* finally and appropriately, stops rewriting. Throughout the novel, however, the typographic identity of Inverarity's name threatens to decompose into an aggregate of signifiers: inverse, rarity, *in veritas,* and so on. Inverarity's only reported speech, significantly, comes in a middle-of-the-night telephone call as a medley of voices imitating a series of mass-media stereotypes. Like so much else of importance in the novel, it is a call that Oedipa can only *remember,* as if "Pierce Inverarity" were a unity-in-multiplicity she must hold in memory amid blank spaces. Yet it is over (this) blank space—of memory and of type—that *The Crying of Lot 49* as text is both written and read. Thus, however the significance of Inverarity's name and legacy is to be interpreted, the novel's final blank page (which in *Gravity's Rainbow* becomes a cinema screen) forces the reader to jump from a hermeneutic to a medial perspective, that is, from the interpretation of meanings to a reading of the effects (and affects) made by a recording of acoustical and optical data as information. By encompassing the limits of both these processes, *The Crying of Lot 49* models the conditions of a contemporary psychic apparatus.

V. If the *The Crying of Lot 49,* like the novel of information multiplicity that follows it, can be said to model the reorganization of the contemporary psychic apparatus, it is because it registers the altered status of consciousness in relation to the new technologies of data storage, transmission, and (as we shall see) calculation. Let us consider this historical/technological change in more general terms by observing how contemporary theorists view Freud's model of the psychic apparatus. In effect, Benjamin's reading is not so much (out)dated as recontextualized in relation to other discourses and other functions. Thus contemporary readings generally emphasize how Freud's model is situated between two paradigms: the thermodynamic paradigm of force, energy, and substance dominant in the nineteenth and early twentieth centuries, and the informational paradigm of organization, information, and control elaborated in the post–World War II period.[34]

No doubt the most extended contemporary reading is the one Derrida advances in his essay "Freud and the Scene of Writing."[35] Derrida's reading (which cannot be treated here with the fullness it deserves) is guided by the fact that for Freud, psychical content is represented by an "irreducibly graphic" text; in other words, "the *structure* of the psychical *apparatus* will be *represented* by a writing machine" (199, Derrida's emphases). The question, then, is not whether the metaphors of writing that run through Freud's attempts to account for memory, the unconscious, and perceptual consciousness—from *The Project for a Scientific Psychology* (1895) to the "Note on the Mystic Writing Pad" (1925)—are good metaphors but rather: "What is a text, and what must the psyche be if it can be represented by a text? For if there is neither machine nor text without psychical origin, there is no domain of the psychic without text" (199).

Derrida argues that since psychic processes cannot be conceived apart from or exterior to a certain "scene of writing," technological devices can no longer serve as mere metaphors. In this instance, Freud's last and most developed model of memory and perceptual consciousness, the "mystic wax writing pad," can no longer be taken to be a metaphor for memory; instead, the writing apparatus "founds memory" and thus makes metaphor possible. If there is an analogy between this child's writing device and the operations of the psychic apparatus, it is because the latter is already inhabited and made possible by a machine, a writing machine. Since this machine "—and consequently, representation—is death and finitude *within* the psyche," it calls for the "historical production of a *supplementary* machine, *added to* the psychical organization in order to supplement its finitude" (228, Derrida's emphases). As Derrida shows, through the strange "logic of the supplement" the invention of a new machine or technology added to what was already functionally complete reveals how the latter was always already a machine. The relation between the two apparatuses, which is also the relation between the present and its representation, between life and death, Derrida calls writing *[écriture]*.

For Derrida, therefore, "the question of technology . . . may not be derived from an assumed opposition between the psychical and the nonpsychical" (228). Indeed, such an opposition would have to assume a form of human being in a pretechnological state. The refusal of this assumption and the displacement of technology "from its traditional problematic," as Derrida puts it, clearly underlie the shift from consciousness to scriptive, informational systems as the site of a new proliferation of information, and hence the formation of information multiplicities. While Derrida provides no sustained analysis of the relationship between information technologies and his theory/practice of writing, he nonetheless demonstrates how writing and written subjects—authors, characters, and readers—can no longer be conceived apart from or existing outside a writing machine: "The 'subject' of writing does not exist if we mean by that some sovereign solitude of the author. The subject of writing is a *system* of relations between strata: the Mystic Pad, the psyche, the society, the world" (226, Derrida's emphasis).

Nevertheless, Derrida's use of the word *system* may seem too general, even metaphorical. In a commentary on Jacques Lacan's "Seminar on the Ego," Friedrich Kittler offers a more technologically precise description of Freud's psychic apparatus.[36] The most salient fact about Lacan's "Seminar on the Ego" is that it is elaborated in relation to cybernetics and information theory.[37] For Kittler the differences between Freud's psychoanalytic model and Lacan's rewriting of it simply reflect the differences in the operating standards of information machines and technical media in their respective epochs. According to the scientific imperatives to which Freud willingly bent himself, ineffable emanations of spirit had to be replaced by systems of neurons that differ according to separable functions, in this case the recording and transmission of data (i.e., memory and perceptual consciousness). In constructing his model of the psychic apparatus, however, "Freud's materialism reasoned only as far as the information machines of his epoch—no more, no less" (63).

For example, storage functions—not only the graphic inscriptions highlighted by Derrida but also the grooves on Edison's newly invented phonograph record—could be conceived only on the model of the engram. For both his case studies and lectures, Freud relies on his own "phonographic memory," as he emphasizes on several occasions.[38] Psychoanalysis ("the talking cure") is actually a form of "telephony," a communication circuit between patient and analyst in which the former's unconscious is transformed into sound or speech and then back into the unconscious. (Kittler notes that a telephone cable was laid in Freud's house—but not in the consulting room—in 1895). Yet Freud did not limit himself to the phonocentric. In *The Interpretation of Dreams* the transmission medium was optical, a cameralike apparatus that converted latent dream thoughts into a system of conscious perception, the virtual images of which Lacan would understand as cinema. In constructing a model of the psychic apparatus, Freud thus implemented all storage and transmission media available at the time: print, phonograph, telephone, and film.

Lacan grasped the importance of these technical media for Freudian theory (as suggested by the titles of his own works: *Ecrits,* the *Seminars, Television,* "Radiophonie," etc.), as well as the extent to which the foundation of psychoanalysis rested on the end of the print monopoly and the historical separation of different media. Thus, for Kittler, Lacan's triple register of the imaginary, the real, and the symbolic corresponds explicitly to the separation of media, that is, to film, phonograph, and linguistic signifiers respectively. For Kittler, however, the Lacanian symbolic corresponds not simply to the system of linguistic signifiers (as Lacan himself puts it, the most complex machine is made of words), but to the entire domain of calculation. For this reason the most important technological invention between Freud and Lacan was the computer, or more specifically, Alan Turing's Universal machine of 1936. In sum, Kittler argues that Lacan's rewriting of Freud should be understood as an attempt to redefine the psychic apparatus according to contemporary conditions of mediality; to do this, Lacan implements in a functional model the most up-to-date media of information storage, transmission, and computation.

The value of Kittler's analysis of Lacan is twofold. First, it points to how Derrida's notion of writing, or *écriture,* needs to be reformulated (or supplemented in turn, as it were) specifically in terms of contemporary information technologies, which no longer depend on the mechanism of the engram for archiving information. And second, it sketches the minimal requirement for a contemporary model of the psychic apparatus, that is, it must implement the full range of today's media in their capacities for information storage, transmission, and calculation. And though Kittler does not read literature itself as a psychic apparatus, he does apply an information processing model to literary analysis. In an essay on the poetry of Gottfried Benn, he writes, "Literature itself, whatever its subjects and topics may be, is first of all a form of data processing; it receives and stores, processes and transmits information in a manner in no wise structurally different from computers." [39] This essay extends his earlier thesis that works of literature provide a "discourse on the discourse" of a specific culture and thus a critical vantage point upon the very hardware of cultural data processing: "The data processing of a given society can be reconstructed by analyzing its artistic media. Being less formal than its systems of knowledge, those media display and propagate the elementary regulations that culturalize the natives of that society. Before anything can be known, there must be rules or signs for identifying things as signs or data; there must be rules defining which persons or devices will be acceptable as source, as emitter, as channel, and as receiver of information." [40]

It should be evident that *The Crying of Lot 49,* with its conspicuous interest in the postal system, the telephone, and the electronic communications industry as well as its problematization of sender and addressee poles, provides a veritable textbook illustration. In fact, if the probability that various marginal groups in America may be in secret communication gives *The Crying of Lot 49* its affective charge and ground tone of runic mystery and subliminal semiosis, the machinery of the Tristero, with its alternating gothic and sinister associations, provides the occasion—and this is what makes the book fictional—for exploring the delirious effects of a new telecommunications environment on its sensitive subjects. At the same time, *The Crying of Lot 49* points to a shortcoming in Kittler's formulation, for the regulations, rules, and signs as well as the roles and positions assumed by subjects in these processes may be strongly contested within the society in question, and therefore within the very "discourse on the discourse" that provides the means of our reflection upon them. To anticipate somewhat, the evidence provided by Pynchon, McElroy, Gaddis, DeLillo, Gibson, and Cadigan (and earlier adumbrated by Burroughs) suggests that "culturizing the natives" (as Kittler puts it) in our society of control amounts at best to a mixed blessing. Perhaps Jean-François Lyotard, in *The Postmodern Condition,* best captures the gist of the matter when he describes contemporary Western society as a cybernetic system or "vangard machine dragging humanity after it, dehumanizing it in order to rehumanize it at a different level of normative capacity." [41]

Lyotard's formulation thus raises the question of the degree to which the novel of information multiplicity merely participates in this process, offering (at best) an enlarged sense of the "normative capacity" of contemporary culture. But if it is not fully isotopic with the discourses circulating in contemporary society and does offer some genuine alternative, as contemporary figurations of the sublime or forms machinically inscribing material and psychic processes not yet integrated or even assimilable, then we must still ask how its critical difference should be assessed and what kind of claims can be advanced on its behalf.[42] The answer, I have suggested, lies in its capacity to model a contemporary psychic apparatus, or at least to point suggestively toward the latter's conditions of possibility and necessary features.

VI. Before proceeding, it may be useful to summarize how the concept of mediality points to internal distinctions of historical/technological difference within the grouping of novels to be considered. As instantiated in *Gravity's Rainbow, Lookout Cartridge,* and *JR,* the novel of information multiplicity emerges exactly between the modernist era defined by the separation of media (film, phonograph, typewriter) and a new era defined by a global communications assemblage in which the television and computer assume essential functions. Subsequently, however, the influence of this communications assemblage and the pervasive sense of a totalized information economy yield a somewhat different kind of novel, designated here as the novel of media assemblages. In this type, represented by DeLillo's novels, as well as by *Vineland, Neuromancer,* and *Synners,* information multiplicity is assumed or conventionalized, and what now matters most is the degree of connectedness among different media systems. In short, a fundamental concern with film, sound recording, and print as separate and separable media in the novels of Pynchon, McElroy, and Gaddis evolves into a concern with culture as a medium produced by the mass media in DeLillo's novels and Pynchon's *Vineland,* and with a global communications network in those of Gibson and Cadigan.

This shift, to be sure, is not absolute and may reflect only an intensification of differences already evident at the outset of the information age. As we have seen, *The Crying of Lot 49* bears witness, if only symptomatically, to the entire reorganization of the psychic apparatus that new technologies of data storage, transmission, and calculation are bringing about. More generally, the novel reveals how uncertainty and undecidability no longer signify an individual existential dilemma but become a pervasive condition in an information-saturated environment. In such an environment, experience and social identity undergo a radical textualization as the social codes that determine psychic identity are constantly redefined through multiple systems of communication, including the mass media.

As one consequence, contemporary writers feel impelled to rewrite the modern. *The Crying of Lot 49* reinscribes the modernist impulse to valorize art, pattern, and design—what German art historians refer to as the "will to form"—as a fictive projection that must repress or ignore the actual material and historical agencies responsible for the production of our subjectivity. Indeed, much of *The Crying of Lot 49* transpires in the shadow of Yoyodyne, a giant aviation and electronics firm whose primary contractor is the Department of Defense and whose engineers are disgruntled by the necessity of signing away their patent rights. *Gravity's Rainbow* and the novels of information multiplicity that follow texualize even further the relationship between technology and forms of subjectivity. In so doing, tracing and diagramming and the mixing of different "regimes of signs," rather than symbol making and the elaboration of modernist, writerly styles, become their characteristic functions. Constructed in part from the discourses of science, mathematics, and technology, these fictional assemblages constitute a form of psychic apparatus that inventories many of the systems, images, and representations that, through various media, shape our cultural space and "write" us as its inhabitant subjects. The modernist notion of the author as a creative, godlike power is rejected, and aesthetic (en)closures are rewritten as paranoid/schizoid systems.

If modernist fictional multiplicities required the textual liberation of language through self-referential strategies (highly visible in writing by Raymond Roussel, Gertrude Stein, and James Joyce), the multiplicities that define and are defined by the contemporary novel of information multiplicity are predicated on the realization that language no longer enjoys a position of sovereignty but is now only one medium among many. As a consequence, the writing machines that translate multiplicities "outside the text" into fictional multiplicities must read and rewrite the effects of other media. In acknowledging their (and our) historically conditioned mediality, the novel of information multiplicity attests that what Kittler calls the discourse network should perhaps be reformulated for the postmodern period as an information network, since the codings and machinic processes produced by and circulating within current Western society involve flows and exchanges that are, strictly speaking, semiotic and asignifying rather than simply linguistic.[43]

part II

The Novel of
Information
Multiplicity

The thought of every age is reflected in its technique.... If the
seventeenth and early eighteenth
centuries are the age of clocks,
and the later eighteenth and the
nineteenth centuries constitute
the age of steam engines, the
present time is the age of communication and control.
- Norbert Wiener

■ ■ ■ ■ ■ ■ ■ ■ ■ ■ ■ 3

Rocket-State Assemblage

Gravity's Rainbow

I. In a review of Wiener's book *Cybernetics*, the source of the epigraph above, his sometime friend and colleague John von Neumann describes Wiener as "one of the protagonists of the proposition that science as well as technology, will in the near and in the farther future increasingly turn from problems of intensity, substance, and energy, to problems of structure, organization, information, and control." [1] In the 1940s and 1950s, this new orientation becomes evident in an emergent discourse network with multiple scientific supports. Both von Neumann and Wiener had been inspired by Alan Turing's study of "computable numbers" and his notion of the Universal machine. Both Wiener and von Neumann knew and drew upon Claude Shannon's mathematical definition of informa-

61

tion and its transmission, and both were influenced by Warren McCulloch and Walter Pitts, two neurologists who, by drawing on Turing's formulations, were able to apply Boolean algebra to the properties of nerve cells, thereby connecting their model of a logic machine with the actual physiology of the human brain.

One day the work of Turing, Wiener, von Neumann, Shannon, and others may seem as essential to the formation of the discourse network shaping postmodern American fiction as psychophysics was to the discourse network of modernism.[2] Even now, what is striking is how much of that work was undertaken and developed under the dark auspices of World War II and the ensuing Cold War. Which is to say, under the shadow of state intelligence networks and the military sponsorship of scientific research. Indeed, World War II can be characterized as a watershed in the slow transformation whereby the most worrisome problems of science changed from the epistemological to the social and political. In brief, the war shredded and stripped away the illusion that science is apolitical; it also brought new economic determinants into play, as the government (or state apparatus) became the primary instigator and support for research.[3]

World War II as a watershed event in the growth of technology and scientific research is precisely the subject of Thomas Pynchon's *Gravity's Rainbow,* whose publication in 1973 endorsed what had already become a given within the sixties counterculture: that *paranoia* no longer designated a mental disorder but rather a critical method of information retrieval.[4] The history that the novel retrieves concerns the birth of a "rocket-state" that will unify as a "meta-cartel" an international network of new industries—plastics, electronics, aviation—growing out of the ruins of World War II. In a tentacular expansion, this network will soon provide the material basis for a new technopolitical world order. *Gravity's Rainbow* emblazons its "history" in the V-2's arc across the sky and in the temporal and spatial trajectory traced by one particular rocket, whose payload promises to yield the secret of the main character's erotic response to its hardware. The construction and firing of this special rocket at the end of the war (and of the novel) bring into focus the ways in which the war functioned as both occasion and means for the transfer and expansion of a whole new weapons system developed in reciprocal alliance with a new form of cinematic (or machinic) perception.[5] Hence this special rocket's *terminus ab quo* in Germany, circa 1945, and its *terminus ad quem* in a movie theater in Los Angeles, circa 1972, where the reader is "watching" a film. As the film burns out on the novel's last page, we are urged to think of *Gravity's Rainbow* itself as an unfilmable movie, a sequence tracing movements and connections we have been trained not to see, like the distribution networks of the metacartel responsible for much of our history.

Of course, more needs to be said about these cartels and how much they still dictate our needs. In Paul Virilio's account, which closely accords with Pynchon's historical assumptions, the military-industrial complex born from World War II undertook an endo-colonization of its own population, the threat of nuclear war enabling it to hold captive the entire civil society of both East and West in a mirror symmetry euphemistically referred to as *détente*.[6] In this respect, the military may have been the true postwar avant-garde, keeping the populace under control until new apparatuses of capture—variously described as the society of the spectacle, consumer or mass-media society—could be set into place and thus secure the operational requirements of an increasingly global, multinational capitalism. *Gravity's Rainbow* assumes that the integration of America's military-industrial complex and the networks of global capitalism depended upon—indeed, was one with—the digitalization of information. Pynchon's prose fictional narrative counters this digitalization by transposing its history into a continuous but indeterminate stream of delirious media effects, as the novel mimics film, radio, dance hall music, drug-induced hallucinations, and séances in which the dead speak.

As a consequence of both its striking contemporaneity and obvious historical complexity, *Gravity's Rainbow* is usually ranked alongside such modernist classics as Faulkner's *Absalom, Absalom!* and Joyce's *Ulysses*. Yet Pynchon reveals a certain distance from his modernist forebears, most noticeably in the particulars of his concern with twentieth-century history and technology. Generally speaking, history for both Joyce and Faulkner is contingency and must be set against the larger, structural frame that myth provides. Myth thus functions as a limit, against which the infinite variety and detail of historical experience appear in outline. Pynchon, in contrast, pursues two related strategies: he shows that the contemporary world is already immanent in the technologies developed during World War II; at the same time, he suggests that the usually assumed historical accounts serve merely to mask the emergence of a new order of power, which administers the needs of these (and only these) new technologies. As a record of the various ways "They" convince us to die for "Them," history itself is reduced to a certain kind of myth, forcing us to locate our own particular contingencies in relation to its increasingly ominous logic. Thus, while remaining committed to history as a form of understanding, Pynchon is deeply suspicious of what our specific history has become.

Even as theme and method, however, paranoia does not suffice to structure the multiple narratives this history entails. Even from a paranoid-conspiratorial point of view, war no longer makes sense in terms of personal experience, since wars are no longer fought between people or nations but between different media, information technologies, and data flows. With *history, myth,* and *personal experience* having become contaminated terms and no longer able to support stable oppositions, Pynchon turned to modern science and technology for alternative concepts of narrative necessity and thematic organization. Specifically, in information theory, mathematics, physics, organic chemistry, and cartography he finds the counterterms necessary for representing the experiences of his fictional subjects. Writing before Virilio, Kittler, and Baudrillard, however, Pynchon could not simply assume these terms but had to embed them in a literary structure. In order to retrieve and link together extraordinarily diverse arrays of information—the development of the V-2 rocket and the technologies that made it possible, the history of colonialism and genocide in German Southwest Africa, the growth of petrochemical industries producing synthetic products, especially plastic and mind-altering drugs, the rise of multinational corporations, the evolution of German expressionist cinema, and the development of Pavlovian and behavioristic psychology, not to mention frequent allusions to Hollywood films, pop culture stereotypes, and primitive myths— Pynchon constructs an encyclopedic and entropic narrative. This narrative, at once overarching and kaleidoscopic, shifts without warning from one point of view to another, from present to past, from one place or country to another, and from reality to fantasy, dream, or drug-induced hallucination.

In a perceptive early review of *Gravity's Rainbow,* Richard Poirier argues that Pynchon's fiction takes the shape it does because it responds directly to how ways of perceiving and imagining are already embedded *in* current technology.[7] Although closely related, the approach taken here builds instead upon Deleuze and Guattari's notion that technologies always operate within and as part of a larger historical assemblage, or a multiplicity in which heterogeneous terms and relations function together in a symbiosis, or "sympathy."[8] According to their pragmatic theory of language, writing (and the production of statements generally) occurs only from within one side of this assemblage, the "collective assemblage of enunciation," which is linked in a relationship of reciprocal determination to a specific distribution of bodies, or a "machinic assemblage." In the assemblage, all statements are collective by nature and operate as "order-words" or "incorporal transformations"; the author of a statement simply functions as a part.[9] Yet Deleuze draws the further distinction between an author and a writer: an author, as subject of an enunciation or statement (like any user of language), can express a feeling or belief, designate a certain state of things, or signify a relationship; a writer, on the other hand, "invents assemblages from the assemblages which invented him, he makes one multiplicity pass into another." The difficulty, Deleuze adds, "lies in making all the elements from a non-homogeneous group conspire . . . [and] function together."[10]

Thomas Pynchon is a writer precisely in Deleuze's sense: in *Gravity's Rainbow* he invents an assemblage out of the historical assemblage that may be said to have formed him (and probably many of his readers as well). Three devices in particular—the method of "mapping on," the concept of the "interface," and a topographical multiplicity designated as "the Zone"—provide the main textual means by which this fictional assemblage is articulated. Like every assemblage, *Gravity's Rainbow* also consists of a mixture of different "semiotic regimes," each one a specific way to conjoin words or statements with a specific disposition of bodies. Pynchon's novel shows how these semiotic regimes all function within the same historical context: one regime provides the means by which a "They-system" of power relations can stifle and overcode the multiplicities out of which it emerges, another offers strategies of resistance, and yet another figures betrayal as the means by which forms of subjectivity are produced.

Before proceeding, it may be worth noting a striking parallel between one of Pynchon's underlying themes and a basic concept informing *Anti-Oedipus* and *A Thousand Plateaus,* Deleuze and Guattari's two-volume work on capitalism and schizophrenia. The reasons for this parallel are no doubt complex, but they probably arise from a similar response to the proliferation of life-denying agencies of coding and control. The frightening conjunctions of destructive power and desire evident in the twentieth century which Pynchon traces as "The Plot That Has No Name" in his first novel *V.* and which are given fuller, more concrete elaboration in *Gravity's Rainbow* are the specific and visible workings of what Deleuze and Guattari designate as an "abstract machine." This abstract machine, which increasingly (re)defines the terms of contemporary social existence, reduces the multiplicities of life to codable and thus manipulatable elements in a structure of power and control that both Pynchon and Deleuze and Guattari identify with the rationalizing dynamic of Western history.

II. Throughout *Gravity's Rainbow,* characters, places, and events constantly map on to one another and to other reference systems, the result being a vertiginous proliferation of orderings and interpretative schemes mixing history, myth, geopolitics, modern science, technology, and the mass media.[11] As a whole, the novel maps or projects a set of concerns, in fact, a whole sensibility conspicuous in America in the late 1960s, onto events in Europe at the end of World War II. More locally, the self-conscious narrator often proceeds by discovering or proposing various possible mappings among the novel's multiple plots and myriad characters. To be sure, not all of these mappings are to be taken with equal seriousness; nevertheless, several examples will indicate how the device of mapping on provides an underlying coherence for a diversity of thematically and stylistically ordered information.

Early in the novel, which is set in London in 1944, we discover that the new German rocket bombs are falling at points that happen to coincide exactly with the "stars" on a map of sexual encounters kept by the central protagonist, the American Lieutenant Tyrone Slothrop. It is also revealed that, as an infant, "Baby Tyrone" had been conditioned by a Pavlovian psychologist at Harvard to get an erection from an unknown "mystery stimulus" (which may or may not have been extinguished) and that, as an adult, Slothrop tends atavistically to see signs of God's presence in the sky, as if the influence of his Puritan ancestry still persisted over generations. Not surprisingly, Slothrop's psychosexual profile is of special interest to a number of Allied intelligence agencies, including the one for which he is working. Ordered to submit to a sodium amytal injection, he experiences an extraordinary cloacal fantasy that begins with a trip down the toilet at Roseland Ballroom in search of his dropped harmonica and culminates in a shoot-out scene in the Wild West. Newly invented psychological tests such as the Minnesota Multiphasic Personality Inventory, to which Slothrop also submits, also reveal that he has a wide variety of personality disorders.

About the same time, the Allied command discovers that the German rocket bombs are falling on London in a Poisson distribution, that is, according to a statistical pattern that can be calculated mathematically. That both the rocket strikes and Slothrop's sexual encounters fall into an essentially random distribution is hardly surprising, but that the two distributions coincide point for point constitutes an anomaly or singularity that initiates *Gravity's Rainbow*'s central plot. Putting into question relations of cause and effect, this enigmatic coincidence brings under critical scrutiny a number of agencies and technologies by which Western culture attempts to define and control reality (most obviously: through behaviorism, missile guidance systems, the cinema, and psychic communication with "the other side"). Yet, between the coincidence and the interpretive systems called upon to explain it, an unbridgeable gap or incommensurability always remains, leaving open the possibility that the central plot is indeterminate.

The presentation of the various characters and their relationships gives rise to a variety of other mappings. When Slothrop realizes that he is being tested and observed, he begins to wonder if he is not the focal point of a plot whose dimensions reach back into his past and are entwined with research efforts somehow linked to the development of the German V-2 rocket. His paranoia intensifies in the war's aftermath when he discovers the existence of a special rocket constructed to house a mysterious "black instrument" (the *Schwarzgerät*), which promises to reveal exactly how his personal past connects with the historical past. Yet, for all its seeming importance, this quest for information is treated parodically—"The Schwarzgerät is no Grail, Ace, that's not what the G in Imipolex G stands for" (364), he says to himself at one point—and gradually Slothrop himself begins to dissolve as the "band-width" of his personality (measured as a function of "time differentials") tends to slope toward zero, as if his paranoid apprehensions about his past were the only thing holding his personality together.[12] In contrast to the apparent solidity insured by the details of his military dossier and psychosexual profile, "Slothrop" begins to scatter and thin, becoming unlocatable in the terms that these coordinate systems and regimes of visibility provide.

Slothrop's quest is doubled by two other searches for parts of the V-2, one by a black African named Enzian and another by Enzian's white Russian half-brother, Tchitcherine, the former in order to save the remnants of his Herero tribe from racial suicide, the latter in order to destroy Enzian and thereby eliminate all trace of his negative, or black, mirror image. Yet these geographically mirroring symmetries are not the only means by which these characters map on to one another: at one point the narrator describes Tchitcherine as "a giant supermolecule with so many open bonds available at any given time" (346), thus encouraging us to think of relations between some of the characters as chemical reactions; at another, the narrator reports that fragments of Slothrop's disintegrating personality may have grown into "consistent personae of their own," thus making some of the novel's population "offshoots of his [Slothrop's] original scattering" (742).

On the German side, a commander of a V-2 rocket battery, the Nazi intellectual Major Weissmann, code name Blicero, provides the basis for a variety of cultural mappings. As his given name suggests and code name underscores (the name is taken from *Blicker,* the nickname the early Germans gave to Death, with its associations of bleaching and blankness), Weissmann/Blicero represents white European man, now plunged deeply into perversion and decadence. Seldom portrayed simply on the level of depicted events but usually in relation to fairy tale, cultural fantasy, history, and myth, Weissmann first appears in a sadomasochistic sexual reenactment of *Hansel und Gretel.* He plays (in drag) the evil witch, while a young German soldier named Gottfried and the Dutch double agent Katje Borgesius (who will later be involved in the plot against her lover, Slothrop) play the parts of the children. Weissmann's perverse relationship with Gottfried recalls an earlier relationship formed in the 1930s with the Herero boy Enzian. While still a young soldier in German Southwest Africa, Weissmann had seduced Enzian with talk of Rilkean "transformation" and "masculine technologies": "Beyond simple steel erection, the Rocket was an entire system *won,* away from the feminine darkness, held against the entropies of lovable but scatterbrained Mother Nature: that was the first thing he [Enzian] was obliged by Weissmann to learn, his first step toward citizenship in the Zone" (324). This system will later become a prop in Weissmann's own demonic scenario of power and transcendance. Having become a cunning administrator with fearful power and strange desires—in many respects, the narrator informs us, he resembles the actor Rudolf Klein-Rugge, famous for the part of Dr. Mabuse in Friz Lang's film—Weissmann manipulates German V-2 rocket engineers such as Franz Pökler into constructing a special housing—the *Schwarzgerät,* or "black instrument"—made of a new synthetic plastic called Imipolex G. At the end of the war, in an atavistic attempt to undo the Abraham-Isaac story and at the same time leap ahead into the future of manned space flight, Weissmann sacrifices his lover, Gottfried, by inserting him into the *Schwarzgerät* and firing him toward the North Pole from Lüneburg Heath. Seeking escape from "the Old European cycle of infection and death," as he calls it, Weissmann reflects on how the Faustian intellectual need to transcend has become "a sterile grace." As a corrupt and corrupting father figure, moreover, Weissmann maps on to the many "Pernicious Pops" in the novel, so that by its conclusion the narrator will refer to him as the "father you will never quite manage to kill" (747).

Wiessmann's construction as a character also reveals a significant historical dimension of the novel's textual mapping. In an article on "Media and Drugs in Pynchon's Second World War," Friedrich Kittler gathers evidence that suggests that the character Weissmann-Blicero represents a form of double exposure based on the two German commanders of Peenemünde during the war.[13] The first, General Walter Dornberger, was an army ordnance officer who discovered Werner von Braun and who later wrote a book about the development of the V-2 (a book Pynchon obviously draws upon). In 1944, "by special decree," Dornberger was replaced by the sinister SS Chief Squad Leader Dr. Hans Kammler. Kittler notes that Kammler, like Pynchon, has destroyed all his photographs, but the important point is that Kammler, like Blicero, disappeared in the aftermath of the war. All that is known for certain is that his bodyguard had strict orders to shoot him if capture by the Allies appeared imminent. Thus, by combining the two historical figures of Dornberger and Kammler in the Weissmann-Blicero character, Pynchon neatly encapsulates much of the history of the Peenemünde military base during the war.

Although Kittler is primarily interested in how "narratability" in *Gravity's Rainbow* must be read in relation to the "semio-technology" of media developed during the war, he points to further evidence of the extent to which Pynchon's various mappings are based on historical fact. Like Flaubert's *Salammbô* and other historical novels, *Gravity's Rainbow* is "essentially founded on documentary sources, many of which—circuit diagrams and differential equations, corporate contracts and organizational plans—are textualized for the first time." However, by simultaneously blurring the distinctions between what is apparently real and the dreams, fantasies, and hallucinations of the characters, *Gravity's Rainbow* often subverts the ontological status of what it depicts.[14] This tendency is clearly motivated by an interest in what lies on "the other side" of the empirical or phenomenal world. Indeed, part 1 is entitled "Beyond the Zero," which means beyond the realm of the empirically verifiable and the limitations of rational, cause/effect thinking, and by extension, beyond death. (The epigraph for part 1 is taken from Werner von Braun's statement that nature does not know death, only infinite transformation.) Many characters, in fact, are visited by eery, often unexplainable intrusions from "the other side": if not snatched by death in the soundless, fiery illumination of the rocket's fall in London, they are touched by the presence of voices or shadowy shapes, such as the giant angel spotted by bomber pilots over Lübeck, the rainbow-colored wind that unpredictably sweeps across Mount Brocken, or the mystical Kirghiz light in south central Asia.

This interest in what lies on "the other side" also motivates numerous psychic mappings of character relationships. The otherworldly communications of Carroll Eventyr, a spiritualist medium employed by an experimental intelligence agency referred to as "the White Visitation," offer a dramatic case in point. Eventyr's "control" in the spirit world is Peter Sachsa, who was, in turn, a medium in Weimar Germany in the late 1920s. Eventyr's connection to Sachsa allows the narrative to move from séances in the novel's present (1944–45) to earlier ones, and then to circulate freely through the minds and activities of characters "on both sides." When Eventyr becomes more curious about the life of his control, he is warned against intruding into forbidden territory. It then occurs to the narrator that Eventyr may be endangering his lover's life as well: "Then will they try to get Nora too? If there are analogies here, if Eventyr does, somehow, map on to Peter Sachsa, then does Nora Dodson-Truck become the woman Sachsa loved, Leni Pökler?" (218). As this and other mappings are subsequently affirmed, the reader is encouraged to map other character relationships as well. In an earlier exchange between Leni and her husband, Franz, a "cause and effect man," Leni herself advocates "mapping on to different coordinate systems" (159) as an alternative to cause/effect thinking.

III. Like the strategy of mapping on, Pynchon deploys the notion of the interface both locally and as a generalized textual device. In the scientific sense, an interface is a membrane or partition that at the same time functions as a conduit for exchange. In *L'Espace critique,* a study of the crisis of space brought about by recent developments in science and technology, Paul Virilio discusses the interface in terms directly relevant to Pynchon's appropriation of it as a textual device. Virilio points out that with the interface, "the limitation of space has become commutation: the radical separation, the necessary crossing, the transit of a constant activity, the activity of incessant exchanges, the transfer between two environments. What used to be the boundary of a material, its 'terminus,' has become an entryway hidden in the most imperceptible entity." The interface thus constitutes a new kind of surface, precisely because it "annuls the classical separation of position, of instant or object, as well as the traditional partitioning of space into physical dimensions, in favor of an almost instantaneous configuration in which the observer and observed are suddenly linked, confused and chained by an encoded language from which emerges the ambiguity of interpretation of represented form-images." [15]

Pynchon takes full advantage of this commingling ambiguity in his treatment of the interface between the two sides of the movie screen. Indeed, the cinema interface so pervades *Gravity's Rainbow,* by entering into and defining the text at various levels and providing numerous instances of textual motivation, that it will require a more lengthy discussion.[16] As we shall see, these cinematic determinations are justified by its multiple importance as a technology crucial to the rocket's development, as *the* modern psychic apparatus that subjectifies through effects of the moving image, and, perhaps most important, as an apparatus that by deterritorializing the image, initiates the becoming-image of the world.

The reciprocal relay effect of rocket and cinema technologies begins with Fritz Lang's film *Die Frau im Mond* (1929), in which a rocket carries passengers to the moon after a reverse countdown sequence that is immediately carried over and applied to real rocket launches.[17] It is this film, mentioned several times in the novel, that so enraptures Franz Pökler and determines his future career as a rocket engineer. It seems hardly accidental, therefore, that there are also significant technical convergences between film and the rocket's experimental development. The construction of the rocket's internal guidance system provides one striking example. Guidance depends not only on the rocket's position and velocity, variables that can be observed externally, but more essentially on the rocket's rate of acceleration, which requires internal monitoring in order to obtain the figures necessary for calculating the double integral equations (406). To solve this problem, German engineers inserted high-speed Askania cameras into a part of the rocket housing containing measuring instruments, whose gauges were then photographed during the rocket's flight: "After the flight the film was recovered, and the data played back. Engineers sat around looking at movies of dials" (407). Furthermore, the rocket launches themselves were always filmed, and these films proved essential to the rocket's future role. Although Hitler had once visited the V-2 rocket test site at Peenemünde, it was only when he saw a film of an experimental firing that he became convinced of its value as a weapon.[18] Thus, from its very inception, the rocket was connected both internally and externally to the cinema as an automatic writing machine or inscription device.

Pynchon's narrator remarks that the very equations that calculate the rocket's trajectory reflect an essential parallelism between the rocket's flight and film as a technical medium, since film also counterfeits movement through a series of infinitesimal increments, or frames: "There has been this strange connection between the German mind and the rapid flashing of successive stills to counterfeit movement, for at least two centuries—since Leibniz, in the process of inventing calculus, used the same approach to break up the trajectories of cannonballs through the air" (407). The narrator then relates how Franz Pökler, the same engineer enraptured by Lang's movie, was "to be given proof that these techniques had been extended past images on film, to human lives" (407).

Pökler's fanatic dedication to work on the rocket eventually estranges him from his wife, Leni, who takes their daughter, Ilse, and abandons him. Years later, Pökler's superior, Major Weissman, locates Pökler's supposed daughter, now a young teenager, and in return for special work on the *Schwarzgerät* allows her to visit Franz once a summer. From the beginning Pökler suspects her identity yet, in his loneliness, accepts the arrangement:

> So it has gone for the six years since. A daughter a year, each one about a year older, each time taking up nearly from scratch. The only continuity has been her name, and Zwölfkinder [a German Disneyland they visit together] and Pökler's love—love something like the persistence of vision, for They have used it to create for him the moving image of a daughter, flashing him only these summertime frames of her, leaving it to him to build the illusion of a single child . . . what would the time scale matter, a 24th of a second or a year (no more, the engineer thought, than in a wind-tunnel, or an oscillograph whose turning drum you could speed or slow at will . . .)? (422)

A study in repression, Pökler knows and doesn't want to know that "his" child comes from the death camps nearby, knows and doesn't want to know that the rockets are weapons of death, not vehicles that will allow him to escape earth's gravity and fly to the moon, as in Lang's *Die Frau im Mond*. When Pökler finally refuses incest with his putative daughter, a refusal his Nazi manipulators had not been counting on, he becomes, the narrator tells us, a real father and achieves a certain release.

Pökler's ethical action, however, is only a social adjustment to machinic (specifically, cinematic) effects. If film is not life but "the rapid flashing of successive stills to counterfeit movement" (407), what is human consciousness or even identity in the film age if not a similarly illusive sequence of images? As the example of Pökler's cinematic child suggests, *Gravity's Rainbow* urges us to ask the question not in metaphysical but in political terms: what agencies and instrumentalities are responsible for our perceptions and the images that ultimately constitute our identity? At the same time, the novel underscores our willingness to participate in such constructed identities and fabricated scenarios and suggests that it may be already too late to reclaim anything like a real self. Slothrop himself illustrates this dilemma.

Midway through the novel, wandering more and more aimlessly in post-war Germany, Slothrop takes up with the aging film star, Greta Erdmann. In part motivated by the absurd coincidence that the phony passport he carries bears the name of her ex-husband, Max Schlepzig, she and Slothrop reenact a sadomasochistic scene from *Alpdrücken* ("Nightmare"), one of her early "porno-expressionist" films. We soon discover that, as a consequence of making this scene, Greta conceived the daughter, Bianca, for whom she is now searching and, further, that this same scene aroused Franz Pökler to father his daughter, Ilse, on the same night he saw the film. Thus the revelation that Bianca and Ilse are "cinematic twins," in both cases the product of a screened or cinematic fantasy, connects a series of parallel relationships within an array of widely dispersed characters and events. In the light of this cinematic interface, Slothrop's later sexual intercourse with Bianca must be seen as a kind of symbolic incest, a reading reinforced by the sequence of events from Franz Pökler's life spliced in between the account of Slothrop's encounters with Greta and Bianca.

Slothrop's emotionally intense encounter with Ilse's cinematic twin, Bianca, is no doubt the more complex and is a turning point insofar as Slothrop's failure to save her life signals the beginning of his own disintegration. In a parody of a Hollywood thirties comedy, he meets her on the *Anubis,* a rich pleasure boat ferrying not the souls of the dead to judgment, as the name and jackal on the bowsprit imply, but an international collection of decadents floridly entwined in daisy chains of sexual intercourse. She's ready for escape, and he's the man for the occasion, since he alone is aware of the danger posed by her mother's murderous obsessions. They soon make love, but as "he disentangles himself . . . he creates a bureaucracy of departure, inoculations against forgetting, exit visas stamped with lovebites . . . but coming back is something he's already forgotten about" (470–471). However, Bianca's last look has an arresting effect and motivates a long cinematic passage composed of flashing images in which she blurs into a generic image of the girl Slothrop left behind:

> Her look now—this deeping arrest—has already broken Slothrop's seeing heart: has broken and broken, that same look swung as he drove by, thrust away into twilights of moss and crumbling colony, of skinny clouded cylinder gas pumps, of tin Moxie signs gentian and bittersweet as the taste they were there to hustle on the weathered sides of barns, looked for how many Last Times up in the rearview mirror, all of them too far inside metal and

combustion, allowing the days' targets more reality than anything that might come up by surprise, by Murphy's Law, where the salvation could be. . . . Lost, again and again, past poor dam-busted and drowned Becket, up and down the rut-brown slopes, the hayrakes rusting in the afternoon, the sky purple-gray, dark as chewed gum, the mist starting to make white dashes in the air, aimed earthward a quarter, a half inch . . . she looked at him once, of course he still remembers, from down at the end of a lunchwagon counter, grill smoke working onto the windows patient as shoe grease against the rain for the plaid, hunched-up leaky handful inside, off the jukebox a quick twinkle in the bleat of a trombone, a reed section, planting swing notes precisely into the groove between silent midpoint and next beat, jumping it *pah* (hm) *pah* (hm) *pah* so exactly in the groove that you knew it was ahead but *felt* it was behind, both of you, at both ends of the counter, could feel it, feel your age delivered into a new kind of time that may have allowed you to miss the rest, the graceless expectations of old men who watched, in bifocal and mucus indifference, watched you lindy hop into the pit by millions, as many millions as necessary. . . . Of course Slothrop lost her, and kept losing her—it was an American requirement—out the windows of the Greyhound, passing into beveled stonery, green and elm-folded on into a failure of perception, or, in a more sinister sense, of will (you used to know what these words mean), she has moved on, untroubled, too much Theirs, no chance of a beige summer spook at *her* roadside. . . .

Leaving Slothrop in his city-reflexes and Harvard crew sox—both happening to be redring manacles, comicbook irons (though the comic book was virtually uncirculated, found by chance near nightfall by a hopper at a Berkshire sandbank. The name of the hero—or being—was Sundial. The frames never enclosed him—or it—for long enough to tell. Sundial, flashing in, flashing out again, came from "across the wind," by which readers understood "across some flow, more or less vertical: a wall in constant motion"—over there was a different world, where Sundial took care of business they would never understand).

Distant, yes these are pretty distant. Sure they are. Too much closer and it begins to hurt to bring her back. But there is this Eurydice-obsession, this *bringing back out of* . . . though how much easier just to leave her there, in fetid carbide and dead-canary soups of breath and come out and have comfort enough to try only for a reasonable fascimile—"Why bring her back? Why try? It's only the difference between the real boxtop and the one you draw for them." No. How can he believe that? It's what They want him to believe, but how can he? No difference between a boxtop and its image, all right, their whole economy's based on *that* . . . but she must be more than an image, a product, a promise to pay. . . .

Of all her putative fathers—Max Schlepzig and masked extras on one side of the moving film, Franz Pökler and certainly other pairs of hands busy through trouser cloth, that *Alpdrücken* Night, on the other,—Bianca is closest, this last possible moment below decks here behind the ravening jackal, closest to you who came in blinding color, slouched alone in your seat, never threatened along any rookwise row or diagonal all night, you whose interdiction from her mother's water-white love is absolute, you, alone, saying *sure I know them,* omitted, chuckling *count me in,* unable, thinking *probably some hooker* . . . She favors you, most of all. You'll never get to see her. So somebody has to tell you. (471–472)

This lengthy passage clearly demonstrates how Pynchon's writing interfaces on multiple levels with cinema. First, the fluid and only seemingly digressive prose creates spatial and temporal montage effects that are both inspired by film and demonstrably worried about the kind of detachment and slide it makes possible. More specifically, through the cinema–prose fiction interface, the look of an abandoned lover is slowly serialized over time into a "boxtop image" as movements in a Greyhound bus across a landscape, memory images, and scenes from both an imaginary film and several unidentified generic Hollywood films all enter and commingle in a phantasmatic space neither completely fictional nor materially real. Second, the narrator's attempt to address Slothrop directly, even though Slothrop is on "the other side" of the interface and cannot respond, adds a different kind of complexity to the passage. For this attempt on the narrator's part to hail or interpellate Slothrop figuratively doubles Slothrop's 'interfacial' questioning of Bianca's reality, and thus it can only confirm the reader's growing sense that Slothrop himself is losing distinctiveness, becoming more and more dispersed within a conglomerate of images and representations, as if the layering of images over time which bestowed upon him substance and consistency ("temporal bandwidth") was no longer holding (him) together.

But while Pynchon often presents film as an apparatus that frames and subjectivizes us, making of us a certain kind of subject, subjected to and by the image, as in Heidegger's description of modern man as *subjectum* of the world picture,[19] he also points toward singular images beyond the apparatus's regulation. Near the end of the novel, the narrator specifically mentions "presences we are not supposed to see—wind gods, hilltop gods, sunset gods—that we train ourselves away from to keep from looking further even though enough of us do, leave their electric voices behind in the twi- light" (720). Moreover, by treating the image as both frame and interface, as a surface where worlds meet and exchanges take place—as in the fleeting presence of Sundial—Pynchon holds out the possibility that the image can be a vehicle for movements that, though framed, are not necessarily cap- tured.

However, the dominant impression or effect created by Pynchon's use of film and the cinematic apparatus in *Gravity's Rainbow* is to erode com- pletely any possibility of a fixed or stable opposition between the world on film and the world unmediated by it.[20] This aspect of the novel is thematized most directly through the career of one of the characters, the filmmaker and black marketeer Gerhardt von Göll, the director of *Alpdrücken* and former associate of the German expressionist film directors Lang, Pabst, and Lub- itsch (112). Von Göll's first film for the Allies is a propaganda film in which British soldiers masquerade as the *Schwarzkommando*, an elite German rocket battery composed of black Hereros from German Southwest Africa. When it is later discovered that the *Schwarzkommando* actually exists, von Göll is convinced that "his film somehow brought them into being"; his mission, henceforth, is "to sow in the Zone seeds of reality" (388). Von Göll's latest film, entitled *New Dope*, is therefore even more ambi- tious:

> There is a movie going on, under the rug. On the floor, 24 hours a day, pull back the rug sure enough there's that damn movie! A really offensive and tasteless film by Gerhardt von Göll, daily rushes in fact form a project which will never be completed. Springer [von Göll's alias] just plans to keep it going indefinitely there, under the rug. The title is *New Dope*, and that's what it's about, a brand new kind of dope that nobody's ever heard of. One of the most annoying characteristics of the shit is that the minute you take it you are rendered incapable of ever telling anybody what it's like, or worse, where to get any. Dealers are as in the dark as anybody. All you can hope is that you'll come across somebody in the act of taking (shooting? smoking? swallowing?) some. It is the dope that finds *you*, ap- parently. Part of a reverse world whose agents run around with guns which are like vacuum cleaners operating in the direction of life—pull the trigger and bullets are sucked back out of the recently dead into the barrel, and the Great Irreversible is actually reversed as the corpse comes to life to the accompaniment of a backwards gunshot. (745)

Though obviously comic, the passage again reveals how film or the moving image generates a multiplicity of connections; it also makes the often evident and essential point that the connection between cinema and drugs is never fortuitous.[21] Like the technologies of rocket and cinema, which both rupture and reverse sequences of cause-effect and therefore problematize any simple relationship with the real, the technology of drugs also operates as a flight apparatus to other worlds. However, with *New Dope*—the pun is not only unavoidable but fully functional—the interface results from a projection not on the wall but on the floor itself, a de-grounding effect hilariously confirmed by the film's subject matter, the discovery of a new drug whose origin disappears with its consumption. Reference to a new drug, moreover, cannot help but evoke associations with Oneirine, a fictional drug mentioned several times earlier in the novel, specifically in connection with its property of "time-modulation" (389). One of the many new drugs produced by synthesizing polymer compounds in the 1930s, Oneirine induces not only paranoia but "hauntings [that] show a definite narrative continuity" (703). Tellingly, Oneirine also happens to be von Göll's drug of choice. Thus, through a subtle network of associations between "New Dope" and Oneirine, Pynchon slyly establishes a self-reflective parallel between von Göll's films and his own prose fictional narrative, but in a convolution that multiplies connections (and slippages) between representations internal to the novel and the novel itself.[22]

It is also through the figure of von Göll that Pynchon introduces the theme of the world's becoming-image. In a rescue mission late in the novel, when Slothrop questions von Göll's prior arrangements with the Russians: "Springer, this ain't the fuckin' *movies* now, come on," von Göll only rejoins: "Not yet. Maybe not quite yet. You'd better enjoy it while you can. Someday, when the film is fast enough, the equipment pocket-size and burdenless and selling at people's prices, the lights and booms no longer necessary, *then* . . . then." (527). In one sense, of course, von Göll's statement simply anticipates the effects of television, effects that Pynchon will later explore in *Vineland*. In another, however, von Göll's "not yet" is pure anachronism. Not only is Slothrop already "in" the film—as Pynchon takes pains to make obvious in Slothrop's relations with women like Katje, Greta, and Bianca—but so are the narrator and reader. Like Burroughs's writing, *Gravity's Rainbow* posits a Bergsonian, machinic world of images in which "the film never stops" and in which privileged instances of subjective perception are always subsumed in a mobile constellation of relationships with other images.[23]

The cinema screen is not the only instance of an interface in the novel. Pynchon extends the notion to a variety of different domains, including an imaginary molecular realm below the threshold of human visibility. In one scene, Enzian rushes in to save a Herero woman from a self-induced abortion, only to encounter her husband, Pavel, hallucinating on "leunagasolin," which makes him see the Moss creature and "The Water Giant, a mile-high visitor made all of flowing water who likes to dance, twisting from the waist, arms blowing loosely along the sky" (523). Pavel is then called by the voices of the "Fungus Pygmies who breed in the tanks at the interface between fuel and water bottom." The point of this microcosmic fantasy is that the other side also has its interfaces with us and its little moments of communication.[24] But the question raised here and echoed more seriously throughout the novel is whether what lies on "the other side" is subject to the same form of organization and control, whether inside and outside simply duplicate the same bureaucratic arrangement, or whether there is an ultimate limit, an interface that might open out onto a real beyond and hence onto some form of absolute exteriority.

IV. This question is most fully explored in part 3, entitled "In the Zone." According to the novel's figurative topography, the Zone is what lies "Beyond the Zero" of part 1. An epigraph drawn from *The Wizard of Oz,* Dorothy's fearful, "Toto, I have a feeling we're not in Kansas any more," signals that if grey and bureaucratic London is anything like Kansas, then the Zone will open out onto a technicolor phantasmagoria. On the level of depicted events, the Zone encompasses the space lying between "the zero," or absolute destruction of an older (mainly European) political order, and "the one," or unity of the newly emerging technological order of the transnational rocket-state. The Zone is thus a space of ruins and the allegories they spawn, where geographies are mental maps and vice versa, but above all a space of indeterminacy and singularity, where no patterns converge. The rocket's *Brennschluss* ("burn-out") points hang in the sky overhead, the narrator tells us (in another instance of mapping on), as "a constellation waiting to have a 13th sign of the Zodiac named for it . . . but they lie so close to Earth that from many places they can't be seen at all, and from places inside the zone where they can be seen, they fall into completely different patterns" (302).

For many of the novel's characters, such as the Argentine anarchists or Enzian's *Schwarzkommando,* the collapse into chaos of the German national state and all social organization also opens up new, even utopian possibilities: "maybe for a little while all the fences are down, one road as good as another, the whole space of the Zone cleared, depolarized, and somewhere inside the waste of it a single set of coordinates from which to proceed, without elect, without preterite, without even nationality to fuck it up" (556). For Slothrop, who enters the Zone with forged identity papers and must assume many roles in his quest for information about the *Schwarzgerät*, the Zone is an existential carnival where identities can be easily assumed and quickly shed, or bartered like secondhand clothes, because of the absence of any socially defined reality. Like his sodium amytol fantasy, it is a plunge into a cartoonish, surreal realm, and thus an opportunity to see what is left out or hidden in the construction of modern social reality.[25] Right away, Slothrop is besieged by all manner of signs and seemingly significant shapes, or, as the narrator puts it, "traffic from the Other Side . . . (no serial time over there: events are all there in the same eternal moment and so certain messages don't always 'make sense' back here: they lack historical structure, they sound fanciful, or insane)" (624).

This collapse of diachronic order (and hence of cause and effect) is anticipated in part 1 in the confrontation between the statistician Roger Mexico and the Pavlovian behaviorist Edward Pointsman, whose total dedication to the "Book" of his master figures a perverse twist on modernism's privileged trope. Whereas Mexico's probability equations can encompass indeterminacy, discontinuity, and points of singularity in the "curve of life," Pointsman's empirically based methodology confines him within the rigid determinacies of either/or, zero/one. Faced with Mexico's distribution curves, Pointsman can only wonder: "How can Mexico play, so at his ease, with these symbols of randomness and fright? Innocent as a child, perhaps unaware—perhaps—that in his play he wrecks the elegant rooms of history, threatens the idea of cause and effect itself. What if Mexico's whole generation have turned out like this? Will Postwar be nothing but 'events,' newly created one moment to the next? No links? Is it the end of history?" (56).

As the concrete realization of Pointsman's fears, the Zone is populated not so much with linked events as with movements and flows in a flux of people, objects, signs, and representations. "It is a great frontierless streaming out here," the narrator proclaims (549), before describing all the nationalities "on the move." However, this nomadic space without direction or hierarchical structure soon becomes the site of a process of disassembly and reassembly. Slothrop himself will be disassembled (but something goes wrong, the narrator tells us, and he is not reassembled), as well as leaders such as Roosevelt: "a being They assembled, a being They would dismantle" (374). In these terms, *Gravity's Rainbow* represents the vast process of modernization accelerated by World War II. The Zone itself figures as the crucible necessary for the meltdown and dissolution of outdated territories, languages, and filiations, of all boundaries, forms, and even human identities impeding the installation of a new order that will take cybernetics as the model in its remaking of the world as a pure instrumentality.[26] As is frequent in Pynchon's fiction, this ominous theme is announced jokingly, when one Zone black market profiteer sighs, "Is it any wonder the world's gone insane, with information come to be the only real medium of exchange?" (258). Most of this information feeds the tentacular growth of the new rocket-state, whose most visible real world manifestation is a proliferating international cartel of petrochemical and plastic industries such as I. G. Farben, Dupont, and Shell Oil.

Do the birth and growth of the new rocket-state—and the order it represents—effectively close the Zone, or does the Zone extend beyond its confines, even providing the space or ground of the rocket-state's condition of possibility? The answer would seem to lie in Slothrop's various movements, not only because his quest for information about the mysterious rocket containing the *Schwarzgerät* articulates the novel's central plot (in both senses), but also because Slothrop's disassembly occurs simultaneously with the formation of this new order. If we are to believe that there is a central plot directed against Slothrop, then we must assume, along with Slothrop himself, that his conditioning as an infant locks him into a vast, overreaching scientific, military, and economic conspiracy. The putative unity of "the Firm," or They-system, as it comes to be called, which is gradually identified with the rocket-state and its supporting multinational cartel, would therefore seem to justify not only Slothrop's but the novel's pervasive paranoia. Paradoxically, this paranoia must effectively deny the multiplicity of forces, events, and singularities that the novel details, *and* yet still be considered valid insofar as this heterogeneity is slated to be homogenized and incorporated into component parts of the They-system.

Gravity's Rainbow frequently insists that this homogenizing process involves the "routinizing" of all forms of charisma, and above all that of the rocket, which powerfully conjoins Eros with Thanatos. At the same time, the extent to which the rocket can be routinized remains ambiguous and indeterminate. At one point, a character named Miklos Thanatz (whose name obviously evokes Thanatos) tells Slothrop that the rocket "really did possess a Max Weber charisma . . . some joyful—and *deeply* irrational— force the State bureaucracy could never routinize, against which it could not prevail" (464). Statements by representatives of the Firm support this view, while also revealing the kind of fear provoked by the irrationality of charisma and therefore the necessity for its bureaucratization. In fact, Dr. Rozsavolgyi, one of Slothrop's malevolent psychological testers, espouses what will become the objective of the rocket-state's bureaucratization: "But if personalities could be replaced by abstractions of power, if techniques developed by the corporations could be brought to bear, might not nations live rationally? One of the dearest Postwar hopes: that there should be no room for a terrible disease like charisma . . . that its rationalization should proceed while we had the time and resources" (81).

With the emergence and growth of the corporate, bureaucratic system of the rocket-state, however, another system or, rather, countersystem simultaneously blossoms. As we see in part 4, entitled "The Counterforce," this countersystem consists of a whole network of countercultural connections and relays, which attempt to subvert and desecrate the rationalizing semiotic processes of the Firm, or They-system, through its own scatological refusals, alternative sign systems, and "drug-epistemologies." Between the two systems, relayed in different ways by both, Slothrop traces a line that extends from his search for the *Schwarzgerät* to the more fragmented "molecular" lines of his dealings with the Counterforce, and then to the final dissolution of his identity in a process of becoming invisible.

V. Either capture by the They-system or disappearance from history: these appear to be the only options *Gravity's Rainbow* presents. Yet the line Slothrop traces hardly defines a stable opposition. Even at the level of plots, there are numerous defections, betrayals, and multiple crossings between the They-system and the Counterforce. Instead of structuring the novel, these two opposed types of organization in fact only make up parts of a complex arrangement of lines and dimensions articulating a multiplicity. In this sense, *Gravity's Rainbow* constitutes a Deleuzian assemblage. As with every assemblage, the novel defines an interface: on one side, or face, we find an overcoding agency or "abstract machine" (effectively identified with the They-system) which organizes subjects, statements, and materials into binary oppositions, thus insuring their convertibility and translatability, in short, their usefulness to the Firm; on the other side, or face, we witness a constant pull toward the outside and the uncodable exactly like the deterritorialized movements that Deleuze and Guattari designate as "lines of flight" *[lignes de fuite]*.

The term refers to the lines in an assemblage where the gradient of deterritorialization and decoding is greatest, in contrast with segmentary lines that cut up or define a territory according to rigid, binary-coded oppositions, and with molecular lines that are tangential, random, and fragmentary. Every assemblage, therefore, is composed of these three types of line: segmentary lines designate the boundaries of "molar aggregates" defined by semiotic regimes that code and overcode; molecular lines are the edges where the latter break down and diffract; and lines of flight are the paths of least resistance or greatest acceleration toward the assemblage's outside, or exteriority. Lines of flight thus trace not only paths of escape from dominant codes and systems of meaning but also map lines of transformation and metamorphosis or "becoming-other." Summarily, then, every assemblage presents two interfaces: one of deterritorialization and decoding, and one of reterritorialization and overcoding.

In *Gravity's Rainbow,* the rocket itself is situated exactly at the interface between these two sides: on the one hand, its flight represents a new vector of deterritorialization, while on the other, and for this very reason, it becomes the focus of institutional attempts to recode and channel (routinize) the energies it releases. On the novel's level of expression, this double valency is reflected in the rocket's polarized thematizations, as (most obviously) in its conjoining of Eros and Thanatos. Furthermore, as a vector of deterritorialization, the rocket is subjected not only to routinization by the rocket-state bureaucracy but also to elaborate interpretation or recoding.

Such interpretations, however, are often subjected to self-reflexive parody. At least one unwary critic understands Pynchon's treatment of the rocket as a "projection," or form of cultural sublimation, a simple Freudian reading that cannot be sustained in view of parodic passages such as the one near the novel's conclusion where the "world-renowned analyst Mickey Wuxtry-Wuxtry" opines that "Jamf was only a fiction, to help him [Slothrop] explain what he felt so terribly, so immediately in his genitals for those rockets each time exploding in the sky . . . to help him deny what he could not possibly admit: that he might be in love, in sexual love, with his, and his race's, death" (738).[27] However, if many passages, beginning with the celebratory banana breakfast early in the novel, are necessarily to be read in relation to the rocket, it is because the rocket functions not simply as a weapon of death but also and more importantly as a Deleuzian "desiring machine" that functions as a means of producing, coding, and channeling desire within a specific sociohistorical field.[28] In Deleuzian terms, the rocket technology and its attendant bureaucracy are not so much an expression of the death drive as a means by which the death drive, as the unknown itself, can be meaningfully recoded and reterritorialized.

As we saw earlier, the rocket operates both within and as part of a cinematic writing machine by means of which images of flight (in every sense) are produced, inscripted, and disseminated, and all at the same time. As a desiring machine, the rocket consequently produces and determines a certain "reading effect" or subjectivity dramatized both in Slothrop's attempt to retrieve the data of his personal past and in the Hereros' attempt to read—as rocket kabbalists and scholar-magicians—the signs of their future destiny. However, the rocket constitutes only part of a larger assemblage, which Pynchon's writing machine gradually delineates. Schematically, one side, or face, of this assemblage defines an enclosed space of paranoid interiority produced by the multiplication of connected points, while the other traces lines of flight passing through those points toward an exterior that defines the They-system's limit. Thus, in the assemblage that *Gravity's Rainbow* articulates, virtually any point of determination in its discourse—whether inscribed in scientific, historical, or mythical terms—also defines an interface with the indeterminate. In other words, the text presents a continuous proliferation of interfaces, and thus a multiplicity.

Again, certain features of this assemblage are anticipated in the intellectual conflict between Roger Mexico and Pointsman in part 1. Unlike Mexico, whose equations generate numerical multiplicities and who lives in a realm of probabilities, Pointsman cannot conceive of any place between one and zero, that is, in the excluded middle domain. "Like his master, I. P. Pavlov before him, he imagines the cortex of the brain as a mosaic of tiny on/off elements. Some are always in bright excitation, others darkly inhibited. The contours, bright and dark, keep changing. But each point is allowed only the two states: waking or sleep. One or zero. 'Summation,' 'transition,' 'irradiation,' 'concentration,' 'reciprocal induction'—all Pavlovian brain-mechanics—assumes the presence of these bi-stable points" (55). But things are not so simple, even for Pointsman's laboratory dogs, not to mention the "monster" Slothrop he seeks to observe and control. There are paradoxical phases, where weak stimuli get strong responses, and transmarginal phases, where stronger stimuli no longer produce stronger responses: "inside and outside remain just as they were, but the interface—the cortex of Dog Vanya's brain—is changing, in a number of ways" (79). Even more peculiar, at one end of experimental results there may be "silent extinctions beyond the zero," while at the other, ultraparadoxical phases in which the idea of the opposite weakens and inside and outside threaten to become part of the same field. Thus, even in a rigorously structured domain of "bi-stable points," binary oppositions break down into an immanent multiplicity of events that manifest themselves precisely at the interface with the external world.[29]

Inevitably, Pointsman comes to think of "the war itself as his *laboratory*" (49, Pynchon's emphasis) and of Slothrop as his "fox." His thinking thus mirrors the mental condition of the patient in the mental ward at the White Visitation who thinks that he *is* the war, newly enlivened after a catatonic period when the Runstedt offensive is initiated. Yet even though Pointsman will wonder if his colleague Spectro was right after all, that "Outside and Inside [could] be part of the same field" (144), he cannot permit himself to think what this might mean.

Pointsman's obsession with control, dramatized in his Pavlovian theorizing and hoped-for experiments with Slothrop, of course raises questions about how scientific research feeds the war effort and the subsequent installation of the technopolitical rocket-state. Indeed, questions about who or what is controlling the war and for what purpose are frequently posed, beginning with the séance for Nazi officers early in the novel in which the voice of Walter Rathenau announces the importance of control to the new technological state. According to Rathenau, the prophet and architect of Germany's first cartel-state economy during World War I, two questions are paramount: what is the nature of synthesis, and what is the nature of control? Later we see how these two questions dovetail in a molecular realm of ionic bonding and polymerization, as the novel retraces a line of development in modern organic chemistry. It begins with an actual event: the German chemist F. A. Kekulé's archetypal dream of a snake with its tail in its mouth ("the uroboros"), a dream that inspired him to try bonding carbonized benzene molecules into rings. This procedure eventually leads to the production of a whole new range of synthetic products, particularly dyes, plastics, and drugs.

The ideological implications of Kekulé's research are brought out through the fictional figure of Laszlo Jamf, who late in his life conceived a personal hatred for the covalent bond: "That something so mutable, so soft, as a sharing of electrons by atoms of carbon should lie at the core of life, his life, struck Jamf as a cosmic humiliation. Sharing? How much stronger, how everlasting was the ionic bond—where electrons are not shared, but captured. Seized! and held! polarized plus and minus, these atoms, no ambiguities. . . . how he came to love that clarity: how stable it was, such mineral stubbornness!" (577) In spearheading a move beyond the frailty and mortality of the organic bond through the synthesis of inorganic rings and chains, Jamf lays the grounds for a new conceptualization and extension of control. Like Pointsman, Jamf illustrates how scientific conceptualizations are implicitly ideological; and like Pointsman's, his statements clarify how the material possibility of the new rocket-state and the intellectual integrations on which it depends ultimately stem from new apparatuses of "capture." It is no playful coincidence, therefore, that Jamf is the scientist who experimented on Baby Tyrone at Harvard and thus is probably responsible for Slothrop's erotic response to the rocket. While the possibility that Jampf substituted an erectile plastic penis made of Imipolex G for Baby Tyrone's natural organ is hinted at but never definitely confirmed, the novel often insists that sexual behavior is the area where human beings are most susceptible to control, and that this vulnerability will always be taken advantage of by the They-system.

Gravity's Rainbow shows how these efforts to capture and control take place at every level, including that of language. About the same time (in the 1930s) that Jamf is developing his theory of polymerization, another character, the Russian intelligence officer Tchitcherine (who is also Slothrop's Soviet counterpart), is assigned to the "Weird Letters Committee" in Asia, probably as a disciplinary warning from the Communist Party. The purpose of this committee will be to impose the New Turkish Alphabet on the Kirghis in Baku. In this respect, the narrator informs us, the committee is very much like the committees on molecular structure, where one hears "how alphabetic is the nature of molecules": "See: how they are taken out from the coarse flow—shaped, cleaned, rectified, just as you once redeemed your letters from the lawless, the mortal streaming of human speech. . . . These are our letters, our words: they too can be modulated, broken, re-coupled, redefined, co-polymerized one to the other in worldwide chains that will surface now and then over long molecular silences, like the seen parts of a tapestry" (355). Neither a coincidence nor an analogy, the parallelism between reshaping words and molecules directly illustrates how an abstract machine working in different domains institutes a recoding of all preexistent "natural languages" into its own language of binary oppositions. Born in varied circumstances, but where the scientific and the political always overlap, this abstract machine brings about a new method of control, one that will be given formal elaboration only with the advent of cybernetics and information theory in the 1950s. What matters in *Gravity's Rainbow*, however, is how the operation of such an abstract machine is systematically effectuated and insured by the newly emergent rocket-state, which can thereby transcend both national and geopolitical boundaries.

Summarily, then, *Gravity's Rainbow* presents World War II as a watershed historical event that brings about a new technopolitical order and structure of power. The novel stages the emergence of this new order in the ruins and opened space of the Zone in terms that can be usefully described as an instance of what Deleuze and Guattari call an assemblage, or a multiplicity of heterogeneous, cofunctioning elements that operate by symbiosis. This assemblage has two sides and thus defines an interface. On one side, the human and material flux produced by the destruction of the war is taken up or captured, organized, and channeled by the rocket-state, which operates as an abstract machine that overcodes everything it has any use for. As an anonymous network and bureaucracy of power (a They-system), it constitutes not a conspiracy but a cofunctioning of institutions and technologies according to immanent criteria of instrumental performance. In this respect, it resembles what Michel Foucault calls disciplinary power.[30] For the same reason, however, paranoia, albeit useful as an epistemological assumption, cannot explain how the abstract machine gives a consistency to this new technopolitical order. The essential features of this order can now be extracted from the account of the novel given thus far:

1. Its codings are always binary. As a system of energized points and enervations, the brain is a multiplicity, but Pointsman, following Pavlov, can treat it only as a binary system.
2. It must capture and recode all primitive languages and territorialities, as in the imposition of the New Turkish Alphabet.
3. It penetrates nature itself and operates at a molecular level. Furthermore, as the examples of Pointsman, Kekulé, and Jampf illustrate, it is capable of capturing an entire scientific discipline, whose discoveries are in no sense ideologically neutral. It is even implied that the abstract machine operates through bureaucracies "of the other side" (478–79), as the narrator describes one such bureaucracy that routes Kekulé's dream from an ancestral, Jungian archetypal pool to the one scientist who would pervert it for the Firm's uses.
4. Its binary codings and recodings define molar aggregates that form the basis of large power blocks. In this way, its semiotic processes become

insinuated with the logic of history itself, from which it becomes inextricable.

VI. That "history" is no longer what "we" thought it was: this is the lesson that both Tchitcherine and Enzian, following Slothrop, eventually learn. Let us therefore consider their stories in some detail. As Tchitcherine himself realizes, he is initially useful to the Soviet Communist Party because his personal pursuit of his black half-brother, Enzian, coincides with its need to pursue and eliminate a heretical rocket-sect, of which Enzian is a leader. Tchitcherine, understandably, loses interest when he is captured by the much older machinations of the witch, Geli Tripping, who falls in love with him. At that point, like Slothrop, he will disappear from the novel.

Throughout most of its length, however, Tchitcherine is positioned on the ideological interface between the conspiratorial apparatus of the Party and the equally paranoia-producing network of petrochemical companies and their techno-scientific alliances. His contact with the latter occurs mainly through the sinister figure of Wimpe, a drug salesman and I. G. Farben representative with whom he has a number of shadowy, Dostoevskian dialogues, which are later echoed by the equally hallucinatory exchanges with the Party representative, Nikolai Ripov. According to the novel's method of narrative uncertainty, his encounter with Wimpe is presented as only a probable occurrence, while his exchanges with Ripov are perhaps only a "haunting," presumably the result of Tchitcherine's ingestion of Oneirine. In neither case, however, is the thematic seriousness of the encounter undercut by the obvious comic echoes set off by their names.

The *Verbindungsman* and self-styled drug salesman, Wimpe, readily admits to Tchitcherine, whose bodily injuries have made him a drug addict, that he is "really trafficking in pain," real pain he insists, and not the imponderables that addiction implies. However, it seems that there is a dilemma built into nature, much like the Heisenberg uncertainty principle in particle physics: "There is nearly complete parallelism between analgesis and addiction. The more pain it takes away, the more we desire it. It appears we can't have one property without the other, any more than a particle physicist can specify position without suffering an uncertainty as to the particle's velocity" (348). And the analogies, as Wimpe elaborates, hardly stop there:

> Think of what it would mean to find such a drug—to abolish pain rationally, without the extra cost of addiction. A surplus cost—surely there is

something in Marx and Engels . . . to cover this. A demand like "addiction," having nothing to do with real pain, real economic needs, unrelated to production or labor . . . we need fewer of these unknowns, not more. We know how to produce real pain. Wars, obviously . . . machines in the factories, industrial accidents, automobiles built to be unsafe, poisons in food, water, and even air—these are quantities tied directly to the economy. We know them, and we can control them. But "addiction?" What do we know of that? Fog and phantoms. No two experts will even agree on how to define the word. "Compulsion"? Who is not compelled? "Tolerance"? "Dependence"? What do they mean? All we have are the thousand, dim academic theories. A rational economy cannot depend on psychological quirks. We could not plan.   (348–349)

From which point, and with implacable logic, it is only a step to "our little chemical cartel" as the model for the very structure of nations in the postwar period.

Wimpe thus spells out the fuller operational imperatives of the new order of the rocket-state: in order to insure ultimate victory—beyond the economic and ideological victory it already enjoys—this order must be capable of regulating human pain and suffering in a rational way. But such a rationalized "libidinal economy" would only further extend the regime of control and repression that the novel increasingly identifies with Western history. Again Wimpe explains:

The basic problem . . . has always been getting other people to die for you. What's worth enough for a man to give up his life? That's where religion had the edge, for centuries. Religion was always about death. It was used not as an opiate so much as a technique—it got people to die for one particular set of beliefs about death. Perverse, natürlich, but who are you to judge? It was a good pitch while it worked. But ever since it became impossible to die for death, we have had a secular version—yours. Die to help History grow to its predestined shape. Die knowing your act will bring a good end a bit closer.   (701)

Thus, on both sides of the Eastern and Western ideological interface, *history* has come to mean "Their" successful effort to get us to die for "Them," to pay for "Their" crimes, to believe in "Their" eternal hegemony. And what makes this perversion of the narrative of human emancipation possible is our unmasterable fear of death.

In his later haunting by the Party representative Nikolai Ripov, Tchitcherine is accused of never having been "of the faith," of having had a "death-bed conversion" to a belief in History. Although he expects to be liquidated for his doubts about the Dialectic, he is informed instead that he is still useful to the Party and needed for the relocation of captured German rocket personnel to Central Asia. But Tchitcherine realizes that this use, unlike his atavistic revenge quest for his black half-brother, Enzian, corresponds to no underlying psychic need of his own. Thus, "in *his* dialectic, his own life's unfolding, to return to Central Asia is, operationally, to die" (706, Pynchon's emphasis). As in the case of Slothrop, life means dropping out of the historical plot in a "becoming-invisible."[31]

Which brings us back to the other side of the interface defined by the assemblage constituted in the Zone. If, as we have seen, on one side, an abstract machine programs or codes all signs and meanings for control by the They-system, to the point of not only saturating this new historical space with plots but making history itself a plot, on the other side of the interface, plots break down into indeterminate uncertainties or functions of probability, as the narrator often emphasizes, in a burgeoning of multiplicities. Thus, while the first side articulates an entropic space of paranoid enclosure and redundancy (meaning as binary use-value), this other side opens upon a space of surprise and singularity where structures undergo decoding and deterritorialization, sometimes even accelerating into movements beyond meaning and significance in Deleuzian lines of flight to the outside and outer limit of the Western cultural/historical field. Slothrop is traveling on one such line of flight, and he eventually disappears from the novel, having passed through various disguises and alterations of his identity (from Ian Scuffing and Max Schlepzig to Rocketman, Schwarzknabe, and Plecha-zunga). His final becoming invisible must be understood therefore as both a dismantling, or deconstruction, of his identity and an escape from history as a structure of repression.

The fate of the Hereros is more ambiguous, inasmuch as it is tied to their attempt to recode their cultural and tribal links through the technology of the rocket. (By a strange, perhaps parodic coincidence, the structure of the rocket's firing mechanism corresponds to the mandala-shaped layout of the Herero village or living space.) However, the Herero effort to reassemble a sacred rocket may also accelerate a suicidal drive already present within them as victims of colonial deterritorialization. In any case, it is against this death drive that their leader Enzian struggles. In a scene echoing Tchitcherine's moment of truth, Enzian also realizes that the war, and therefore history itself, is not what he thought it was. Riding through a bombed-out area, he happens upon an oil refinery, Jamf Ölfabricken Werke AG, which he discovers is not in ruins at all but in perfect working order, just waiting for the right connections to be set up. Thus far he has supposed that the Herero Destiny is to be the Kabbalists or scholar-magicians of the Zone, with the rocket as their Torah and Holy Text. But what if *this* is the Real Text, he asks himself, and "I'm riding through it right now":

> It means this War was never political at all, the politics was all theatre, all just to keep the people distracted . . . secretly, it was being dictated by the needs of technology . . . by a conspiracy between human beings and techniques, by something that needed the energy burst of war, crying, "Money be damned, the very life of [insert name of Nation] is at stake," but meaning, most likely, *dawn is nearly here, I need my night's blood, my funding, funding, ahh more, more. . . .* The real crises were crises of allocation and priority, not among firms—it was only staged to look that way—but among the different Technologies, Plastics, Electronics, Aircraft, and their needs which are understood only by the ruling elite. (521, Pynchon's brackets and emphases)

As Enzian realizes, this new Text gives rise to other texts, each one a possible cover-up for something else, and so on indefinitely.[32] Yet, for the Hereros, the search for the Real Text must continue, since it is the only thing holding the tribe together ("Somewhere, among the wastes of the World, is the key that will bring us back, restore us to our Earth and to our freedom" [525]). Unlikely as it may sound, the rocket provides the only focal point for their reterritorialization.

Situated between the paranoia inspired by the despotic bureaucracy of the rocket-state and the antiparanoia or chaos of the nomadic, deterritorialized space of the Zone, Enzian thus figures a third possibility. True to the textual methods already adumbrated, his name derives from both fictional and documentary sources. The narrative reveals that Weissmann named Enzian after the German poet "Rilke's mountainside gentian of Nordic colors" (101). But it turns out that the name Enzian—"a sound for chanting" (321)—has magical associations in the Herero language; as a consequence, Enzian is "being used for his name" by the political faction led by Ombindi. Finally, and perhaps most important, Enzian was the German code name for one of the unrealized V-2 rocket projects.

Enzian's special position in the narrative may encourage readers to understand his scene of interpretation as a privileged, self-reflexive moment, as if *Gravity's Rainbow* here turns back on itself and reveals the logic or key of its own construction. Enzian's difficulty ascertaining the Real Text and what it might mean would accordingly signal that any attempt to locate the novel's Real Text will prove equally difficult and problematic. Either the textual doubling of a paranoid structure ruins the possibility of establishing a Real Text, and all interpretations become projections, that is, the generation of other texts; or the doubling, self-reflexive sense of *plot* evident from the outset must be seen as a metafictional strategy, providing the reader with a way to bracket the paranoia and interpretive delirium.[33] However, neither interpretive possibility seems fully satisfactory, at least as the basis for a privileged reading, inasmuch as the novel puts into play a number of distinctly different semiotic processes, or what Deleuze and Guattari call regimes of signs, no single one of which subsumes the others.

VII. In *A Thousand Plateaus*, Deleuze and Guattari isolate four specific regimes of signs, each of which produces significance and a structure of reference through a different mechanism or means of coding. In the "pre-signifying regime," which is usually found in primitive social organizations or societies, the coding is inscribed in multiple and nonhierarchical forms—on the body, in dance, ritual and myth—and takes as its ultimate referential territory the body of the earth itself. In the "signifying or semiotic regime," certain signs or signifiers are singled out and undergo a "paranoid" reorganization, as they are overcoded into a highly formalized system wheeling about a center (the despot's face) and requiring constant (re)interpretation to insure this privileging of certain signs over others. This regime corresponds to a barbaric or despotic social organization, and it always includes a priest or professional class whose function is to maintain this formal semiotic system through interpretation (overcoding). The "counter-signifying regime" subverts this overcoding by generating numerical and spatial multiplicities; it describes the practices of nomadic and marginal groups who refuse the imperial and state bureaucracies of the despotic regime. Finally, the "post-signifying regime" is what allows forms of modern subjectivity to appear; it operates through the simultaneously double process of a betrayal or "turning away" from the despotic, semiotic regime and the emergence of a "point of subjectification" that splits the subject into a subject of the utterance *[énonciation]* and a subject of the statement *[énoncé]*.[34]

All four of these regimes of signs operate in *Gravity's Rainbow*. Functioning as a paranoiac-despotic organization, the They-system identified with and integral to the rocket-state constitutes a signifying or semiotic regime. Born of a desire for mastery and control, this regime semiotizes the world according to binary codes that allow it to totalize and interpret everything through fixed molar categories and taxonomies and to impose criteria of instrumental reason and performativity. In the early sections of the novel, Slothrop is caught in the webs of this regime, as he becomes suspicious of the plot against him and begins to read various signs in accordance with the paranoia it produces. With his entry into the Zone, signs continue to multiply, as he finds himself reading mandalas, crosses, swastikas, trout entrails, paper scraps, and graffiti, in addition to the shapes in the sky to which he has always been peculiarly sensitive. But as Slothrop also realizes, these signs no longer refer necessarily to any plot against him (in other words, they no longer appear to be overcoded). All of which suggests that he has moved into a pre-signifying regime in which all nature speaks to him and no sign is privileged through the redundancy of interpretation.

Slothrop's experience is clearly paradigmatic for *Gravity's Rainbow* as a whole. In relation to the field dominated by the signifying or semiotic regime of the rocket-state, the Zone constitutes an exteriority or "outside," and sustains a mix of different regimes of signs. Thus, once "in" the Zone, Slothrop encounters various counter-signifying regimes characteristic of nomadic peoples opposed to the imperial bureaucracy and state apparatus. The most obvious example, the Counterforce, operates according to a semiotic predicated on "stoned" as opposed to "straight" consciousness, that is, on sub rosa, marginalized or repressed connections, as the narrator emphasizes: "Those like Slothrop, with the greatest interest in discovering the truth, were thrown back on dreams, psychic flashes, omens, cryptographies, drug-epistemologies, all dancing on a ground of terror, contradiction, absurdity" (582). Thanatz, the Zone's leading proponent of "Sado-anarchism," provides another example. In a humorous perversion of the signifying regime, Thanatz argues that if "S and M could be established universally, at the family level, the State would wither away" (737), since the state would then be deprived of its capacity to coopt us into its games of dominance and submission. Thanatz himself is a reader of whip scars, just as Saure Bummer reads reefers and Eddie Pensiero reads shivers, to name several of the Zone characters who read all manner of signs, but not in accordance with any rationalized semiotic. These various alternatives to the signifying or semiotic regime of the rocket-state emerge not accidentally in the Zone, which as a multiplicity supports a whole range of different regimes of signs.

The failure of the Counterforce gives rise in turn to a post-signifying regime that enables individualizing modes of subjectivity to appear. Deleuze and Guattari understand this regime as a transformation of the semiotic or paranoid-despotic regime. Conceived as a concentric system in which all signs are interpreted in relation to a central point of significance (the despot or focus of paranoia), the paranoid-despotic regime necessarily entails the possibility of deception (do the signs all point to a conspiracy?). All signs that do not are channeled out of the system along a negative line of flight toward a scapegoat figure who functions as the despot's negative or inverted image. A double turning away—of both the despot and the subject—brings about the post-signifying regime. First, the negative line of flight becomes a positive line when the central point is replaced by multiple points of subject-ification. Each one of these points then commences a linear, segmental trial, or proceeding, in relation to which the subject is doubled into a subject of the utterance and a subject of the statement. This doubling of the subject initiates a back-and-forth relay between a mental reality issuing from the subject of the utterance and a dominant (social) reality referred to by the subject of the statement; the difference between the two realities is what subjectifies. Whereas the radiating visage of the despot always raises the possibility of deception, the doubled subject of the post-signifying regime exacts an endless process of betrayal.

Pynchon's narrator seems to understand this process all too well; indeed, his very appearance and admission to "betraying" all the characters (739) confirm the presence of the post-signifying regime. In a passage worthy of Foucault, the narrator explains that what splits the Counterforce as subject (and therefore constitutes its most important point of subjectification) is a "double-minded" allegiance to the system, of which the Ego is Their personal representative:

Well, if the Counterforce knew better what those categories [of world economics] concealed, they might be in a better position to disarm, de-penis and dismantle the Man. But they don't. Actually they do, but they don't admit it. Sad but true. They are as schizoid, as double-minded in the massive presence of money, as any of the rest of us, and that's the hard fact. The Man has a branch office in each of our brains, his corporate emblem is a white albatross, each local rep has a cover known as the Ego, and their mission in this world is Bad Shit. We do know what's going on, and we let it go on. As long as we can see them, stare at them, those massively moneyed, once in a while. As long as they allow us a glimpse, however rarely. We need that. And how they know it—how often, under what conditions. (712–713)

In Lacanian terms, the Counterforce is divided between (or mistakes) its own desire and the desire of the other. More disturbing, if the Ego is always already installed as the system's "Branch rep," the very possibility of paranoia is at once totalized and liquidated. Hence the necessity of the Counterforce's failure, since the counter-signifying regime it incarnates can only lead to the subjectivities of the post-signifying regime.

Money, of course, or the structure of power it represents, is not the only point around which the doubling process of subjectification occurs. As Deleuze and Guattari point out, love and consciousness are the two privileged modes in which this doubling most regularly occurs. In *Gravity's Rainbow*, these two modes are enacted, respectively, in Roger Mexico's consuming passion for Jessica Swanlake, who eventually betrays their love for her conformist husband, Jeremy, and in Edward Pointsman's futile quest for the Nobel prize. Significantly, Pointsman feels betrayed by Clive Mossmoon and others in the Firm for having abandoned him to minor administrative functions. Although betrayal is only one specific feature of the post-signifying regime, its pervasive presence in *Gravity's Rainbow* indicates that for Pynchon, betrayal and response to betrayal constitute the primary acts whereby modern subjectivity is formed, further ramifications of which he will to explore in *Vineland*.

With the demise of the Counterforce and the now terrible "Oedipal situation in the Zone" (747), entropy becomes what the text desires (and perhaps the reader as well). As it approaches an end, the increasingly fragmented narratives of the novel are displaced by various interpretations—of the rocket's meaning and Slothrop's disappearance, as if the strategies of recovery and continuity which interpretation entail were a necessary compensation for a final dispersal of energies and a betrayal, or at least a (re)containment, of the lines of flight the novel has traced. The narrator willingly participates in this interpretive regime. In the closing pages, he will read Weissman's and Slothrop's Tarot cards and comment on various interpretations offered by Kabbalistic and Gnostic sects of "Rocket-state cosmology," all while recounting the final stages and countdown of 00000, the mysterious rocket containing the *Schwarzgerät* launched at Lüneburg Heath at the end of the war. With its silent reentry over a movie theater in contemporary Los Angeles, the narrator positions the reader inside the theater, drawing our attention to "the darkening and awful expanse of screen," where there is "a film we have not learned to see" (760). Just as the rocket is about to descend in fiery destruction upon us, we are exhorted to join together in singing an apocalyptic hymn composed by Slothrop's Puritan ancestor and the author of the treatise *On Preterition*. The song may be paraphrased as follows: though each of us will die, time itself will continue until the "Light" that will level the land has found the "last poor Pret'rite," and every road in the Zone has its "sleeping Riders"; at which point, the Zone will have a "face on ev'ry mountainside" and a "Soul in ev'ry stone." Yet, in this projected (re)animation of the Zone, the text itself defers the very apocalyse it announces.

But apocalypse, or rather its modern version known as entropy, also means the enlivening rush of maximum information, which the text can only mime in a dizzying mix of modes. For what is most striking about this final section is not so much the increased importance of interpretation as the fact that the text suddenly splinters and proliferates into a multiplicity of inscriptions and interfaces with other media, as if *Gravity's Rainbow* suddenly revealed itself to be a multidimensional film or kaleidoscopic space in which various media interface. In this respect, while surely a novelistic tour de force for its diversity of presentational strategies and reading effects, the final section doesn't differ essentially from Pynchon's manner of presentation throughout. But if Pynchon's writing machine—interfacing with and mixing different representational styles, modes, tones, languages, and narrative vantage points—produces a unity of effect, it is obviously not because it functions according to any simple expressive necessity. Nor does this unity follow dialectically from the novel's fundamentally contradictory attitude toward history: on the one hand, *Gravity's Rainbow* is engaged, even obsessed, with historical events, but on the other, it presents history, such as "the Allied Home Front" in the war effort, as "something of a fiction and lie, designed, not too subtly, to draw [lovers] apart, to subvert love in favor of work, abstraction, required pain, bitter death" (41). What accounts most fully for this mix of semiotic regimes and presentational modes, rather, is simply the necessity to situate this historical contradiction in relation to the multiplicity out of which it arises. To accomplish this, *Gravity's Rainbow* must continually counteract and thwart at its own formal level of presentation the rationalized semiotic that prevents this multiplicity from attaining visibility. In other words, the novel must produce "a zone" in order to depict "the Zone" that made possible its own historical existence. This explains why the narrative makes no attempt to represent World War II directly as a historical event but instead assumes a whole range of prior depictions— historical, literary, cinematic—onto which its own representations interface and map on. The result, as we've seen, is a dizzying mix in which everything suggests itself as a sign or analogy for everything else and all representations float in a delirious mixed space of communication.

All of which suggests that the historical separability of media which *Gravity's Rainbow* assumes but textually subverts now matters less than the translatability of media in different regimes of signs. Of these different regimes, only one (the signifying regime) is based on language, and it is clearly identified with a new lingua franca of control, or language reduced to coded and exchangeable information. Hence, in these terms, the importance of Pynchon's counterstrategy. For it is only by means of a multiplicity in which no signifying system or regime of signs attains dominance and no expressive or discursive unity can take hold that the historical assemblage responsible for this shift—and the formation of the postwar world—can be written.

These distributed content-discriminations yield, over the course of time, something *rather like* a narrative stream or sequence, which can be thought of as subject to continual editing by many processes distributed around in the brain, and continuing indefinitely into the future. This stream of contents is only rather like a narrative because of its multiplicity; at any point in time there are multiple "drafts" of narrative fragments at various stages of editing in various places in the brain.

▪ Daniel Dennett

4

Narration, Delirium, Machinic Consciousness

Lookout Cartridge

I. Like *Gravity's Rainbow, Lookout Cartridge* exemplifies how the languages and assumptions of information theory, modern technology, and film have come to mediate and define our experience, thereby offering new possibilities for novelistic exploration and formal experimentation while also suggesting that the novel distinguishes itself through its capacity to appropriate and reflect upon other "scriptive systems" and technical media. And like *Gravity's Rainbow, Lookout Cartridge* is a large-scale, encyclopedic novel of information multiplicity in which the generative principle is proliferation: not only of plots, characters, objects, scenes, bodies of knowledge, cultural allusions, and patterns of significance, but also of perspectives by which we are enticed to make sense of a burgeoning narrative always threatening to overwhelm us. Unlike other "maximalist" novels, however, the multiple perspectives and narrative vantage points in *Lookout Cartridge* are all anchored to the consciousness of the first-person narrator, William Cartwright, whose quest to discover why the film he made with his friend Dagger DiGorro was mysteriously destroyed provides the basis for the novel's central plot. In contrast, then, to writers such as Pynchon and Gaddis, McElroy seeks to represent in concrete and exacting detail the movements and multiple connections of a complex consciousness. Yet this is a machinic consciousness, rendered not as a Bergsonian stream, as in modernist novels, but as the articulation of "multiple drafts," in many respects anticipating Daniel Dennett's model based on computer architectures.[1] Moreover, as we shall see, McElroy's narrative consciousness is machinic precisely because its complex registrations are inseparable from a media assemblage designated metaphorically in the novel as a cartridge.

McElroy's explicit depiction of the movements of a consciousness commits him to forms of realism that these other practioners of the maximalist novel have for the most part eschewed. In an interview conducted by Tom LeClair, McElroy admits to being "a realist," although "possibly in some new way I'm not sure about."[2] This qualification can be understood in relation to what McElroy says at another point in the interview, when he speaks of his novels up through *Lookout Cartridge* as attempts to create "a collaborative network which human experience is" (242). As he goes on to explain, such a network is not mere metaphor: "In the process of understanding the network, one sees innumerable correspondences, and these yield what we may call metaphor. Sexual relations between two people may be like telepathy. But always I wanted to make these comparisons, these analogies, these metaphors have a stronger status so that my books would not seem to be literary artifices but would seem to be pretty desperate, sober explorations into what the larger network of the world really is" (243). McElroy's comments in the interview suggest that what we might call his conceptual realism follows from his interest in the perceptual clarities of scientific and technological forms. What is not clarified is the nature of the relationship between human experience conceived of as a collaborative network and the kind of narrative consciousness depicted in *Lookout Cartridge*. Is the network simply a mapping of consciousness onto the external world, or is it an emergent field of interdependent relations?

The question brings into a focus a novelistic dilemma: how can a narrative cause information to proliferate from varied perspectives and thus sketch a collaborative network, all while remaining attached to the consciousness or point of view of a single individual subject? In novelistic terms, how can a sense of human experience as a collaborative network be conveyed from within the limiting constraints of first-person narration? McElroy's solution in *Lookout Cartridge* is to direct our attention constantly toward what lies between the narrator, Cartwright, and what Cartwright himself refers to as "the great multiple field of impinging informations."[3] In other words, toward what lies between consciousness and the "collaborative network which human experience is." As we shall see, this space between becomes a multiply cross-hatched site of displacements and substitutions, where an attempted narrative (ful)filling remains forever incomplete because it can never be fully occupied or accounted for by any individual subject.

II. The simplest means by which to create a narrative space of "betweenness" is to have the narrator jump back and forth between different spaces and times, and this is exactly how *Lookout Cartridge* is structured. In little more than one hundred pages and within a time span of seven days, Cartwright arrives in New York from London, flies back to London, returns to New York, and again flies back to London. Soon thereafter he takes a train to Glasgow, flies to Stornoway (in the Hebrides), hitchhikes to the Stones of Callandish, and walks to a hut near Mount Clisham. Then, from Dagger DiGorro's apartment in London several days later, Cartwright jumps, or as he puts it, "loops" ahead forty hours to New York (404), where he will remain until the novel's conclusion after another week of intense shuttling back and forth between apartments, lofts, warehouses, and taxis.

Inserted into Cartwright's narrative of the various encounters that animate these movements are memories of specific scenes and exchanges with family, friends, and business associates and set pieces in which he recounts earlier episodes—most prominently, the shooting of different scenes of the destroyed film. As a consequence, the "present" of the narrative or the events as they "now" unfold and to which Cartwright responds is laminated into a dense temporal structure constitued by memories from the past and associations in the present, and it jumps ahead into future events or anticipated recollections of future events that somehow "insist" in the present. The net effect, of course, is that Cartwright as narrator is *always* located in that "dimensionless space between" different times and places. Paradoxically, the present moment in Cartwright's ruminating consciousness loses all temporal and spatial specificity in the very act of defining itself in relation to the events before and after which frame it.

This paradox would seem to be inherent in any phenomenological presentation of experience, and *Lookout Cartridge* is nothing if not unremittingly phenomenological.[4] In both conception and realization, McElroy's novel rests squarely upon phenomenological premises: it privileges a central knowing consciousness defined by its own project of intending possible meanings in the world, even while that project is constantly menaced by a background disorder that, while sometimes falling into patterns of interference, keeps any totalizing order just beyond its grasp. More specifically, Cartwright's elicitation of meaning through his "readings" of film and diary as well as through his interaction with the various groups of people who surround him takes place within a burgeoning and often delirious multiplicity that is never wholly recuperable as narrative "meaning."

In every sense, then, *Lookout Cartridge* pushes at the limits of phenomenological understanding, not only by multiplying the positions from which an intentional consciousness grasps the world but also by suggesting that these positions are all slots in a structurally determined system that necessarily implies a blind spot as their condition of possibility.[5] In these terms, *Lookout Cartridge* can be said to position or inscribe itself within the cultural space between phenomenology and structuralism, the two most rigorously systematic of contemporary attempts to define the terms of individual experience. In *Lookout Cartridge* itself, however, this state of betweenness must first and last be understood in relation to mediality, that is, in relation to the new possibilities and limits of information as it is mediated by the technologies of film and sound recording. Always moving between different accounts and inscriptions, Cartwright's "consciousness" consists of reflections on the unwritable data flows of these technologies as supplemented by the *aide-mémoire* of a typewritten diary.

Despite the obvious importance for McElroy's narrative of multiple jumps in time and space, then, these jumps are not in themselves the novel's primary concern. They simply draw our attention to what is important, namely the extended exploration of the gap between perception and consciousness, between what we have seen and what we think we know and conversely, between what we know (or feel that we know) and what we have actually seen. Like *The Crying of Lot 49, Lookout Cartridge* explores the possibility of a fully contemporary psychic apparatus in which what is registered is written over a blank (or blind) spot.

What are most striking are the specific means, both scriptive and otherwise, that constitute this exploration. "I have in my head things I may not have exactly seen, just as you who read this have me" (6), the narrator Cartwright states in the novel's opening pages, and then he follows with an image of a hand entering the glass wall of a laboratory through "large elastic lips sleeving a glove port." It is indeed a familiar image, one that we all "have in our heads," as Cartwright reminds us; and subsequently, throughout his narrative, he will often return to the metaphorical implications of this glove by which dangerous materials can be touched or moved. In Cartwright's ensuing efforts to bring into consciousness and account for what he has seen or somehow knows, the glove becomes his metaphor for how we can extend ourselves into a potentially dangerous space. Later he will refer to the camera itself as a glove that reaches for but does not touch "the thing it takes" (91). But more important, Cartwright's written account also functions as the reader's virtual glove, thus enabling Cartwright to address the reader directly as "you who have me here." "Like me," he continues, "you have in your head things you may not have exactly seen" (6). Unlike Cartwright, however, the reader "may never be called to account for what [he or she has] seen."

Part of what Cartwright has seen was recorded on the film he made with Dagger, part of it was written in the film diary he kept during the film's shooting, and part of it comes to him as he ruminates over these images and words while reaching for a new understanding of the information he gathers in his encounters with others. That Cartwright's account of what he has seen will ultimately have to be a *narrative* follows specifically from the fact that the film that he and Dagger conceived and shot together has been destroyed, and Cartwright wants to know why. His search to discover the exact reason soon provokes other narrative questions, beginning with why he was deliberately pushed from behind down a subway escalator soon after his arrival in New York, and then why his old college friend Jim Wheeler mysteriously disappeared after fatally stabbing a man with a car aerial as Cartwright approached him on his way to an appointment with Dagger's niece, Claire.

As these and other narrative questions rapidly begin to accumulate, so do both the amount and kind of information Cartwright introduces in his attempt to grasp what is going on around him and how the destruction of his film fits into the "large endless harmony" his friend "the Druid" claims it is part of. "Information," Cartwright says, "and the prospect of more dragged me toward some final grid" (460). However, the immediate effect of this proliferation is one of near delirium from information overload. As

McElroy himself admits, the reader is left "teetering on the edge of not understanding" while simultaneously being "tantalized by the sense that the information is all here if he just knew how to understand it."[6] In this respect, the reader occupies a position very much like Cartwright's. But while Cartwright eventually discovers what happened to his film and foils a terrorist plot, thus bringing about conditions for a certain kind of narrative closure, the reader is left with many unanswered questions. Indeed, although *Lookout Cartridge* appears to advance toward some larger, hierarchically structured master narrative within which all the minute details can be subsumed and all the questions resolved, such a narrative remains only immanent, waiting on the horizon to be pieced together out of a plethora of other narratives that promise to connect or interlace but often bifurcate and fray into uncertainty. At the novel's end, we may feel, or intuit, that we understand Cartwright's part in the "large endless harmony," but we are not likely to be able to give a complete narrative account of it.

This is because all of what Cartwright has in his head cannot be conveyed in the form of a single, all-encompassing narrative, although it can gradually be made to fill the space of the novel. For one thing, Cartwright's search for the answer to why his film was destroyed precipitates so many interconnected events (including the theft of his film diary) that no reconstruction of a single sequence ever becomes possible. For another, many of the details of the film's making, as well as the events from Cartwright's past life, assume significance only retrospectively, in the light of future events and the revelations that he will elicit from them only in a future "now." Indeed, as Cartwright jumps back and forth with increasing frequency between scenes past and yet to come, a cluster of larger, stereoscopic and looping narratives begin to emerge out of a complex spatial and temporal multiplicity.

Within, or indeed *as part of* these narratives, Cartwright describes the scenes—often in vivid, riveting detail—that he and Dagger shot in Corsica, at Stonehenge, in the London Underground, in an unlocated room, and in the Marvelous Country House, as well as the multiple associations he recorded in his diary and the memories triggered in his consciousness as he ruminates over these images. The reader, however, soon begins to sense that what will become most important are not so much these images and their associations as what lies between them, in the space they both articulate and prevent from becoming visible. In order to fill in these gaps and to make them yield unforeseen meanings, Cartwright must both conceal his own lack of information and uncertainty and become more active by adopting strategies that will prod other characters into revealing what they know (or don't know).

As information proliferates, so do ways of dealing with it, as Cartwright introduces concepts and analogies drawn from film and computer technologies, speculations about Mayan calendars, the rocks of Stonehenge, the drawings of Frederick Catherwood, the bridges of Isambard Kingdom Brunel, the structure of liquid crystals, and mythic stories about past events. Out of all these various connections an entire relational network and fictional topology emerges, articulated primarily by metaphoric extensions of the way Cartwright inserts himself like a cartridge into the various spaces and systems that constitute his world.[7] In this way, the basic epistemological premises of the detective story at the novel's base are expanded to their fullest and most varied dimensionality. And while the destroyed film remains the ostensible focus for the resolution of the detective story plot, the reach of Cartwright's consciousness extends far beyond the film itself, until, by the novel's end, it enables him to intuit his "place in a multiple system" (439).

In these terms, the immanent but always deferred and therefore incomplete master narrative can be thought of as only the occasion for a "space reached into existence" (488), a space that envelops Cartwright because it has been created by his very effort to insert himself between various groups and factions and to push and probe from his own position within "the great multiple field of impinging informations" (465). Like his childhood friend Ned Noble's time machine, Cartwright's own self-elected status as a "lookout cartridge" between friend and foe becomes "less a device to go back and forth than a pictured formula for slipping between and creating a space that was not there before" (436).

This space, and within it Cartwright's state of betweenness, is amplified and developed both at the level of represented events and at the level of their narrative accounting, levels that fuse to make the space of the novel an expansive field of images, movements, and mental actions articulated through narration, description, and rumination. Indeed, whether the result of McElroy's scientific preoccupations or not, *Lookout Cartridge* constitutes a vector-field of images and interacting sets of information, of which Cartwright the narrator is both an observer and a self-consciously active support. To comprehend fully how this space, or field, is constituted, it would be necessary to consider both the diverse components that make up its elements and the unique grammar or syntax by which they are linked or positioned with respect to one another.[8] Here several brief indications must suffice.

Cartwright himself defines the most essential elements and their primary syntactical relations in his often technological vocabulary and scientifically inflected ruminations. As noted earlier, film and memory images, as well as objects such as liquid crystals, Mayan calendars, Brunel's bridges, and Catherwood's drawings, frequently recur as privileged referents for cognitive events. These referents possess no obvious thematic consistency, either physically or as ideas; in their seemingly random heterogeneity, however, they can be understood as the memes that populate Cartwright's consciousness.

In *The Selfish Gene* (1976), Richard Dawkins coins the term to designate replicators (of ideas, catch phrases, ways of doing things) that operate on the cultural level in much the same way as genes do on the biological, that is, according to evolutionary laws of natural selection. In *Consciousness Explained,* Dennett appropriates Dawkins's notion for his model of the evolution of consciousness and argues that it is the infestation of memes and their constant reprogramming by the brain as a virtual machine that allows the human mind to emerge. Dennett writes that, like genes, "memes are invisible, and are carried by meme vehicles—pictures, books, sayings (in particular languages, oral and written, on paper or magnetically coded, etc.). Tools and buildings and other inventions are also meme vehicles. A wagon with spoked wheels carries not only grain or freight from place to place; it carries the brilliant idea of a wagon with spoked wheels from mind to mind. A meme's existence depends on a physical embodiment in some medium; if all such physical embodiments are destroyed, that meme is extinguished." [9]

Whereas Dennett emphasizes how memes behave according to laws of proliferation, natural selection, and parasitism, what stands out in *Lookout Cartridge* is the extent to which Cartwright's consciousness constitutes an activity in which specific memes are isolated and their potential for extension or use in new contexts is tried out. In Dennett's model, however, this is what consciousness *is,* and he describes it as the constant reorganization and "editorial revision" (or what he calls "multiple drafts") by various virtual machines in the brain such as perception, speech, and memory. By suggesting that the human brain, like the computer, is a virtual machine (an idea first proposed by Alan Turing) but that human mind or consciousness is the result of its multiple, always competing operations, Dennett avoids the usual crude and reductive comparisons. Unlike that of a computer, Dennett says, the architecture of the brain is "massively parallel, with millions of simultaneously active channels of operation. What we have to understand is how a Joycean (or, as I have said, 'von Neumannesque') serial phenomenon can come to exist, with all its familiar peculiarities, in the parallel hubbub of the brain" (214). As we shall see in a moment, McElroy's narrator, referring to the differences between serial and parallel processing, also wonders about this relationship. More important, the differences between the two, or rather between the spaces in which they occur, point to an essential feature of the space and architecture of *Lookout Cartridge*.

If memes and the various operations to which they are submitted provide the content of Cartwright's consciousness, they constitute nevertheless a response to a series of actions in the external world. Words such as *catch, push, loop, insert, slot, cartridge,* and *shtip* indicate the nature of many of these actions and provide the basis not only for Cartwright's complex articulations or syntax but for those of the novel as a whole. As one reader observes, *Lookout Cartridge* is precipitated by a "push," then organized around a "catch." [10] The essential thing, however, is that these words are all multiply interactive. The Yiddish word *shtip,* for example, conveys multiple senses of push or pushing, with obvious sexual connotations. In the novel, accordingly, it evokes the German Jewish world of Cartwright's ex-lover Tessa and the circle of her family and friends. Yet for Cartwright *shtip* also

> exemplifies the multiple and parallel sorties which raise our brain above the digital computer to which it is akin; the digital computer works its yes and no operations faster than the brain yet is confined to serial single-file one quest-at-a-time circuit-seeking; but the human natural Body Brain (as my Druid terms it) sends countless of these single files not one at a time but all at once circulating down the deltas, through the gorges and moving targets and (like parties of Indians—Brooklyn, Hindu, Maya, Hollywood or, as the English call the American, *Red*) athwart axes of all pulsing fields. (447)

To extend Cartwright's computer analogy, these key words provide the means by which the text performs feats of parallel processing. Recurring in various contexts, they denote actions, movements and relationships that are fundamentally interactive, both at the microlevel of depicted events and at that of the novel's structure and composition, assuming of course that these levels can be separated. That key actions are always *interactions* is made strikingly apparent in both the murder of Jim Wheeler and the narrator's killing of the Indian assassin Krish: neither is an act of violence inflicted by a willful subject upon a passive body. Both take place as if the recipient thrust himself or moved into the deadly point as a step in a complex dance.

The integration of component parts and their constant interaction is also suggested more simply at the level of the novel's chapter divisions: inserted between the sequentially numbered chapters are intercalated sections with titles such as "Vacuum Insert," "Yellow Filter Insert," "Dagger-Type Cassette," "Love Space," and "Corsican Montage." These inserts effectively give *Lookout Cartridge* the appearance of a constructivistlike assemblage and allow it to reflect not only the modular structure of Dagger and Cartwright's film but the machinic world of which Cartwright is a part. Described in terms of interlocking systems, wheels within wheels, cassettes and cartridges, insertions, plug-ins, branchings, circuits, loops, and connections, it is a world largely defined by human and technological interaction. Indeed, the need to emphasize the fundamental heterogeneity of elements and their machinic constellation of relationships in *Lookout Cartridge* is all the more important, given that the novel's multicentered, self-organizing, and emergent assemblage of articulations (as well as McElroy's formulations concerning experience as a collaborative network) anticipate in broad but striking ways recent theories about neural networks and connectionism in cognitive science.[11]

We can now return to the difference between the serial file operations of the digital computer and the parallel processing of the human brain. The space of *Lookout Cartridge* is modeled on and attempts to encompass both. Just as memes, whether images, words, or ideas, can be processed only one at a time, so Cartwright's awareness can take place only in time. Yet, through memory, rumination, and accumulation, he can aspire to a simultaneous totality of linkages in which all connections light up in a single moment of understanding. The tension between the temporalized tracks of action and inscription, on the one hand, and the saturated grid of instantaneous information, on the other, thus characterizes the space through which Cartwright moves and his consciousness is defined.

This space becomes meaningful, however, only in relation to the novel's larger narrative outlines and trajectories. These we will examine by looking more specifically at the film Cartwright and Dagger made together, the role of Cartwright's film dairy, and the networks of characters involved in both. Like the nonnarrative elements that function through analogy and semantic interaction, these narrative trajectories assume their importance as lines of connection within the "multiple field of impinging information" where Cartwright comes to view himself as only one center among many. Unlike nonnarrative elements, however, these trajectories outline the boundaries of the space "reached into existence," as Cartwright aptly describes the space opened up by his own activities. Thus they are both the measure of Cartwright's reach and the indication of certain structural limits. Consequently, they raise inevitable questions about how *Lookout Cartridge* as a whole must be situated in relation to the narratives that in turn can be used to frame it.

III. Cartwright first discusses the film the day after his arrival in New York with Dagger's niece, Claire, who is employed by Outer Film, the company that had offered to help finance at least part of the film's shooting in Corsica. That evening, Cartwright provides the first extended description of the film in a meeting Claire sets up with Monty Graf. Apparently intimate with Claire, Graf appears to be an interested third party especially inquisitive about the film's extant footage and possibilities for its future development. His questions to Cartwright center on the ideas behind the film, as well as on which parts have been destroyed; he even raises questions about the existence of a second film, either to be made or already made. Graf's questions thus point to gaps or limitations in Cartwright's own knowledge about both the existence and the identity of the film he made with Dagger. As it turns out, "their" film has no ascertainable single identity, not only because material parts of it have been destroyed but also because its existence as an idea has different meanings for different people. As a collaborative effort between Cartwright and Dagger, the film was also the fruit of collaborations between Dagger and others about which Cartwright at the time remained unaware. In a further complicating twist, Cartwright later discovers that several of "his" ideas about the film are viewed by certain people as Jan Aut's ideas and that a second film was being made by Outer Film which doubled certain parts of the film he made with Dagger.

Moreover, since Jan Aut is both the wife of Phil Aut, who owns Outer Film, and the sister of Monty Graf, the various interests vying for the film have family ties as well. In fact, the family as a filiating connection becomes increasingly important. From the outset, Cartwright's activities pose a danger to his own family's well-being and future existence. During his trip to New York, his house in London is broken into and the original version of his film diary stolen. While he shuttles back and forth between New York, the Hebrides, and London, his wife, Lorna, begins to dally adulterously with a young musician in her singing group. But most important, Cartwright discovers that his daughter Jenny's boyfriend, Reid, who is also involved with Jan Aut, may be using Jenny to obtain information about Cartwright and that her life is increasingly endangered by Cartwright's various maneuverings. Jenny had typed his film diary and appears to know much more about the actions described in it than Cartwright ever assumed. But this is true of others as well. In ruminations precipitated by the film's loss, he comes to understand a number of important relations between the film and his family life, including certain revelations about his former adulterous relationship with his wife's friend Tessa. And finally, Cartwright discovers that the very existence of the film poses a dangerous threat to yet another family—the Flint brothers Gene, Jack, and Paul. Late in the novel, Cartwright pieces together the simple truth that Jack Flint wants the film destroyed because it implicates the Flint family in a terrorist network. Significantly, Cartwright discovers the network's existence through June, a fashion model in New York, who warns him about the threats of her brother Chad, one of its members. Altogether, then, these various filial connections indicate the extent to which the novel also explores what lies between families, as well as what ties them together.

Positioned between Cartwright and a number of competing interests with differing conceptions as to its meaning, the film constantly displaces our interest from Cartwright toward this space between. But it turns out that the film itself is also implicitly concerned with this state of betweenness. As a collaboration between Cartwright and Dagger, it emerges in the give and take between their differing ideas about how it should be made and put together, and therefore about what it might ultimately mean. When Cartwright describes the film to Monty Graf, he states that he feels that it was about power: "Power shown being acquired from sources where it had momentum but not clarity"; or as he puts it later: "power poached on or tuned in on when it lacked direction but had momentum" (77, 180). The film itself conveys no specific direction to this power, since its episodes are displaced and decontextualized into what Cartwright calls a documentary daydream. It possesses a documentary status because it operates according to a realist epistemological premise: at a certain time and place, the camera recorded a series of specific images of people doing and saying certain things; yet it is also a daydream because these images, constantly rearranged in different sequences without any overall narrative connection, were about different things in the minds of the two filmmakers, not to mention the associations they would evoke in the minds of different viewers. Encompassing both document and daydream and articulating a space between, the film both defines and occupies a multiplicity.

In obvious ways, nevertheless, the filmed images originate in or implicate some kind of power—military, religious, technological—which, though lacking a specific political context, resonates historically through various countercultural allusions and associations typical of the early 1970s. The filmed sequences include: a U.S. Army deserter in an unplaced room talking with a Marxist revolutionary; a softball game in Hyde Park; religious mystics dancing around a bonfire in Wales; an Hawaiian hippy playing his guitar in the London Underground; a country house where menacing characters converse while outdoors on the rainy patio a deserted TV under an umbrella is receiving images of the moon from Apollo 15; a Corsican montage featuring an international seminar on ecology; the rocks at Stonehenge; bombers taking off from a U.S. Air Force base; a suitcase slowly packed; a bridge; hands laying out TNT; fingers dismantling a kitchen timer; people with black faces and white hair; stray objects, bits of music, and voices for "the times we live in." Cartwright in particular feels that these images were "lurking on the margins of some unstable, implicit ground that might well shiver into revolution." And though he wanted to show "America and England in some dream of action and peace . . . through all the scenes mingling England and America and deliberately unplacing the scenes, there was the cool theme of America itself" (70). By implication, then, the film depicts America as a state of mind and site of dislocation, decontextualization, and disassociation.

Not surprisingly, the "collaborative network which human experience is" turns out to be neither completely certain nor reassuring. Cartwright gradually discovers that he has been used by his best friend, Dagger, who deliberately kept him ignorant both of the identities of certain of the people they filmed and of the real purpose for which the film (or parts of it) was made. Moreover, to a undetermined extent, Dagger and Cartwright (unknowingly) also collaborated in the making of Jan Aut's film, which both overlaps with and doubles their own. While shooting the Stonehenge sequence, Cartwright had noticed a second person filming at the same time, but it had never occurred to him that their own footage was to become part of someone else's film. As Jan will later explain to Cartwright, her film was to be about "how we don't know enough": "That was what a friend had said months ago and it had crystallized her idea and then her husband Phil my associate (she said) had strangely not turned it down. His interest was a pretext financial or other, but the end sustained itself and could even transform her husband's motive" (405). And further: "But everyone not knowing enough wasn't the only point; another was just not tricking up some neat script-story but taking power in process, other people's ongoing energies and tying into them, that's the way I express it but I got the idea from someone else and that's appropriate too" (419).

The irony here is multiple. For one thing, the reader knows that Cartwright himself was the originator of these ideas. What's more, many of the other characters, Jan included, think Cartwright's motive for participating in the making of a film (with Dagger or her) was economic all along, whereas Cartwright was never simply a businessman interested in a profit; at most, he admits, "I . . . had deliberately used this thing as a point through which attention might be distributed" (443), and for "speculations" of an entirely different order. If anyone, it was Dagger who secretly harbored an economic motive. As he admits to Cartwright late in the novel, their "shooting Jan's wild portrait of Jerry [her son by Phil Aut] had been designed to insure a little last-minute leverage if only to sustain Phil Aut's concern with a film which to his strangely inhibited but intense protectiveness might thus seem to implicate in left wing activities the two human beings he told Jack Flint in a rare moment of frankness he would make any sacrifice for" (442). But, as Cartwright realizes, this only made Dagger "one open and neat part of Aut's exploitation of Jan's plan" (442), since Aut was also using the film project as a means of maintaining control over his wife, Jan, and their son, Jerry. Jan, in turn, thought that her husband and Jack Flint together were making a science demonstration film for children. Nevertheless, amid these complications of both motive and purpose, Jan's idea for a "pan-human film" ultimately explains why Cartwright and Dagger's film records the faces of a terrorist network and thereby threatens to expose it.

As Jan recounts to Cartwright, her film was intended

> in one ninety-minute peace-montage to bring together clashes of practice, doctrine, color, and geography among . . . certain revolutionary groups: interviews, glimpses, faces sometimes only half seen which Jan believed would say implicitly not just that their human aspirations were more kin than foe to each another, but more (and this to the ordinary audiences who would see the film if only on their television sets) that such groups were full of passionate love which might lean toward violence but only in answer to what there was no point in her spelling out. It was to be the deed of her life, plain black and white. Aristotle had said Man was a political being and a being endowed with speech—so a film of silent faces would not do—she left the execution to Phil and John and (though she had not pressured him herself) her son. (408)

Thus, when Dagger and Cartwright film the dancing religious mystics in the Wales bonfire sequence, it is not by accident that their camera records the image of the revolutionary leader Paul Flint fleeing into the woods and that other faces filmed at other scenes turn out to be connected in completely unexpected ways. Although the bonfire idea was Cartwright's, this particular event was known in advance by Dagger through his niece, Claire, who of course was working for Phil Aut at Outer Film.

But while the film's existence turns out to be the result of a complex collaboration among many people with varying motives and differing understandings of what it was about, its destruction finally proves to be a comparatively simple matter. From the beginning, Cartwright has only Dagger's word that the footage—all except for the eight-millimeter sequence of the first-strike bombers taking off—was in fact destroyed, and Dagger eventually proves to be altogether unreliable. As Cartwright moves out through denser and denser loops in his quest, he begins to think that "since Glasgow I had cared less about the film and some meager muddle of my past that it held, for what I wanted was information that would carry me into the future" (340). Cartwright will move into that future when he simultaneously recovers and destroys the film. That moment comes late in the novel when he finally meets up with Dagger in Claire's apartment. At this point, he is not certain whether or not any of the film still exists, but he is relatively sure why its existence poses a special threat to both an international terrorist network and the wealthy businessman and entrepreneur Jack Flint:

> I was about to ask where Claire was and why Dagger had wished to put the Softball Game between the Hawaiian-in-the-Underground and the Suitcase-Slowly-Packed [it is precisely by puzzling out the answers to such questions that Cartwright has learned to read what is registered on the film], but I reached down without looking and touched the familiar bulk of an untouched Sunday *Times* and was glad the film was probably destroyed, maybe I could conquer my weightlessness and sell the destroyed film to Jack Flint who must not wish his brother Gene's wife and house on view, nor his agent Krish in the Softbal Game, nor his brother Paul the guru in transit at the Bonfire in Wales (near where Brunel's timber viaduct over the Usk burned and was replaced by him with iron)—nor would Jack want his brother, his youngest his magnetic brother Paul's voice on a Nagra tape or his face in a stone doorway at the probable scene of Jim Nielsen's liquidation. (473)

Just after this moment, Dagger asks Cartwright to wait at Claire's apartment for a delivery man while he takes the dog out for a walk. Cartwright suspects a setup but acquieces anyway. Then, on an impulse, he checks the carton of audio gear Dagger has brought over from England and discovers their film—carefully dated and placed—concealed underneath. He then dumps the film into the building's garbage incinerator, "liquifying his assets," he thinks to himself, and fills its emptied space with pages from the *Times* just before the delivery man arrives to pick up the carton for Outer Film.

Cartwright's destruction of his own film is not simply intended to foil Claire's double-dealing scheme and Dagger's betrayal and put an end to the spiral of violence in which he himself has become entwined. Early in the novel, musing about a drive-in movie screen that suddenly toppled over one summer night, Cartwright reflects that the "image became yours by disappearing" (7). The same could be said for his film, which by disappearing has become his in a way that it never could if it had remained intact. Cartwright had also wanted the film to change his life—it was, after all, a film in every sense about revolution—but ironically it is the loss of the film that has brought him to the loops and turns he is now moving through. Having come to possess the film in every sense except the physical, he can only hope to move beyond it into a safer future by destroying it.

IV. During the making of the film, Cartwright had kept a diary, which both doubles the events recorded on the film and mediates them in a more explanatory and reflective mode. But the immediate effect of keeping the diary was to alter Cartwright's perception: "Why did I begin a diary? Did I foresee the film's ruin? I learned to look more closely in order to see what Dagger was seeing through the viewfinder. But later to recall what ought to go into the diary. But perhaps always to take for myself a depth that was in our film if not on it" (402). It would seem therefore that Cartwright can recall the film images so vividly because he has trained himself to recall them for his diary; but he also has a similar recall of the diary, and his memory or voice often works to fill in what was neither on the one nor in the other. As he will later think to himself, in an extraordinary passage we shall later return to, "I became the film's sound, not at all an echo but (from a written diary) a delayed voice now printed on the original film's absence" (100).

When Cartwright first describes the Wales bonfire sequence to Claire early in the novel, he mentions that "Claire didn't yet know I was recalling my diary" (26), and then moments later he remembers, in silent answer to her seemingly innocent query, that he did not include in the diary a written description of the elusive character (Paul Flint) in the grove. Such incidental points seem to matter little at first, and only retrospectively does it become clear what is behind Claire's question. Initially, the reader's attention will most likely be captured by the physical details of the filming, as Claire's appears to be in this early scene, particularly as they are rendered in the sections titled "Unplaced Room," "Corsican Montage," and "Marvelous Country House," which are written in the present tense and give precise accounts of what is being recorded by the camera. These sections suggest what the diary is like and doubtlessly will be taken for extracts from it by some readers. Not surprisingly, the diary is also read by a number of characters within the novel who respond variously to just this evocative power: both Jerry Aut and Savvy van Ghent claim that the diary "sounds better than the film"; Cartwright's daughter, Jenny, who types most of it for him, responds to its literary qualities; and for Cartwright's wife, Lorna, it raises questions—"I was reading the scene you call Marvelous Country House, right? And suddenly I'm in the middle of my friend Tessa" (124)—requiring a rather delicate explanation from Cartwright. But for Cartwright himself the diary is never really separate from the film. As he puts it in an odd sexual simile, before again affirming his resolve: "Diary and film parted and came together, hiding one another, parted and came together like some flesh breathing, an organ like a creature, and I must turn only to the ruining of the film, who did it, who had done it, and why" (158–159).

The purpose of the diary, Cartwright tells Lorna, was "to explain some of what the film couldn't have shown" (122). In this way, the diary provides the reader with a very specific account of what the camera records as well as its surrounding context, and therefore of what the film was supposed to mean, at least to Cartwright. This information is extremely important for the reader, since so much significance resides in the gap between what Cartwright thinks he and Dagger are doing or seeing and what they have actually recorded in the eyes of various others, known and unknown. For example, the Wales bonfire evokes "the trend toward eastern modes, organic community, dislodging from the city" (70). In Cartwright's ruminating consciousness, Wales was "passion and sorcery, heroes and deceptive mountains and music and boozing and hidden communes up behind a misty hill and lambs bleating in the gorges" (220), as well as the story of the hound dog Gelert and a myriad of other associations, both personal and cultural. But what matters most in relation to the plots wheeling around Cartwright is simply that the diary records the presence of Paul Flint, who is hiding in a Welsh commune.

It is this simple fact—and others like it, the recorded images and words of the violent terrorist Len Incremona in the Marvelous Country House, for instance—that makes the diary an object of special interest to the terrorist network. Cartwright, sensing this, uses the diary from the outset of his quest as a lure and means of obtaining information about both the film and those who are interested in it. Indeed, in a curious reversal, the diary becomes evidence in the eyes of the terrorists of a knowledge they attribute to Cartwright but which he does not always possess. And Cartwright, also sensing this—in a second loop, as it were—uses this knowledge to increase his power. Listening outside Paul's hut near Mount Clisham to the brothers Gene and Jack Flint (who possess Cartwright's stolen diary), Cartwright thinks: "It seemed to me they knew different things, and this might be why or how they were going round in circles" (330). Like the film, in fact, the diary is inherently ambiguous and divisive: displaced into the space between different groups or factions, it becomes an object of double-dealing and a focal point where cross-purposes reveal themselves.

In a later scene inside a New York taxi driven by Mike the revolutionary, Cartwright responds to the question as to why he wasn't looking out for his daughter, Jenny, with one of his own: "Was she looking out for me by letting my diary go?" (403). To which Mike retorts: "Listen . . . we know what Jack told you. But suppose he burned one copy for Gene to see but kept the other?" (403). By asking such questions, Cartwright gradually learns that the terrorists are divided by their differing degrees of knowledge and that he can take active advantage of their differences by playing them off against one another, "undermining the ring of violent exiles by sowing confusion among them" (415), as the woman Lana puts it in Cartwright's "lookout dream." The diary itself, of which there are multiple copies—both carbons and Xeroxes—serves as an essential means for doing this. Like the film, the diary thus takes on a curious life of its own.

In the climactic confrontation with the terrorist group, Cartwright, even while captured and held prisoner, is able to use his knowledge of what the diary contains in order to sow confusion. When one of the terrorists, John of Coventry, proposes Cartwright's house arrest, Nash explodes: "House arrest? said Nash, house arrest? Where do you get house arrest? He blew Bill and Ronnie at South Ken. How many copies of the diary are there? He's got connections, connections" (483). The diary, like the film, is a legible record of Cartwright's connections, both with and between others; and, like the film, Cartwright will learn to read it by filling in around what it doesn't say and by extrapolating from what others think that it does.

V. In a novel in which betweenness figures so prominently, we should not expect the objects and actions depicted in it to have a simple status or single identity. True to this expectation, *Lookout Cartridge* bulges in profusion with doublings and multiplications, ambivalences and polarities. This is true not only of the film and diary—not to mention the curious objects, such as liquid crystals and semiconductors, that populate the novel's space—but also of the novel's many characters. From the outset, we are often reminded of the striking resemblance between Cartwright's daughter, Jenny, and Dagger's niece, Claire (and thus we are prepared for Incremona's mistaken killing of Claire in Jenny's place). Indeed, many of the characters, at least on a first reading, appear to proliferate or replicate without ever achieving clearly distinct identities: Len and Nash, the two Johns (John of the loft and John of Coventry), the two Jims (Wheeler and Nielson), Mary and Marie, Elizabeth and Elspeth, Chad and Savvy, Cosmo and Krish, and many more. Although we eventually sort most of them out, the initial effect is dizzying. But more important than the separate identities of the many minor characters is the curious split identity of the terrorist network—or system, as Cartwright refers to it—which is both revolutionary in the best sense and violently terrorist in the worst.

These two poles are represented by the charismatic Paul Flint and the explosively violent Len Incremona, but their positions are in turn doubled by the intellectual Chad and the silent but dangerous Nash. The initial evidence suggests that the network is revolutionary mostly in the terms of the late-sixties countercultural movement; that is, its primary activities include harboring U.S. Army deserters who are against the Vietnam War, moderate drug pushing in the underground, and setting up communes—first in Wales, later in Chile—to provide material support for alternative life styles. It turns out that Cartwright's own friend and "wholistic physician," Mr. Andsworth (also known as "the Druid"), adumbrates the philosophy. However, the most important leader and powerful influence in the group is clearly Paul, who has such an impact on Chad and Jim Nielson that both decide to change their lives. Significantly, Paul himself seems two-sided: he is described by Jan as beautiful and charismatic and someone she wishes her son to emulate and by Mike "as dangerous in his purity, and in danger like a Weatherman who doesn't know enough but sets out to make an impact-bomb by turning TNT back into nitroglycerine" (406). Thus, if Cartwright is able to sow dissension in the group, it is because a rift already exists, and it seems to have come about as a result of Paul's decision to leave the group. As Jan explains to Cartwright:

> Paul had opted out, she said, but not because of the big projects discussed—a symbolic war on children waged against school buses; or slowly, through many collaborators, assembling the parts of two bazookas in a Washington rooming house with a roof and shelling the President during a scheduled lawn function; or simply bombing the White House in order to precipitate martial law and with it consequences leading to change. No, on the contrary, Paul had made a mystic parallel between public political action and the family firm now so complex in its indirect holdings that possibly not even Jack had it all in his head. And since effective political action no longer seemed feasible, Paul had conceived a small community in New England which would be neither as remote as he had felt himself to be in that Hebridean hut nor as socially involved as he had really been both through his power in a movement and through his location so useful to certain American exiles. (405–406)

But if Paul finds "in stones and stars a calm beyond revolutionary purpose, beyond even peace and contemplation," his brief cameo appearance driving yet another of the taxis Cartwright takes in New York is enough to establish that he can be of little help in Cartwright's effort to prevent the terrorist violence planned by the remainder of the group—Chad, Nash, Incremona, Gene, John, and the Frenchmen. The details remain sketchy but indicate that it will probably include dynamiting one of the Flint warehouses where children may be present as part of a science demonstration film. Cartwright's unexpected presence in the adjacent warehouse, where he and the terrorists discover that Jack has set up video equipment to film whatever goes on in his own warehouse next door, has the effect of disorienting the terrorists, and the plan is apparently aborted. The explosion Cartwright witnesses from the helicopter above Manhattan—"the silent flash there in the city's grid" (3) which begins the novel and to which we loop back at its end—turns out to be only a police tow truck dynamited by Len Incremona. Finally, on the novel's last page, when Cartwright, with his friend Sub's mostly ignorant collaboration, heaves the latter's new TV set out of Sub's apartment window onto Incremona in the street below, the terrorist network appears to be effectively squelched.

In the context of this seemingly most resolute and definitive of gestures which concludes the novel, Cartwright's last words—"I was not sure what

I had seen but I knew what we had done" (531)—give pointed iteration to the gap between perception ("what I had seen") and what can be narrativized ("what we had done"). But the question all along, both in the novel's overall structure and in the movement from page to page, has been whether this gap can indeed be filled and whether this sometimes slight but ever present difference can be overcome or transcended through the act of an intentional consciousness. In thus asking whether narrative—or indeed a proliferation of narratives—can be made to subsume and thus include the multiplicity between what has been seen and what can be made to emerge explicitly into consciousness, *Lookout Cartridge* raises pressing questions about the limits of narrative, the precise nature of which must now be considered.

VI. According to the Freudian model, the unconscious process of repression operating on the contingencies of memory and childhood experience makes it difficult (though not impossible) for the unaided individual to account fully for his or her own experience. *Lookout Cartridge* is clearly not concerned with the unconscious in this Freudian sense, except perhaps in a modified structuralist version (like that of Jacques Lacan) according to which the individual always occupies a "subject position" by virtue of a symbolic structure. As Cartwright becomes more and more active as a knowing subject (or, in Lacanian terms, as "the subject who is supposed to know"), he comes to recognize the extent to which he is only one of many "centers" acted on by necessities operating outside and beyond the consciousness of any single individual. Moreover, his hyperawareness of how he occupies a place in a "multiple system" (439) is charged with both positive and negative valencies. Negatively, his quest reveals how he is "looping inside someone else's plan" (280) as a functional part of "someone else's system." Positively, the quest confirms his desire that his own life reflect a larger life (401), as well as his belief that "you must build yourself into the life around you" (410). In these terms, Cartwright's quest both enacts and tests the senses in which human experience *is* a collaborative network.

Nevertheless, an unresolvable tension or contradiction between wanting to know and wanting to be a part of remains essential to Cartwright's consciousness. Approaching the end of his quest, he thinks to himself: "I wanted to take home a tale to my family they could understand. But it might be too late. They were dispersed" (421). This simple, even homely truth qualifies Cartwright's final sense of how intricately and on how many levels he is indeed subsumed into what the Druid calls a "large endless harmony."

As Cartwright finds himself "between blind coghood and that sinister hint of god-head or godbody in me issuing from my place in a field of multiple impingements" (459), he also experiences a deadly weightlessness. And as he passes through accelerating loops of renewed understanding, he also formulates a law: "You will not have both power and the understanding of it" (504). But finally, within the maze of systems and subsystems reflecting and wheeling off one another within the novel, it is not clear whether such discursive contradictions are finally transcended or merely suspended. For in Cartwright's feeling of weightlessness between forces, which means a great increase of personal power but also brings him close to death, or in the narrative loopings that deliriously de-center and re-center Cartwright while permitting no large narrative resolution, the space of betweenness within which he ceaselessly moves and creates is revealed to be a multiplicity of ambivalences and polarities that can be neither reduced to a signifying structure nor escaped.

When McElroy speaks of *Lookout Cartridge* as a "rhythm of gatherings together and dispersions," he could well be alluding to the way in which the narratives constantly converge only to be propelled out again into alternately wider and narrower trajectories.[12] When Cartwright describes "the energy in process [we were] tying into here" as "an energy constantly disturbed in its course or starting out again and again at new points" (350), he could likewise be describing the narrative energies that continually move the reader through digressions that eventually loop back through central narrative points. The risk, of course, is that this sideways thrust and return of the narrative will stall out in an accumulating profusion of details or simply dissolve in an always threatening delirium. But even while building the reader's confidence that the details are hardly fortuitous and that they will eventually dovetail in an intelligible structure, *Lookout Cartridge* persistently poses questions about the narrativity of the experience it recounts. Specifically, it questions the possibility of a totalizing narrative within an environment in which information constantly proliferates and new technical media separate, into distinct visual and aural data streams, what formerly constituted the material of collective and individual experience.

When Cartwright conceives of himself as a "delayed voice now printed on the original film's absence" (100), he indicates something essential about the writing machine generating the novel and the psychic apparatus it models. First, the statement suggests that, when Cartwright's ruminating consciousness must explicitly acknowledge its own mediality, or dependency on some medium—whether film or diary or indeed digital computer—it can do so only in a delirious form. Thus, while the novel registers mediality as a difference between multiple inscriptions, the awareness of this difference is registered as an assertion of a necessary supplement to an absent text (not only the missing film but the missing diary), in an experiential moment of self-identification and perhaps even self-origination. For most of *Lookout Cartridge*, this delirium is warded off by the impulse to narrativize and to account for the self in relation to others. At the same time, delirium continues to menace Cartwright in another form, as a burgeoning excess of connections within an always "impinging information field." These two aspects of Cartwright's position within the narrative can perhaps best be described by the Lacanian figure of the "subject who is supposed to know."

Lacan introduces this notion to account for the transferential relationship in psychoanalysis and the basis for intersubjectivity in general. Simply stated, between any two partners the subject supposed to know acts as a third, as "the pivot from where everything that goes on in transference is articulated." [13] In *Lookout Cartridge*, it is through Cartwright's diary—in Lacan's language, the signifier introduced in the discourse instituted by it— that Cartwright comes to occupy this pivotal position as the subject who is supposed to know. However, as we've already seen, Cartwright's shifting positionality within the narrative is defined not simply in relation to others but by means of and in relation to the mediations of diary, film, and sound recording. In McElroy's novel, at least, the subject who is supposed to know is very much the subject of technical media.

Friedrich Kittler's insistence on the convergence of the "methodological distinctions of modern psychoanalysis and technical distinctions of the modern media landscape" are therefore essential for understanding the significance of Lacanian theory as it might be applied to McElroy's novel.[14] Kittler argues that "the historical synchronicity of cinema, phonography, and typewriter separated the data flows of optics, acoustics, and writing and rendered them autonomous. . . . Lacan's 'methodological distinction' between the real, the imaginary, and the symbolic is the theory (or merely a historical effect) of this differentiation" (114). Specifically, Lacan's notion of the symbolic corresponds not just to language but to "the signs of language in their materiality and technicity" (114), the imaginary to the optical images of cinema, and the real to the data of sound recording. In McElroy's novel, these three separable data streams are registered as they impinge on Cartwright's consciousness, whose ruminations in turn build toward a narrative. It is a narrative, however, menaced by and inseparable from an immanent delirium; in fact, Cartwright's verification of narrative relations is what prevents his consciousness from being merely the record of delirium. Thus, whereas for Kittler "a delirium written down [as literature] coincides with what the sciences and media themselves were doing," [15] *Lookout Cartridge* attempts to maintain the separation of media in its fictional representations and, at the same time, to divert the delirium that follows from this separation into a sense-making narrative device.

In these terms, *Lookout Cartridge* can be said both to anticipate and to complicate some of the questions about postmodern narrativity and technology that Fredric Jameson raises in his essay "Postmodernism, or the Logic of Late Capital." [16] Taking Lacan's formulations as a "suggestive aesthetic model," Jameson seeks to confront what he calls the "schizophrenic breakdown" of temporal forms of organization and hence the incapacity to narrativize evident in much postmodern art and literature. As Jameson acknowledges, however, the very absence of strong narrative connections makes available new, free-floating "intensities" that displace the older modernist affects of alienation and anxiety. Corresponding to this breakdown in the rendering of temporality is the emergence of a new kind of dizzying and disjunctive space—"postmodern hyperspace"—which Jameson finds exemplified by John Portman's Los Angeles Bonadventure Hotel. In its labyrinthine, apparently noncommunicating spaces and passages, the Bonadventure "has finally succeeded in transcending the capacities of the individual human body to locate itself, to organize its immediate surroundings perceptually, and cognitively to map its position in a mappable external world" (83). For Jameson, nevertheless, these postmodern mutations in the rendering of time and space ultimately have a simple explanation: they "stand as the symbol[s] and analogon[s]" of our present incapacity to locate ourselves and map our experience in relation to the global, de-centered communicational networks of multinational capitalism.

Viewed in this perspective, *Lookout Cartridge* can be seen as an effort to write a prose fictional equivalent of a hyperspace and the drama of one character's attempt to trace his own cognitive map of its contours and passages. The story McElroy's narrator struggles to tell would thus have to be paraphrased a little differently. It is certainly about a lost film that registers the lost idealism and frustration of sixties counterculture and the emergence in the seventies of a new kind of cynical terrorism; but it is also about how this story cannot be fully conveyed because it is also marked, perhaps even determined, by a more profound historical change, also depicted within the novel: the creation of an environment in which new technologies and mass-media images not only throw into question the authority of any ultimate referential truth behind appearances (and which it would be incumbent upon an historically responsible narrative to reveal), but make experience, or at least the evidence of the senses, inseparable from technical media.

Thus, while these two stories may involve different orders of events, *Lookout Cartridge* suggests that they cannot actually be separated. For consciousness itself, as it is represented in the novel, is always a matter of mediality: it always emerges as the product of different registrations or inscriptions of experience. Specifically, it arises in the gap between what is registered on the film and what is registered in memory, or between what is on the film and what is in the diary, or in the discontinuities between different narrative accounts. In *Lookout Cartridge,* then, consciousness must be said to arise or to constitute itself *in* a difference and *as* a difference, a difference that requires different media of perception and recording for its articulation.

In the novel's primary system of metaphors, this space between is either defined by or identified with a cartridge (for film, tape, or gun) as the means by which one system is inserted into another larger system. Shuttling between different places and various groups associated with his film partner, his daughter, his wife, and those who were filmed, as well as between different times—the shooting of the film, conversations that took place in the past or would later take place—the narrator, Cartwright, becomes this cartridge between spaces, times, and groups of people, even between different accounts of events. Indeed, Cartwright's self-insertion into events makes the cartridge a constantly changing multidimensional frame and hence the site of a burgeoning multiplicity. As the site of multiple and contradictory inscriptions, this cartridge or writing machine also delineates a blind spot, by marking the place of the narrator's insertion into transindividual networks of control and determination which are at once familial, social, economic, and political and which can never become totally visible no matter how many times or places the narrator may come to occupy.

Committed to Marxist hermeneutics, Jameson wants to maintain that "our faulty representations of [i.e., our failure to narrativize] some immense communicational and computer network are themselves but a distorted figuration of something even deeper, namely the whole world system of present-day multinational capitalism" (79). Seeking a new form of realism, McElroy's *Lookout Cartridge* demonstrates not only how our experience, and hence our awareness of contemporary events, cannot be assumed to exist apart from the technologies, scriptive and otherwise, by which those events are registered but also how those technologies always extend experience beyond their intended end, and therefore beyond the ends for which those technologies were presumably designed. And whereas Jameson believes that contemporary technology is fascinating precisely because "it seems to offer some privileged representational shorthand for grasping a network of power and control even more difficult for our minds and imaginations to grasp" (79–80), McElroy discovers that technology can hardly be thought of as any representational shorthand" and that its relationship with any "network of power and control" will be necessarily excessive and incommensurate.

If the novel as a literary assemblage offers a convenient means for the investigation of this relationship, it is through its capacity to proliferate narratives in which an information multiplicity arises in the "dimensionless space between" events and their registration. But finally, this space "reached into existence" by a writing machine endlessly rewriting prior inscriptions cannot be separated from the space of the book itself. Also another cartridge, but now inserted into the reader's own "field of impinging information," *Lookout Cartridge* thus becomes the site of a lasting difference, the one between the book we have in our heads and the one we hold in our hands.

. . . . **5**

Capitalism and Entropic Flow

JR

I. No doubt the most striking fact about
William Gaddis's novel *JR* is that it consists almost entirely of talk, much of it over the
telephone, transcribed with a minimum of authorial interruption. The streams of conversation and cacophony of voices which make up *JR*
proceed, moreover, as much by disconnection as
by connection and move according to rhythms
of flow, or repeated disruption and renewed
flow, rather than according to meaningful or lo-
gocentric principles of logic and rhetoric. Which
immediately raises questions about what impels
and governs this flow and how it can be accounted for in novelistic or representational
terms.

Almost any page in *JR* will serve to illustrate
this point, but consider the following passage,

where the General Roll company secretary, Terry, is talking to another employee, Myrna, who speaks first:

—I can't make it like that, like that time with Ronnie I'm always scared somebody's going to walk in right when you're wait is that all the pink polish?

—We made it four times up there Monday before he went, I'll get more at lunch you want to go shopping? I saw this like silky yellow blouse over on Steinway it would go real nice with your coloring turn it up a little . . .

and save four dollars on genuine leath . . . your gospel station. And ye shall . . . motion to dismiss a class action suit by . . . viernes sabado y domingo, el . . . market is down sixteen cents. The . . . for tomorrow, partly sunny windy and too . . .

The voices met, parted, rose over the scratch of emery boards, dropped for the sound of the phone—no he went out of town for a couple of days Mister Shapiro, could I do something for you . . . ? no come on now don't get fresh . . . paused to dial,—yes I'm calling Mis . . . no ma'am no I'm not the lady selling free dance less . . . no for Mister Bast, is he . . . he's where . . . ? answered again—that last order I got the order right in front of me it says twenty pound stock yeah . . . and silence, finally, with—wait out here for me, I forgot to turn off the lights . . .

inbound traffic on the Gowanus Exp . . . favor, send your mouth on a vaca . . . and rain, the present tem . . . no tiene nada . . .

—Turn it off I swear, if he wasn't so cheap we'd have Muzak. How come you came in so late this morning.

—I got the worst cramps I been, wait. Hello . . . ? No he's out of town, he went yesterday Mis . . . tomorrow I think, I'll tell him to call you okay? Goodbye now . . .[1]

Here, as throughout *JR*, human speech is distinguished from a more encompassing hum or murmur only as a series of modulations, wherein sexual confessions, chatter about shopping, business on the telephone, and radio broadcasts merge and flow with the same value and intensity. But if human speech is not given automatic priority or preeminence, perhaps it is because speech itself is only one form of flow, neither more nor less important than the flow of people in and out of the office, the flow of traffic outside, the flow of paper goods and cheap consumer objects, the changes in the weather, the flows of the body, and the flow of time itself. *JR* thus raises the question of how flow and circulation could become so generalized that sounds, objects, and bodies could all have the same status in regard to the novel's economy of representation.

It would not be irrelevant to consider this flow in relation to television, whose diffusion of images since the mid-1970s has brought about similar leveling effects. In a pathbreaking study of television published in 1974, just one year before *JR* appeared, Raymond Williams proposed "flow" as the central concept for its analysis.[2] For Williams, television constituted a radical new medium of communication simply because its messages no longer form discrete units, and interruption is transformed into something like its opposite, continuity. As we shall see, *JR* can be similarly described.

However, Gaddis's novel relates flow most directly to the abstract exchanges of contemporary capitalism, and stock trading on Wall Street is one of its overt subjects. *JR* is concerned with the movement and effects of capital as they incarnate a new regime within the larger history of American corporate capitalism. What above all characterizes this regime is the almost complete subordination of use-value to exchange-value, with the corollary that the production and circulation of information—of objects as signs rather than goods—now functions as the economy's primary motor. Corporate raiding, buyouts, takeovers, leasebacks, buying on margin, trading on credit, using tax credit as capital—all the various strategies that typify the current system as it is represented in *JR*—now seem to operate according to a logic of their own, with seemingly little relationship to earlier economic theories based solely or principally on supply and demand. Like the weather, or indeed any turbulent system, the stock market becomes as a consequence highly sensitive to small fluctuations in trading. Always susceptible to these erratic shifts and therefore unpredictable even in the short term, the market increasingly appears to teeter on the edge of chaos.

At first sight, *JR* appears less concerned with the dynamics of such a system than with the chaos it wreaks on individual human lives. Yet further inspection reveals that the two are not easily separable. In Gaddis's novel, capitalism is not simply portrayed as a mode of production and exchange operating in the background, as an economy in the restricted sense, but as an entire mode of being in which words and things are defined in a certain manner and for which human life functions as both agent and *materiel,* its subject and object positions governed by an elaborate and highly abstract operational logic no longer amenable to a collective human will or rationality. According to Jean Baudrillard, the operational logic of contemporary capitalism is dictated by "the force which rules market value: capital must circulate; gravity and any fixed point must disappear; the chain of investments and reinvestments must never stop; value must radiate endlessly and in every direction."[3] In sum, the value of what is produced in the current capitalist economy is measured and even determined by the extent and rate of its circulation, not its consumption.

This compulsion to make capital flow and circulate through every sector of human being and social life not only defines objects primarily in relation to their sign or information value but also calls for a new form of operational subject. Such a subject functions not as a centered and autonomous agent, engaging other agents in a scene of dramatic action, but as a screen, interface, terminal, or switching node within multiple networks and relay systems. For a subject emerging within the purely operational context of information flow and exchange, however, there is no dialectic between subject and object which would allow the subject to reflect upon and thereby transcend him- or herself. As Baudrillard again appropriately remarks, the "scene and mirror" that once enabled this dialectical drama to unfold have ceased to exist: "In place of the reflexive transcendence of mirror and scene, there is a nonreflecting surface, an immanent surface where operations unfold—the smooth operational surface of communication."[4]

Jean-François Lyotard offers a similar account of the subject as located at "nodal points" of specific communication circuits. "One is always located at a post through which various kinds of messages pass," Lyotard asserts, quickly adding that "no one, not even the least privileged among us, is ever entirely powerless over the messages that traverse and position him [or her] at the post of sender, addressee, or referent." Little consolation, however, if contemporary society is now a giant cybernetic machine operating by feedback, seeking to combat its own entropy through ceaseless movement and communication, with performativity its only criterion for success; for, as Lyotard asserts, everything in it must become "operational (that is, commensurable) or disappear."[5]

JR relentlessly shows what the society theorized by Baudrillard and Lyotard looks like at the level of everyday life. First, as a side effect of the operational logic of late or cybernetic capitalism, the entire human world seems catastrophically disorganized, as if it had fallen under the baleful spell of some disruptive and noisy machine that operates by inefficiency, producing only accidents, spillage, waste, breakdown, and misunderstanding.

Most of the novel's characters experience this machine as an "infernal machine" in which they are all caught up and swept along. It is infernal not only because it appears to function by systematically frustrating their every volitional act and attempt at communication but also because of its strange power of attraction and energizing effects. The machine is also totalizing in its extension and effects: there is neither an "outside" or place of respite beyond its reach, nor by the same token, no "inside" or locatable center. In short, the machine is coextensive with and completely immanent to the world of the novel. Finally, the machine has no memory; it does not recognize the past as a source of value but only circulation and exchange in the present.

Within this machinic world, human beings are represented as voices and speech acts, that is, not as individual or autonomous selves but as conduits and networks through which information flows and various kinds of exchange take place. On the one hand, the characters' dysfunctionality at the referential level signals a form of resistance to this new machinic regime, even if this resistance can be expressed only symptomatically. On the other hand, this psychological reading is not quite exact, for the characters in *JR* are not depicted as separate from the heterogeneous arrays of information and objects with which they combine in working arrangements, which become most visible when these arrangements become hilariously dysfunctional. In the scene quoted at the outset, Terry is represented as only a regulator of flows within multiple networks of exchange that everywhere exceed her. In this respect, the scene is no different from later scenes such as those in the principal's office in the Long Island school or the 96th Street Manhattan apartment. What characterizes all three scenes is a multiplicity of objects and signs in which the characters provide the means for their fluid interaction. What differs from scene to scene is merely the speed and intensity with which these elements interact and the diverse effects their flows produce on the characters involved.

However, if we want to account for the new subject who emerges there, we must do so in terms that are directly responsive to the way in which *JR* registers them. Which means in the machinic language of flow—of represented objects and sounds, but also of signs on the printed page. The term *machinic,* which for Deleuze and Guattari designates "working" relationships that are neither vitalistic nor mechanical among functional parts of an assemblage *[agencement],* is appropriate therefore in at least two senses: as a novel, *JR* depicts the world of contemporary capitalism as a machinic universe; but the machine driving the novel also enters into its composition and (dis)organization, defining not only its content but the very form of its expression.[6]

What, then, is the subject of this machinic language? Proceeding only by interruption, by constantly breaking down and starting up again, speech in broken and disrupted flows constitutes *JR*'s most basic form of expression. Its conversations make up so many little "desiring machines," as Deleuze and Guattari call the coupling of an energy-producing machine or one that produces flow (of any material whatever) with another that breaks, cuts into, or syphons off part of that flow.[7] Nature itself is a "machinic phylum," a multiplicity of partial objects, some overlapping with others, connected through breaks/flows and forming connective syntheses in an endless binary linearity. The sun and the eye, the air and the mouth, a breast and a mouth: in each case there is a flow and an organ or partial object that breaks that flow, siphoning off part of it. In Deleuze and Guattari's theory, the word *machine* in no way indicates that these connections constitute an objective structure, with subjective positions and coordinates of reference. Desiring machines simply arrange and connect flows, without recognizing any distinctions between persons and organs, the material and the semiotic. Furthermore, as heterogeneous, Rube Goldberg–like constructions, they "work" by continually breaking down: starting, stopping, starting again, in a process of flow-cut-stoppage-flow-cut-stoppage that goes on indefinitely.

In *JR,* it is capitalism—and only secondarily society—that organizes de-siring machines into subjects and objects that function in circuits of commu-nication and exchange. As a giant cybernetic machine that "capitalizes" not only all subjects and objects of exchange but all forms of flow and communication within society, contemporary capitalism calls up a new kind of subject out of the human multiplicity, whose activities are no longer to be understood as those of a dramatic agent interacting with other agents on a scene but as a functional node or terminal in a communications network. Schematically, then, *JR* can be said to be about the flow of words in relation to the movements of bodies in the widest possible sense: not only integral human bodies, but also body parts, objects, money or capital, messages, or whatever assumes corporal form. When these flows conjoin, as in the buy-ing and selling of stock, language speeds up in a process of deterritorializa-tion, as if the already highly deterritorialized trading of stock deterritoria-lized speech itself, leaving in its wake a new kind of human subject.

The novel's central character, JR, illustrates what this new subject looks like, and the other characters, how subjects formed by an older regime of capital have become dysfunctional by comparison. The two other major characters, the composer Edward Bast and the science teacher Jack Gibbs, straddle the two regimes; both attempt to realize projects conceived from within the older regime while participating in the new one. If both fail, it is because they are unable to translate their artistic and critical projects into the terms that the new capitalist regime demands. However, failure in *JR* is not a simple matter, for there are no wholly successful "translations" within *JR*—even Frigicom, the new scientific attempt to translate noise pollution into "shards," eventually fails. All of which confirms the novel's tacit theme that failure and machinic breakdown are not the unfortunate results but the necessary conditions of a new regime, one that takes specific form in JR's Family of Companies and Typhon International.

Whereas the conventions of traditional novelistic representation were developed to represent the social world of a stage of capitalism now rapidly receding into the past, an older world represented in Gaddis's novel by the Bast family and its company, General Roll, the conventions of *JR* seem to have been invented in order to represent the newer world of corporate capitalism. More precisely, *JR* can be said to encompass the two worlds corresponding to these two regimes of capital and to articulate their difference in both the form and content of its language. As a consequence, *JR* acquires a layered, temporal depth and a complexity in what otherwise might appear as too flat a rendering of the surfaces of contemporary American life.

In order to see how *JR* encompasses these two worlds and functions in relation to their difference, a more detailed inventory of the novel and its machinic effects must first be provided. A summary of the first hundred pages or so will indicate the basic themes and method of presentation. With the formation and meteoric rise of JR's Family of Companies, which takes place in roughly the novel's middle third, information, characters, and events begin to proliferate at such a frenetic and less dramatically apprehensible pace that it becomes difficult to keep them sorted out according to conventional novelistic assumptions. With these assumptions serving as something like a ghostly scaffolding, *JR* turns into something stranger, a becoming-assemblage whose flows in many ways resemble JR's own paper empire. The novel's three main characters, JR Vansant, Edward Bast, and Jack Gibbs, function as subjects of this assemblage, both as characters in their own right and as speaking voices supporting thematically inflected discursive networks. Each in his own way is pulled toward delirium and thus participates in the acceleration of flows and the becoming-delirious that gives *JR* its special momentum.

II. In the opening exchange between the Bast sisters, Anne and Julia, who are thinking back to the first time they saw paper money, *JR* announces its concern with a theme (money), a medium (paper), and an important historical change in capitalism's medium of exchange (from gold to paper money):

> —Money . . . ? in a voice that rustled.
> —Paper, yes.
> —And we'd never seen it. Paper money.
> —We never saw paper money till we came east.
> —It looked so strange the first time we saw it. Lifeless.
> —You couldn't believe it was worth a thing.
> —Not after Father jingling his change.
> —Those were silver dollars.
> —And silver halves, yes and quarters, Julia. The one from his pupils. I can hear him now.   (5)

The dialogue is then interrupted by an authorial observation: "Sunlight, pocketed in a cloud, spilled suddenly broken across the floor through the leaves of the trees outside" (5). This striking anthropomorphism suggests that sunlight, like gold coins, has spilled across the floor (the verb *spill* will recur in a variety of contexts throughout *JR*), as if the processes of nature here participate in or mimic human gestures rather than constituting an order of otherness or difference.

When the dialogue resumes, it now includes a third speaker, a lawyer named Mister Coen, who has come to the Bast sisters' Long Island home to clear up certain matters pertaining to the recent (intestate) death of their brother, Thomas Bast. As the legal representative of Thomas's company, General Roll (which originally manufactured piano rolls), Coen seeks to know who in the Bast family might be in a position to exert claims on Thomas's estate, which consists primarily of a controlling interest in General Roll. Coen, however, is unable to make himself understood and is constantly frustrated by the Bast sisters' explanatory but to him confusing and digressive stories about Father, Thomas, and their brother James.

Although Coen insists that he only wants to ascertain the basic facts—"The law seeks order, Miss Bast. Order!" (8)—the facts are just what he is not able to determine. Mainly interested in the status of Edward Bast, the young nephew of the Bast sisters who resides with them, he departs without knowing Edward's exact age or, more importantly, his paternity. Doubts arise from the fact that Edward's mother, Nellie, first married Thomas, then cohabited with and later married James, with Edward's birth falling somewhere in the transition period. Curiously, this uncertainty about James's paternity is sustained graphically, since the very name Edward Bast cannot help but evoke—both visually and aurally—the word *bastard*.

The conflict between the order sought by the law and the entangled profusion of the Bast family history comes out in the comically confused conversation between Coen and the Bast sisters, which always moves at cross purposes, with misunderstanding begetting further misunderstanding, and threatens to escalate into cacophony and verbal chaos. It is not only that the Bast sisters lack a sense of relevance, their comments moved by a logic of association and reminiscence; but Coen adds to the confusion by using words in their strictly legal rather than common sense and is frequently carried away in a near delirium of legal jargon and equally irrelevant citations of legal precedence.

This incommensurability of two realities, the past history of the Bast family and the law as a quasi-autonomous discursive mechanism, results in a disorder increased rather than reduced by the things temporally and physically present which would normally facilitate communication. Notably, the local newspapers add to the confusion by using James's prewritten obituary to report the death of his brother, Thomas, so that "it's hard even knowing who's dead" (6). And the Bast house itself is the site of an always threatening and sometimes eruptive menace of physical disorder. Hammering and cutting noises constantly intrude, and the latch to the side or back door—no one is certain which—is faulty. Coen breaks off the arm of his chair, spills his papers, drops and breaks his glasses, all while one of the sisters busily tries to replace a missing button on his coat.

Meanwhile, a curious typographical device both registers and signals the misapprehension that will push the dialogue in diverse directions. When Coen first identifies himself to the ladies—there is never any authorial introduction of characters, who simply appear suddenly as voices—he says that his name is spelled without an *h*; yet, whenever either of the aunts speaks his name, it is spelled Co*h*en. That his name visually evokes *coin*—associated with spillage on the novel's first page—further indicates how typography (or a logic of material signifiers) plays an active role in the generation of the text. By means of a simple graphic strategy, Gaddis conveys the fact that the sisters have failed to grasp his correct name.

As an instance of what the Russian formalists call a "baring of the artistic device," this strategy signals that everything taking place in the social space imagined by the reader has to be conveyed exclusively by the resources of print as a medium. Throughout *JR*, in fact, information is made significant graphically, most often by spelling and/or typographic "error." In this way, Gaddis not only draws our attention to thematically important signifiers and the novel's material surface of inscription but also indicates how the "space" of *JR* will be defined: as a space "opened" by the noncoincidence of the human voice with its graphic registration as signs on the printed page. In this sense, *JR*'s acknowledgement of its own mediality determines its thematic interest in other inscriptions of meaningful sound, that is, in piano rolls, sheet music, newspaper ads, manuscripts, and the (purely fictive) device Frigicom. Formally and thematically, these compositional strategies draw attention to *JR*'s surface and frustrate the reader's escape into the imagined depths of a depicted social world.

This feature is also evident in the way Gaddis manages transitions from one particular scene of dialogue to the next by following a movement articulated *within* or immanent to that first scene. When Coen leaves the Bast house in his car, we follow its rapid motion (for two descriptive paragraphs) through a suburban landscape into the center of an unnamed town to a curb in front of the local bank, where once again we are immersed in another conversation among a different set of characters: Mr. Whiteback, who is both president of the bank and principal of the local elementary school; Amy Joubert, who teaches at the school; and Edward Bast, who has recently become the school's composer-in-residence through a Ford Foundation grant. We then move quickly in Whiteback's car to the school, follow Whiteback's gaze upward to Jack Gibbs standing at the window of his science class just as the lesson is ending, follow Gibbs's gaze back down to the front of the school, and then follow Dan diCephalis into the principal's office, where the principal, Whiteback, the curriculum specialist, Miss Flesch, Major Hyde, a member of the school board, and Vern Teakell, the district superintendent, are discussing the school budget, which mostly involves the purchase of expensive equipment (a minimum is spent on books) and the resurfacing of the parking lot. Other characters enter and leave, the most significant of whom is Mr. Pecci, the local congressman, who is representing Flo-Jan, the company that will do the blacktopping. Meanwhile, telephones ring and sounds and images appear on the audiovisual monitor of the in-school television circuit. At a certain point, Dan diCephalis, in charge of testing (for which this expensive equipment has been purchased, but no one can calibrate the holes in the paper) leaves the office for the Jewish temple, where students are rehearsing the production of Wagner's

Das Rheingold, the school cafeteria where they would normally rehearse having been taken over by drivers' ed. class. There we come in on Edward Bast leading the students through a practice session, playing one-handedly on the piano (he has injured his other hand) while Major Hyde's son interrupts with a "Call to Colors" on the trumpet (the only music he knows) and an unidentified old man from music therapy class accompanies them on the saxophone. The session ends when JR Vansant, in the role of the dwarf Alberich, who will steal the Rhinegold after renouncing love, apparently steals the money (actually, he gives it to another teacher, to be set aside for the class to purchase a stock certificate on their upcoming field trip to the New York Stock Exchange).

Once again in his car, diCephalis drives Bast back to the in-school television programming studio. On the screen of a studio monitor an image of Smokey the Bear appears, and it is via this image that we return to the principal's office, where representatives of the Ford Foundation (Whiteback mistakenly thought they were to come the following week) are viewing a demonstration of the in-circuit TV educational system. They decide to watch an audiovisual presentation of Mozart's life as a composer. However, the inexperienced Bast, while doing the pre-scripted voice-over presentation, becomes exasperated by its "fairy-tale" style and soon departs from the text. Emphasizing Mozart's oppressive money problems and quoting scabrous excerpts from Mozart's letters (such as the epigrammatic "Believing and shitting are two different things"), Bast deliriously narrates the bleak details of Mozart's death and pauper's funeral. Meanwhile, in the principal's office, panicked school officials attempt to cut away from Bast's scandalous presentation to a "resource" film on Wall Street shown to Amy Joubert's class, and then to Ann diCephalis's film on the silkworm, but a faulty knob (which later falls off) prevents them from controlling the equipment, and eventually they have to unplug it. At this point diCephalis leaves the principal's office, drives to the programming studio to pick up his wife, and takes her home.

This twenty-seven-page sequence, in which we move into and then away from the school in a multiplicity of discontinuous but related movements, is characteristic of Gaddis's mode of presentation throughout. We also note that surfaces—particularly inscriptive surfaces—often come into play. As the number of characters and the number of activities in which they are engaged increases, so does the level of the noise, confusion, and number of accidents; at the same time, a great deal of information about the characters, their activities, and their environment is conveyed. Characters come to life solely through what they say, but the reader quickly learns to recognize them through their distinctive verbal ticks and obsessive motifs. For example, the principal, Whiteback, never departs from an abstract bureaucratic jargon ("tangibilitating the utilization potential"), Miss Flesch reduces language to jibberish ("PRwise it can't hurt us educationwise"), Vern repeatedly emphasizes his perspective ("see it on the corporate level all the time"), and Major Hyde returns obsessively to the topic of his home nuclear fallout shelter, supposedly "what America's all about."

The school sequence also follows the opening section by developing further the already introduced double theme of the conflict between business and art and business and education. Both conflicts already appear in the Bast family history, in effect defining Edward's family inheritance. Father, the founder of General Roll, the Bast family business, was also a musician and teacher of music. In the next generation this split is externalized in Thomas, who took over the business, and James, who became a composer. (Significantly, James never appears in the novel but remains in exile in Europe.) In the school sequence, the conflict between art and business (or money) is conveyed symbolically through the Mozart and Wagner material, while the conflict between business and education is treated with satirical directness: the school is run as a business in which teaching is done by audiovisual technologies ("books cause too many problems"), while also operating as a clearing house for consumer products in which students and objects are actually confused (students institutionally designated as "retards" are at one point displaced by newly resurfaced automobile tires, or "retreads"). But the school is not simply a place where business as a mindset is inculcated ("what America's all about"); it also functions as a site where new subjects are programmed to accept content in a highly specific form: as merely one interchangeable component in an information circuit. This reduction is comically illustrated by Coach Vogel's science film in which electronic parts and human sexual organs are presented as completely interchangeable.

At the school, impositions of order usually produce disorder. The science teacher, Jack Gibbs, makes this theme explicit when he addresses the class in a series of statements that run directly counter to the school's new educational program:

> —All right let's have order here, order . . . ! he'd reached the [television] set himself and snapped it into darkness.—Put on the lights there now.

Before we go any further here, has it ever occurred to any of you that all this is simply one grand misunderstanding? Since you're not here to learn anything, but to be taught so you can pass these tests, knowledge has to be organized so it can be taught, and it has to be reduced to information so it can be organized do you follow that? In other words this leads you to assume that organization is an inherent property of the knowledge itself, and that disorder and chaos are simply irrelevant forces that threaten it from outside. In fact it's exactly the opposite. Order is simply a thin, perilous condition we try to impose on the basic reality of chaos.   (20)

Gibbs tries to press upon his students the sense in which knowledge has no inherent organization but is rather a construction or fragile order imposed upon "the basic reality of chaos." Though his logic is not altogether clear, Gibbs understands that the reduction of heterogeneous realms of knowledge to a single audiovisual language ("information") promotes the illusion that chaos is something threatening us from outside, and that the order apparently formed by this reduction to information in fact produces a much greater disorder.

Gibbs's name evokes that of Josiah Willard Gibbs, the nineteenth-century American physicist responsible for introducing statistics into the study of thermodynamic systems and an early theoretician of entropy (the tendency of closed systems to lose energy). In *The Human Use of Human Beings: Cybernetics and Society,* which Jack Gibbs later cites explicitly (see p. 403), Norbert Wiener explains how, by introducing statistics and probability theory into physics, Willard Gibbs sounded the death knell not only of Newtonian ideas of order but of an entire conception of the physical world: "in a probabilistic world we no longer deal with . . . a specific, real universe as a whole but ask instead questions which may find their answers in a large number of similar universes. Thus chance has been admitted, not merely as a mathematical tool for physics, but as part of its warp and weft."[8] As Weiner explains, "Gibbs' innovation was to consider not one world, but all the worlds which are possible answers to a limited number of questions concerning our environment. His central notion concerned the extent to which answers that we may give to questions about one set of worlds are probable among a larger set of worlds" (20). Gibbs further postulates that as the universe grows older, entropy, or the measure of this probability, tends naturally to increase. Order is least probable and chaos most probable, but fortunately there are enclaves where order may actually increase, at least temporarily. Biological life systems are one such instance, the various exchanges between human beings and between human beings and machines another.

The new field of cybernetics, as Wiener christened it, stems from the application of Gibbs's ideas to the "theory of messages" (23) conceived specifically as a method of control, which is accomplished by means of what Wiener calls feedback. In a feedback system, output, or the results of a past performance, is reinserted into the same system as input in order to form a self-regulating loop. Wiener's pronouncements, however, depend upon a specific *interpretation* of early formulations in information theory concerning the relationship between entropy in thermodynamics and entropy in information theory. As Wiener himself puts it:

> Messages are themselves a form of pattern and organization. Indeed, it is possible to treat sets of messages as having an entropy like sets of states of the external world. Just as entropy is a measure of disorganization, the information carried by a set of messages is a measure of organization. In fact, *it is possible to interpret* the information carried by a message as essentially the negative of its entropy, and the negative logarithm of its probability. That is, the more probable the message, the less information it gives. Clichés, for example, are less illuminating than great poems. (31, my emphasis)

Wiener's version of information entropy was contested by Claude Shannon, the information theorist who derived the mathematical formula for computing information in a communication channel. Unlike Wiener, who understood the relation between information and entropy to be inversely proportional, Shannon saw them as the same thing; that is, information *is* entropy.[9] As a system's disorganization increases, more information becomes available; chaos is simply maximum information, and hence a highly unlikely (or improbable) state.

Like *The Crying of Lot 49* and the novels of information multiplicity that follow it, *JR* opens up the space between these two conceptions. As we shall see, not only do the feedback mechanisms that, in Wiener's theory, control disorder only produce more disorder in an escalation of effects, as in a runaway system,[10] but the entire novel plays on the inherent ambiguity of information as a measure of a message's entropy. In the torrent of words unleashed by JR, Gibbs, and others, what counts is less their semantic or information value than the effects they have in relation to other flows, both semiotic and material.

JR also draws an implicit contrast between this scientific model of order and disorder and Empedocles' classical mythic model in which the universe consists of a sphere in which elements constantly combine and fall asunder according to ever recurrent rhythms of Love and Strife, the two cosmic forces that act on all elements.[11] Although for Empedocles the cosmos has no origin or telos, it does have four stages, or phases, through which it continually cycles: "two polar stages represented by the rule of Love and the rule of Strife, and two transitional stages, one from the rule of Love towards the rule of Strife, and the other back again from the rule of Strife towards the rule of Love." Beginning (but only logically) with the rule of Love, where all elements are combined in such a uniform way that "nothing whatever can be discerned in it," Empedocles traces the evolution of life through four successive generations, thus also suggesting that his cosmogony consists of cycles within cycles. In the first generation, there are only fragments of bodies: "Here sprang up many faces without necks, arms wandered without shoulders, unattached, and eyes strayed alone, in need of foreheads." In the second generation, "solitary limbs wandered about seeking union [. . .] but these things fell together as each chanced to meet the other," resulting only in the formation of monsters. In the third generation, under the influence of Strife, "wholenatured forms" at last appear, but they are sexually undifferentiated. Finally, the increased influence of Strife yields the "present" phase of sexually differentiated fully human beings.

Experiencing the world as fragmentary and disordered, Gibbs often makes use of imagery from Empedocles' first generation. As he walks through New York's Penn Station, where "elbows found ribs and shoulders backs," he directly echoes Empedocles: "place like the dawn of the world here, this way . . . countless hands and unattached eyes, faces looking in different directions" (161). In his earlier conversation with Mr. Gall, Gibbs also appeals to Empedocles for an image of primitive chaos, before the imposition of order, "when limbs and parts of bodies were wandering around everywhere separately" (45). The context of this reference suggests moreover that Gibbs (perhaps unconsciously) associates this disordered state with a critique of capitalism, since he brings up Empedocles' name in reply to Mr. Gall's query about the source of the Greek motto inscribed over the entrance to the school. As the reader realizes (or will later discover), the inscription is only disguised as Greek and can be deciphered as the first three words of Karl Marx's heralded "From each according to his ability, to each according to his needs." And finally, Empedocles' language of unattached body parts is registered in the authorial descriptions of Gibbs's idyllic weekend of passionate lovemaking with Amy Joubert (see pp. 483, 489–490), where this time a profusion of entangled limbs and body surfaces seeking one another is presented under the sign of Love rather than Strife.

III. The next extended sequence, the school field trip to Wall Street, where Amy Joubert's social studies class will purchase a share in Diamond Cable, develops the theme of business and education in relation to the workings of corporate capitalism. (A subsidary theme, the relationship of parents to their children, also becomes paramount.) The lesson is supposed to illustrate how buying stock and becoming a shareholder is a form of participatory democracy, but this is undercut by almost everything that happens.

As the class is guided from the stock exchange on Wall Street to Crawley and Company, where they buy a share in Diamond Cable, and then to Typhon International for an instructional film and a box lunch (which they never receive), we see how the children's curiosity and desire to know is systematically frustrated. At Typhon they are taken in charge by David Davidoff, a public relations specialist who intends to play up their visit in the corporate annual report. But Davidoff only adds to the general confusion, often excusing himself to attend incompetently to "brush fires," as he calls problems that arise while he is "on deck." Meanwhile, signs indicate that the value of Diamond Cable stock is slowly dropping and that Typhon International is engaged in an ambitious international mining operation in Africa, the success of which depends on major capital investment by the U.S. government, tight control over corporate manipulations vis-à-vis both the Securities and Exchange Commission (SEC) and "the liberal press," and cooperation on the part of Congress and the military (a number of generals are involved). To facilitate this scheme, Amy Joubert's father, Monty Moncrief, resigns on the day of the class visit so that he can take a post in Washington.

Of course, none of this is imparted to the kids, who are abandoned in the boardroom to watch an educational film they have already seen. When introduced to the class, all that Governor Cates, director of Typhon International, can manage to say is, "as long as you're in the game you may as well play to win" (107). Nevertheless, JR and Hyde's son do get a glimpse of what corporate dealing is like when they overhear Cates and the corporation's lawyer Beaton talking in the bathroom (a site that turns out to be symbolically highly significant). In an unmistakable tone of crass manipulation, certain operational directives ("buy for credit, sell for cash"; "the trick's to get other people's money to work for you") come across loud and clear. Although JR doesn't understand all that he hears or reads (he picks up numerous brochures), he gets a good introductory lesson in how corporate capitalism actually works.

The lessons of the school field trip are soon put into practice. With increasing speed and no other resources than energy and ingenuity, the eleven-year-old JR will juggle together a conglomerate of worthless companies into a financial empire that eventually threatens the stability of the market and the future of Typhon International. Yet JR's creation is neither as incredible nor as fantastic as it sounds, not least because the stock market functions in many ways like a game played by remote control, over the telephone or through the mail, that is, through communications media that by nature operate without any authorized verification of the sender's identity. This is a lesson that JR grasps early on. After being reprimanded for unauthorized use of the school telephone, JR contrives to have the telephone company install a booth from which he can conduct his business operations in one of the school corridors. When Hyde's son warns him that he will get into trouble for forgery, JR replies: "What do you mean forgery I just scribbled this here name which it's nobody's down at the bottom where it says authorized by, I mean you think the telephone company goes around asking everybody is this here your signature? All they care it says requisition order right across the top so they come stick in this here telephone booth" (185).

Just as JR grasps that his own personal identity never has to be "arthurized" in order to have the telephone installed, he soon understands that the business of buying and selling operates in a manner similar to the school telephone setup: as circuits that he can connect together without his having to stand as their "authorized" guarantee.[12] To make things work in the business world, he only has to manage connections and to direct flows and exchanges in circuits that are already established, like a skilled player of video games. In other words, he knows he has to function not as an origin that would require or involve an identity defined by its capacity to initiate something on the basis of its own authority but as a switching mechanism that taps into, directs, and manages flows. What makes this flow and its acceleration possible is not just the change from metal to paper currency (a change the elderly Bast sisters can clearly remember) but the shift from currency to the even more abstract exchanges of the credit system. (Significantly, JR often confuses the words *loan* and *borrow*, but apparently to no ill effect.)

The growth of JR's financial empire parodically illustrates what this change makes possible. JR first opens a bank account in Nevada in the same way he got the telephone installed. Scouring newspapers and mail order catalogues, collecting free samples of whatever strikes him as possibly useful, he gets his first idea for a business deal from an entry in a "spot bid catalogue," which he obtains in a trade with Hyde's son: he will buy nine thousand surplus picnic forks from the navy on credit and then unload them on the army for a profit (later a shipment of the forks mysteriously turns up at the school). Meanwhile, taking Davidoff at his word (Davidoff had told the class that even the owner of a single share could bring suit if unsatisfied), JR threatens to sue Diamond Cable, and Davidoff himself settles out of court with a cash payment without looking into the origin of the threat. With this money JR buys debentures (at seven cents on the dollar) on Eagle Mills stock, a decrepit upstate New York mill. Using the cash from the Eagle Mills employees' pension fund, JR rapidly begins to acquire an assortment of bankrupt companies and near worthless vested interests. These include a Midwestern brewery, a publishing house, X-L Lithography, Triangle Paper Products, a shipping line (its only vessel capsized), a chain of nursing homes and funeral parlors, pork bellies, sheep-gut condoms, plastic flowers—all of which, through tax write-offs and wheeling and dealing, JR consolidates into a corporate "family of companies," an obvious caricature of the family he never had at home.

Most of these deals are parlayed over the telephone, a "snot rag" disguising JR's adolescent voice, or worked out by "Edwert Bast," JR's "business representative [sic]," as the business card JR acquires for Bast reads. Other employees also join the company: Davidoff, Miss Flesch, diCephalis, a general—even the cynical Gibbs helps out; but no one except Bast knows who JR is. As it expands, the corporation's headquarters move from a telephone at a seedy downtown diner to rooms at the Waldorf Hotel, with the deliriously chaotic 96th Street apartment functioning as uptown headquarters. Although only a paper empire, to various competing interests JR's Family of Companies soon appears to be a vast consortium of companies and a fantastic commercial juggernaut.

However, just when the "JR Corp" begins to threaten the stability of the stock market, its own instability and disorganization, increasing in proportion to its growth, lead to its unraveling. (The subsequent SEC investigation finds nothing illegal in JR's operations, most of the corporation's mistakes having been made against its own advantage.) In a last exchange following the dramatic end late in the novel, when U.S. marshals appear at the door of the 96th Street apartment with subpoenas for the corporation's records,

JR and Bast try to assess its demise. Still under the sway of Davidoff's public relations gimmick to promote him as financial wizard and "man of vision," JR refuses to acknowledge any personal accountability, his speech sliding from one "could I help it if . . ." or "was it my fault that . . ." to another. In a long passage (see p. 656) summarizing the life of JR's corporation, Bast counters that JR knew all the time that the "man of vision" ploy was all "trash." In exasperation, Bast forces JR to listen to a piece of music and to tell him what he hears, but he is then so angered by JR's response that he launches into a long harangue in which he accuses JR of ruining or degrading everything he touches. JR responds, first, with a reminder of all he has done to further Bast's musical interests (unlike other capitalist entrepreneurs in the novel, JR displays no prejudice against art per se), and second, with a surprisingly detailed indictment of the systemic constraints on the free enterprise capitalist system.

Earlier JR had brought it to Bast's attention that their difficulties could be attributed to the operations of a new city bank:

> —It's this here new branch of one of these same banks that's screwing us too I mean they never lose these banks don't, I mean where we're getting screwed Crawley's getting screwed everybody's getting screwed except these here banks they never get screwed, they're always in there getting this percent of everything I mean I should have thought of it . . . [. . .] I mean some bank getting some bank I should of thought of that by myself hey? Like where this newspaper just said the parent company I mean that's me, how the parent company is going after this SSS Savings and Loan with these big cash reserves that's how I thought of it I just saw it in the paper, like where the paper's always saying the parent this the parent that I mean that's me the parent! See I hardly got started hey once we get things fixed up I had all these plans . . . his teeth were chattering—I mean like banks we could have these different kinds of banks like this regular bank and these blood banks these eye banks these bone what, where you going . . . (653–654)

As JR himself begins to realize, the system is clearly out of control (note the prescient reference to the Savings and Loan). Not only does chance play a major role in stock market speculation, but frequent reversals of intention and effect make intention something one reads about in newspaper accounts, the result of clever *post facto* interpretation. Hence the importance of public relations people such as Davidoff, who, as JR observes on the class visit, creates the news before it happens. But finally, given this chaotic state of affairs, it can be said that JR draws the correct lesson from his experience when he returns in his exchange with Bast to the central importance of banks: "I should have just went after some bank myself right at the start!" (662). JR's experience and "education" have taught him that since capital must circulate (that's the way the game works), banks are the most profitable, since they profit from circulation itself and appear to be less obstructed by opacities in the system, that is, by human worries and problems that slow down the circulation of capital. From this perspective, the problem with JR's Family of Companies is that it attempted to move capital too fast, without having the personnel who could deal adequately with the human resistance to this movement.

The disastrous human consequences of JR's financial manipulations inevitably raise the question of whether JR is to be seen as an inhuman monster or simply as another unknowing victim of a system he did not create. Gaddis himself, in an interview, has revealed that *JR* is the novel he cares most about, "because I'm awfully fond of the boy himself." [13] By way of explanation, he points out that JR, having no past or parents around him, is "obliged to invent himself . . . in terms of what he sees around him" (67). What he sees, of course, is a school managed like a business with no educational content in a culture that gives prime importance only to "tangible assets." Gaddis then comments on the significance of JR's age:

> The reason he is eleven is because he is in this prepubescent age where he is amoral, with a clear conscience, dealing with people who are immoral, unscrupulous; they realize what scruples are, but push them aside, whereas his good cheer and greed he considers perfectly normal. He thinks this is what you're supposed to do; he is not going to wait around; he is in a hurry, as you should be in America—[to] get on with it, get going. He is very scrupulous about obeying the *letter* of the law and then (never making the distinction) evading the *spirit* of the law at every possible turn. He *is* in these ways an innocent and is well-meaning, a sincere hypocrite. (68, Gaddis's emphases)

Gaddis's understanding of his character JR and his "liberal" response to capitalism are all of a piece. In the interview he describes capitalism "in the end as really the most workable system we've produced"; the problem is not "the system itself, but its abuses . . . *within* the letter of the law" (68–69). By calling attention to and satirizing these abuses, *JR* makes it clear that "our best hope lies in bringing things under better and more equitable control, cutting back the temptations to unmitigated greed and bemused dishonesty

. . . in other words that these abuses the system has fostered are not essential, but running out of moral or ethical control can certainly threaten its survival" (69).

While *JR* can of course be read as Gaddis conceives of it—as a satire on contemporary abuses of capitalism—the novel also contests Gaddis's liberal view, above all through JR's own words and activities, which display an amoral but more realistic understanding of how capitalism actually works. Since capitalism recognizes only the value of circulation and exchange, and thereby constitutes an intrinsically amoral system, its abuses cannot be said to be extrinsic. As a case in point, when Cates tells Beaton to find the legal loopholes that will enable him to do what he wants—advice that JR will later repeat to his lawyer Piscator—it is not an abuse of the system but an inevitable consequence of capitalism's operational logic.

At first, the Typhon corporation appears to be *the* model of a successful capitalist enterprise, but it turns out to be no more substantial or *real* than JR's Family of Companies; in this universe, *real* can only mean operational and pragmatically efficacious. Thus, comparison shows *not* that Governor John ("Black Jack") Cates, the director of Typhon International, is the real thing next to whom JR is a paltry imitation but that both are versions of the same kind of operational subject: the subject as a switching mechanism for information and material flows. To be sure, Cates understands the system like no other character in the novel, and his voice conveys the authority of knowledge and experience. Callously indifferent to the human consequences of his actions, as when he reacts to news of human death only in terms of possible financial gain, he shows no interest in anything except the stock market and his financial dealings. Though he seems to be part of Amy Joubert's family, this connection only provides a means for hiding assets and keeping things secretly under his own control. Like JR, he loses control by failing to attend to the human factor, and, outside the circuits of flow and exchange he "governs," he appears to have even less of a personal identity. This is comically confirmed late in the novel when Cates enters the hospital to have one of his prosthetic parts replaced. As he continues to direct operations by telephone even as he is being prepared for surgery, his companion, Zona Selks, threatens his lawyer, Beaton, that she will sue him for "impersonating himself":

—Beaton you tell him if he tries that I'll sue him for, dried up old raggedy Andy with his tin heart I'll sue him for impersonating himself for impersonating Mister Katz he's nobody, he's a lot of old parts stuck together he doesn't even exist he started losing things eighty years ago he lost a thumbnail on the Albany nightboat and that idiot classmate of his Handler's been dismantling him ever since, started an appendectomy punctured the spleen took it out then came the gall blatter that made it look like appendicitis in the first place now look at him, he's listening through somebody else's inner ears those corneal transplants God knows whose eyes he's looking through, windup toy with a tin heart he'll end up with a dog's brain and some nigger's kidneys why can't I take him to court and have him declared nonexistent, null void nonexistent why can't I Beaton. (708)

While nudging us to see Cates as an assemblage of artificial body parts without organic unity, the passage also participates in an entire network of references to the circulation of body parts, linked on the one hand, to the new imperative of circulation and exchange brought about by contemporary capitalism, and on the other, to the disconnected human limbs in Empedocles' cosmogony first mentioned by Gibbs in the principal's office. On the class visit to Wall Street, as they leave Crawley and Company, JR and Hyde's son see a man lying in a doorway without any hands or face (89). Tellingly, they refer to Crawley himself as "the man with all the heads." Later, when the two are discussing JR's first "business deals," it comes out that JR has just received in the mail a "deluxe portable vibrator" or "vibropenis," as it is called, "another first in the marital relations field" (170).

These associations, when read in conjunction with Zona Selk's description of Cates as a collection of body parts and with JR's expressed desire to own not only a money bank but also blood banks, eye banks, bone banks, and so on, reinforce the idea that for the current capitalist regime the human body is already a commodified object or collection of parts with a certain exchange value and that it must circulate like everything else. Such an operational imperative is now intrinsic to the system and is clearly of a piece with the view of human identity revealed in JR's assumptions about what authorizes or initiates action.[14]

IV. If both Typhon International and JR's Family of Companies illustrate the logic of this new capitalist regime, the Bast family company, General Roll, offers a picture of an earlier and less developed stage. Founded by Thomas Bast to manufacture piano rolls, the company has gradually expanded its production to include other paper products; even so, it remains a small-scale operation in which all the employees know one another. The company's uppermost concern, voiced by Norman Angel, Stella Bast's husband and the firm's general manager, has always been to produce quality products and to keep the company in the Bast family. Profits have always been invested back into the company itself, and shares in the company have never been sold on the open market.

Aside from the larger question as to who will assume control of General Roll now that Thomas Bast is dead, Norman Angel, as manager, faces two significant problems. The first concerns tensions among employees caused by Terry, his sexually attractive secretary. Already involved with the salesman Lenny (whom Angel will have to fire for incompetence), Terry attracts the attention of Angel's assistant, Leo. When Terry rebuffs him, Leo circulates pornographic photographs of a nude young woman who appears to be Terry. Although the circulation of these photographs has no economic implications—this exchange being limited to the personalized libidinal economy of the company (which would also include Stella's sexual seduction of Edward)—it recalls the mail order ad for pornographic photos that JR carries around and the pornography that Hyde receives in the mail when he orders a baseball glove for his son. An implicit contrast is thus established between a generalized economy in which sexual images circulate indeterminately like any other commodity and a smaller, more restricted one in which they have a specific reference and charge.

The more serious problem plaguing General Roll is the huge estate tax imposed on the company as a result of Thomas Bast's death. Angel and the company lawyer Coen estimate that in order to finance this debt burden, the company will have to "go public" and sell its stock on the open market; in other words, take the step that will destroy the company's present identity. Thus another implicit contrast emerges between the way economic relations are defined in relation to the federal government: in the case of General Roll, the federal government is an entirely distinct, even antagonistic entity; in the case of Typhon, relations are so complicitous that the operations of corporate capitalism cannot be separated from those of the government. Their separation, regulation, and control is only an impossible liberal dream.

▪ ▪ ▪ ▪ ▪

The question of who will inherit controlling interest in General Roll drives JR's overarching plot, but it cannot be posed without considering a subsidary question: why does Edward Bast, who stands to inherit a substantial claim on his family's company, take absolutely no interest in its fate?

Early in the novel, his cousin Stella Bast, who displays the most interest in the inheritance, tells her husband, Norman Angel, that "maybe Edward's suddenly afraid he's not Uncle James' son" (114), implying that Edward fears that he might not have inherited James's artistic talent. Edward himself seems to assume that his family inheritance is split: a talent either for business or for art. Since he never questions the necessity of this opposition and his single, unwavering ambition is to be a composer, he must deny or repress any interest in General Roll.

However, this split inheritance does not explain why Bast is so easily enticed into helping JR, and subsequently into a maelstrom from which he will be extricated only when taken to the hospital in a state of delirious exhaustion at the novel's conclusion. Bast becomes so involved that to trace his increasing participation as JR's business "representative" would require tracing the mushrooming growth and final demise of the JR Family of Companies itself. It all begins, innocently enough, when JR lends him the money to pay for the kids' train tickets on their return from the visit to the stock exchange (Amy Joubert having forgotten to give them to him); but it becomes more serious when he agrees to have Crawley look at JR's portfolio when Bast himself visits Crawley to dispose of various Bast family stockholdings for his aunts. At this point, the fatal connection is made, since Crawley offers to pay Bast to compose some "zebra music" for a film he is putting together which will advocate the stocking of American parks with wild game from Africa. Having been fired from his teaching job, and unable to find work as either a composer or a practicing musician, Bast accepts the offer, even though it means commercializing his artistic talent.

Bast is soon trapped in a double bind familiar to artists in a capitalist society, wherein he must work at some unrelated job in order to finance the time necessary for his art. For Bast this double bind soon reaches absurd limits, for the only time left for him to compose serious music, that is, when not negotiating for JR or writing "zebra music" for Crawley or listening on earphones to radio stations to note illegal (i.e., improperly patented) emissions, is the dead of night. As a result, Bast's life becomes a comic nightmare of displacements and juggling acts in which he is never doing what he is supposed to be or wants to be doing. When Gibbs asks him about the orchestra piece he is scoring, Rhoda, the transient inhabitant of the 96th Street apartment, cuts in with the truth of Bast's situation: "Man like don't let him get started I mean when he starts explaining like why he can't do this one thing until he does this other thing he's not doing either because there's like something else he has to do as soon as he finishes this other thing I mean can you move your foot" (567).

One reason Bast is pulled into working for JR is that it does not appear to be a *real* job: he receives no salary, only stock in another of JR's schemes; he has no regular working hours, only business trips upstate and then to the Midwest which prove to be increasingly exhausting; and no office, only a cafeteria telephone and then the 96th Street apartment, which is only supposed to replace the destroyed Long Island studio as a place where he can compose music. That Bast acts simply as JR's business "representive" allows him to maintain the illusion that, as only a representative of these schemes, he somehow stands outside and apart from them. In other words, he may represent JR's business interests, but *he* is not represented by them. But the machinic logic of being JR's business "representive" is more insidious and works in two ways to undermine Bast's assumptions. First, it masks an inhuman mechanism by obscuring how Bast gives a human face to an inhuman process. The main reason the Eagle Mills deal goes through is that the townspeople think they are dealing with Bast, whose sincere personal appearance hides the manner in which they are being manipulated. And the same is true of Bast's part in JR's scheme to defraud the American Indian tribe of its mineral rights. Yet Bast seems unaware of his own complicity in JR's financially successful but humanly disastrous schemes. Second, the logic of the business representative undermines or at least reveals the insupportability of Bast's assumption that art can somehow stand outside the commercial logic of the business world, even though—at least in its material aspects—both he and it are dependent upon them. *JR* contests this assumption, as well as Bast's assumption that he could work for capitalism while keeping the best part of himself outside it.

Once Bast begins to work for JR, he is repeatedly forced to scale back his musical projects. He begins with high ambitions, having conceived a romantic opera inspired by Tennyson's *Locksley Hall* and his barely controlled adolescent sexual feelings for his cousin Stella. The project is nurtured in the barn behind the Bast residence which James had converted into his studio. As Bast explains to Stella herself: "it's the one place an idea can be left here you can walk out and close the door and leave it here unfinished the most, the wildest secret fantasy and it stays on here by itself in that balance between, the balance between destruction and realization until . . ." (69). However, the world represented by the studio is soon desecrated by intruders (who literally defecate on the piano), ironically on the same night Edward discovers that Stella's sexual interest in him is only a cover for her financial interests. Later the studio is destroyed, just as the Bast house (and the historical order it represents) will be removed in order to make room for suburban development.

As Bast himself recalls, while composing music, Wagner never looked at the path outside his window, because it was along this path that the world came rushing in. In the 96th Street apartment, where Bast will try to compose a cantata (having abandoned the more ambitious opera), the world is literally rushing in through every crack, crevice, and conduit. Through the partly unhinged door, floods of mail arrive daily for JR Corp. and a number of Gibbs's cronies, including the fictitious proprietor, Mr. Grynszpan, adding to the growing piles of newspaper, paper bags, manuscripts and notes, film canisters, reference works, and cartons and boxes of sundry objects including an electric letter opener (courtesy JR Corp.) and tie rack already littering the apartment. Water gushes uncontrollably from sink and bathtub taps, a buried and unlocatable radio blares on and off according to whether a passing human body momentarily functions as its antenna, while a dingy lamp flickers on and off and the clock runs backward. Amid this disorder, Rhoda drifts in and out, dispensing sexual favors and leaving melting pizzas and oily concoctions from the local delicatessen in her path. The telephone rings ceaselessly, but even to answer it or sort through the daily mail proves more than one character can manage. As Gibbs sums up the chaotic conditions: "Problem Bast there's too much leakage around here, can't compose anything with all this energy spilling you've got entropy going everywhere. Radio leaking under there hot water pouring out so God damned much entropy going on think you can hold all these notes together know what it sounds like? Bast?" (287).

Although Bast finally manages to complete a piece of "zebra music" for Crawley, it is not until he finds relative tranquility in the hospital while recovering from exhaustion and a nervous breakdown that his own artistic ambitions are in some way realized with a short work for the cello. The diminution of Bast's ambitions and the relative insignificance of his achievement thus raise a question about the possibility of art in the almost totally commodified world that *JR* depicts.

While the question is raised directly by Bast's fate as an artist, it is more fully addressed by Gibbs, both in his comments to Bast and the other characters and in his failed attempt to complete a book begun sixteen years earlier about "mechanization and the arts, the destructive element" (244). As Gibbs struggles to define a historical relationship between technology, art, and the fate of a number of artists of his own generation, the *Türschluss* or "closed door" generation, as he calls them, who all seem afflicted with paralysis of the will, he brings a significant intellectual dimension to the novel and gives its thematic concerns historical definition. Meanwhile, his own fate as a character suggests how his generation is implicated in the new operational subject produced by the current regime of capitalism.

Gibbs's life story, which in certain details resembles Gaddis's own, provides a schematic mapping of *JR*'s major concerns.[15] As a young man, Gibbs had left a good job at General Roll in order to write a book tentatively entitled *Agapé Agape*. Upon his departure, Thomas Bast gave him five shares of company stock, which he subsequently gives to his ex-wife as a bargaining ploy in his attempt to gain access to his daughter. While these two facts tie Gibbs to *JR*'s central plot question (Who will ultimately control General Roll?) and to one of its most significant thematic nodes (the relation between the disintegrated family and money), Gibbs's impact as a character derives more fundamentally from his failure to pull his life together. Having failed to complete his book, Gibbs has slid into a dissolute, near alcoholic life, supporting himself as a high school science teacher but also gambling habitually at a Long Island racetrack. An earlier affair with Stella Bast had come to nothing when she decided to marry Norman, her father's company manager. In the novel's present, a long weekend affair with Amy Joubert following upon a big win at the track inspires him to return to his unfinished book. However, in the chaotic 96th Street apartment he is unable to work back into the material, with its daunting intellectual ambitions, and he ends up abandoning both the project and any future with Amy, who then marries her counterpart in the corporate world.

As Gibbs describes his book to Amy, it was to be "a book about order and disorder more of a, sort of a social history of mechanization and the arts, the destructive element" (244). From the pieces provided and Gibbs's various pronouncements, we gather that the book is mostly concerned with the elimination of the artist in modern society. Gibbs provides a clear example in a conversation with Bast:

> —Problem writing an opera Bast you're up against the worst God damned instrument ever invented, asked me to tell you about Johannes Müller didn't you?
> [. . .]
> —Asked me to tell you about Johannes Müller didn't you? Told you you're not listening I'm talking about Johannes Müller, nineteenth-cen-

tury German anatomist Johannes Müller took a human larynx fitted it up
with strings and weights to replace the muscles tried to get a melody by
blowing through it how's that. Bast?

—Yes it sounds quite . . .

—Thought opera companies could buy dead singers' larynxes fix them
up to sing arias save fees that way get the God damned artist out of the
arts all at once, long as he's there destroy everything in their God damned
path what the arts are all about, Bast? that's why you hid it?   (288)

As Gibbs explains to Rhoda while reading passages from his manuscript in
the 96th Street apartment, increasing mechanization is not simply a matter
of saving money but one of "invention . . . eliminating the very possibility
of failure as a condition of success precisely in the arts where one's best is
never good enough." [16] His favorite example, which draws from both his
former employment at General Roll and careful study of Oscar Wilde's lec-
ture tour of the American West in the 1890s, is the invention of the player
piano, which of course allows the saloon owner or customer to "shoot the
pianist." Although Wilde's perceptions of America remain pertinent, Gibbs
realizes that invention also makes Wilde's doctrine of "art for art's sake . . .
obsolete." As one of his handwritten notes, reproduced on page 587, states:
"The arts must accept the new conditions and make the most of them."
Specifically, the new conditions imposed by invention, by which Gibbs
means technology and the mechanization of art, spell the end of art conceived as either personal expression or pure esthetic form.

   The problem that Gibbs could never solve is how art is to make the most
of these new conditions, to which neither art as personal expression nor art
for art's sake can provide an adequate response. Although Gibbs never
comes up with an answer, he suggests one possibility in an altogether different set of circumstances when he tries to explain to Amy his sometimes
erratic behavior: "I mean sometimes there are situations that just don't seem
to have a solution in their own context do you, do you see what I mean?
And the only way to, the only thing to do is step in and change the whole
context" (496). Until the context can be changed, it would appear that
Gibbs and others interested in the arts can only remain immersed in "the
destructive element." (Gibbs alludes specifically to Stein's advice to Jim in
Conrad's *Lord Jim* at an earlier moment, and the phrase resonates through
much of *JR*). For Gibbs, the context appears to change when two unpredictable events from outside the deterministic rationality of his daily life—a big
win at the track and his passionate love affair with Amy—suddenly lift him

out of the destructive element. At this point he decides to complete the book, but his ambition falters and then dissolves when he returns to the old context, that is, the 96th Street apartment.

Although registered more symptomatically, the dilemma that Gibbs faces intellectually and tries to live through by immersing in the destructive element also afflicts the three members of the *Türschluss* generation who are his friends. All three are artists: Thomas Eigen is a novelist, Schepperman an abstract painter, and Schramm a screenwriter who had earlier failed to write an autobiographical account of his experiences in World War II. According to Gibbs, all suffer from what he calls the "*Türschluss* syndrome," which sets in when they begin "to see the doors closing all sad words of tongue or pen to see the same God damn doors Schramm saw closing." In Gibbs's view their various failures—and Schramm's actual suicide—result from their inability to resolve the nihilistic question of why "anything should be worth doing." Thus, Schramm committed suicide not because he could no longer write but because he could no longer convince himself that writing itself was a meaningful activity.

Rhoda, however, sees not only her former lover, Schramm, but Eigen (and by extension the whole *Türschluss* generation) as men too ego-centered and invested in themselves either to trust one another or to take the risks that artistic creation requires. As a free-floating hippie who easily adapts to the chaotic flux of 96th Street, Rhoda senses the limitations of these selfish and self-centered men, an insight graphically supported by Eigen's name, which suggests via its German meaning what is proper to or owned by the self.

These clashing views of the *Türschluss* generation fold into a larger problematic, for *JR* hints at a correspondence between the technological/commercial imperative within twentieth-century capitalism to eliminate the artist and a psychological reluctance on the artist's part to take risks, including the risk of psychological breakdown. The artists in the novel who (like Eigen) have a strong sense of personal identity may be able to withstand "the destructive element" but seem unwilling to undergo or incapable of undergoing the kind of breakdown that may be necessary for a creative breakthrough.[17]

This particular generational problem, moreover, parallels another (already adumbrated in Bast's family): an inability to acknowledge the extent to which creative energies may be challenged rather than threatened by contemporary capitalism. Curiously, capitalism makes them come alive like nothing else, as Gibbs himself illustrates. On two occasions in telephone conversations with JR Corp.'s lawyer Piscator, Gibbs gives shrewd and direct advice on how to handle a crisis situation. Unable to work on his book in the 96th Street apartment, he answers a telephone call "just to help Bast out." After nearly a page of fragmented replies to Piscator's concern over the impending loss of several tax credits, Gibbs assesses the situation and directs him to do as follows:

> All right look take on the whole thing get rid of that two and half million cash outlay in carrying charges by dumping these four smaller studios well under book value, say you sell them off at two million and bring your tax credits up around forty million just hang onto the big studio rate this Leva's going you'll be . . . problem getting hold of their stockholders list quote the book value at a hundred and sixty-eight a share real God damn point's how active it is, stockholders probably watching these losses sitting on their look I don't know the whole story shouldn't be trying to . . . can't no I told you I'm working on something I . . . help Mister Bast out yes but he didn't say anything about a . . . Didn't mention that either no he . . . no look I . . . didn't tell me about that either damn it look Mister Piscator trying to help out but I've got something here I'm working on that's . . . I don't know when I'll finish it no! Now will you . . . you're welcome yes good . . . I will yes goodbye. (572–573)

Surprisingly, but perhaps not surprisingly, a little later Gibbs calls Piscator back with an idea, and within a few minutes on the phone, Gibbs sounds every bit as knowledgeable and authoritative as Governor Cates.

The point is not that Gibbs is smart and can play that game but that he attains an energy and coherence unavailable to him as an analyst of contemporary culture simply by connecting to the corporate business world through the telephone. As becomes comically (but also painfully) evident in Gibbs's attempted revision of his manuscript, cultural analysis requires a language not only *un*supported but actually assaulted by the sights and sounds of the immediate environment. In this environment, the clarity and difficulty of Gibbs's prose is so incommensurate with the flux of his experience that he cannot decide whether any phrase "makes sense" or needs to be rewritten. Thus he continually wavers between revisions and the earlier version of his manuscript. In contrast, the highly fragmented, incomplete speech of moneymaking "works" because both activities operate according to a syntax of substitution and the plug-in of interchangeable, interconnectable parts. Accordingly, a congruence—even relay effect— emerges between the flux of capital in its acceleration of exchange value and its bias toward communication flow, the flux of a new environment shaped by development, the flood of consumer objects and mass-media messages, and the flux of an agrammatical language that directs other flows by means of switch words and which no longer stands in any analogical relation to experience or knowledge. Since the telephone already deterritorializes speech, it is not surprising that this further deterritorialization occurs in business calls spoken over the telephone.[18]

V. Bast's fate at the end of *JR* suggests one kind of resolution of the contradiction facing the artist in a late-capitalist society. Returning from his business trip to the Midwest for JR Corp. totally exhausted and near delirium, Bast ends up in the hospital with a nervous breakdown after he discovers that his home on Long Island has literally been removed and his aunts have disappeared. After working as JR's business "representative," Bast's speech has come to sound increasingly like JR's, which is marked by expletives such as *holy shit* and the adjectival phrase *this here*. In the hospital, Bast ceases to speak altogether, although listening intermittently to his roommate Isadore Duncan's account of *his* experiences with the JR Corp. and, more positively, of how a Beethoven piano piece once affected him. Whereas Duncan dies as a result of a nurse's incompetence, Bast recovers enough from his harrowing experience with JR and apparent loss of self to create a small work of art, a piece for unaccompanied cello. Thinking that it can't be worth much (his actual words suggest that he had discussed with Duncan the question of value in terms that echo the nihilistic problematic of the *Türschluss* syndrome [see p. 715]), Bast throws his composition in the trash. Yet, in a final confrontation with Stella Bast, who now controls General Roll, he decides to retrieve it: "No, no I've failed enough at other people's things I've done enough other people's damage from now on I'm just going to do my own, from now on I'm going to fail at my own here those papers wait, give me those papers" (718). Bast then leaves the hospital with a new resolve.

It is difficult, however, to avoid the conclusion that art conceived as Bast conceives it can only issue in work of minor scale and ambition, especially when compared to Gaddis's own novel.[19] In a system tending toward total commodification, the artist seems not only unnecessary but an actual obstacle to the commercialization of his or her work, as statements by capitalist entrepreneurs such as Cates and Crawley underscore.[20] *JR* also draws attention to the contradiction under capitalism between the making and appreciation of art on the one hand, and its acquisition, reproduction, and distribution on the other. Since art has no tangible value until it circulates in the public domain—indeed, art cannot be identified as such until it does—its production *as art* cannot be financed in advance. Bast himself comes to something like this realization in his final words, spoken to Eigen on his last visit to the 96th Street apartment: "I mean until a performer hears what I hear and can make other people hear what he hears it's just trash isn't it Mister Eigen, it's just trash like everything in this place everything you and Mister Gibbs and Mister Schramm all of you saw here it's just trash!" (725).

Whereas Bast has apparently worked through the *Türschluss* syndrome, Gibbs seems doomed to remain within it: in the novel's last few pages he is slowly reading Broch's *Sleepwalkers* to Schepperman ("been on page thirty-five for two hours") (724). Yet *JR* ends not with either Bast or Gibbs but with a recording of JR's voice made earlier by Bast: "for all these here letters and offers I been getting because I mean like remember this here book that time where they wanted me to write about success and like free enterprise and all hey? And like remember where I read you on the train that time where there was this big groundswill about leading this here parade and entering public life and all? So I mean listen I got this neat idea hey, you listening? Hey? You listening?" (726). For Gaddis, presumably, what matters is that as readers we are still "listening" and that we are hearing what the performer hears. Which would mean that even JR's last words are not "trash," even though—and this is what hearing means—the words literally suggest that they are part of "this big groundswill."

As a novel, *JR* seeks to resolve the dilemma resulting from the opposition between art and capitalism, first, by having the characters themselves spell out the terms in which the problem is to be addressed, and second, by having the novel itself "perform" the solution. On this reading, *JR* could be said to take the conditions of its own production as part of its overt subject matter, framing these conditions as a contradiction expressed by the characters, and offering a resolution of the contradiction through its own performance. Summarily, the terms are: the risk the artist takes or refuses, the increasing threat to eliminate the artist altogether, and the new technical and social conditions that make art for art's sake obsolete and to which new art must respond. Among these new conditions, changes in the conditions of mediality are paramount, and it is no accident that Gaddis draws attention to various media—both artistic and technical—in the novel's last pages.

The ways in which *JR* responds to each of these terms can now be spelled out seriatim. First, there can be no doubt that with *JR*, Gaddis takes great risks, for never has a novel gone so far in mimicking noise, almost to the point of becoming confused with it, in order to "take it in" and somehow redeem or transform it. Second, while the disappearance of the artist as a direct guiding presence has been an essential strategy in modern fiction since Flaubert and Joyce, Gaddis's twist on this strategy is twofold: on the one hand, he has made explicit the historical conditions that have made it necessary; on the other, he has resolved the technical problem of the artist's disappearance in an innovative (if extreme) way. For, unlike Joyce or Faulkner, Gaddis no longer relies on stylistic shifts and changes in point of view. Not only is *JR* composed solely of reported speech, but it is speech more fractured and redundant than ever recorded in a novel. By reducing the authorial function to an apparently neutral recording device that registers flows observable only in a specific location, Gaddis redefines "the literary" to accord more fully with the conditions of art's production and reception in the era of late-capitalist flows and technical media. In short, literature becomes the recording of delirium by machinic means. In *JR* the contents of this delirium are the refuse, trash, noise, and failures rejected by or not integratable within the new regime defined by contemporary capitalism.

Remarkably, the highly fractured language that renders this noise also opens out upon a vast outer world, with an existence all its own. What is perhaps most striking about this chaotic and fragmentary world, in which everything seems to have fallen under the baleful spell of late capitalism, is its temporal, historical depth, which is layered or striated in terms of both human generations and the stages, or phases, of capitalism. In this regard, Empedocles' notion of "generation," rather than Love and Strife—obvious metaphors for the forces of unification and dispersion respectively—is the more significant machinic figure. As the world represented by the Bast family and General Roll is superseded by the world represented by JR Corp. and Typhon International, *JR* makes it clear how this new generation both demands and produces, as in the examples of Cates and JR, a new kind of human subject.[21]

For Gaddis, the subject is first and last a way of rendering discourse in a novel. Whereas this older world was easily represented by the traditional novel—indeed, the novel was invented expressly to represent it—the new world of corporate capitalism can no longer be transcribed into the terms and conventions of novelistic representation. *JR*, in fact, can be said to contain within it all the materials of a traditional novel without at all being one, as if the older world looms as an afterimage or as something seen through a fragmented rearview mirror. But while we know how to describe the language and novelistic conventions of the world receding into the past, those that would render and make palpable the present world are more uncertain. The question is: how can this world be described in its full positivity, without falling back on merely negative terms? *JR* proposes an answer through its articulation of a machinic language.

VI. Early in *JR*, Bast responds to Amy Joubert's query "about creating an entirely different world when you write an opera, about asking the audience to suspend its belief," with an uncharacteristically firm and direct assertion: "No not asking them making them, like that E flat cord that opens the Rhinegold goes on for a hundred and thirty-six bars until the idea that everything's happening under water is more real than sitting in a hot plush seat with tight shoes on . . ." (111). Does Gaddis's own novel strive for some analogous effect? Critics have pointed out that Wagner's opera *The Ring of the Nibelungen* provides structural parallels to *JR*'s action much as Homer's *Odyssey* does for Joyce's *Ulysses*.[22] Suggesting that *JR* is the most ambitious attempt to do in writing what Wagner does in music, Steven Moore identifies themes that recur and function like musical phrases or leitmotifs.[23]

But can the analogy with music be pushed further? While these parallels are essential to *JR* as a meaningful structure, they are less relevant to the question of whether *JR*'s highly fragmented language brings about anything like the "molecularization" of sound achieved by Wagner. For in fact, *JR* does more than orchestrate the cacophonies of late capitalism with recurrent leitmotifs and literary allusions; its intensive, deterritorialized speech renders noise while remaining clearly distinguishable from it. Following the example of Wagner, Gaddis pulverizes language, reducing it to a stream of linguistic particles in order to construct a language machine producing effects not only symptomatic but expressive of the current regime of capital, and which may even escape its coding mechanisms.

The first instances where language begins to unstick and float free of its anchoring in a specific dramatic context are those in which the characters are impelled toward an incipient delirium. In Coen's recitation of legal precedent in the opening conversation with the Bast sisters, he exhibits a tendency toward a verbal delirium, his language taking off in a quasi-autonomous discursive spin. Similarly, when Edward Bast delivers the Mozart presentation on the school audiovisual program, we witness a flow of words going out of control. An even more striking instance occurs when Edward begins to rant and rave in James's studio after his attempted sexual intercourse with Stella Bast is interrupted by the arrival of her husband, Norman, with a policeman to investigate the studio's trashing by vandals (see pp. 141–142). Yet, in all three examples, the heterogeneity of the different languages remains visible, and the elements retain their identity within a verbal patchwork.[24]

With Gibbs's clipped speech and alcoholic murmurings, however, we notice an acceleration effect, no doubt produced by his tendency to drop articles and often the grammatical subject, making the language tend toward agglutinative verbal streams. In these instances, the stammering effect characteristic of much of the broken, incomplete utterances of the characters breaks into a stream or flow of words. Governor Cates directing the flow of capital and attendant communications at Typhon International achieves exactly this kind of speed and fluidity, as when he addresses Beaton, the Typhon lawyer (see p. 692).

Finally, with the telephonic communications of JR and Bast, the stammer and flow that typifies talk in the novel attains a maximum speed and intensity (see pp. 464–471 for a lengthy unbroken stream). In these passages, speech is so particle-ized, syntax so streamlined, that language becomes a torrent of affectively charged sounds that speed up and slow down according to the dynamics of flow. These passages thus approach a delirious machinic language in which the voice of the individual begins to give way to something else speaking, a molecular assemblage of enunciation which both corresponds to the decoded flows of the new regime of capitalism and reveals itself as the source from which the new subject of this regime will draw its individual voice.

Speech thus decoded or deterritorialized cannot be understood as one extreme instance in a variegated spectrum of verbally satirical deformations. On the contrary, these instances of transcribed speech incarnate *JR*'s central dynamic, which is to render everything as part of a generalized flow: the flux of words, the flux of money, the flux of subjects and objects. All must move and circulate—even the old Bast house in Long Island, where rustling voices are besieged by encroaching sounds of hammering and cutting, until the house itself is literally carried away. At the other end of the novel's trajectory, the 96th Street apartment in Manhattan, these various flows achieve their highest degree of saturation, but also—the apartment being the site where the highest number of communication circuits cross—their inevitable rupture and collapse. Thus, if the Bast house marks *JR*'s *terminus ab quo,* the apartment is the most extreme point in the novel's becoming-delirious, where flows of communication among Wall Street investment firms, flows of consumer objects, and stockpiled information—papers, notes and manuscripts, sheet music, and film in cannisters—reach the greatest density of concentration and spillage.

The invention of Frigicom late in the novel offers a striking counterpoint to the chaos of flows in and out of the 96th Street apartment. Significantly, Frigicom is first described by another operational subject, the public relations specialist David Davidoff, in a press release he reads over the telephone:

Dateline New York, Frigicom, comma, a process now being developed to solve the noise pollution problem comma may one day take the place of records comma books comma even personal letters in our daily lives comma, according to a report released jointly today by the Department of Defense and Ray hyphen X Corporation comma member of the caps JR Family of Companies period new paragraph. The still secret Frigicom process is attracting the attention of our major cities as the latest scientific breakthrough promising noise elimination by the placement of absorbent screens at what are called quote shard intervals unquote in noise polluted areas period operating at faster hyphen than hyphen sound speeds a complex process employing liquid nitrogen will be used to convert the noise shards comma as they are known comma at temperatures so low they may be handled with comparative ease by trained personnel immediately upon emission before the noise element is released into the atmosphere period the shards will then be collected and disposed of in remote areas or at sea comma where the disturbance caused by their thawing will be make that where no one will be disturbed by their impact upon thawing period new paragraph. While development of the Frigicom process is going forward under contract to the cap Defense cap Department comma the colorful new head of research and development at the recently revitalized Ray hyphen X Corp Mister make that Doctor Vogel declined to discuss the project exclusively in terms of its military ramifications comma comparing it instead to a two hyphen edged sword by the alliance of free enterprise and modern technology which promises to sever both military and artistic barriers at one fell swoop in the cause of human betterment period. Citing as his original inspiration cap p Pater's line describing cap v Venice as frozen music comma Vogel emphasized the possible importance of Frigicom comma a name he coined from the cap l Latin words for cold and communicate comma to the fields of music and literature period with the perfection of the thawing process comma Vogel envisions concerts comma entire operas comma and books read aloud and preserved by the Frigicom process comma stressing its importance to longer works of fiction now dismissed as classics and remaining largely unread due to the effort involved in reading and turning any more than two hundred pages period new paragraph getting all this? (527)

By "freezing" sound rather than recording it, Frigicom presents an alternative or even technological transcendence of both paper and electronic media and their systems of encoding. As the references to literature and music suggest, it represents a futuristic vanishing point beyond which current forms of artistic production and consumption would become obsolete, ominously subsumed within a conglomerate of blurred interests (the military, capitalism, and modern technology) which are masked by "the cause of human betterment."

Frigicom thus represents an effort outside the novel to deny not only the medium on which the novel itself depends but also the very idea of mediality. As a literalized form of deterritorialized sound, Frigicom would give physical or apprehendable shape and substance to a limit beyond which a form of content and form of expression can no longer be distinguished, since it represents the condensation of a medium of expression (sound) into an object, or "shard." Both the antithesis of aural flux and its parodic apotheosis, Frigicom represents within *JR* the limit of its language-flight, its fictional endpoint, as it were. Not surprisingly, Gaddis calls attention to its importance through typographical means: in the only passage set off by the conventions of the press release, the description of Frigicom inverts and literalizes the convention operating throughout the novel—that we are reading sounds recorded by printed language.

The deterritorializing of human speech and the introduction of the fictional device Frigicom are therefore not only closely related but essential to understanding how *JR* works and what it is about. Both reveal aspects of the machine driving the novel: on the level of expression, the machinic inscription of deterritorialized speech becomes the novel's primary means of expressing the effects of late capitalism on human behavior, whereas on the level of content, Frigicom represents the inherent tendency of capitalism to absorb or ally itself with the latest developments in military research and technology. Significantly, both fail: Frigicom breaks down in a comic castastrophe, and deterritorialized speech can always be folded back into the symptomatolgy of delirium.

Yet these are not failures in any simple sense, any more than the failures of the characters. As a novelistic representation and transcripted verbal per-

formance of the processes of late capitalism, *JR* is both a product of capital
and a document that critically inscribes capital's excesses. Which means,
finally, that *JR*'s critique is doubly embedded: in its obviously satirical representations of the operations of capitalism, and also in the way it shows how
capitalism constantly produces effects that exceed its intended limits and
necessarily bring about its failures. *JR* itself is one such effect, its failure
inscribed historically through its self-reflexive relationship to the institutions of art and literature. Through JR's rise and fall, it suggests that failure
and breakdown are less personal or individual issues than processes already
inscribed in the capitalist machine, as means by which it reprograms itself
to increase its own performativity. By making failure and breakdown not
simply thematic but a function of its own method of composition and articulation, *JR* also makes itself a fully machinic novel.

To describe this process more precisely, let us return to Deleuze and Guattari's theory of the assemblage. In *A Thousand Plateaus,* they compare the
two planes of the assemblage to the two planes of writing which the French
novelist Nathalie Sarraute proposes in *The Age of Suspicion:*

> a transcendent plan(e) that organizes and develops forms (genres, themes,
> motifs) and assigns and develops subjects (personages, characters, feel-
> ings); and an altogether different plane that liberates the particles of an
> anonymous matter, allowing them to communicate through the "enve-
> lope" of forms and subjects, retaining between them only relations of
> movement and rest, speed and slowness, floating affects, so that the plane
> itself is perceived at the same time as it allows us to perceive the impercep-
> tible (the microplane, the molecular plane).[25]

In *JR,* these two types of plan(e) correspond to the differences between the
language of novelistic representation and machinic language. More precisely, when we consider the characters as represented subjects and the motifs and themes as meaningful articulations, we appeal to the novel's
"plan(e) of organization" as an assumed structural principle governing its
representation. On the other hand, if we consider the novel a recording of
flows within which certain effects of language are produced that are not
easily accountable according to the codes of representation—effects of
speed and slowness, intensity and repetition—then we must appeal to a different dimension, one that would be defined by the novel's "plan(e) of immanence." In Sarraute's description, these effects are produced as a way of
making the reader see the "imperceptible"; they operate to produce a form
of novelistic representation with a higher, more microscopic power of reso-

lution. In *JR*, in contrast, they arise directly from the operations of late capitalism, understood as a cybernetic machine out of control.

If in *JR* these effects have an expressive value, they are expressive of a machinic assemblage within which human beings serve mainly to complete a circuit of heterogeneous parts. Even the author of the novel, William Gaddis, occupies a position within the machine, that of a recording apparatus, transcribing flow in the medium of print. Neither the origin nor the inventor of machinic or cybernetic capitalism, Gaddis simply engineered a writing machine that makes it expressive, that is, that renders the logic of its effects in literary, prose fictional terms.

Gaddis does this by making the characters' speech function as so many little desiring machines that start and stop according to rhythms of flow and indirectly by the actions and gestures their words refer to or imply. While both kinds of effect are closely associated with the workings of capitalism, the relationship between them is neither causal nor expressive in any representational sense. Psychosocial motivations, such as greed and the desire for profit, while clearly depicted, hardly account for the operations of either capitalism or of Gaddis's novel. In *JR*, particular forms of represented content (the flow, or circulation, of objects and bodies) are linked or enmeshed with particular forms of expression (speech acts and forms of inscription). What matters in this double articulation is not any simple determination of one by the other but their reciprocal relationship of influence and relay, contamination and proliferation.

This effect is especially evident in *JR*'s depiction of the daily life of capitalism, where the use of the telephone and the visual monitoring of stock market activity speed up the processes of trading, which in turn makes new forms and terms of credit mandatory. New forms of credit create new reasons for buying and selling stock, as well as new forms of stock to buy. As a result, the system produces entangled loops and feedback effects, and disorder burgeons as a direct consequence of new forms of order. As information ceaselessly proliferates, it undermines the distinction between order and disorder. Instead of responding to the governing effects of feedback and control envisioned by Norbert Wiener, contemporary capitalism produces an information multiplicity whose terms always exceed the *telos* of the system's functioning.

In order to depict contemporary capitalism as a dynamic system and its issue as an information multiplicity, *JR* proliferates into a paper multiplicity teetering on the edge of chaos and deterritorialized in two distinct domains, or planes: on the plane of content, where subjects and objects—not only

JR's paper empire but the world of capitalism that envelops it—are carried away in a maelstrom of flows and ramifying disorders, and on the plane of expression, as speech is similarly pulled into a deliriously accelerated cacophony of switch-words and verbal streams. This assemblage can emerge, however, only as a result of Gaddis's attention to the resources of writing and the print medium, that is, to writing's material existence as a series of marks on the page and to its capacity to render or transpose the effects of other media.

To put it inversely, Gaddis's writing traces and intensifies those lines of disorganization which capitalism's inhuman and asocial forces inscribe upon human life in its various social forms. To do so, he must further disorganize conventional novelistic forms (fully developed characters, dialogues, scenes, and plots) and, in light of these forces and the new technologies that mediate them, construct new methods of composition. The result is a machinic novel whose consistency is given neither by the subject nor by the objects of the writing but in the invention of a new type of literary multiplicity.

part III

The Novel
of Media
Assemblages

There is always a hidden camera somewhere. You can be filmed without knowing it. You can be called to act it all out again for any of the TV channels. You think you exist in the original-language version, without realizing that this is now merely a special case of dubbing, an exceptional version for the "happy few." Any of your acts can be instantly broadcast on any station. There was a time when we would have considered this a form of police surveillance, today we regard it as advertising.

- Jean Baudrillard

6

Fictions of the Culture Medium

The Novels of Don DeLillo

I.
In *Gravity's Rainbow, Lookout Cartridge,* and *JR,* the proliferation of information seems barely contained by the novel as a formal structure; novelistic conventions are present, but they operate primarily as the necessary scaffolding of a literary assemblage. In Don De-Lillo's fiction, genre functions as a framing device and thereby becomes an essential component of his writing machine. This use of genre as a framing device corresponds directly to the increased importance of the mass media. In contrast to the interest displayed by Pynchon, McElroy, and Gaddis in film, sound recording, and print as separate (and separable) media, DeLillo explores the ambient spaces and character types that have precipitated out of a new medium, "a particular social and cultural medium," as he

165

calls it, in which his characters "float."[1] Indeed, the difference between separable media and a syncretic medium produced by the mass media accounts for many of the most distinctive features of DeLillo's writing.

Although DeLillo doesn't spell out the connection, it is obvious that this new medium is inseparable from—though not reduceable to—the images and simulations of contemporary mass media, the implosive effects of which result in apathy and indifference for the masses as a new social category.[2] DeLillo's writing machine functions as an offshoot of this mass-media assemblage, taking its representations and social codings as so much material for novelistic reflection. Like Jean-Luc Godard's films or David Salle's paintings, DeLillo's fiction thus assumes that the world is not simply out there, waiting to be registered firsthand. For these postmodern artists, rather, experience seems "always already" framed, mediated by multiple agencies, and available only through competing and contradictory codes, images, and representations. Confronted with these viral replications, the postmodern artist counteracts our automatic and naturalized tendency to perceive less by questioning and shifting the frame. Similarly, the power of language to capture and order perception is countered by presenting language as a cultural—rather than natural—site of struggle, conflict, and contestation into which new languages and idioms are always entering. Working primarily with the words, images, and ready-made representations of the contemporary American social and cultural medium, DeLillo deploys both strategies in order to render visible this medium's special properties and to explore its expressive possibilities.

A rapid enumeration of his published novels will indicate the extent to which DeLillo appropriates novelistic subgenres as an explicit framing device: *Americana* (1971) is a *Künstlerroman,* or artistic autobiography, of a young executive in the television industry who drops out to make a self-reflexive film about the nation's spiritual state; *Endzone* (1972) is a sports novel about a football player obsessed with Wittgenstein and nuclear warfare; *Great Jones Street* (1973) is a pop novel centered on a rock musician who withdraws from the public world in order to contemplate the source and effects of his music; *Ratner's Star* (1976) combines science fiction with satire in a rewriting of Lewis Carroll's Alice books which exposes the implosion of contemporary scientific knowledge; *Players* (1977) is a thriller about a Wall Street stock exchange employee who gets involved with terrorists while his girlfriend unwittingly destroys a homosexual marriage; *Running Dog* (1978) is a spy novel propelled by a quest for an allegedly pornographic film made for Hitler in the last days of the bunker; *The Names* (1982) is an international intrigue about American innocents abroad who become fascinated by a series of cult murders; *White Noise* (1985) combines college and disaster novels in recounting how a professor of Hitler studies is first exposed to a "toxic event" and then discovers that his wife is addicted to a mysterious drug; *Libra* (1988) is both a "docu-fictional" portrait of Lee Harvey Oswald and an espionage-conspiracy thriller centered on JFK's assassination; finally, *Mao II* (1991), another *Künstlerroman*, centers on a reclusive writer who, after allowing himself to be photographed, journeys to Beirut in search of a terrorist group.

While the list tends to highlight the ambiguity of DeLillo's status as a writer (is he popular or highbrow?), a more interesting question is whether these novels are to be read as modernist fictions stylized for a larger audience or as a series of postmodern fictions that operate as pastiche of older genres.[3] Neither reading, however, accounts for the fact that in each novel the subject matter or content normally associated with a conventional genre or popular form is crossed or overlaps with at least one other kind of content. Repeatedly, the resulting mix offers both a striking internal variety and the articulation of unusual narrative vantage points, or novelistic spaces of suspension and crossover. This (re)combination of materials associated with different subgenres short-circuits conventional expectations and directs attention elsewhere.

I suggest that we understand DeLillo's appropriation of novelistic subgenres not as a literary strategy but as a critical engagement with a logic something like the one governing the replications and simulations of the mass media. DeLillo assumes that certain mass-media forms, notably espionage thrillers and detective story plots, function not simply as entertainments but also as "ready-mades" structuring public perceptions of complex events. To open these forms to novelistic investigation and new expressive possibilities, he recombines them and introduces material not circumscribed or predetermined by their specific genre expectations. By subtracting, reframing, and recontextualizing what is perceived to be the subgenre's typical contents and codes of understanding, he introduces new angles of perception on the "culture medium" as a new domain of images whose interactions are fixed by technological devices and secret systems and out of which a new form of subjectivity emerges.

However, DeLillo only gradually arrives at the full implications of this fictional procedure. His novels can be read therefore as an evolving sequence in which various component parts and textual strategies finally coalesce in a fictional assemblage that is most fully articulated in *Libra*. The evolution of this assemblage is marked by the way in which word and image, film and televisual effects are reconfigured as aspects of an englobing media assemblage, or multiplicity, within which the "de-multiplication" of human identity and the collusion of agencies and institutions are the most striking consequences. The coalescence of this assemblage, moreover, allows a new conception of the event to emerge in novelistic form. Whereas the earlier fiction constantly evokes a certain kind of nonrepresentational event, but only negatively, through narrative inversions and lacunae, De-Lillo finds in the multiplicity of dispersions and contaminations which *is* the Kennedy assassination not only a site where the different effects of this media assemblage first "light up" but also the means to render the type of event this media assemblage gives rise to.

II. DeLillo builds the early novels around tour de force narratives usually rendered by a detached and sophisticated narrator and often punctuated by "frontal" or "pop-out" declarations by various zany and distempered characters. Seldom explored psychologically, these characters' novelistic interest lies almost entirely in their capacity as vehicles of special languages and speech acts. Frequently unstable, they appear to be essentially linguistic constructions, tending to decompose and recombine much as pieces of language do, as if their frequently delirious outpourings were so many throw-away set pieces.

To be sure, the characters usually segue from personal or private obsessions to utterances of cultural importance. In *Endzone,* when the narrator's three-hundred-pound roommate, feeling guilty about his Jewish identity, asserts that "history is guilt," the narrator replies: "It's also the placement of bodies. What men say is relevant only to the point at which language moves masses of people or a few momentous objects into significant juxtaposition. After that it becomes almost mathematical. The placements take over. It becomes some sort of historical calculus. . . . A million pilgrims face Mecca. Think of the power behind that fact. All turning now. And bending. And praying. History is the angle at which realities meet."[4] When the narrator's girlfriend, Myna Corbette, also overweight, describes herself, she expresses in psychological terms a state that *Endzone* is interested in exploring only as a set of apparently self-perceptive assertions; that is, as a certain kind of speech act: "I don't want to be beautiful or desirable. I don't have the strength for that. There are too many responsibilities. Things to live up to. I feel like I'm consistently myself. So many people have someone else stuck inside them. Like inside that large body of yours there's a scrawny kid with thick glasses, inside my father there's a vicious police dog, a fascist killer animal. Almost everybody has something stuck inside them. Inside me there's a sloppy emotional overweight girl. I'm the same, Gary, inside and out" (67).

These speeches, in which the characters often give the impression of speaking out directly to the reader but without revealing an inner depth, reflect the influence of film, particularly those of Jean-Luc Godard. In fact, DeLillo acknowledges the influence of film—"the strong image, the short ambiguous scene, the dream sense of some movies, the artificiality, the arbitrary choices of some directors, the cutting and editing"—in terms that clearly work against the development of character and plot.[5] The ideas expressed by the characters in speeches, such as those quoted above, are seldom put to the test in the characters' actions or even explored in detail through the movement of the narrative. Instead, as DeLillo himself came to realize, they define and are defined by a particular social and cultural medium.

Although never far from satire, DeLillo's early fiction is clearly motivated by an interest in the power of modern jargons to define and order the movements of bodies and thereby to keep messy and menacing realities at a distance. In *Endzone*, for example, it is less the macho violence of football and nuclear warfare that provides the basis for metaphorical parallels than the precision and vectorial power of their languages. In a brilliant play-by-play account of a grinding football match against West Centrex Biotechnical College, the quarterback barks out signals like: "Monsoon sweep, string-in-left, ready right, cradle out, drill 9 shiver, ends chuff, Broadside option, flow-and-go" (116). In the narrator's Dostoevskian dialogues about nuclear war games with an air force ROTC officer, we hear about "perimeter acquisition radar, slowmotion countercity busting, super-ready status, dose-rate contours, fallout hazard, spasm response" (42). *Endzone* draws our attention to these specialized languages, but only to show how each one correlates with a particular disposition or ordering of bodies. Specifically, the novel insists that football creates an efficient, even ascetic illusion of order, as the ceaselessly renewed meshing of bodies is given cultural definition and meaning through organized forms of language: "impressions, colors, statistics, patterns, mysteries, numbers, idioms, symbols" (112). Nuclear warfare, on the other hand, outstrips and impoverishes language: "There's no way to express 30 million dead," the narrator exclaims, "No words . . . they don't explain, they don't clarify, they don't express. They're painkillers. Everything becomes abstract. I admit it's fascinating in a way, I also admit the problem goes deeper than just saying some crypto-Goebbels in the Pentagon is distorting the language" (85). But if *Endzone* demonstrates that football is violence given ritual form, at once goal and endlessly replayable end of civilization, whereas nuclear warfare is its terrible obverse, an endgame that can never really be played at all, the demonstration is made in and about their languages.

Nevertheless, DeLillo's early fictional works are neither "novels of ideas" in the manner of, say, Aldous Huxley, nor even "novels of language," in which obsessive speech acts and professional jargons collide and enter into dialogue and contestation.[6] More to the point, the specific languages in this early fiction are always seen as imbricated with and ordering specific kinds of behavior ("the placement of bodies"). Linked to setting or place as much as to the ideas expressed, the psychology that attaches to such behavior is to be understood as an effect rather than a cause. In these terms, the novels operate as Deleuzian microassemblages, articulating words and bodies in a relationship of reciprocal determination.[7] Thus, whereas the football games at Logos College, the narrator's affair with Myna (which ends when she loses weight, thereby becoming conventionally glamorous), and his encounters with the air force ROTC officer are all events that occur in different languages, these languages ultimately make sense only in relation to the placement, movement, and meshing of bodies in games, sexual love, and mass holocaust, respectively.

Yet if *Endzone* can be said to articulate a line along which language and the movement of bodies meet and define each other, such a line cannot easily be made into a plot line, which must be defined by some necessity that develops over time. In *Endzone,* contrarily, time is marked by the sudden and aleatory intrusion of death and silence on body and word: a teammate is killed in an auto accident, the college president dies in a plane crash, one coach commits suicide, another succumbs suddenly to a debilitating illness, the star running back withdraws into mysticism, and the narrator himself, in the novel's last paragraph, spirals into brain fever. Singly and collectively, these events threaten to disrupt the language-body relationships from some undefinable "outside."

In *Great Jones Street,* DeLillo's next novel, the line articulating language with behavior becomes a plot line, but only through a narrative convolution. This pop novel is interesting primarily for the way in which it replays quintessentially modernist themes of silence, death, and language in relation to the feedback effects of the mass media, that is, in relation to a logic of reversibility and the collapse of cause and effect. The plot involves a rock musician's attempt to withdraw from his audience in order to contemplate the source of his art, as well as the social insanity it both partakes of and feeds into. In the implosive channels of the culture medium, they amount, finally, to the same thing.

Fascinated by silence and the void he creates by withdrawing from public life, Bucky Wunderlick's sense of having come to the end of something can be resolved only through his own suicide. But this is what his fans desire anyway, most of all a group of urban freaks called the Happy Valley Commune, who want to secure the legend of privacy his disappearance has created and on which their cohesiveness depends. Paradoxically, Bucky's "interest in endings, in how to survive a dead idea," is both brought about by new technical media and lived out in a delirium of its new possibilities. The last tape he made before dropping out was an attempt at sheer glossolalia, an effort to tap into raw or less mediated realms of experience. In the age of technical media, or so Bucky seems to believe, originality can be achieved only in a meltdown of all data channels and addresses.

As it charts the "mad weather of language," *Great Jones Street* also ventilates a number of rather stringent social observations, usually conveyed by satirical and caricatural social types such as Klobke, the business mogul and head of Transparanoia Enterprises, or Dr. Pepper, the scientist of the underground who appears only in disguise. DeLillo's next novel, *Ratner's Star,* abounds with such types, wacky scientists and mind managers who congregate in the hothouse atmosphere of a think tank in the Chinese desert in order to decipher and then respond to a message received from a distant star. The setting allows DeLillo to explore language not in relation to silence but as it proliferates in the special codes and nomenclature of modern mathematics and science. Again a narrative convolution brings the novel to a close: the signal from outer space turns out to have originated on earth, but earth conceived of as a "mohole," a void core or multidimensional negative energy state theorized by Orang Mohole, Nobel laureate of alternative physics. Almost simultaneously, Maurice Wu, an archeologist and explorer of bat caves, discovers evidence of a human civilization as advanced as our own that mysteriously regressed, perhaps as the result of a nuclear catastrophe. And the message itself, decoded by the fourteen-year-old genius mathematician Billy Twillig, refers to a particular time at which something momentous *will* happen. Yet this heralded event is perhaps only a repetition or return, confirming Wu's suspicion that the theory of the big bang also applies to human civilizations.

What makes *Ratner's Star* compelling, however, is less the antics of its absurd characters than its abstract architecture and curious topography of boomerang shapes and holes: black holes, "moholes," holes in the earth. DeLillo calls *Ratner's Star* a "naked structure" generated from a "structural model," and clearly it represents his first attempt to construct a novel explicitly as a fictional assemblage.[8] As the writing carries to a limit the antinovelistic impulse that has marked his fiction from its beginnings, conventionally novelistic sections such as the flashbacks to Billy Twillig's family life read like vestigial remnants or simulacra of a superannuated form. At the same time, the narrative inversions that typify the early fiction here achieve a new functionality. As the plot moves toward an inversion of the quest that propels it, it stages an implosion of knowledge, underscoring how the models invented to explain aspects of reality have now completely absorbed that reality and how scientific and mathematical theory have become "pataphysics." Through this involution, *Ratner's Star* enters the realm of what Jean Baudrillard calls "simulation" and "Moebius-spiraling negativity," wherein representational forms inevitably bend back on themselves and no longer reflect any stable external reality.[9]

Displaying affinities with both Menippean satire and science fiction, *Ratner's Star* seems neither, and to label its deployment of hybrid genre markers as postmodern only acknowledges a problem that leaves DeLillo's particular appropriation and mixing of subgenre forms unexplained.[10] *Ratner's Star* makes it clear that for DeLillo genre functions as a matrix or generative model, while establishing that the fiction thus generated assumes that the reality to which it refers is so contaminated by images and representational forms that it can no longer be distinguished from them. As a character in *Libra* aptly puts it, we are now in "curved space," where the old truths no longer hold. This condition of curved space to which DeLillo's inversions and narrative convolutions respond is simply that of the new culture medium.

III. Doubts about representation reverberate through DeLillo's next two works of fiction as well. Heralding a (re)turn to the more properly novelistic, *Players* and *Running Dog* do so only by means of that well-wearing popular subgenre, the thriller. In both novels, parallel plots chart the movements of a man and a woman initially together but then pulled in divergent directions; in both, the narrative cuts back and forth in cinematic montage between short, truncated scenes often consisting of little more than brief passages of elliptical dialogue set within abstract, disconnected spaces. What is most important, film enters the composition of both novels in order to raise questions about representation and the subject's positioning in regard to the image. However, this shift in attention from conspicuous language to the cinematic image indicates not so much a new direction—*Americana*, after all, is about the making of a film—as a more insistent focusing on the specific properties of the contemporary social and cultural medium. Indeed, as DeLillo approaches more directly his most fundamental subject, film comes to occupy a privileged place, much as language—in speech acts and the ordering of bodies—does in his earlier fiction. But what interests DeLillo the writer is not simply the influence of cinema and the image per se but a new mode of perception which might be called postcinematic, in that it assumes a totalizing omnipresence of cinema and hence the transformation of the world itself into a universe of interacting images. In attempting to render this new style of perception and the ways in which it alters our perception and behavior, DeLillo explores the becoming-image of the world adumbrated by von Göll in *Gravity's Rainbow*.

Postcinematic perception assumes a foundationless state in which the world appears to have lost all substance, anchoring, or reference points, except in relation to other images or what are conceived as images. In *Matter and Memory* (1896), Henri Bergson makes a philosophically plausible case for such a view, but more useful here is Gilles Deleuze's appropriation of Bergson in order to define the cinema's component elements. For Deleuze, the cinema assumes that not only the world but also its perceivers can be defined as interacting images:

There are images; things themselves are images, because images aren't in the head, or in the brain; on the contrary the brain is one image among others. Images ceaselessly act on and react to one another, produce and consume. There is no difference between images, things and movement. But images also have an inside, or certain images have an inside and are experienced from the inside. These are subjects. There is in effect a gap between the action undergone through these images and the executed response. This gap gives them the power to store other images, that is, to perceive. But they store only what interests them in other images; to perceive is to subtract from the image what interests us; there is always less in our perception. We are so filled with images that we no longer see those outside for themselves. On the other hand, there are sound (or sonorous) images. . . . Certain among them have a reverse side that we can call ideas, meaning, language, expressive traits, etc. through which sound images have the power to contract or capture other images or a series of other images. A voice assumes power over a set of images (the voice of Hitler). Ideas, functioning as slogans, are embodied in sonorous images or waves and tell us what must interest us in other images: they dictate our perceptions. There is always a central blotting device to normalize images, by subtracting what we must not see. So it is possible to make out two currents, due to the gap already mentioned: one goes from external images to perceptions and the other from dominant ideas to perceptions. Thus we are held in a chain of images, each in its place, each in itself an image, and also in a web of ideas functioning as slogans [mots d'ordre].[11]

In Deleuze's terms, subjectivity occurs as a movement of perception through images and representations, as one image is framed by another through a continuing shift in the frame of reference. Subjectivity is accounted for as a "subtractive" moment, the image or thing (they are ultimately the same), minus that which does does not interest us as a function of our needs.

This conception of subjectivity as the framing of one image by another can clarify DeLillo's depiction of character in both *Players* and *Running Dog*, where the characters remain immanent to their perceptions and have no other life—mental or otherwise—outside the images that define them and to which they react with private and ritualized reorderings. In one sense, of course, they are hardly characters at all, inasmuch as they lack a significant mental life and seldom reveal signs of a complex psychological interiority. It may be more accurate, therefore, to view DeLillo's characters as sites where a particular configuration of forces and social pressures in the culture medium crystallize or precipitate out as patterned sets of recognizable interests and responses. Their seemingly perverse refusal to transcend their cultural contexts (and thereby become more human) must be understood in relation to a larger displacement, in which the seat of what was formerly regarded as the will or intentionality shifts from the individual to the institutions and instrumentalities (or what DeLillo calls devices) in and through which the individual acts. Thus, not surprisingly, this displacement of subjective agency in the regime of the image is accompanied by the emergence of sinister networks of power articulated through and across collusive agencies and secret or nearly invisible systems.[12]

Players opens with a film, or rather with the still unnamed characters in a jet airliner watching a soundless but bloody film of terrorists slaughtering American men on a golf course, all to the mocking accompaniment of a piano recital by one of the passengers. "The simple innocence of this music undermines the photogenic terror, reducing it to an empty swirl," the narrator tells us.[13] Just as the music expresses the characters' insulation from the horror of the filmed event, so their later playing in a real drama will reduce it to no more than an empty swirl of images. This preliminary scene, moreover, gives the reader the model, or blueprint, that will generate the fiction to come. Fewer than than two hundred pages later, *Players* concludes with an equally abstract scene in a motel where the main character disappears in a sudden exposure to a blinding light.

Between these brief scenes of filmic appearance and disappearance, *Players* recounts the separate and secret efforts of a young Manhattanite couple to escape from their emotionally buffered existence. Lyle works on the floor of a Wall Street stock exchange; Pammy for a firm called Grief Management Council, with offices at the World Trade Center. Together they watch TV, dine with friends, engage in casual yet obligatory sex. When a man is shot on the stock exchange floor, Lyle insinuates himself into the group of terrorists responsible, even agreeing to plant a bomb on the exchange and thus carry out the attempt foiled by the first man's shooting. At the same time, he hedges his bets by vaguely informing on the group and plays at being a double agent. But it turns out that J. Kinnear, Lyle's doppelgänger and the terrorist with whom he establishes a strange and complicitous relationship, is also a double agent, having already contacted the federal agents supposedly monitoring the terrorists. The promise of Lyle's involvement in a more tonic reality later dissolves when Kinnear fails to show at a motel rendezvous in Canada, sending instead a former lover who appears in Lyle's room wearing a dildo. The telephone call that will reveal information about Lee Harvey Oswald in exchange for the money Lyle supplies (so that Kinnear can forge a new identity) never comes. Meanwhile, Pammy takes off for Maine on holiday with her co-worker Ethan and his lover, Jack. Enchanted by Maine's pastoral simplicity, Pammy, who believes such things as "follow your instincts, be yourself, act out your fantasies," cannot resist what she assumes will be casual and healthy (though secret) sex with Jack. But Jack is a deeply disturbed person, and soon thereafter he commits suicide by burning himself beyond recognition.

Although engaged in "compulsive information gathering" (129), Lyle displays almost no interest in the terrorists' hatred of capitalist abstraction and electronic money, which is supposedly what moves them to action. As one terrorist explains: "Rafael wanted to disrupt their system, the idea of worldwide money. It's this *system* that we believe is their secret power. It all goes floating across that [stock exchange] floor. Currents of invisible life. This is the center of their existence. The electronic system. The waves and charges. The green numbers on the board. This is what my brother [Rafael] calls their way of continuing on through rotting flesh, their closest taste of immortality" (107). As for Pammy, it never occurs to her to wonder about Jack's relationship with Ethan and how her sexual playing with Jack might affect the lovers' relationship. Returning to New York alone, she achieves a "sobbing release" only after watching a sentimental movie on TV. Out on the street again, she finds herself confused by a sign beneath a flophouse marquee that reads TRANSIENTS: "It took on an abstract tone, as words had done before in her experience (although rarely), subsisting in her mind as language units that had mysteriously evaded the responsibilities of content. Tran-zhents. What it conveyed could not itself be put into words. The functional value had slipped out of its bark somehow and vanished" (207).

Even reduced to "language units," these deterritorialized signs and peripheral conversations appear far more significant than Lyle's or Pammy's thoughts and actions, no doubt because these thoughts and actions cannot be said to issue from subjects who are morally responsible. *Players* insinuates that a full understanding of the characters' actions is precluded by an indeterminism or undecidability inherent to the culture medium: in their shadowy collusions and symmetries, the terrorists and the police become indistinguishable; similarly, sexual repression and sexual liberation seem impossibly confounded.[14] For these characters floating in a medium of images in which everything seems detached from both their physical and emotional needs, the electronic and placarded exchanges of capitalism announce the alpha and omega of social reality. As players in a drama not their own, their gestures appear and disappear without consequence, mere points of singularity in an abstract, disconnected space.

Though similarly focused on a narrow, even minimalist range of behaviors, *Running Dog* cuts a wider swath through the culture medium. Glen Selvy, trained in intelligence gathering and paramilitary procedures, works for Radial Matrix, a formerly secret intelligence operation that, having broken away from the CIA, has mutated into an autonomous form of "system management." The very existence of Radial Matrix, in fact, indicates a growing indistinction among and between government agencies, military and corporate interests, a point emphasized by the fact that the Mafia, with its distinctive ethnic, lower-class identity, functions as its parodic other. Selvy himself lives deliberately according to an archaic and austere warrior code, which he refers to as "the routine." However, when he breaks the rules by sleeping with an *un*married woman involved in his current assignment and unwittingly destroys his company's listening device, he doesn't question the company's decision to have him liquidated, or "adjusted," but turns it into a suicidal game. After eluding his assassins in a New York sex parlor, where he picks up a prostitute who specializes in sex stories—eroticism having thus far been identified solely with "the moving image"—he heads directly toward his former paramilitary training ground in Texas, where he first adopted the code.

When Moll Robbins, another major character, drifts into an affair with Selvy, she is a journalist for *Running Dog,* a formerly radical magazine that carries sensational exposés without any particular political import. Moll is investigating Senator Percival, primarily because of his secret collection of pornographic art but also because of his investigations into PAC/ORD, the governmental funding agency ultimately responsible for the existence of Radial Matrix. In the maneuverings of these shadowy, collusive agencies, Moll's investigation is gradually deflected onto interest in a reputedly pornographic film of Adolf Hitler in the last days of the bunker, an object like "the Maltese falcon" for which a number of agents are vying for possession and distribution rights. Thus, whereas Selvy's perception is limited and contextualized by a code he strictly adheres to, even if it demands his death, for Moll the quest for information and larger frames of reference is displaced onto an object of fetishistic interest and historical fascination. *Running Dog* concludes by cutting back and forth between scenes of Selvy's execution and decapitation, by two former Vietnamese army regulars employed by Radial Matrix, and Moll's viewing of the film.

Whereas in *Players* film prefigures the action to follow, in *Running Dog* film serves as the first and last frame of reference. It also performs the inversion that, up to this point, has been the function of DeLillo's narrative. Early in *Running Dog,* Selvy and Moll see Charlie Chaplin's *Great Dictator.* The film Moll sees at the conclusion is the fictional inversion of the Chaplin film: a film not of pornographic acts but of a figure who appears to be Hitler playing at being Chaplin for a group composed mostly of children; not images of "the madness at the end . . . the perversions, the sex," as everyone has expected, but of relative innocence, of innocence confounded with an evil of history.[15] Chaplin imitating Hitler, Hitler unwittingly imitating an imitation of himself. What connects them is an empty signifier: "the world's most famous mustache." Is history (and the novel itself) thereby reduced to images of masquerade, repeating itself as farce? The filmic frame, as well as *Running Dog*'s insistence upon visually deceptive appearances, implies that there is no substantial reality behind or beneath surfaces, only images and representations obscuring and displacing other images and representations.

These mediating constructions, however, are never neutral. As part of an entire apparatus of surveillance and control, they acquire substantiality whenever they are used to frame us. Thus Lightborne, a connoisseur of and dealer in pornographic art, complains:

> "Go into a bank, you're filmed," he said. "Go into a department store, you're filmed. Increasingly we see this. Try on a dress in the changing room, someone's watching through a one-way glass. Not only customers, mind you. Employees are watched too, spied on with hidden cameras. Drive your car anywhere. Radar, computer traffic scans. They're looking into the uterus, taking pictures. Everywhere. What circles the earth constantly? Spy satellites, weather balloons, U-2 aircraft. What are they doing? Taking pictures. Putting the whole world on film."
>
> "The camera's everywhere." (149–150)

Earlier, Earl Mudger, the head of Radial Matrix, tells Moll: "You can't escape investigation. The facts about you and your whole existence have been collected or are being collected. Banks, insurance companies, credit organizations, tax examiners, passport offices, reporting services, police agencies, intelligence gatherers. It's a little like what I was saying before. Devices make us pliant. If *they* issue a print-out saying we're guilty, then we're guilty" (93). Mudger then threatens Moll with a taped version of her conversation with the senator, embellished with spliced-in sounds of sex.

As the head of Radial Matrix, Mudger represents both a new type and a throwback to a more archaic figure. Described as combining "business drives and lusts and impulses with police techniques, with ultrasophisticated skills of detection, surveillance, extortion, terror and the rest of it" (76), Mudger's part in U.S. military intelligence operations during the Vietnam War enabled him to establish a "feudal barony" (84) and to become a high-tech warlord who knows how to implement "systems planning." Radial Matrix is the result. Because Mudger is interested in Moll, whose long-legged walk excites him sexually, he is willing to explain its basic operational assumptions. First is the collusion among institutions in which the very distinction between agents and agencies dissolves: "Loyalties are so interwoven, the thing's a game. The Senator and PAC/ORD aren't nearly the antagonists the public believes them to be. They talk all the time. They make deals, they buy people, they sell favors. I doubt if Lomax knows whether he works for PAC/ORD or Lloyd Percival, ultimately. You have to understand, agencies allow this to go on all the time. People know what's happening. But they allow it. That's the nature of the times. You go to bed with your enemies" (89–90). Indeed, we later find Grace Delaney, Moll's boss and the editor of *Running Dog* magazine, in bed with Lomax discussing the feasibility of publishing Moll's article.

Second is the correlation between advanced technology and a lack of individual commitment. Again Mudger explains: "There's a neat correlation between the complexity of the hardware and the lack of genuine attachments. Devices make everyone pliant. There's a general sponginess, a lack of conviction" (91). When technology reaches a certain level, Mudger continues, "people begin to feel like criminals. . . . It's the presence alone, the very fact, the superabundance of technology, that makes us feel we're committing crimes" (93). Ironically, Mudger will later weary of the mechanisms he has set into motion to acquire the allegedly pornographic film, which originally stirred his interest because of its "human interest," the "pacts and alliances and accommodations" that represented an alternative to the "essentially sterile concepts" of systems (139).

A world of systems is a world of "connections, links, secret relationships" (111), in which Hitler and Lee Harvey Oswald become icons of mysterious and powerful forces. It is the world not only of collusive institutions but also of the moving image. When Moll finally attains access to the senator's private collection of pornographic art, she is struck by how it is "strictly private, isolated from the schemes and intricacies" (80) that surround the senator's life. She feels, moreover, that the artwork is innately limited: "The modern sensibility had been instructed by a different kind of code. Movement. The image had to move" (80). Moll's experience thus confirms Lightborne's earlier remarks concerning the necessity of "movement, action, frames per second" (15). As Lightborne explains: "[A] thing isn't fully erotic unless it has the capacity to move. A woman crossing her legs drives men mad. She moves, understand. Motion, activity, change of position. You need this today for eroticism to be total" (15). Variously registering the code by which the moving image assumes this new primacy, *Running Dog* also suggests that the cinema, strictly defined, merely participates as one instantiation in a regime of the image that everywhere exceeds it.

Effects of this relative deterritorialization of the image are clearly visible in the street and bar scenes, which minor characters experience as if they were cameras, or directors filming their own movies. (See *Running Dog*, pp. 114–115, for a particularly vivid instance.) In both novels, however, an absolute deterritorialization of the image traces a line of flight that carries away the male protagonists. In *Players*, Lyle frames his perceptions in relation to a terrorist group and his own playing at having a secret, double life.

But Lyle's double, J. Kinnear, is already a double, a double without an original and already moving toward invisibility. Not surprisingly, Lyle's pact with Kinnear springs him loose from his own fixed identity and sets him off on a similar line of flight into the unknown. But with Kinnear's disappearance, Lyle undergoes a bleaching de-multiplication and final loss of definition. In the final scene in a motel room, *Players* registers Lyle's becoming-invisible as if he were a film image exposed to bright light. In *Running Dog,* the method of conceiving of character according to the framing and substraction of images is internalized directly through what Selvy refers to as the routine. Basically, the routine circumscribes the context according to the functionality and protocols imposed by an institution. Yet what makes Selvy interesting is his refusal to change the game (or the context) when he discovers that maintaining the routine means his own death, that all his training and discipline was a "course in dying. In how to die violently. In how to be killed by your own side, in secret, no hard feelings" (183). Having finally returned to his own site of origin at Marathon Mines and once again experiencing the intense cold of the desert training ground, Selvy comes to thinks of concentration as a "steadiness of image," as if his line of flight has been a movement toward the vanishing point of his own death: "All behind him now. Cities, buildings, people, systems. All the relationships and links. The plan, the execution, the sequel. He could forget that now. He'd traveled the event. He'd come all the way down the straight white line" (192). As a vector of deterritorialization, this "straight white line" graphs the plot for DeLillo's typical male heroes as an escape from the image and the ultimate substraction.[16]

In *Players* and *Running Dog,* images no longer simply reflect a reality they presuppose but define and interact with it through relationships of framing, implication, and complicity. In *Running Dog* especially, images enter the novel's texture so completely that the distinction between film as a representation of an external reality and film as an image related only to other images becomes problematic. And this blurring extends to the genre frame as well. John Frow has argued that *Running Dog* is set within the frame of the thriller only to subvert its structural assumptions. But like Fredric Jameson's assertion that DeLillo "tended to work in older genres, reviving them self-consciously across the distance of pastiche," this view fails to account for how DeLillo works *with* their assumptions and associations.[17] For DeLillo's strategy is not to subvert these subgenres through irony or to deform them into pastich but rather to treat them as mass-media ready-mades that have been displaced onto and now structure whole areas of public perception, most obviously in the worlds of sports, rock music, science, and government espionage. As public frames of perception, they can be subtracted from, dislocated, and recontextualized in such a way as to render visible new forms of deterritorialized subjectivity.

IV. DeLillo's next two novels, *The Names* and *White Noise*, set this new regime of the image against a ritual form of terrorism in the former and a new invisible realm in the latter. In both cases, the functional role of novelistic subgenres is much diminished. Although *The Names* harks back to the Jamesian international novel about American innocents abroad and *White Noise* combines elements from both the college novel and the environmental disaster novel, in neither case do genre problems threaten to subvert subgeneric structural assumptions. Instead, we find a fuller articulation of words and images with the characters' perceptions and behavior, resulting in a complex series of powerful contrasts. Whereas *The Names* meditates on the often enigmatic separations of image, word, and landscape for Americans living in foreign places, *White Noise* registers how a domestic, middle-class consciousness attempts to come to terms with the infusions of biotechnology and the blurred mediascape of contemporary America. What the two novels share is an interest in the boundaries and delineations that death brings into play.

The Names begins and ends with the narrator's relationship to an image, that of the Greek Acropolis on the hill overlooking Athens. James Axton, an American insurance analyst working abroad, admits that he has stayed away from the Acropolis—"The weight and moment of those worked stones promised to make the business of seeing them a complicated one," he tells us.[18] In the end he makes the visit, and so the novel is framed by this historic image of "beauty, dignity, order, proportion" (3). But not quite, because this clarity is haunted and diffused by the arbitrariness of other languages and the complete otherness of anticlassical cultural orderings. *The Names* actually concludes with an excerpt from the manuscript of Axton's son, a novelistic retelling of Owen Brademas's autobiographical reflections and specifically of his failure as a child to join with his community and speak in tongues at a Penetecostal church revival meeting, and then his forlorn departure into "the nightmare of real things, the fallen wonder of the world" (339). This nested narrative connects to the central narrative through Brademas's discovery of a mysterious Near Eastern cult that practices a curious method of ritual murder: the victim is chosen when the initials of his or her name link up with a specific place name, to which the victim is then lured for execution. Through Brademas, an anthropologist learned in Eastern languages and script, both Axton and Frank Volterra, a New York experimental filmmaker, become obsessed with the cult; Volterra even tries to film one of the murders from the safe distance of a helicopter.

The plot culminates in an obvious contrast between the last cult murder and the assassination of David Keller, Axton's American friend and a banker, by political terrorists in Athens. It is not clear which one is the actual target. As tools of multinational capitalism, both deal in the abstractions of a bureaucratic system. Axton's job as a risk analyst is to provide data about the safety of American capital investments in the Near East, but it turns out that, unbeknown to him, his employer is the CIA. By the native inhabitants, however, both men are viewed as technicians of a new order of death. As Axton himself puts it: "Banks, loans, arms credits, goods, technology. Technicians are the infiltrators of ancient societies. They speak a secret language. They bring new kinds of death with them. New uses for death. New ways to think about death. All the banking and technology and oil money create an uneasy flow through the region, a complex set of dependencies and fears. Everyone is there, of course. Not just Americans. They're all there. But the others lack a certain mythical quality that terrorists find attractive" (114). The contrast between the cult murders and political terrorism is supplied by Brademas, who describes the cult as an antiterrorist group: "They mock our need to structure and classify, to build a system against the terror in our souls. They make the system equal to the terror. The means to contend with death has become death" (308).

As Axton points out, killing in America is "a form of consumerism," the "logical extension of consumer fantasy." In other words, killing in America is "pure image. . . . No connection to the earth" (115). *The Names* explores this putatively American disjunction through a systematic examination of various relationships among name, image, and geographic site: specifically, through the passion of Axton's wife, Kathryn, for the earth as revealed on the archeological dig on the Greek island, the nomadic wanderings and ritual murders of the cult, and the obsessive movements of the Americans across different spaces and cultures, with Athens serving as the densest point of intersection. To focus this series of contrasting relations, each of the novel's four parts—"The Island," "The Mountain," "The Desert," "The Prairie"—is concerned with a specific geography and typical type of movement.[19] But always behind the characters' intelligent talk and observation about the roots of culture in the age-old mysteries of language, religion, and even madness loom the stark incursions of American money and technology, with their power to deterritorialize. Between the logic of capital and the implacable logic of the cult murders, there is only a disjunctive contrast and no possibility of a linking event.

Whereas *The Names* resolves a foreign landscape into a series of separated words and images, *White Noise* shows the American suburban environment to be a ubiquitous blurring or dissolution of word and image, as if a new medium were being constituted out of the pollution of mass-media ads and the codes of consumer society. Early in the novel the narrator and main character, Jack Gladney, a professor of "Hitler Studies" at a small Midwestern college, takes his family to the local grocery store. Strolling down an aisle of fruit that is "sprayed, burnished, bright," he realizes "the place was awash in noise. The toneless systems, the jangle and skid of carts, the loudspeaker and coffee-making machines, the cries of children. And over it all, or under it all, a dull and unlocatable roar, as of some form of swarming life just outside the range of human apprehension." [20] He then bumps into his New York friend and colleague, Murray Siskind, who finds the supermarket full of "psychic data": "Everything is concealed in symbolism, hidden by veils of mystery and layers of cultural material. . . . Energy waves, incident radiation. All the letters and numbers are here, all the colors of the spectrum, all the voices and sounds, all the code words and ceremonial phrases. It is just a question of deciphering, rearranging, peeling off the layers of unspeakability" (37–38). Earlier, Gladney had taken Murray to see "the most photographed barn in America" (12). Murray responds by wondering if we can ever know what the barn looked like before it was photographed thousands of times, if we can ever get outside "the aura" that now surrounds it. [21] His answer is that we can't, that we're now part of it. *White Noise* concerns the narrator's attempt to maintain a comfortable suburban domestic life as "part of the aura."

However, there are pervasive signs of danger and a vague but unintelligible menace to which the children seem especially sensitive. As the novel proceeds, the Gladneys' world is dramatically exposed to a toxic cloud, during which Jack receives a possibly lethal dose. This event is followed by the family's discovery that the wife, Babette, is addicted to an experimental drug that she believes will cure her of an overwhelming fear of death and for which she has been exchanging sexual favors with a shadowy figure named Mr. Gray. The narrator's intellectual obsession with Hitler, on the other hand, is finally revealed to be a screen for his own obsession with death, which he attempts to resolve by tracking down and shooting his wife's lover.

Whereas the fear of death drives the novel's two-part, cantilevered plot, its texture registers the transfusion of communications technology and the mass media into what the narrator calls "the dark underside of consumer consciousness." The totalizing impact of television as a "wrap-around environment"—as Marshal McLuhan famously called it—makes itself felt with ominous insistence, as media voices constantly dictate or displace the speech of the characters. Word and image fragments such as *Panasonic, Mastercard, Kleenex Softique,* and *Dristan Ultra* punctuate the narrative, as if their penetration into consciousness were wholly assumed and required no response. A woman walking in the street utters the words: "A decongestant, an anti-histamine, a cough suppressant, a pain reliever" (262). Characters experience persistent "brain fade" and constant déjà vu and live in a state of dazed uncertainty, anxious and unsure about who they are and what they are saying or thinking. In part 1, entitled "Waves and Radiation," Gladney's son Heinrich responds to such uncertainties by appealing to "brain chemistry, signals going back and forth, electrical energy in the cortex" (45). In part 2, the arrival of the toxic event produces a pure Baudrillardian moment of reversal when an evacuation unit called SIMUVAC arrives to use the "real event to rehearse the simulation" (139). Curiously, the event is never fully reported on TV; instead of instigating controversy and investigation, it is absorbed and disappears as a nonevent.

Technically, the words *white noise* signify an undifferentiated blending of visual and auditory stimuli, but several characters wonder if death itself is not best described in these terms. At one point, the narrator's colleague in neuropsychology tells him that "it's a mistake to lose one's sense of death, even one's fear of death. Isn't death the boundary we need? Doesn't it give a precious texture to life, a sense of definition? You have to ask yourself whether anything you do in this life would have beauty and meaning without the knowledge you carry of a final line, a border or limit" (228–229). *White Noise,* like Pynchon's *Vineland* after it, shows how this "final line" is ceaselessly blurred by the entire apparatus of image and ad culture.

On the novel's last page, having noted that the shelves at the local supermarket have all been rearranged, the narrator observes:

> Only the generic food is where it was, white packages plainly labeled. The men consult the lists, the women do not. There is a sense of wandering now, an aimless and haunted mood, sweet-tempered people taken to the edge. They scrutinize the small print on packages, wary of a second level

of betrayal. The men scan for stamped dates, the women for ingredients. Many have trouble making out the words. Smeared print, ghost images. In the altered shelves, the ambient roar, in the plain and heartless fact of their decline, they try to work their way through confusion. But in the end it doesn't matter what they see or think they see. The terminals are equipped with holographic scanners, which decode the binary secret of every item, infallibly. This is the language of waves and radiation, or how the dead speak to the living. And this is where we wait together, regardless of age, our carts stocked with brightly colored goods. A slowly moving line, satisfying, giving us time to glance at the tabloids in the racks. Everything we need that is not food or love is here in the tabloid racks. The tales of the supernatural and the extraterrestrial. The miracle vitamins, the cures for cancer, the remedies for obesity. The cults of the famous and the dead. (326)

White Noise thus closes on a theme that infuses much of recent American fiction: the tremendous expansion of the culture's "realm of the dead." This expansion, which *Vineland* takes up more fully (as we shall see in the next chapter), follows from the greatly increased storage and transmission capacities of contemporary technical media. Overtly satirized in Murray's pop culture theorizing, this theme extends beyond DeLillo's exploration of a death obsession, since it is determined at a deeper level by the new conditions of mediality brought about through saturation of the environment by the "language of waves and radiation." DeLillo himself clearly feels the need to situate his novel in relation to this new space of the aura, as Murray calls it, created by the media. Though not written in the "language of waves and radiation, or how the dead speak to the living," *White Noise* nonetheless rewrites the effects of that language in its own novelistic terms, thus meeting the challenge posed by the paradoxical object of its representation. For whether characterized as the aura, white noise, or "a peculiar kind of American medium," it sweeps up the characters in a mode of individuation for which the German word *Stimmung* perhaps best conveys the multiplicity of effects.

Yet, even while *White Noise* offers the fullest anatomy of the effects of the contemporary media assemblage and the culture medium it produces, these effects do not stem from a specific event—the toxic event itself simply being another effect. With the Kennedy assassination, however, when this media assemblage first emerges in the light of a national trauma, DeLillo focuses precisely on the new kind of event that most fully characterizes the culture medium. In rewriting this event, the assemblage that he has been writing all along jells into a constellation of resonating themes and devices.

V. At first view, *Libra* appears to offer a fictionalized portrait of Lee Harvey Oswald by way of a Maileresque "true life novel" about the Kennedy assassination.[22] But this "true documentary fiction" is complicated by Oswald's depicted entanglement in a CIA-inspired conspiracy, which in turn connects the novel to both the subgenre of the espionage-conspiracy thriller and the increasing "nonfictional" efforts of investigative journalists to bring to light, finally, the "truth" about the Kennedy assassination. This generic complexity allows DeLillo to deploy the fictional as a way of exploring the historical, as well as the inverse: to deploy history as a way of exploring the nature of fiction and fictionality.[23]

From the outset, the Kennedy assassination has led something of an underground existence in DeLillo's fiction. In his first novel, *Americana,* David Bell's camera-picaresque wandering across America ends with a drive past the Texas School Book Depository in Dealey Plaza, inaugurating a series of covert references to the assassination which silently reverberate through subsequent novels. However, in "American Blood: A Journey through the Labyrinth of Dallas and JFK," an article DeLillo published in 1983, the event surfaces directly, where it is characterized as an explosion of social and epistemological certainties. Indeed, DeLillo attributes an epochal importance to the assassination: what came unraveled on that Dallas afternoon, he says, was "the sense of a coherent reality most of us shared."[24] At that moment, he continues, we entered "a world of randomness and ambiguity," a world so "totally modern" that it "shades into" the "literature of estrangement and silence." Not only did the violence of that day put "a warp in the texture of things," but its prolongations in time and space have rendered suspect both perception and memory, in fact all the methods we have at hand for verifying the physical evidence of the event:

> There are jump cuts, blank spaces, an instant in which information leaps from one energy level to another. Dallas is a panorama of such things, a natural disaster in the heartland of the real, the comprehensible, the plausible. The lines that extend from the compressed event have shown such elaborate twists and convolutions that we are almost forced to question the basic suppositions we make about our world of light and shadow, solid objects and ordinary sounds, and to wonder further about our ability to

measure such things, to determine weight, mass and direction, to see things as they are, recall them clearly, explain to waiting faces what happened.

In attributing special status to the Kennedy assassination, DeLillo tempts us to seek in its uncertainties a key to the specific ethos and delineations of his own fiction. In an interview given shortly after *Libra*'s publication, he admits that it may even have "invented" him as a writer.[25] However, instead of looking for (or at) foreshadowings and antecedents in his earlier fiction, with it now in mind that the Kennedy assassination was a primal or originating cause ("the dark center") and that the novels are secondary and consequent effects to be tracked and assessed, it is more important to understand how *Libra* brings together and reactivates DeLillo's recurrent fictional interests. His own reflections suggest two things at once. First, that *Libra* functions in the manner of Freudian *Nachträglichkeit,* of deferred action and retroactive animation, in relation not only to his earlier fiction but to the Kennedy assassination itself, the "jump cuts" and "blank spaces" of which reverberate cinematically—but in some new way yet to be formulated—into the social and historical present. And second, that it puts into fictional practice a different understanding of the event, one that will finally allow us to begin to read the Kennedy assassination, less, however, as an aesthetic or epistemological break than as a multidimensional, unrepresentable information multiplicity whose every manifestation is entangled with conflicting versions and contaminated physical evidence. Out of this information multiplicity, moreover, conspiracies proliferated and political lines of force suddenly constelled into a new audiovisual regime in which public discourse is defined by mass-media images.

It has been widely observed that the Kennedy assassination, followed by those of Martin Luther King and Robert Kennedy, inaugurated a period of profound cynicism and distrust of the U.S. government, and, at the same time, that Kennedy's death and funeral brought together an enormous collectivity of viewers through the agency of television. In *The Geopolitical Esthetic,* Fredric Jameson sees the emergence of paranoia and conspiracy film in the sixties as a direct symptom of this conjunction.[26] But, however we interpret paranoia as a pervasive sixties theme, it has since become clear that the investigation of Kennedy's death was a cover-up that helped to bring about a much greater degree of integration of the diverse powers within the federal government, giving rise to new methods of control of, and complicity with, the mass media. This integration and complicity are evident not only in the congruence between the *Life* magazine portrait of

Oswald as "psychotic assassin" and the *Warren Commission Report,* but also in the largely successful efforts to block or diffuse independent investigations and assessments.[27]

The Kennedy assassination thus lights up a new mass-media assemblage and brings into view an entire multiplicity of effects. *Libra*'s subject is precisely this event as multiplicity. Moreover, by staging a historical event as a multiplicity out of which information proliferates, *Libra* exhibits certain similarities to Pynchon's *Gravity's Rainbow.* Both novels construct a Deleuzian assemblage out of the historical assemblage that may be said to have formed them (and many of their readers as well). However, whereas *Gravity's Rainbow* achieves a topographical expansion through dream, fantasy, and hallucination, *Libra* is strikingly linear and diagrammatic, qualities that characterize DeLillo's conception of novelistic writing in general. Both character and plot are delineations, of course, and in *Libra* these delineations could be said to extend real lines (in the sense of information boundaries) into fictional or imagined space. DeLillo's obvious interest in devices, diagrams, networks, and systems only further confirms the sense in which his novels can be conceived as multidimensional drawings or assemblages of lines, as in a Deleuzian multiplicity.

The most immediately apparent line reactivated in *Libra* is plot as a "death vector." Win Everett, the renegade ex-CIA operative in the novel who fashions a plot—which soon goes out of his control—to shoot at but not kill Kennedy in order to arouse anti-Castro sentiments in the United States, explains the idea: "He believed that the idea of death is woven into the nature of every plot. A narrative plot no less than a conspiracy of armed men. The tighter the plot of a story, the more likely it will come to death. A plot in fiction, he believed, is the way we localize the force of the death outside the book, play it off, contain it."[28] This idea, implicit in *Great Jones Street* and *Running Dog* and made explicit in *White Noise,* achieves a further complexity in *Libra,* not simply because the idea is voiced as a metafictional reflection by one of the characters who, as a conspirator, fabricates a plot (and a character too, as we shall see), but also because the idea itself is both realized and unraveled in the novel's larger context. This is brought about by having it played off against an altogether different conception of human events, as voiced by another character. About two-thirds of the way into the novel, when David Ferrie is trying to nudge Oswald into taking part in the conspiracy to shoot the president, he says this to Oswald:

Think of two parallel lines, . . . One is the life of Lee H. Oswald. One is the conspiracy to kill the President. What bridges the space between them? What makes a connection inevitable? There is a third line. It comes out of dreams, visions, intuitions, prayers, out of the deepest levels of the self. It's not generated by cause and effect like the other two lines. It's a line that cuts across causality, cuts across time. It has no history that we can recognize or understand. But it forces a connection. It puts a man on the path of his destiny. (338)

Libra opens up and unfolds in the space defined by these two conceptions, specifically as they might be applied to the Kennedy assassination or, better yet, as they might provide it with a kind of diagrammatic coherence. Both conceptions share a certain notion of linearity, of course, but as we shall see, the second conception, that of "the third line," assumes a superlinearity more complex than either linear history or novelistic plot. This superlinear third line, moreover, is essential to *Libra*'s structural design inasmuch as its logic determines its convergent double plot structure and thematic resonance of parts.

Structurally, *Libra* alternates between sequential segments of two gradually converging lines of action until the two lines finally intersect in Dallas on November 22, 1963. Specifically, chapters marked by place names, in which scenes from Oswald's life are depicted, alternate with chapters marked by dates, in which the machinery of the developing conspiracy is slowly being set up and moved into place. The first chapter portrays Oswald as a schoolboy in the Bronx, riding the New York subways, feeling on the edge of "no control." In alternating subsequent chapters, a recognizable Oswald begins to emerge from his heterogeneous experiences as student in New Orleans, soldier in the marine corps in Japan, defector in Moscow and Minsk, husband and father in Fort Worth and Dallas, and political activist in New Orleans. Oswald's own plot line culminates with his participation in the Kennedy shooting, even as Oswald himself holds out several distinct and contradictory possibilities as to what his participation might mean. As we shall see, however, Oswald's emergence as a fictional character must be viewed critically, as an effect of a conspiratorial construction that *Libra* self-reflexively reproduces.

Inaugurating the second line, and depicting events that occur much later than the events of the first chapter, the second chapter jumps to a meeting of the three conspirators who will plot to assassinate the president: Win

Everett, Laurence Parmenter, and T. J. Mackey—all agents or former agents of the CIA who participated in the Bay of Pigs debacle and who would like another crack at reclaiming control of Cuba. Before passing to this initial conspirators' scene, *Libra* pauses briefly in the room of Nicholas Branch, a retired senior analyst at the CIA who has been hired by the agency to write a secret history of the assassination. As a metahistorical reflection on the novel's other two fictional lines, and unfolding even later in time, Branch's ultimately futile attempt to write a historical account of the assassination of President Kennedy constitutes another track, or line, yet one still distinguishable from what Ferrie calls the third line.

Although Branch never sheds any light on the assassination, his efforts prove essential to *Libra*'s structure. To understand why, we must examine his role in light of the "Author's Note" appended to the novel's last page, where DeLillo explains how "any novel about a major unresolved event would aspire to fill some of the blank spaces in the known record." To do this, DeLillo says, he "altered and embellished reality, extended real people into imagined space and time, invented incidents, dialogues and characters." In these terms, *Libra* does not sound so different from the historical novel as analyzed by Georg Lukács.[29] But as DeLillo acknowledges, the historic events his novel chronicles are shrouded in uncertainty and suspicion, official subterfuge and conflicting sets of evidence; they constitute a site where "a dozen labyrinthine theories all mingle, sometimes indistinguishably." However, *Libra*'s fictional status prevents it from being "one more gloom in a chronicle of unknowing." Thus, DeLillo concludes: "because this book makes no claim to literal truth, because it is only itself, apart and complete, readers may find refuge here—a way of thinking about the assassination without being constrained by half-facts or overwhelmed by possibilities, by the tide of speculation that widens with the years."

In light of these authorial reflections, Branch appears to assume at least a double role in the novel's economy of representations. First, he represents the failures of a strictly historical, empirically governed account and its incapacity, when faced with the multiplicity of proliferating information generated by the event, even to represent it as a coherent totality, much less explain it. Overwhelmed by the documents, statistics, memos and "grisly exhibits" sent to him by the CIA's curator, Branch gradually despairs of establishing even the simple facts: "Powerful events breed their own network of inconsistencies. The simple facts elude authentication. How many wounds on the President's body? What is the size and shape of the wounds?

The multiple Oswald reappears. Isn't that *him* in a photograph of a crowd of people on the front steps of the Book Depository just as the shooting begins?" (300). Second, by acknowledging the inherent failure of these exhibits and other heterogeneous collections of data to make sense or coalesce into an meaningful set of relations, Branch also seals off the rest of the novel from contamination by an unintelligible chaos, thereby allowing it to stand "apart and complete."

But this particular fiction—that *Libra* can stand apart and complete—although literally authorized by DeLillo's appendix, cannot be maintained except as an authorial fiction. While we are encouraged to read Oswald's life through the lens of a novelistic construction, Branch's reflections also serve to remind us that the coherence of this construction is achieved by denying the uncertainty and even fictionality of much of the historical data. For two examples of how fictional much of the historical evidence now appears, let us consider Oswald's alleged Marxist leanings and the report of his trip to Mexico City several months before the assassination.

In the *Warren Commission Report,* allegations of Oswald's Marxist sympathies were based almost solely on the testimony of Kerry Thornley, one of Oswald's marine buddies. Of the twelve or so other marines questioned by the Warren Commission, none could report witnessing any interest on Oswald's part in communism or Marxism. However, Thornley's testimony was not only published in a separate section from the affidavits of the other marines, which of course contradicted it, but it was also given greater attention by the media. Most researchers now view Oswald's "Marxism" as part of his legend, or cover identity, which enabled him to infiltrate certain left-wing groups. Perhaps more intriguing, years before the assassination, Thornley had written *Idle Warriors,* a novel about a young marine, based on the Oswald he knew, who defects to the Soviet Union. Which means that before Oswald became "Oswald" he was already doubled by a literary representation.

Oswald's alleged trip to Mexico City two months before the assassination is also shrouded in uncertainty. Oswald's wife, Marina, has always claimed that he never took any such trip, and even several members of the Warren Commission expressed scepticism regarding the CIA's "evidence" that Oswald had visited the Soviet and Cuban embassies. (The "evidence" included a photograph of a man—purportedly Oswald—who bore no resemblace to Oswald.) More recent scholarly analyses in fact support the view that the entire trip was fabricated by the CIA.[30] In any event, as a direct result of these two problems, President Johnson agreed that the Warren Commission hearings should not only be closed to the public but also tightly controlled.

Does all this mean that the account of Oswald's life that *Libra* offers is merely a fictional construction made (up) from historical material, a construction that assumes that other selections, other constructions, other versions of Oswald would be possible and perhaps equally plausible? Clearly, *Libra*'s guiding aim is to enable the reader to make sense of the event in ways that Branch's attempt at a strictly empirical account cannot. Specifically, *Libra* will depict Oswald as a stabilized and intrinsically intelligible character, while also acknowledging the multiplicity of his contradictory appearances; it will acknowledge the complexity and indeterminism of plot while also ratifying a specific sequence of events. It would seem, therefore, that *Libra* achieves its identity as a novel precisely through this kind of delimitation—a delimitation, it is essential to note, forced upon DeLillo not by any experimental or imaginative impulse but by the extremely problematic nature of the historical material itself.

In this sense, *Libra* can be said to be actually "about" a certain body of historical material—a vast, untidy assortment, much of it apparently meaningless—collected in the *Warren Commission Report* and then transmitted to the American public in a highly fictionalized form, that is, as a simplistic narrative about a "lone-nut" assassin. It follows, then, that *Libra* does not simply offer yet another version of the Kennedy assassination. Instead, through the historical fiction of Branch's "secret history" and the novelistic representation of a historically real character and putatively real plot, *Libra* attempts to establish a different kind of relationship between the historical material and the fictions that surround it and give it form. This relationship—which for the moment I shall simply designate as a "resonance effect"—becomes evident in the unusual novelistic measures forced upon DeLillo in his treatment of plot and character, measures that ultimately reflect an understanding of the Kennedy assassination as a new kind of event.

One of the most striking ways that the two lines—the plot line to assassinate Kennedy and Oswald's life line—communicate or resonate is through multiple patterns of coincidence. When David Ferrie first meets the young Oswald in New Orleans, he tells him: "I've studied patterns of coincidence. . . . Coincidence is a science waiting to be discovered. How patterns emerge outside the bounds of cause and effect" (44). Through this notion of coincidence Ferrie intuitively seeks a new conception of the event, one the novel itself attempts to depict. In fact, *Libra* hints that coincidence offers an alternative to the conclusion arrived at by Nicholas Branch, who, at the novel's end, "has learned enough about the days and months preceding November 22, and enough about the twenty-second itself, to reach a determination that the conspiracy against the President was a rambling affair that succeeded in the short term due mainly to chance" (441). The alternative is precisely what I am calling a superlinear event: it arises conceptually out of the distinction between a plot (as a sequence of events linked by cause/ effect) and coincidence, and concretely in the resonant series of devices by which, on the one hand, Oswald is "scripted" into the assassination attempt, and, on the other, Oswald himself fabricates a range of alternate identities.

It begins with Win Everett's efforts to "script a gunman out of ordinary dog-eared paper, the contents of a wallet," having first devised "a general shape, a life" (50). Everett wants to set up not just a simple fall guy but someone with a fabricated trail leading back to the Cuban Intelligence Directorate and behind that, at a deeper level, to the CIA's attempt to assassinate Castro. But the conspirators also need "a name, a face, a bodily frame they might use to extend their fiction into the world" (50). To this end, Mackey would "find a model for the character Everett was in the process of creating" (50); meanwhile, Parmenter would obtain blank documents from the records branch of the CIA. However, at a lunch with a Soviet CIA contact, George de Mohrenschildt, it is Parmenter who hears about an attractive "model": Lee Harvey Oswald, an ex-marine who has recently taken a shot at the right-wing racist, General Edwin T. Walker. But then, before Everett can "build an identity, a skein of persuasion and habit, ever so subtle" (78), Oswald disappears. In quest of a substitute, Mackey goes to see Guy Banister in New Orleans, a former FBI agent with CIA connections who runs a private detective agency as a front for anti-Castro paramilitary activities. Incredibly, he discovers that Oswald, supposedly looking for an undercover assignment, has just been to see Banister. But what appears to be a bizarre coincidence and lucky break for the conspirators is only apparently fortuitous, for as the reader knows, Oswald has been sent to Banister by the FBI's Agent Bateman to gather information on Banister's anti-Castro activities.

Looking through Oswald's room for a sample of his handwriting soon after Oswald's resurfacing in New Orleans, Mackey uncovers evidence that Oswald too has been fabricating names, documents, alternate identities, in fact a paper trail not unlike the one Everett is fabricating for Oswald. At first somewhat reluctant to confront the fact that "Lee Harvey Oswald existed independent of the plot" (178), Everett feels displaced and even experiences a sensation of panic when he hears about Oswald's forgeries, which so eerily mirror the fictions that he himself has been so carefully devising. Furthermore, the conspirators discover that other plots to assassinate the president are being hatched in Chicago and Miami. Amid these complications, Mackey reflects, it is now only Oswald who gives their plot its coherence:

> Oswald wanted his path to be tracked and his name to be known. He had private designs, a hero's safe haven in Cuba. He wanted to use the rifle that could be traced to him through the transparent Hidell. Mackey was cautious. The kid had a dizzying history and he was playing some kind of mirror game with Ferrie in New Orleans. Left is right and right is left. But he continued to fit the outline that Everett had devised six months earlier. There were the homemade documents, the socialist literature, the weapons and false names. He was one element of the original plan that still made sense. (303)

Thus, if the ultimate coincidence between the gunman Everett is scripting and the "Oswald" that Oswald himself is creating finally enables the conspirators' plot to assassinate Kennedy to become a realizable event, it is precisely because the conspirators maintain this fiction of an identifiable Oswald, even as they (and Oswald himself) work to subvert it. Nicholas Branch, on the other hand, noting the proliferation of Oswalds in New Orleans, Dallas, and Mexico City in the months before the assassination, comes to think of "Lee H. Oswald" as a "technical diagram, part of some exercise in the secret manipulation of history" (377).

Since none of the conspirators wants to get close to Oswald, the task of "bringing him in" falls to David Ferrie. But it turns out that Ferrie has already picked him up, after overhearing his voice in Banister's office and recognizing him from the old days when Oswald was one of his cadets in the civil air patrol. In addition to his overt homosexual interest in "Leon," Ferrie knows that Oswald is a focal point of interest among the intelligence networks all around him. But most of all, he finds Oswald fascinating because, in the ambivalences and antithetical tendencies of his life, Oswald illustrates his theory of coincidence. As Ferrie admits to Oswald, he knows Lee is spying on Banister, that he is pretending to be anti-Castro when it is clear that he is a "partisan, a soldier for Fidel" (316). But Ferrie also senses that Lee "is capable of seeing the other side," that he "harbors contradictions"; in short, that he is a Libran, "sitting on the scales, ready to be tilted either way" (319). Through Ferrie's theory of coincidence and his capacity to convince Oswald of its relevance to his own life, a certain kind of device for bringing the various Oswalds into alignment for the assassination is thus set into place.[31]

As the day of Kennedy's visit to Dallas approaches and it is announced that Kennedy's motorcade will pass directly under the window where Oswald works, Ferrie attempts to convince Oswald that this convergence cannot be mere coincidence in the ordinary sense: "We don't know what to call it, so we say coincidence. It happens because you make it happen" (384). He then delivers the pitch to Oswald: "You see what this means. How it shows what you've got to do. We didn't arrange your job in that building or set up the motorcade route. We don't have that kind of reach or power. There's something else that's generating this event. A pattern outside experience. Something that jerks you out of the spin of history. I think you've had it backwards all this time. You wanted to enter history. Wrong approach, Leon. What you really want is out. Get out. Jump out. Find your place and your name on another level" (384).

Oswald, for his part, begins to sense coincidence all around him, ramifying everywhere he looks: "everything he heard and read these days was really about him. They were running messages into his skin" (383). One series of coincidences connects him to Kennedy: "Coincidence. Lee was always reading two or three books, like Kennedy. Did military service in the Pacific, like Kennedy. Poor handwriting, terrible speller, like Kennedy. Wives pregnant at the same time. Brothers named Robert" (336). Another series, this time of Hollywood films, connects him to the act of assassination. One night, visiting his wife, Marina, who now lives with Ruth Paine in Dallas, they decide to watch a movie on TV. As if preselected for him alone, the movie is *Suddenly,* with Frank Sinatra, about an attempt to assassinate President Eisenhower, although the president is never named. Oswald feels "connected to the screen. It was like secret instructions entering the network of signals and broadcast bands, the whole busy air of transmission" (370). With Marina asleep in his lap, he watches a second movie, *We Were Strangers,* in which John Garfield plays an American revolutionary in Cuba in the 1930s who plots to assassinate the dictator. Again, the effect is immediate: "Lee felt he was in the middle of his own movie. They were running this thing just for him" (370). And beyond these coincidental series, a third series of significant times in Oswald's life seemed to be gathering for some momentous repetition:

It wasn't only the movies that made him feel a strangeness in the air. It was the time of year. October was his birthday. It was the month he enlisted in the Marines. He shot himself in the arm, in Japan, in October. October and November were times of decision and grave event. He arrived in Russia in October. It was the month he tried to kill himself. He'd last seen his mother one year ago October. October was the missile crisis. Marina left him and returned last November. November was the month he'd decided with Dupard to take a shot at General Walker. He'd last seen his brother Robert in November.

Brothers named Robert.

He got Marina settled in bed, then sat next to her and murmured serious baby talk to help her fall asleep again. He felt the power of her stillness, a woman's ardor and trust, and of the child she carried. He would start saving right away for a washing machine and car. They'd get an apartment with a balcony, their own furniture for a change, modern pieces, sleek and clean. These are standard ways to stop being lonely.   (371)

The last sentence is curiously haunted, as if Oswald, even as he recognizes or acknowledges the "standard ways to stop being lonely," seems inclined to choose—indeed has already chosen—another way, the way of desperate men in small rooms. That this other way was always or inevitably his is soon confirmed by his thoughts just after the assassination, when he has been captured and once again—a recurrent experience in his life—finds himself alone in a small cell:

Lee Harvey Oswald was awake in his cell. It was beginning to occur to him that he'd found his life's work. After the crime comes the reconstruction. He will have motives to analyze, the whole rich question of truth and guilt. Time to reflect, time to turn this thing in his mind. Here is a crime that clearly yields material for deep interpretation. He will be able to bend the light of that heightened moment, shadows fixed on the lawn, the limousine shimmering and still. Time to grow in self-knowledge, to explore the meaning of what he's done. He will vary the act a hundred ways, speed it up and slow it down, shift emphasis, find shadings, see his whole life change.   (434)

Curiously, Oswald here begins to anticipate the activities of Nicholas Branch, another solitary individual in a small room, as if in the brief span of time between the assassination and his murder by Jack Ruby, Oswald is already becoming his future interpreter(s), just as in his televised death, witnessed live by millions of TV viewers, he becomes part of American consciousness in a way unique to its history.

Libra's conclusion doubly emphasizes the indeterminate and inherently ambiguous aspect of Oswald's identity by focusing on two contrasting representations, his image and his name. His image is captured by the television camera just as Oswald is gunned down by Jack Ruby. The wife of one of the conspirators, Beryl Parmenter, registers its affective power: "There was something in Oswald's face, a glance at the camera before he was shot, that put him here in the audience, among the rest of us, sleepless in our homes— a glance, a way of telling us that he knows who we are and how we feel, that he has brought our perceptions and interpretations into his sense of the crime. Something in the look, some sly intelligence, exceedingly brief but far-reaching, a connection all but bleached away by glare, tells us that he is outside the moment, watching with the rest of us" (447). Oswald's detachment from himself, his awareness that he doesn't coincide with his image, gives the image its disturbing power, a power suddenly magnified when the viewer sees that detachment destroyed, as Oswald's face crumples into deadly pain. Oswald thus appears to be at once part of and outside the image as it merges with the television viewer and the larger public consciousness. But is it a jump out of or into history?

A similar ambiguity haunts *Libra*'s final scene, where Oswald's burial is filtered through the consciousness of his bereaving mother, left to wonder miserably "who arranged the life of Lee Harvey Oswald?" (455). The novel concludes with her single consolation that no matter how much "they" schemed against her, "[Lee Harvey Oswald] was the one thing they could not take away—the true and lasting power of his name. It belonged to her now, and to history" (456). But in what sense does Oswald's name, now so fully dispossessed of any exact referent, belong to her or to history? As if to underscore this disjunction between name and referent, we are reminded earlier in the scene that the body of Lee Harvey Oswald was buried under a "last alias," William Bobo, "for security reasons" (454).

The central ambiguity of Oswald's identity is framed by and resonates through the series of men in small rooms who echo and repeat one another throughout the novel. Win Everett initiates the series when he begins the process of inventing "Oswald." Doubling Oswald's own efforts to fabricate alternate identities, Everett's invention is both self-referential and metafictional. His sense that "some things we wait for all our lives without knowing it" (27), as he says to his fellow conspirators, clearly echoes Oswald's feeling that his (Oswald's) life was leading toward a momentous event in

which he would finally realize his historic destiny. For Oswald, this fulfill-
ment means breaking free of the series of small rooms that has hitherto
defined his life's trajectory. Ironically, Nicholas Branch reflects upon and
becomes a part of the series when he acknowledges that "it has taken him
all these years to learn that his subject is not politics or violent crime but
men in small rooms. Is he one of them now? Frustrated, stuck, self-watch-
ing, looking for a means of connection" (181). And finally, appending his
"Author's Note," DeLillo literally inscribes himself as the last frame of the
series.

Everett, Oswald, Branch, and by extension DeLillo, the author, thus
form a series of men in small rooms both aligned and differentiated through
variously embedded assumptions about the difference between fiction and
reality and about how history is to be defined in relation to both. At the
center of this complex of relationships is Oswald himself, who is not simply
an actual historical personage around whom DeLillo constructs a quasi-
documentary fiction but, in a very critical sense, a fiction already created by
various intelligence agencies and police networks, then refined and amplified by the Warren Commission and mass media—all with different motives
and design criteria. In the *Rolling Stone* article cited earlier, DeLillo acknowledges this remarkable fact: " 'Lee Harvey Oswald' often seems a secret design worked out by men who will never surface—a procedural diagram, a course in fabricated biography. Who put him together? He is not an
actor so much as he is a character, a fictional character who first emerges as
such in the year 1957. . . . Oswald seemed scripted out of doctored photos,
tourist cards, change-of-address cards, mail-order forms, visa applications,
altered signatures, pseudonyms."[32]

The extent to which Oswald himself participated in his own fabrication
is more enigmatic. The historical evidence reveals that there was not only
this fictitous, "scripted" Oswald but also a plurality of alter egos and fake
identities disseminated by the (or a?) Lee Harvey Oswald, who seems to
have employed an astonishing range of names and variants for purposes of
identification or whenever a signature was required. All of which leads De-
Lillo to hazard that "Oswald was his own double." But which Oswald was
whose double? In this convergence of conspiratorial fabrication and schizophrenic dispersion, human identity is so radically uncertain and "de-
multiplied" that the very notion of a double seems somewhat anachronistic,
if not completely obsolete. And clearly, the world of espionage in which
Oswald operated was such a dizzying labyrinth of reflecting and refracting
surfaces that it is quite possible, as DeLillo himself speculates, that Oswald

might have worked for one intelligence agency while appearing to work for another, without ever knowing which was which.

When we turn to consider how DeLillo has inscribed—or rather rein-scribed—Oswald in *Libra*, it may appear initially as though he has tried to contain this dispersion of Oswald's identity through the notion of the dou-ble, or rather, more exactly, through Oswald's creation of his own double through the fiction of "Hidell." Yet Hidell is less a fictional double of Os-wald than a cryptonym, a device by which the self introjects and harbors a foreign element within itself.[33] By means of this foreign element, which re-mains within the self but is not incorporated by the self, as if encrypted as a cyst, Oswald can create and maintain "a world within the world" and thereby not succumb to the claustrophic solitude of the small, confining rooms through which he moves and which bestow a certain unity on his diverse experiences. Not only does this self-authored fiction allow Oswald to communicate with the energy of the secret and thereby with the possibil-ity of transforming his life-world, but it is through this fiction, or device, that those resonances among discrete events which Ferrie calls coincidence begin to emerge.

Hidell first appears in Atsugi, Japan, as Oswald's introjection (or inter-nalization) of his marine sergeant, Alec Heindell, who is also known as "Hidell." Thus, not only is Hidell originally another's double, but it is also a name that consolidates or inscribes in a verbal matrix a series of earlier moments in Oswald's life. The act of introjection occurs at a specific mo-ment. Having wandered into a bar in Tokyo, Oswald realizes that the cus-tomers are only men, many of whom wear "bright kimonos and bright swirling wigs, their mouths precisely painted, faces layered in chalk" (89). Departing precipitately, at the door he suddenly sees Heindell walking in the street; in order to avoid the shame and disgrace that would fall upon him if seen leaving what he presumes is a gay bar, he turns back inside and drinks a beer. Later, after he emerges, he thinks to himself that "Hidell" means "don't tell." He then goes directly to another bar, the Queen Bee, where he meets his Japanese acquaintance Konno. For the first time, he lets it be known that he is willing to divulge information he has acquired as a radar operator about the top-secret U-2 spy plane that operates out of his marine base. From this moment, he is no longer completely "himself": "He paused, measuring how he felt. Inside the bouncy music and applause, he occupied a pocket of calm. He was not connected to anything here and not quite connected to himself and he spoke less to Konno than to the person Konno would report to, someone out there, in the floating world, a collector of loose talk, a specialist who lived in the dark like the men with bright lips and spun-silk wigs" (89).

Thus begins Oswald's secret life as a spy. Later that evening, while waiting with Konno for the hostess Tammy, Oswald muses to himself:

> Take the double-*e* from Lee.
> Hide the double-*l* in Hidell.
> Hidell means hide the *L*.
> Don't tell.   (90)

Oswald's mental acrostic may nudge us to recall "a secret he'd never tell" (83), revealed only a few pages earlier: that he experienced difficulty reading words on a page, and couldn't spell more than a few words without getting the letters mixed up. But it also evokes an earlier episode in Oswald's life, when he secretly read Marxist books:

> The books were private, like something you find and hide, some lucky piece that contains the secret of who you are. The books themselves were secret. Forbidden and hard to read. They altered the room, charged it with meaning. The drabness of his surroundings, his own shabby clothes were explained and transformed by these books. He saw himself as part of something vast and sweeping. . . . The books made him part of something. Something led up to his presence in this room, in this particular skin, and something would follow. Men in small rooms. Men reading and waiting, struggling with feverish ideas. Trotsky's name was Bronstein. He would need a secret name. He would join a cell located in the old buildings near the docks.   (41)

In this striking sequence of passages we first sense the logic by which the name *Hidell* comes to inscribe, or encrypt, the secret forces acting on Oswald's life; it is a logic according to which something small, private, secret, inner—be it book or cell—can link Oswald to something larger, sweeping, and outside. Yet there are further ramifications.

Some time after the meeting with Konno, when Oswald is thrown into the brig for possession of an unauthorized weapon with which he has shot himself in the arm (apparently as a ploy to remain in Japan), he reflects on his earlier reading of Trotsky in Brooklyn and on the meaning of history: "History means to merge. The purpose of history is to climb out of your own skin. He knew what Trotsky had written, that revolution leads us out of the dark night of the isolated self. We live forever in history, outside ego and id. He wasn't sure he knew exactly what the id was but he knew it lay hidden in Hidell" (101). Later, trying to will himself asleep while his cell mate, Bobby Dupard, masturbates against the wall, Oswald thinks:

> Hidell means don't tell.
> The id is hell.
> Jerkle and Hide in their little cell.   (101)

Later still, after his fictional or faked—in any event, self-cancelled and therefore finally undecidable—defection to the Soviet Union, Oswald finds himself being interrogated by a KGB officer named Alec, a name he himself will use while in the USSR and which is already inscribed in his alter ego (or id), Alex Hidell. In Russia, moreover, it is Hidell's "theatrical, self-mocking" voice he hears "when he set to work on his suicide attempt" (211). Finally, as he lies on a stretcher after being shot by Ruby, his dying thought is that "die and hell [are] in Hidell" (440).

From this evidence we can infer that "Hidell" functions as a matrix of otherness for Oswald, a device not only de-centering and dispersing his identity but also inscribing the loss of identity which death itself will bring. The contrast between this cryptonymic function and the name's empirical manifestation becomes evident precisely in what the conspirators make of it. Searching Oswald's room in New Orleans for a handwriting sample or material that would help Everett "script" Oswald for their plot, Mackey discovers, among other things, that

> There was a draft card in the name Lee H. Oswald. There was a draft card in the name Alek James Hidell.
>
> There was a passport issued to Lee H. Oswald. A vaccination certificate stamped A. J. Hideel. A certificate of service, U.S. Marines, for Alec James Hidell.
>
> There were forms filled out in the names Osborne, Leslie Oswald, Aleksei Oswald.
>
> There was a membership card, Fair Play for Cuba Committee, New Orleans chapter. Lee H. Oswald is the member. A. J. Hidell is the chapter president. The signatures, according to Mackey, were not in the same hand.   (179)

Mackey, naturally, thinks that Hidell, transparent in its simplicity, is Oswald's fake identity; he is even "inclined to fault the boy on technicalities Hidell, Hideel)" (180). Everett knows better, and senses that Oswald's fabrications may hide some deeper, more elusive purpose.

To assert that Hidell is Oswald's simple fake identity, as Mackey is inclined to do, assumes of course that there is a real Oswald, an Oswald that is or possesses a coherent, stable identity, transparent to itself, in relation to which Hidell would be a fake. However, as we have seen, this is not a claim that can be sustained in view of the way Hidell actually functions. As Oswald's cryptonym, *Hidell* opens a space within Oswald that at the same time connects him to an outside, and to a different configuration of forces. As a result, the original Oswald becomes unlocatable (or undefinable), except perhaps as a retrospective fiction, and begins to communicate or resonate with other Oswalds. In this sense, Nicholas Branch, noting the proliferation of Oswalds in New Orleans, Dallas, and Mexico City in the months before the assassination, is entirely correct to think of Lee H. Oswald as a "technical diagram, part of some exercise in the secret manipulation of history" (377). What makes it possible for Oswald to be considered a technical diagram is the fact that his de-multiplied identity has become entirely relational and perspectival, as a consequence of the resonance produced when Oswald-Hidell enters the field of forces gathering for release by the Kennedy assassination.

Rather than think of Oswald as a double of himself, as DeLillo puts it in his *Rolling Stone* article, it seems more usefully exact to understand Oswald as a simulacrum—a double or copy without an original—who brings together many heterogeneous series into resonance. Many of these recurring series of items and situations have already been enumerated, to which Oswald himself can now be added. However, and precisely because of the Hidell effect, Oswald as a diverse series of appearances cannot be resolved into any essential core of identity. More important, it is through Oswald-Hidell that these diverse series in the novel begin to converge and communicate, or resonate. Indeed, what Ferrie conceives of as coincidence and the third line can now be seen to adumbrate an intuitive and somewhat rudimentary understanding of this resonance. More obscurely, *Libra* hints that the medium through which this resonance occurs is constituted by the new realm of images disseminated by the movies and other mass media.

In relation to this medium, *Libra* can be said to function as what Gilles Deleuze has called an "intensive system."[34] According to Deleuze, an event is produced by the sudden convergence and coupling of any number of independent and heterogeneous series. This coupling produces an "internal resonance" in the system, from which derives a forced movement that sweeps through and envelops the various constitutive series. What is important about such a system is that it enables us to conceive of an event in terms no longer defined by the protocols of representation, where bounded entities, or wholes, communicate or are related through their assumed likeness or identity. By contrast, an event in Deleuze's sense is instantiated in differences through which parts or part-objects communicate. In such an intensive system, an event is always set off by a simulacrum, which Deleuze calls the "dark precursor."

In *Libra* this is the role of Oswald-Hidell, who as a simulacrum brings the various ramifying series that make up the novel-as-system into a state of resonance. Several series unremarked thus far cluster around Kennedy himself and suggest that he too is something of a simulacrum, or a construction in which Kennedy's personal identity has been displaced and remade by mass-media projections and political machinations. When Kennedy arrives at the Dallas airport—his first appearance in the novel—it soon becomes evident that the whole point of his visit and participation in the motorcade is to (re)affirm as real what for most people is only an image. Thus Kennedy wants "maximum exposure as the ad men say" (393), whereas the crowd wants to confirm that "he looked like himself, like photographs" (392). Indeed, the physical presence of the Kennedys literally produces jubilance in the crowd: *"They're here. It's them. They're real"* (394, DeLillo's emphases). Earlier in the novel, Kennedy's photogenic charisma had been linked explicitly by Banister to the power of secrets: "The man with the secrets gives off the glow" (141). In fact, Banister believes that Kennedy is always accompanied by ten or fifteen look-alikes, multiplying his appearance as a diversionary precaution. But Banister's response is only a symptomatic reaction to Kennedy's potent multiplication and transmission as a mass-media image, comparable in that to Marina Oswald's feeling that Kennedy "floats over the landscape at night, entering dreams and fantasies" (324).

In his *Rolling Stone* article, DeLillo rejects the idea that Oswald is Kennedy's "secret sharer" (in the Conradian sense) with whom he enters into a "mysterious communication." However, as simulacra, Oswald and Kennedy do indeed communicate, through the resonance of multiple and heterogeneous series that define the assassination as an event in the Deleuzian sense. That this communication cannot be conceived in representational terms points to its complexity, which exceeds the parameters of historical thinking without invoking extrahistorical elements. What is different, of course, is the configuration of elements and the space of their articulation.

This Deleuzian conception of the event both accords with DeLillo's expressed interest in devices and diagrammatic structures and provides a philosophical basis for certain statements DeLillo has made concerning his interest in systems. For example, in the interview cited earlier, he makes the following remark: "It is just my sense that we live in a kind of circular or near-circular system and that there are an increasing number of rings which keep intersecting at some point, whether you're using a plastic card to draw money out of your account at an automatic teller machine or thinking about the movement of planetary bodies. I mean, these systems all seem to interact to me."[35] DeLillo implies that conventional history may be only one possible system, one that has screened out most "rings" and whose "points of intersection" are strictly defined by patterns of cause and effect. However, if history is conceived instead as an open system or an aggregate of interacting systems, then the opposition between random events and cause/effect sequences would no longer obtain: certain occurrences would appear to be random only because they are located on rings that are not intersecting at visible points, and certain "patterns [could] emerge outside the bounds of cause and effect," just as David Ferrie believes. Such a conception brings DeLillo's conception of history close to chaos theory, as Richard Lehan has suggested. Referring specifically to *Libra,* Lehan points out that DeLillo's narratives imply that a hidden order can emerge from disorder, "that randomness can be contextualized and recontextualized because there is a larger stability within the system."[36] But beyond this rather general similarity, the point to be underscored is that conventional history reposes on a classical representational scheme, whereas both Deleuze and DeLillo are interested precisely in effects that cannot be represented within such a system.[37]

In an intensive system it does not make any difference whether the terms are fictional or historical; what counts is not their identity but their articulation in series that resonate across boundaries through the agency of a simulacrum. And this is surely the case in *Libra.* Not that the distinction between the historical and the fictional does not matter; what matters, rather, is that the opposition is a relative one, defined by a specific configuration of political forces, social agencies, and media that have conspired to define how the Kennedy assassination is to be or can be represented. *Libra* is designed to free us from that constraint, but without offering a discursive analysis of how it came to be emplaced. This is what finally makes it a novel, not the fact that its rendering of the assassination is in some way fictional.

Nevertheless, it should now be clear that *Libra*'s depiction of the Kennedy assassination, including of course Nicholas Branch's reflections on what remains of the physical evidence, is profoundly corrosive of the official version, which increasingly appears to be a tissue of fictions. Inversely, DeLillo's supposedly fictional depiction of Oswald and his involvement in a

CIA conspiracy closely resembles the historically more responsible version constructed in the wake of recent public disclosures and newly released official documents. But if *Libra* thus goes a certain distance toward deconstructing the difference between the fictional and the historical, it does so by opening the genre conventions of character and plot to precisely those forces outside prose fiction that these conventions were meant to internalize, and thereby to contain.

In these terms, Nicholas Branch's cryptonymic function should also be acknowledged. As a historian introjected into the novel, he nevertheless retains his foreign, outside status while also remaining part of the Kennedy assassination, a branch of the event, as it were, and a reminder of its yet to be deciphered traces. Not surprisingly, given *Libra*'s constant interlacing of the literary and the historical, the fictional and the real, the impossible historical task before him brings to mind an example from literary history. Puzzling over the *Warren Commission Report* and its twenty-six accompanying volumes, Branch thinks of the "mind-spatter" of the language—"an incredible haul of human utterance" (181), and the "desolation" of its photographs. For him it is "the megaton novel James Joyce would have written if he'd moved to Iowa City and lived to be a hundred" (181). But if the report can be said to be "the Joycean Book of America . . . the novel in which nothing is left out," as Branch calls it, *Libra* itself demonstrates how such an encyclopedic collection can generate a novel of information multiplicity in the age of media assemblages and interactive systems: by attending closely to how nonrepresentational series can link up and resonate in the emergence of a new kind of event.

I'm not sure whether these systems still allow us to observe a difference between observation and observer, since all units and knots of these systems by definition observe and control each other.

▪ Claude B. Shannon

7

An American Book of the Dead

Media and Spectral Life in *Vineland*

I. Pynchon's *Vineland* offers a somewhat different look at the culture medium produced by contemporary media. Rather than concentrating on the effects of this medium, it holds up for scrutiny how various media—particularly film, television, and computer—provide the basic terms in which the characters attempt to make sense of their lives. Indeed, like *The Crying of Lot 49* and *Gravity's Rainbow*, *Vineland*'s very texture responds to and reflects the conditions of a contemporary subjectivity mediated by communications technologies. Historically, the novel offers a Janus-faced view of America in the 1980s: it looks back to a period in which social revolution "went blending into commerce" and "the highest state of the analogue arts [was] soon to be eclipsed by digital technology" and forward, on the technological horizon, to a media assemblage in which information is completely digital, carried by fiber-optic networks and mediated through a computer interface.[1] As we shall see in chapter 8, this futuristic assemblage on the horizon underlies William Gibson's cyberpunk novel *Neuromancer,* published six years earlier, in 1984. In the meantime, as *Vineland* attests, the historical present continues to be defined by an assemblage composed of partially connected media systems.

The co-presence but lack of integration among these partially connected media systems goes a certain way toward explaining *Vineland's* heterogeneity, its polyphony of voices and mixed universes of reference, its shifting topography of alternate worlds. But it also accounts for the novel's complex temporality and the multiple times that inhere in its "present." Since the time of information is not yet instantaneous (i.e., various incompatible media allow or require different rhythms of access), time is the issue not only *of* but also *in Vineland's* narrative.

As Friedrich Kittler observes, any flight on a jumbo jet airliner will illustrate such a partially connected media system. More densely connected than in most places, media on a jet airliner remain separate according to their technological standard, frequency, user allocation, and interface. Thus the crew members, who can already be replaced by computers, are connected to radar screens, diode displays, radio beacons, and nonpublic channels, whereas the passengers, as Kittler puts it,

> can benefit only from yesterday's technology and are entertained by a canned media mixture. With the exception of books, that ancient medium which needs so much light, all the entertainment techniques are represented. The passengers' ears are listlessly hooked up to one-way earphones, which are themselves hooked up to tape recorders and thereby to the record industry. Their eyes are glued to Hollywood movies, which in turn must be connected to the advertising budget of the airline industry. . . . Not to mention the technological medium of the food industry to which the mouths of the passengers are connected. A multi-media embryonic sack supplied through channels or navels that all serve the purpose of screening out the real background: noise, night, and the cold of an unlivable outside. Against that there is muzak, movies, and microwave cuisine.[2]

Kittler's example is easily extended to *Vineland's* media-saturated landscape; for some readers it may even evoke the California-Hawaii flight in which the character Zoyd Wheeler is employed as a musician playing a "baby-grand synthesizer" in a "747 gutted and refitted as a huge Hawaiian restaurant and bar" (62). Pynchon often deploys such comic transformations of familiar technologies to draw attention to the odd surreality of contemporary life among partially connected media systems. Yet in *Vineland,* even untransformed technology never serves to "screen out the real background": "Mucho went to the stereo and put on *The Best of Sam Cooke,* volumes 1 and 2, and then they sat together and listened, both of them this time, to the sermon, one they knew and felt their hearts comforted by, though outside spread the lampless wastes, the unseen paybacks, the heartless power of the scabland garrison state the green free America of their childhoods even then was turning into" (314).

Nevertheless, such insistent reminders of the novel's real background—and of what has happened in America since the publication of *Gravity's Rainbow*—are only points or dots in a more complex moiré of implied delineations. For one thing, paranoia no longer provides automatic access to the contemporary political unconscious, which is not so much repressed as articulated in, or as part of, a new mediatized collective assemblage of enunciation. Pynchon's updated history of the present, consequently, entails a mode of presentation somewhat different from the rich profusion of Technicolor interfaces, extended fantasies, and song-and-dance routines that we find in *Gravity's Rainbow.* In *Vineland,* signs and images are more particleized, and they open only momentarily onto other worlds, as if the narrative could not mobilize or move through these threshold mediations but could only register them in passing. At once part of and other than the media-saturated landscape, these signs nonetheless register "molecular perceptions" as evidence of an unconscious realm, a realm that appears to offer the only site of resistance to the mediatized (re-)Oedipalization of America which Pynchon suggests *is* the political legacy of the 1980s.

II. Set mostly in Northern California in 1984, *Vineland* focuses on the seemingly final demise of the sixties counterculture amid the Reaganite repression masked by the "war on drugs" and television's omnipresent diffusions. With these historical events repeatedly foregrounded, every exchange and allusion in the novel acquires a political resonance. Curiously, in this world teeming with mass-media images and unavenged acts of political repression, one is never really alive, and the dead are not completely dead. Specters walk the land, which either lingers in a "prefascist twilight" or has already succumbed to a darkness penetrated only by the light "from millions of Tubes all showing the same bright-colored shadows" (371).

How, then, are we to understand the implicit contrast in *Vineland* between the politically charged film images produced by Frenesi Gates and the 24fps film collective in the sixties, and the mind-numbing triviality of television in the Reagan era? One character of the younger generation, Isaiah Two Four, thinks that television was what defeated the counterculture. As Isaiah explains to the ex-hippy Zoyd Wheeler: " 'Whole problem 'th you folks's generation,' Isaiah opined, 'nothing personal, is you believed in your Revolution, put your lives right out there for it—but you sure didn't understand much about the Tube. Minute the Tube got hold of you folks that was it, that whole alternative America, el deado meato, just like th' Indians, sold it all to your real enemies, and even in 1970 dollars—it was way too cheap' " (373).

Television, in fact, intrudes directly into Zoyd's life in *Vineland*'s opening pages when he discovers that his own annual act of maniacal defenestration has been "rescheduled" (3) without his agreement or prior knowledge. Although an expected and to a certain extent prepared media event, Zoyd's maniacal act had still been *his* act. Now, however, not only are time and place dictated by others, but the only source of danger that gives it an index of authenticity has been removed. As Zoyd senses at the moment of impact, "something was funny" [with the glass] . . . it all felt and sounded different, no spring or resonance, no volume, only a sort of fine, dulled splintering" (11–12). As he later discovers, the glass window of the Cucumber Lounge through which he had jumped had been replaced by a stunt window made of clear sheet candy.

Zoyd's yearly repetition of the act had been a signal to the federal authorities—in return for which he received a monthly mental disability check and parental custody of his daughter, Prairie—that he remains voluntarily in a state of cooptation, albeit refusing actual cooperation. But now, it seems, this fine but essential distinction may also be threatened, for it turns out that among the police and TV and media crew sits Zoyd's old enemy and longtime pursuer, the Drug Enforcement Agency field agent Hector Zuñiga. Tellingly, when Zoyd wonders if these changes in his annual media event are actually Hector's way of sending him a message, a message Zoyd "knew he didn't want to read anyway" (13), he imagines it as coming to him on the television show *Wheel of Fortune,* but without the "genial vibes" of host and hostess. In these terms, the simulated act that initiates *Vineland* hints at an ominous but familiar (and familial) dynamic of complicities among an unwilling but compliant subject, the apparatus of television, and the authority of the state.

Vineland as a whole, however, doesn't fully support Isaiah Two Four's negative view of television and suggests that even tubal mindlessness can have its subversive appeal. In a journalistic article on sloth for the *New York Times Book Review,* Pynchon asserts that the invention of the remote control and VCR promotes a "nonlinear awareness" perhaps incompatible with "the venerable sin of sloth," which seems to have moved on from the TV couch potato to "more shadowy environments" such as computer games, cult religions, and "obscure trading floors in faraway cities."[3] With remote control and VCR, Pynchon explains, "television time is no longer the linear and uniform commodity it once was. Not when you have instant channel selection, fast-forward, rewind and so forth. Video time can be reshaped at will." All of which breeds the illusion, Pynchon adds, that we can control time, even escape it.

As a novel, *Vineland* seeks to restore the pressure of real historical time to this video time. Hence its interest not only in generational differences but also in the family, where these differences are first produced and acknowledged (or denied). *Vineland* suggests that the historical period in which television increasingly saturates American consciousness (i.e., from the 1970s through the Reagan-Bush era) saw significant changes in the mechanisms of social control set into place in the 1960s. As Hector Zuñiga admits to Frenesi, there was no more need for the overt repression of indigenous Americans: "Yeah, PREP, the camp, everythin, they did a study, found out since about '81 kids were comin in all on their own askin about careers, no need for no separate facility anymore, so Brock's budget lines all went to the big Intimus shredder in the sky, those ol' barracks are fillin up now with Vietnamese, Salvadorans, all kinds of refugees, hard to say how they even found the place" (347). Reagan's budget cuts, in fact, bring about several turns in *Vineland*'s plot; notably, Frenesi and Flash are dropped from the federal snitch support system, and Brock Vond fails to capture Prairie at the novel's conclusion when Reagan officially ends the political repression exercise known as REX. More generally, *Vineland* implies that capitalism's free market ideology and the distractions of television (as well as rock music) make overtly repressive control by the state apparatus no longer necessary. The question of whether the state can actually whither away under these conditions, replaced by global, monolithic corporations, as in Gibson's *Neuromancer,* remains peripheral, yet not all that far away.

Hector shows up in Frenesi's life (in *Vineland*'s present) because now that she is off the government payroll and her own deal with the federal authorities effectively nullified, he thinks he can persuade her to return to Vineland

and direct an antidrug film about the sixties. As Hector explains to Zoyd early in the novel, because Frenesi is "a legendary observer-participant from those times," he wants to "bring her up out of her mysterious years of underground existence, to make a Film about all those long-ago political wars, the drugs, the sex, the rock an'roll, which th' ultimate message will be that the real threat to America, then and now, is from th'illegal abuse of narcotics?" (51)

The ironies here are multiple. Such a film could not possibly convey "the truth" about the sixties but could only pervert the kind of message Frenesi and the film collective 24fps had tried to communicate. For the collective, the camera was a weapon to be used in the political struggle against abuses of American power; the images it recorded took the form of a judgment that all could read. Usually, the group simply went out looking for trouble: "they found it, they filmed it, and then quickly got the record of their witness someplace safe. They particularly believed in the ability of close-ups to reveal and devastate. When power corrupts, it keeps a log of its progress, written into that most sensitive memory device, the human face. Who could withstand the light? What viewer could believe in the [Vietnam] war, the system, the countless lies about American freedom, looking into these mug shots of the bought and sold?" (195). Yet the film collective's objective is only as good as the people who put it into practice, and Frenesi is eventually seduced by the federal prosecutor Brock Vond, who becomes the real director of the footage the collective shoots at College of the Surf, where an alternative to the state, the People's Republic of Rock and Roll, precipitately attempts to constitute itself. It is there that Weed Atman's framing (in both senses) and murder unequivocally undercut any argument about the efficacy and truth of the film collective's practice.

There is a further irony in that the corrupted circumstances of Hector's proposed film inevitably recall Frenesi's first political education: "Frenesi had absorbed politics all through her childhood, but later, seeing older movies on the Tube with her parents, making for the first time a connection between the far-off images and her real life, it seemed she had misunderstood everything, paying too much attention to the raw emotions, the easy conflicts, when something else, some finer drama the Movies had never considered worth ennobling, had been unfolding all the time" (82). The "something else" Frenesi gleans from her parents' response to the credits has to do with the political history of Hollywood, with scabwork, complicity, and selling out, a history from which her father, Hub, never remained completely immune. Furthermore, like most of the characters in *Vineland*, not only Frenesi's politics but her very identity is predicated on a response to media (film in particular) and hence indissociable from—because shaped by—certain "reading effects."

More humorously, there is also obvious irony in the fact that Hector's movie-for-TV project is hopelessly entangled with his own fantasy of a career move from drug enforcement to a television series, thus parodically enacting a reconfiguration of power *Vineland* as a whole understands more seriously. As his associate Sid Liftoff observes, "The fucker . . . wants to be the Popeye Doyle of the eighties. Not just the movie, but Hector II, then the network series" (338). A recent escapee from a "Tubaldetox center" whose sanity is questioned by several characters, Hector "is the real thing all right," Frenesi's son Justin proclaims: "[you] can tell by the way he watches television" (355).

Far from decrying or undercutting "Tubal nuances," awareness of which establishes Hector's credibility within American hyperreality, Pynchon assumes the position of an observer-participant working in both fictional and real registers.[4] Fictional movies for TV such as Woody Allen's *Young Kissinger* and Sean Connery in *The G. Gordon Liddy Story* evoke perceptions of similarity which ironically undercut obvious oppositions, while perverse appropriations such as the tow truck drivers Vato and Blood's rearrangements of the Chip'n'Dale theme song ring out with gruff but tonic anarchy: "After listening to the chipmunk duo's Theme a couple of times, getting the lyric and tune down, Blood, turning to Vato during a commercial for re-enlistment, sang, 'I'm Blood,' and Vato immediately piped up, 'I'm Vato!' Together, 'We just some couple of mu-thuh-fuckers/Out—' whereupon disagreement arose, Vato going on with the straight Disney lyric, 'Out to have some fun,' while Blood, continuing to depart from it, preferred 'out to kick some ass,' turning immediately to Vato. 'What's 'is "have some fun" shit?' " (181). As a medium of popular culture, television can incite working people (as it clearly does Pynchon) to serious but abrasive play. Under the Tubal eye, however, the actions of tow truck drivers can only appear as pre-cartooned; as a condition of their own authenticity, they must aspire to the hyperreal. What counts, then, is not what television *is* but what it does and how the characters manage to turn its effects to their own purposes. This they do in various ways, for both good and ill. Not incidentally, Brock Vond achieves a new stage of control freak mastery when he learns to repress a laughing fit set off by something on the Tube.

This is not to deny that television, having swallowed up the world of Hollywood movies, now constitutes a labyrinth of images within which the real becomes shadowy and difficult to identify. One character, Takeshi Fumimota, thinks that television weakens the border between life and death (218), a perception confirmed in *Vineland* by the uncertain existence of the Thanatoids. Nevertheless, it is within this labyrinth of images that a serious and systematic search for the real is enacted in Prairie's attempt to find out "the truth" about her mother, Frenesi Gates, and what she did in the politically turbulent sixties.

III. A good part of *Vineland*'s narrative is structured by Prairie's quest, which is initiated by "a scene of reading" in which Prairie pulls up texts and images on a computer monitor and later watches film footage her mother shot, just before the 24fps film collective's archive is destroyed. Prairie comes to no great revelation about her Mom, even though the quest takes her "back to and through an America of the olden days she'd mostly never seen" (198). Which seems to be the main point, that and Sister Rochelle's "kunoichi disillusionment" that "the knowledge won't come down all at once in any big transcendent moment" (112). What Prairie sees— or reconstructs through technological mediation and discussions with her mother's former friend and sidekick, DL—comprises something like a novelistic version of the film Hector wants Frenesi to make. As Prairie learns to feel her mother's physical presence behind the camera filming the images she watches, her search is absorbed into and becomes an essential part of a tonally complex narrative constantly shifting from present to past and back again, with the past impinging on the present as much as the present on the past, and within which Frenesi's actions and putative motives are repeatedly held up for scrutiny and assessment. Consequently, when Prairie actually meets her mother at the Becker-Traverse family reunion that concludes *Vineland*, there is little left for her to say. It would seem that her access to her mother's experience through these technological mediations proves sufficient for a narrative resolution of sorts while at the same time raising questions about how that narrative is constituted and what it must necessarily leave out.

The dramatic question for Prairie comes to center on Frenesi's active part in the murder of her lover, Weed Atman, a mathematician and leader of the student revolt at the College of the Surf campus. Weed's murder is the vectored event toward which Prairie's search through the past must inevitably move and in which it must culminate, since it represents not only her mother's betrayal but the effective end of sixties counterculture. For this reason it is also the event from which the events in *Vineland*'s present can be said to date or flow. Given the novel's temporal organization around this critical moment, it is all the more striking that the moment itself is not represented: the narrative moves up to and away from it, with the actual ellipsis occurring in the attempt of the 24fps collective to both "frame" and "shoot" (i.e., inculpate, kill, and film) Weed Atman. Although the physical event is inaugurated in a complex handling of camera, light, sound, and gun by the various members of the film collective who activate these devices, the actual event makes an impact only in and through its aftereffects, registered first on the filmed faces of the participants, and now (in the novel's present), by Prairie as she watches the footage some sixteen years later.

The narrative allows the event to emerge amid a complex overlay of doublings and exchanges, verbally conveyed by puns and double entendres ("That's when Frenesi killed the light, that's how the shot ended"). In effect, the event figures/enacts a textual collapse of two opposed worlds previously set apart in Brock Vond's tempting of Frenesi to choose between the "make-believe" and the "real." Frenesi speaks first:

> "I can't bring a gun in the house."
> "But you can bring a camera. Can't you see, the two separate worlds—one always includes a camera somewhere, and the other always includes a gun, one is make-believe, one is real? What if there is some branch-point in your life, where you'll have to choose between worlds?"   (241)

What grounds the substitution of gun for camera, however, is not this or any other exchange in *Vineland* but a specific understanding of filming: not as a simple doubling or reproduction of the real but as a penetration or cutting into it, which thereby opens a space prerequisite for the emergence of a new form of photographic (or cinematic) subjectivity.

In *Gravity's Rainbow,* Pynchon explores such openings primarily through the device of the interface, but in *Vineland* an interest in the materiality of film and other media leads to a complication of this textual strategy. The shooting/filming of Atman explicitly constitutes an interface, but it also defines a bifurcation point ("some branch-point in your life") rendered in turn as a reading effect: on one side of the film are "shapes that may have moved somewhere in the frame, black on black, like ghosts trying to return to earthly form" (246), while on the other are the faces captured by the light, above all the close-up of the murderer Rex's gleaming eyeball and "Frenesi herself, dark on dark, face in wide-angle distortion, with an expression that might, Prairie admitted, prove unbearable" (247). The gunshot, in contrast to these filmic effects, is resolutely part of the real, a re-closing or suturing of the space momentarily opened by the sequence of film shots, physically continuous with, while also signaling, the collapse of Weed Atman into lifeless materiality. The separation of media—the series of simultaneous instantiations by which Howie "missed the actual moment" with the camera but "Krishna got all the audio" while Frenesi searches for the floodlight cables—produces automatically a spatial and temporal multiplicity within which the narrative must attempt to bridge the distance from a wholly disparate real to a socially credible version of reality.

Within the force field delineated by these intersecting but separate technological media, the status of consciousness becomes uncertain, implicitly reduced or equivalent to reading effects, which, as Prairie discovers, may "prove unbearable." It is worth noting that Prairie, although a viewer of the filmed scene, is not the one from whose point of view it unfolds. Her reading, like the insinuations of Frenesi's rememberings or retrospective reflections into the narrative, constitutes a re-doubling of a scene that is fissured from the outset and thus exists nowhere in the plenitude of objective reality. In this sense, Pynchon renders the scene not only as the collapse of two opposed worlds but as a textual imbrication of both the scene's recording and its viewing.

In this collapse and imbrication, consciousness appears as exactly what it is: the interiorized reflection of current media standards. In accord with contemporary theory, Pynchon assumes that consciousness can appear only as a secondary effect, the result of a machinic interplay between a perceptual apparatus, recording device, and a symbolic system. In Jacques Lacan's account (in which "the brain is a dream machine"), consciousness is (at best) a partial reflection or anamorphosis, with the unconscious insistently emerging in the ruptures of representation; as he puts it in one formulation, it erupts in those "parts of the real image which can never be seen . . . where the apparatus seizes up, where it blocks up." [5] The breaks, discontinuities, and temporal doublings that characterize Pynchon's rendering of Weed Atman's murder suggest something like this unconscious, but as multiple foldings over an unrepresentable moment between perception and consciousness.

Narrative, as a consequence, becomes a problematic assertion of relationship. On the one hand, as a sense-making device, it must be anchored to a perspective and thus to a center of intentionality, which is what Prairie's viewing provides. On the other hand, if the event that organizes it cannot be represented but only registered as a series of mechanical instantiations and reading effects, the narrative itself is reduced to a record of machinic breaks inscribed but necessarily edited out, repressed, or in some way glazed over (in the constitution of a thin, transparent film, as it were) in order that consciousness as intentionality can project (or follow) a ribbon of temporal continuity. Thus, whereas Pynchon's text provides a legible record of these breaks and doublings, what matters for Prairie is less her trajectory through or across them than the meaning she gleans from her reading of a filmic image of Frenesi's face.

In this sense, Prairie's quest reaches a culminating point when she sees the footage of Weed Atman's murder shot at College of the Surf:

> Her mom, in front of her [Prairie's] own eyes, had stood with a 1,000 watt Mickey-Mole spot on the dead body of a man who had loved her, and the man who had just killed him, and the gun she'd brought him to do it with. Stood there like the Statue of Liberty, bringer of light, as if it were part of some contract to illuminate, instead of conceal, the deed. With all the footage of Frenesi she'd seen, all the other shots that had come by way of her eye and body, this hard frightening light, this white outpouring, had shown the girl most accurately, least mercifully, her mother's real face. (261–262)

A number of troubling effects, however, inhibit Prairie's quest from coming to any firm or definite closure. First, as we've seen, Prairie's scene of reading integrates information from various media into the narrative by implicitly overriding or bridging the separation of media at exactly the point at which this separation figures a gap or fissure in the real itself. Second, while this narrative may be construed as driven by an Oedipal desire (a point to which we shall return), in *Vineland*'s televisual world, Oedipal identifications are never more than partial. For *Vineland* insists that not only the imaginary identifications that constitute personal identity but the image itself harbors an unexpected complexity.

As Prairie partly realizes, Frenesi's identity has been split into a real and a cinematic self, without any possibility of the one being definitively separated from the other. When Frenesi betrays Weed Atman, she becomes a double of herself, from then on "walking around herself, haunting herself, attending a movie of it all" (237), condemned to a state of self-estrangement. Although this doubling can be read psychologically as expressive of the inner division between Frenesi's thinking self and acting self, and thus as a symptom of Frenesi's inability to choose or commit to anything, it is more pertinent to note that Frenesi has always already been doubled and captured by the imaginary.[6] The narrator, in fact, often reminds us that members of the film collective spend a lot of time filming themselves, and even Frenesi herself, long before Weed's murder, senses that there is no simple real life counterpart to her celluloid and immortal double. As Jean-Luc Godard remarks in a voice-over commentary in his film *Histoire(s) du cinéma* (1989), in the twentieth century life passes *into* the image. There is no simple opposition.

Whereas Frenesi's identity is split by the cinema, Prairie's identity is fractalized, constructed through a series of partial identifications with television characters: Bionic Woman, Police Woman, Wonder Woman, even Brent Musberger, not to mention

> the junior-high gymnasts in leotards, teenagers in sitcoms, girls in commercials learning from their moms about how to cook and dress and deal with their dads, all these remote and well-off little cookies going "Mm! this rilly *is* good!" or the ever-reliable "Thanks, Mom," Prairie feeling each time this mixture of annoyance and familiarity, knowing like exiled royalty that that's who she was supposed to be, could even turn herself into through some piece of neglible magic she must've known once but in the difficult years marooned down on this out-of-the-way planet had come to have trouble remembering anymore. (327)

The very length and dispersive syntax of the sentence suggest the wandering, diffracted kind of attention produced by television (and the mall culture in which Prairie also participates), in contrast to cinema's fascinated gaze and the primarily voyeuristic identifications it sponsors. While it would be perhaps too easy to say that these two technological regimes—one cinematic, the other televisual—establish the primary parameters for the construction of the subject (split, or fractalized), it is clear that in *Vineland* they provide contrasting means by which these two characters view themselves and attempt to negotiate the social.

IV. In contrast to film's splitting and penetration of the real, computer technology in *Vineland* is identified with a realm of factual omniscience. Prairie's first scene of reading at the Sisterhood of Kunoichi Attentives' retreat already points in this direction. Seated before the computer monitor, she becomes "a girl in a haunted mansion, led room to room, sheet to sheet, by the peripheral whiteness, the earnest whisper, of her mother's ghost" (114). Observing "how literal computers could be—even spaces between characters mattered," she wonders if ghosts are literal in the same way, that is, only responsive to the needs of the living. Prairie soon discovers that she can "summon to the screen" ghostly images of Frenesi, images she gradually learns to read and interpret. However, at the end of this first evening of her quest, after she has logged off and gone to bed, the narrative picks up again: "Back down in the computer library, in storage, quiescent ones and zeros scattered among millions of others, the two women [Frenesi and DL], yet in some definable space, continued on their way across the lowlit campus, persisting, recoverable, friends by the time of this photo for nearly a year" (115). And so the narrative, now independent of Prairie's search, continues, recounting further details of Frenesi and DL's friendship, and only returning to Prairie at the computer again some thirteen pages later, at the chapter's end.

In this sequence, then, the notion of computer memory as a ghostly realm accessed through a kind of magic provides the transition from third person to omniscient narration, a transition relying on an assumption made explicit at the very beginning of the next chapter when Ralph Wayvone tells DL, "We know your history, it's all on the computer" (131). In fact, throughout *Vineland* the characters often acknowledge the computer as a site (even agency) of omniscience, with a temporality quite different from that of other media. No doubt the clearest instance occurs in a sequence of scenes from Frenesi's present life. Summarily, when Frenesi thinks about her life with her current husband, Flash, both of whom work as paid snitches for the federal authorities, she takes comfort in the fact that as long as their files are "on" the government's computer system, they are guaranteed a spectral sort of life. Conversely, when they discover that their computer files have been erased, they are suddenly condemned to paranoia and the terror of the unknown. The narrative itself underscores the digital discreteness of these two states of being—one on, the other off—in Frenesi's two moments of illumination.

The first moment comes when Frenesi, now on the federal payroll after having betrayed the counterculture and abandoned Prairie and Zoyd, still has to face the onset of Nixonian repression. It is then that she sees a certain truth about her condition, that the reality, or price she must pay for her betrayal, is servitude in a world of limited freedom: "Come into her own at last, street-legal, full-auto qualified, she understood her particular servitude as the freedom, granted to a few, to act outside warrants and charters, to ignore history and the dead, to imagine no future, no yet-to-be-born, to be able simply to go on defining moments only, purely, by the action that filled them. Here was a world of simplicity and certainty no acidhead, no revolutionary anarchist would ever find, a world based on the one and zero of life and death. Minimal, beautiful. The patterns of lives and deaths" (71–72). One and zero: life and death reduced to the minimal but beautiful language of pure information. Yet it is this digital language that forces Frenesi to realize that she and Flash have "been kept safe in some time-free zone all these years but now . . . must re-enter the clockwork of cause and effect" (90); in other words, they must reenter the world of real time.

Pynchon stages the scene of Frenesi's second "moment of undeniable clairvoyance" in a supermarket, where she tries to cash her last government check a few hours after Flash returns home with the paranoia-provoking news: "Turns out, a lot of people we know—they ain't on the computer anymore. Just—gone" (85). Gazing down the frozen food aisle, waiting for her check to be approved, Frenesi's realization that the Reaganomic ax blades are swinging leads to a vision of God as a hacker:

> there would be a real ax, or something just as painful, Jasonic, blade-to meat final—but at the distance she, Flash and Justin had by now been brought to, it would all be done with keys on alphanumeric keyboards that stood for weightless, invisible chains of electronic presence and absence. If patterns of ones and zeroes were "like" patterns of human lives and deaths, if everything about an individual could be represented in a computer record by a long string of ones and zeros, then what kind of creature would be represented by a long string of lives and deaths? It would have to be up one level at least—an angel, a minor god, something in a UFO. It would take eight human lives and deaths just to form one character in this being's name—its complete dossier might take up a considerable piece of the history of the world. We are digits in god's computer, she not so much thought as hummed to herself to a sort of standard gospel tune, And the only thing we're good for, to be dead or to be living, is the only thing he sees. What we cry, what we contend for, in our world of toil and blood, it all lies beneath the notice of the hacker we call God.   (90–91)

Frenesi's musings are brought up short by the night manager's appearance. Holding her check as if it were a "used disposable diaper," he patiently explains how payment has been stopped: "The computer," he says, ". . . never has to sleep, or even go take a break. It's like it's open 24 hours a day" (91).

Omniscience, life and death, the ultimate order of appeal, what differentiates real time from play time (as we'll see in a moment)—all point to the perhaps surprising fact that in *Vineland* computer language figures the Lacanian order of the symbolic, that is, the autonomous order of the machine that makes human life possible.[7] For Lacan, the symbolic is simply the encoding of the real in cardinal or digital numbers. This encoding translates unlimited chance (the real) into a syntax, or system, of regularities and thus into a set of laws. Lacan himself did not hesitate to identify this order with information machines and the feedback circuits of cybernetics, although his most elaborated example is an incident of counting "odds and evens" taken from an Edgar Allan Poe story.[8]

Pynchon's text assumes (or embeds) this Lacanian principle, as a consequence of its engagement with the textuality (or textual effects) of technical media (already evidenced in both *The Crying of Lot 49* and *Gravity's Rainbow*). Lacan's relevance to such contexts is thus easily explained: his "methodological distinction" between the real, the imaginary, and the symbolic is nothing more or less, as Friedrich Kittler puts it, than "the theory (or merely the historical effect)" of the differentiation of media.[9] Whereas earlier in *Vineland* the technologies of sound recording and film figure the Lacanian registers of the real and the imaginary respectively, the introduction of the computer both completes the triad of contemporary technical media functions (the storage, transmission, and calculation of data) and indicates the agency by which the characters will negotiate their relationship to the real (the stochasticism of bodies) and the imaginary (the phantasmatic identifications that constitute their identities).

These terms spell out the precise sense of Frenesi's second scene of revelation. While it may be tempting to read the scene as the drama of a mystified consciousness suddenly brought up short by the grim reality of Reaganite America,[10] the force of the scene actually derives from Frenesi's realization that she is now inescapably back in the world of real time. In Lacanian terms, her encounter with the symbolic—the discourse of the computer circuit is the discourse of the other, as Lacan himself implies[11]—brings Frenesi back from the realm of the imaginary, figured not only by film but also, if the two can be separated, by her seduction by Brock Vond.

Vineland hints that it is Frenesi's need to escape real time that leads to her seduction. The nature of this enticement—as an escape from time—is suggested through dream images and whispered exchanges, as when, having just given birth to Prairie (whose father is either Brock or Zoyd), she is violently repelled not only by her new daughter but by her mother as well. Here is the most striking in this series of passages:

It was in those hours of hallucinating and defeat that Frenesi had felt Brock closer to her, more necessary than ever. With his own private horrors further unfolded into an ideology of the mortal and uncontinued self, Brock came to visit, and strangely to comfort, in the half-lit hallways of the night, leaning darkly in above her like any of the sleek raptors that decorate fascist architecture. Whispering, "This is just how they want you, an animal, a bitch with swollen udders lying in the dirt, blank-faced, surrendered, reduced to this meat, these smells. . . ." Taken down, she understood, from all the silver and light she'd known and been, brought back to the world like silver recalled grain by grain from the Invisible to form images of what then went on to grow old, go away, get broken or contaminated. She had been privileged to live outside Time, to enter and leave at will, looting and manipulating, weightless, invisible. Now Time had claimed her again, put her under house arrest, taken her passport away. Only an animal with a full set of pain receptors after all. (286–287)

A few pages later, Frenesi imagines her intermittent life with Vond as a video game played "among the back aisles of a forbidden arcade," his erect penis her joystick, its events unfolding in its own time, "no longer the time the world observed but game time, underground time, time that could take her nowhere outside its own tight and falsely deathless perimeter" (293).

Frenesi could not resist Vond's seductive power (and neither, at *Vineland*'s conclusion, can Prairie). The question raised is, What does it mean to be turned on by the fascist male, dressed in uniforms that evoke what the narrator refers to as "the dark joys of social control" (83). In her analysis of the snitch and kinship systems in *Vineland*, N. Katherine Hayles has suggested that for Frenesi, with her politically leftist family background, the truly radical act is to conspire with the fascists; hence her fascination with Brock.[12] But what clearly fascinates Frenesi is Brock's offer of escape from human time through a demonic scenario of transcendence. What Frenesi cannot resist is Brock's challenge, through the exercise of power and control, to the constraints of ordinary human life. As Brock tries to explain in the interplanetary space parable that he and Zoyd improvise in their jail-cell exchange (300), he sees Frenesi not at all as Zoyd does but as a rebel whose fate is not to be bound to the human time of reproduction, of family and domestic commitments. Frenesi, for her part, puzzles over her attraction to Brock and never comes to any full understanding.

On Vond's motivation, however, the narrative is clear: Vond sets up Weed's murder as an experiment in social control, simultaneously eliminating both a threat to the state's hegemony and his own sexual rival. Described by Weed's interlocuteurs as either "a rebel cop, with his own deeply personal agenda," or as "only following the orders of a repressive regime based on death" (366), Vond is placed in something like a double perspective, with Pynchon leaving it entirely open as to whether or not these contrasting views are necessarily incompatible. On the one hand, Vond is a functionary in the state apparatus, manipulated by the "Real Ones" above, caught up in and subject like everyone else to the "Jasonic blade." Thus Prairie and DL speculate about whether Vond's liason with Frenesi is simply part of a "little boys' arrangement" in which she is just the medium for a communication with other males in a scenario of homosocial "fucking over." But Vond is also menaced by dreams of procreation with women who come from above, and he "carried with him a watchful, never quite trustworthy companion personality, feminine, underdeveloped, against whom his male version, supposedly running the unit, had to be equally vigilant" (274). Indeed, in dreams that couldn't be "denatured by drugs or alcohol," Vond is visited "by his uneasy anima in a number of disguises, notably as the Madwoman in the Attic" (274).

Vond's dreams thus conjoin—with unmistakable intertextual markers—C. G. Jung and current feminist theory. One can only wonder, therefore, at the degree of irony implicit in Vond's construction. If, as Molly Hite argues, "Vond's psychic battle to maintain his masculinity by expelling contingency from his own life finally makes him unpredictable, and thus useless to the white men, the Real Ones, that run him," then by the same logic, the very thing that makes Vond *Vineland*'s most visible masculine representative of the repressive state also makes him historically anachronistic.[13] Despite Hite's insertion of "white men" in the preceding sentence and her general argument that *Vineland*'s They-system is unequivocally white and male, the Real Ones above Vond in the order of power are simply defined as a "level where everybody knew everybody else, where however political fortunes below might bloom and die, the same people, the Real Ones, remained year in and year out, keeping what was desirable flowing their way" (276).

What is striking, then, in a novel that seldom refrains from naming names, is the essential invisibility of this class and its inaccessibility even to the likes of Vond. Vond himself only represents Their interests; he is the visible face of Their power: white, ruthless, cunningly cynical, yet also actively conversant with a reality that many (especially in the counterculture) have difficulty acknowledging. That the power Vond both represents and embodies has become ever more inaccessible to the characters (i.e., most Americans) while remaining unmistakably visible in Vond himself is indeed his most important attribute as a character. This is why, to Weed Atman and the Thanatoids killed in Vietnam, Vond appears—glowing with a kind of white radiance—at power's visible threshold, just before it fades into invisibility. As Weed confides to Prairie when she asks if he thinks about avenging his own murder: "Used to think I was climbing, step by step, right? toward a resolution—first Rex, above him your mother, then Brock Vond, then—but that's when it begins to go dark, and that door at the top I thought I saw isn't there anymore, because the light behind it just went off" (366). In contrast to the Real Ones, Vond inhabits—as a liminal figure, and Their intercessor—the visible realm. He therefore appears most often in highly visible means of transportation: the black chauffeur-driven limousine, and the Huey helicopter (the *deus ex machina* associations of which are played on at *Vineland*'s conclusion). In his various machinations, Vond acts as both application point and *medium* of a godlike power that appears most brightly in the political realm. It is hardly accidental, then, that the content of Vond's dreams and the dynamic of his other side are supplied by feminist theory, since feminism remains one of the few oppositional movements that still takes a visibly political form.

V. Like all images, the image of Frenesi's face is not only a lure and continually deferred object of Oedipal identification but also a realm where other, less narrativizable forces are at work. Beyond Brock Vond's glowing visibility lies a supermundane realm of wealth and power (inhabited by mysterious Real Ones) seldom revealed to most Americans except through the oppressive machineries of everyday life. Curiously, *Vineland* is composed of many such topographically distinct but interconnected realms, often articulated thematically through notions of the visible and invisible, the conscious and unconscious. Two realms in particular—one that identifies a Time outside time, first with film images and then with video arcade games, and a second that identifies a return to real time with the computer and its omniscience—are explicitly associated with technical media. In many of these instances, moreover, the narrative brushes up against a limit, a non-narrativizable realm to which access is made through technical media, and the border between life and death becomes shadowy.

Not only *Vineland*'s curious topography but much of its overt content stem from the fact that technical media, which include both cinematic and televisual images as well as computer files, operate as flight apparatuses to other worlds. Friedrich Kittler points out that the realm of the dead has the same dimensions as the storage and emission capacities of its culture: "If grave stones stood as symbols at the beginning of culture, our media technology can bring back all the gods. . . . In the media landscape immortals have come to exist again." [14] While this seems especially true of television and film images, in *Vineland* it is also true of the computer: while reducing the complexities of human life *and* death to one and zero, presence and absence, and functioning as a technological means of surveillance and control through the storage, retrieval, and transmission of data in a timeless global network, the computer also provides a means of access to something like the realm of the dead.

Considered in light of this relationship between the culture's media storage capacity and its realm of the dead, much of what otherwise might appear peripheral to *Vineland*'s narrative suddenly acquires a different kind of significance: notably, the ghost imagery throughout, as well as explicit mention of the *Bardol Thodol* or *Tibetan Book of the Dead* (218); various Yurok Indian stories recounted or alluded to, particularly those of the *woge,* little autochthones who withdrew from the Northwestern landscape when humans appeared; the voices "not chanting together but remembering, speculating, arguing, telling tales, uttering curses, singing songs" (370) which Brock Vond hears near Shade Creek, located not accidentally near Tsorrek, the land of the dead (186); not to mention the faceless predators who come out of Time's wind (383), and even the "Wineland" evoked by the Norse epic of betrayal *Vineland* obliquely echoes; and finally the Thanatoids themselves, characters who are neither alive nor dead and who, near *Vineland*'s conclusion, curiously come alive as never before, perhaps, the narrator speculates, as an effect of television (363). Weed Atman himself returns as a Thanatoid; but whereas the Thanatoids are "officially alive," Atman is "officially dead." Not incidentally, the Thanatoids have their own radio station, Radio Thanatoid, which broadcasts "Direct, though not necessarily live" (384), a Pynchonian joke that summarizes a condition of modern technical media.

Critics, for the most part, have ignored or not known how to read this burgeoning multiplicity of subliminal events on the margins of *Vineland*'s narrative, events that register and even bring about a number of uncertainties and confusions about the real (and the Lacanian symbolic and imaginary as well). Like the pervasive television and movie images and references, these events constitute a heterogeneous and non-narrativizable realm reflecting the sudden and immense expansion of late-twentieth-century America's media storage capacities, and consequently the expansion of its realm of the dead. Kittler observes that nineteenth-century photo albums establish an infinitely more precise realm of the dead than Balzac's *Comédie humaine.*

His observations recall those of Paul Virilio, who refers to the cinema as a ghost industry "seeking out new vectors of the Beyond." [15] These and other media, including the computer and its communications networks, not only provide a greatly and suddenly expanded realm of the dead but also bring about more varied possibilities for "flight into other worlds." As a consequence, *Vineland* must somehow register the fact that if the dead remain in the memory of the living and the threshold for flight is everywhere, it is no longer because of writing and oral narrative.

These other worlds—whether accessed through television, movies, radio, newspaper reportage, Indian myth, tales of reincarnation, or Norse epic—are all immanent to *Vineland*'s narrative while not being fully integrated within it. Each of these narrative sources implies a different information technology and a different time and mode of address. As a sense-making device, the narrative must somehow integrate these other worlds, each with its distinctive threshold for flight, while also acknowledging that these effects are not inherently connected and thus enjoy a quasi independence. In this double obligation, the narrative registers that we still live among partially connected media systems, with incompatible data channels and differently formatted data. Thus, in *Vineland*, the differences between and among media still count, producing not only different kinds of subjectivity and the possibility of different reading effects, but also a complex form of temporality in which a mythic past, two distinguishable historical moments (the 1960s and the 1980s), as well as a different technological future are all simultaneously present. This future, augured in Prairie's technologically mediated quest as well as in various comments about the increasing digitalization of all analogical media, announces a new kind of communications network in which the heterogeneity of information in a partially connected media system will disappear. Media as such will then be merely different interface possibilities accessed through a computer terminal on an optical fiber network. In the meantime, the more or less contemporary present is defined by an assemblage of partially connected media.

However, there is one striking instance of a partially connected media assemblage which not only enters *Vineland*'s narrative but establishes a direct connection with the realm of the dead. I refer to Takeshi Fumimota's story and the whole apparatus of "Karmic adjustment." To be sure, it is not a mass-media assemblage, but it is an assemblage nonetheless, one that connects a machine (the Puncutron) to an institution (the Kunoichi Retreat) to a set of highly self-reflective practices of body-spirit liberation (the Taoist *chi*) to a business (Takeshi and DL's Karmic Adjustments) and to the Thanatoids killed in Vietnam. In fact, from Takeshi's first experiences on the Puncutron, which corrects karmic imbalances through electrical stimulation of the nerves and which is also a kind of writing machine, to his computerization of "karmic chits," a number of circuits are traversed which touch on virtually all of *Vineland*'s thematic concerns.[16] Most significant in this respect are two exchanges: first, when Takeshi, referring both to computer chip memory and Reaganite economic policy, explains to the Thanatoid Ortho Bob how there "arose a system of deferment, of borrowing against karmic futures" in which Death "got removed from the process" (174–175); and second, when Weed Atman explains to Prairi how, just after his death and "looking for the magical exact film frame through which the dispossessed soul might reenter the world," he almost became Prairie in what he thought was Frenesi's idea to exchange "a life for a life, zero out the account" (364). Prairie then adds that the computer makes such an accounting—and a sense of one's personal identity—less complicated. What we see in these exchanges is a newly emergent discourse, pieced together to make some money as well as some sense of their lives by characters who are not yet completely sure they know what they are talking about.

This late-twentieth-century partially connected media assemblage offers therefore a visible contrast to that other image of retribution and cosmic justice in *Vineland,* the one proposed by Emerson and read annually at the Becker-Traverse family reunion. Significantly, the quoted passage is taken from William James's *Varieties of Religious Experience:* "Secret retributions are always restoring the level, when disturbed, of the divine justice. It is impossible to tilt the beam. All the tyrants and proprietors and monopolists of the world in vain set their shoulders to heave the bar. Settles forever more the ponderous equator to its line, and man and mote, and star and sun, must range to it, or be pulverized by the recoil" (369). What the contrast brings out is not that the formulations are determined by (obvious) differences in technology but, rather, how in both instances technology enters into and mediates a machinic conjunction of natural forces, human activities, and a language of accounting (in other words, the realm of the symbolic). In each case, technology is embedded within a two-sided assemblage: on one side, a machinic assemblage of bodies and forces, and on the other, a collective assemblage of enunciation. But in relation to the latter, a significant difference clearly emerges: whereas the same Emerson passage is read, quoted, memorized, and passed down directly at a family gathering where its meaning is taken to be self-evident, "karmic adjustment" is a new discourse fashioned in the Vineland community by adapting a very old discourse to new technological and historical conditions, where it circulates along diverse and unpredictable paths.

VI. Deleuze and Guattari, who make a guest appearance in the novel as the authors of the *Italian Wedding Fake Book* (97), understand the collective assemblage of enunciation as composed of verbal utterances, articulated in different semiotic regimes or mixtures of different semiotic regimes. This collective assemblage is, like any delimited mass of "indirect discourse," always prior to direct discourse:

> Direct discourse is a detached fragment of a mass and is born of the dismemberment of the collective assemblage; but the collective assemblage is always like the murmur from which I take my proper name, the constellation of voices, concordant or not, from which I draw my voice. I always depend on a molecular assemblage of enunciation that is not given in my conscious mind, any more than it depends solely on my apparent social determinations, which combine many heterogeneous regimes of signs. Speaking in tongues. To write is perhaps to bring this assemblage of the unconscious to the light of day, to select the whispering voices, to gather the tribes and secret idioms from which I extract something I call my self *(Moi)*.[17]

Vineland is enveloped by just such a collective assemblage of enunciation—call it the Vineland molecular unconscious—in which a whole gamut of "whispering voices" are registered as such, not only the voices of the media and those from the realm of the dead, but also voices that directly haunt the characters, as when Frenesi hears Brock's night voice amid the sleek raptors of fascist architecture whispering, "This is just how they want you, an animal, a bitch with swollen udders lying in the dirt, blankfaced, surrendered, reduced to this meat, these smells" (287). What Pynchon brings to light through this polyphony of voices and their various frames of reference, as well as through the characters' dreams and the temporally layered scenes, is the collective assemblage of enunciation from which *Vineland* draws its own distinctive shape and texture. But whereas Deleuze and Guattari conceive of the assemblage of enunciation exclusively in terms of words, voices, and murmurings, Pynchon's assemblage includes stories, images, texts, computer files—the whole range of contents that contemporary media make available.

In all of his novels, Pynchon builds his characters not out of closed-off personal traits but of perceptions variously adaptive to the social structure.

In contemporary America the social structure is represented most insistently by the media, particularly television. In *Vineland,* however, the various allusions to cop shows (enactments of law and order), family shows (reinforcements of the Oedipal triangle), and game shows (thinly disguised celebrations of commodity fetishism) assume this obvious "social ordering" function while at the same time providing opportunities for the characters either to divert or to subvert it. Mourning his lost relationship with Frenesi, Zoyd refuses to commit suicide in Hawaii because he doesn't want to hear Dano (from *Hawaii Five-O*) utter "Book him!"; Frenesi masturbates to images of motorcycle cops on TV; Justin's friend, when he needs some distance from his family, thinks of his parents as a television program (351). And, as noted above, Prairie reacts to television through a shifting slide of partial identifications which always allow her a space of critical differentiation. As these and other Pynchon characters constantly demonstrate, media signs and messages can always be decoded and recoded in ways that subvert their intended meaning or effect.

Such decoding and recoding must not be understood exclusively in semantic terms, as Stuart Hall discusses television viewing in his article "Encoding, decoding." [18] If taken in Deleuze and Guattari's sense, the terms can provide a more satisfactory account of the way media actually work, in *Vineland* as in everyday life. Because media harbor a potential for radical, schizophrenic deterritorialization, or flight, they can also operate as a powerful apparatus of social control. Although both delivered and authorized by the media as a control network, or site where capitalism attempts to recode the flows it unleashes, the structures of meaning (redundancy) necessary for recoding and overcoding are never sufficient or complete. Decoded flows (not just of capital, but of sounds, images, and texts) ceaselessly engender new flows that inevitably escape, providing take off points along lines of flight for the characters, however momentary and short-lasting.

Even so, decoding and recoding do not entirely account for *Vineland*'s assemblage of enunciation, especially for the critical importance of drugs, which heighten and de-familiarize the body as a medium of perception, making of its sensations another kind of flight to other worlds. In *Gravity's Rainbow,* Pynchon establishes a fundamental connection between drugs and the cinema through what he calls "Time Axis Manipulation," but in *Vineland* drugs assume a wider importance, because, like alcohol during Prohibition, they are essential to the current economy and structure of power. In general, Pynchon makes unavoidable the often repressed fact that American writing in the twentieth century is intimately linked to the use of drugs and alcohol, obviously in writers such as Hemingway, Faulkner, and Burroughs, but also in a writer such as John Updike, Pynchon's antithesis in the sense that Updike's *New Yorker* gin-and-tonic style re-familiarizes and normalizes through a sophisticated literary style the de-familiarizing effects produced by ingesting "foreign substances." *Vineland* suggests both political *and* literary reasons why drugs are a necessary aspect of Pynchon's writing. It is Deleuze, however, who provides an understanding of the logic of this necessary linkage when he draws attention to an implicit connection between "drugs *as* the American community" (my emphasis) and a molecular and machinic form of perception he calls gaseous.[19]

According to Deleuze, gaseous perception is a "genetic and differential state of perception" beyond both solid and liquid perception, either of which can be subjective or objective, formal or material. Gaseous perception, in contrast, assumes an interaction of images in a state of universal variation, that is, of images no longer subjected to the human eye or human vision; it corresponds to a Cézannian vision of a prehuman world, of a pure perception of images in themselves. Gaseous perception, therefore, is "not subject to time" but "has 'conquered' time" or "reaches the negative of time" (81). Deleuze also cites Carlos Castenada's program for "stopping the world" through drugs in order to experience a form of molecular perception, wherein one sees "the molecular intervals, the holes in sounds, in forms" (85). Tellingly, Deleuze finds this gaseous form of perception embodied in works of American experimental cinema by Brakhage, Snow, Nelson, Jacobs, and Landow.

Whereas *Gravity's Rainbow* is pervaded by gaseous forms of perception and the representation of "stoned" states of drugged consciousness, *Vineland* is haunted by their absence or marginality. In this regard, Mucho Maas turns out to be a key character. In *The Crying of Lot 49*, Mucho's advocacy of LSD is accompanied by his own account of perceptions—such as the spectrum analysis of music he does in his head—which directly illustrates Deleuze's description of molecular perception. Reappearing in *Vineland,* Mucho observes that the primary effect of drugs taken in the sixties was to make one feel immortal. Drugs, therefore, posed a direct threat to state control and the power of life and death it holds over its citizens. At the same time, Mucho's personal history since the sixties points to the necessary entwinement of illegal drugs with the growth of the music industry (just as Hector Zuñiga's personal history indicates the necessary complicity between the illegal drug trade and U.S. law enforcement). After enduring a serious cocaine addiction, Mucho is now "on the Natch" and has become an advocate of abstention as the only way to beat a system that aspires to total control: " 'Cause soon they're gonna be coming after everything, not just drugs, but beer, cigarettes, sugar, salt, fat, you name it, anything that could remotely please any of your senses, because they need to control all that" (313). In the meantime: "They just let us forget. Give us too much to process, fill up every minute, keep us distracted, it's what the Tube is for" (314). Humorously, however, even overexposure to television requires control measures applied at Tubal Detox Centers. According to *Vineland*'s pervasive irony, what makes television an effective narcotic and means of control also makes it dangerous. Control itself must be controlled, which is what the government does.

For Pynchon's characters, the media assemblage is both a substitute for and blockage of the possibility of gaseous perceptions, which, unlike the media, elicit not a totalizing view but a schizophrenic multiplicity of views implicitly suggestive of the limits of the human, and necessarily of the limits of human control. Thus, as a novelistic embodiment of a collective assemblage of enunciation, *Vineland* functions not to deny the media but to counteract its totalizing effects by molecularizing or particle-izing specific Tubal references, or nuances, as the narrator calls them. Liberated from molar narratives and politically oppressive schemes of redundancy and control, such nuances enter the novel's associative, deterritorialized stream in the same way that peripheral signs and messages from other worlds enter it, that is, as implicitly gaseous or fractal perceptions that remain peripheral or only immanent to the narrative. (Significantly, the word *fractal* appears in several instances in relation to perception, e.g., "fractal smells" and the "fractal halo" around DL's hair.) These gaseous perceptions, which remain almost imperceptible or illegible, are very much like the signs and messages haunting the consciousness of all the major characters. Early in the novel, the pattern is clearly established when Zoyd recounts to Prairie his out-of-body attempts to visit Frenesi in the night:

> "Where's it you go, then? Where is she?"
> "Keep trying to find out. Try to read the signs, locate landmarks, anything that'll give a clue, but—well the signs are there on street corners and store windows—but I can't read them."
> "It's in some other language?"
> "Nope, it's in English, but there's something between it and my brain that won't let it through." (40)

While Pynchon's writing frequently refers to orders other than the visible, in *Vineland* such non-narrativized signs and gaseous perceptions delineate the shifting, evanescent contours of a molecular unconscious. In this sense, Vineland can be said to designate Pynchon's mapping of the collective assemblage of enunciation that typifies America in the late 1980s. Deleuze and Guattari conceive of the molecular unconscious as given only in "microperceptions," and thus it stands in opposition to both the perception-consciousness system *and* the projections or translations of the unconscious into molar constructions such as the Oedipal structure. In contrast to Oedipal structures, microperceptions are likened to "holes in the world allowing the world lines themselves to run off."[20] Thus they are also escape routes, lines of flight toward an uncoded outside. In *Vineland* these microperceptions offer lines of flight from the menacing pressure of (re-)Oedipalization, and the normalization that follows as its consequence. Indeed, the possibility of microperceptions—of cracks and holes in the social structure, of moments of pure perception beyond any socially imposed meaning—is what allows the characters the only opportunities they have for instantaneous flight and hence some form of resistance to the re-Oedipalized enclosure that Pynchon insists *is* contemporary America.

In these terms, drugs (or rather their repression) acquire their political significance, as Pynchon makes absolutely explicit in the numerous references to, and several imagined scenes that depict, the most important repressed historical narrative immanent to *Vineland,* namely the U.S. military's large-scale invasions of the marijuana-rich growing areas of the Northwest coast ordered by Reagan in the early 1980s. The consequences for Vineland County (where Holytail is located) are stated unequivocally: "Sooner or later Holytail was due for the full treatment, from which it would emerge, like most of the old Emerald Triangle, pacified territory—reclaimed by the enemy for a timeless, defectively imagined future of zero-tolerance drug-free Americans all pulling their weight and all locked in to the official economy, inoffensive music, endless family specials on the Tube, church all week long, and, on special days, for extra-good behavior, maybe a cookie" (221–222). In relation to *this* narrative, and all that it implies about the viability and power of the Oedipal structure in Reagan-era America, Prairie's quest no longer seems necessarily or exclusively Oedipal but appears to be driven by a desire for access to the sixties as a moment of historical otherness, when "sex, drugs, and rock 'n' roll" made a genuinely significant political difference.

An important difference between the narratives of *Gravity's Rainbow* and *Vineland* can now be spelled out. Whereas in *Gravity's Rainbow* the narrative sketches a network of indeterminate relations (a multiplicity) and then fragments wildly in fierce defiance of the "terrible Oedipal situation" in the Zone at the novel's conclusion, the narrative in *Vineland* stages a convergence of a reconstituted nonnuclear family in which an assortment of mother- and father-figures—both symbolic and real—cluster around Prairie, who understandably takes off for the woods, "feeling totally familied out" (374). But Prairie's resistance to further enactments of the family romance is just what makes her available to Brock Vond, who is the other side of the sixties countercultural experience. For several reasons, then, Prairie's direct confrontation with her mother's seducer in *Vineland*'s closing pages, when Brock attempts to abduct/seduce her, is structurally predetermined.

As every reader will remember, Prairie's reaction is double: she first rejects Brock with a teenage insult, but later, speaking to a now empty sky from which he has permanently departed, she utters a wistful desire that he return, that he take her any place he wants. Fittingly, then, as Prairie falls asleep on the novel's last page, she is pulled between "Brock fantasies" and molecular perceptions ("the silent darkened silver images all around her" [385]). On the one hand, a pull toward the dark seducer ("every woman loves a fascist") or the Oedipal father; it hardly matters which, since both are molar configurations of desire. On the other hand, a flight toward the silver realm of molecular perception. This realm, this time outside time, is the Vineland molecular unconscious. Paradoxically, it offers both a realm of escape from human responsibility (as in Frenesi's life) and the only site of resistance to the omnipresent effort to re-Oedipalize and recode the deterritorialized flows unleashed by Reganomic capitalism. Like *Vineland*'s implicit inventory of what is in our government files as well as our realm of the dead, perceptions of this realm offer a resistance to precisely the narratives by which this recoding of control is both established and authorized.

At some stage we should have
to expect the machines to take
control.
 ▪ Alan M. Turing

▪ **8**

The Disappearance of Media

Cyberspace in *Neuromancer*

I. Widely heralded as a stylish exemplar of
cyberpunk fiction and a compelling blend
of science fiction and postmodern themes, *Neuromancer*'s critical import has more to do with
its assumptions about information and its inventive modeling of the new "world spaces" of multinational capitalism. Indeed, what Gibson
imagined in 1984—the year of *Neuromancer*'s
publication—actually points to a new becoming
on the technological horizon: a totalized, global
information economy in which information and
the digital "dance of biz" do not simply extend
capital and its logic of commodification (capital
and information already being nearly indistinguishable) but effectuate a conjunction of human being and silicon. In the new information
manifold, "data is made flesh," as well as the
reverse.

In *Neuromancer* information is assumed to be the becoming of science and capital. Science itself is no longer conceived (or conceivable) as a language or discourse network that describes nature but as a techno-virus that transforms nature into a new machinic phylum.[1] Mind-body dualisms reappear out of the alien matrix that *is* the future, but these Cartesian avatars are now molecular assemblages articulating the posthuman: on the one hand, the cyborg body, on the other a neuro-electronically accessed communications system providing a "consensual hallucination" in "cyberspace," as Gibson prophetically denominates it.[2] Doubly articulated in cyberspace and "sim-stim" units, the human psychic apparatus becomes a fully technological construct; cyborg culture becomes the only culture.

Inasmuch as cyberspace is a spatialized information field, *Neuromancer* would thus seem to extend into the realm of science fiction the trajectory traced by Burroughs, Pynchon, McElroy, Gaddis, and DeLillo. In obvious ways, however, *Neuromancer* and the two novels that follow it, *Count Zero* and *Mona Lisa Overdrive*, usually referred to collectively as the "Sprawl trilogy," are no longer concerned with information per se, except as a given whose status is wholly assumed. The appearance of cyberspace fiction thus obliges us to confront the possibility that the stakes may have changed and that the fictional articulation of information multiplicities has been superseded by another kind of fictional challenge. Technologically, this new challenge is made possible by a fully electronic communications assemblage in which all information is digitalized and transmitted by fiber-optic cables. In this completely integrated technological assemblage, differences between media disappear, leaving in their stead only different programed outputs or interface effects at a computer terminal.

Gibson's fiction assumes something like this new assemblage and renders its consequences—or new possibilities—in (con)figurations of cyberspace and virtual reality, the Net, and the autonomy of artificial intelligence. But if Gibson's fiction displaces or subsumes the production of information multiplicities into novelistic representations of "consensual hallucinations" or global data constructs in cyberspace, it also raises the question of whether the fictional modeling of cyberspace—and the communications assemblage of which it is a part—bring into play another kind of multiplicity, both representationally and for the novel as a prose fictional form.

II. Two early stories in the collection entitled *Burning Chrome* define more precisely what will be at stake in Gibson's fiction.[3] In "Johnny Mnemonic," the title character (and also the narrator) is a carrier of information to which he has no access. As a consequence of biotechnological implants, hundreds of megabytes have been stored in his head, making him a human-cyborg storage unit and consequently the target of various agents for whom the information is valuable. The point of the story is that he must not only avoid these agents but somehow get the information out of his head and passed along if he is to survive. This he does, thanks in large part to two other cyborgs, a female street-samurai type named Molly (who will reappear in *Neuromancer* and *Mona Lisa Overdrive*) and a heroin-addicted dolphin. The nature of the forces arrayed against them is suggested in the following paragraph:

> Somewhere beneath us, Jones [the dolphin] would be circling his tank, feeling the first twinges of junk sickness. The police would be boring the Drome regulars with questions about Ralfi. What did he do? Who was he with before he stepped outside? And the Yakuza [a high-tech version of the Mafia] would be settling its ghostly bulk over the city's data banks, probing for faint images of me reflected in numbered accounts, securities transactions, bills for utilities. We're an information economy. They teach you that in school. What they don't tell you is that it's impossible to move, to live, to operate at any level without leaving traces, bits, seemingly meaningless fragments of personal information. Fragments that can be retrieved, amplified. (BC 17)

The passage clearly evokes the territory already mapped by Pynchon and DeLillo. In Gibson's story, however, the content of the information stored in Johnny's head is not important beyond a highly generalized assessment of its exchange value: "it was probably research data, the Yakuza being given to advanced forms of industrial sabotage" (BC 17). In order for the story to work, therefore, the reader need not know—any more than Johnny—the exact contents of this information. In short, information here has no cognitive value, as it does for the characters in novels by Pynchon, McElroy, Gaddis, and DeLillo; having only exchange value, it is a matter of concern to Johnny only because he is being used for its storage.

What makes the story interesting, then, is how this information is extracted from Johnny's head and put back into circulation and how Johnny is protected from the agents who are after him. Just as Johnny's own crude attempt to extricate himself from his dilemma with a shotgun hidden in an Adidas bag is about to fail, Molly suddenly appears and effectively intercedes on his behalf. A cyborg "razor-girl" with a "jacked-up" nervous system, eye implants, and deadly razor blades that protract from her fingers,

Molly works for neither the Yakuza nor legitimate corporate interests but is an independent street agent with formidable skills and knowledge. It turns out that she knows about a "war surplus" cyborg dolphin implanted with a sensing device used to detect submarines during the recent war, and it is through this device that the dolphin, though now addicted to heroin, can read the code of the memory program buried in Johnny's head. When the code is spoken to Johnny, he instantly goes into a trancelike state, or "idiot/savant mode," and utters its contents. After recording the information and sending it to a *post restante* mail box in Sydney, Molly and Johnny are able to deal actively as players rather than hunted victims in the information exchanges that Gibson refers to in *Neuromancer* as "the dance of biz." [4]

As for the problem of how to escape the Yakuza assassin hot on their trail, again Molly has the answer: "you hide in the Pit, in the lowest circle, where any outside influence generates swift, concentric ripples of raw menace. You hide in Nighttown. Better yet, you hide *above* Nighttown, because the Pit's inverted, and the bottom of its bowl touches the sky, the sky that Nighttown never sees, sweating under its own firmament of acrylic resin, up where the Lo Teks crouch in the dark like gargoyles, black-market cigarettes dangling from their lips" (BC 8–9). Nighttown itself lies at one extremity of an abandoned mall, its neon arc lights shot out and geodesic dome darkened by "decades of cooking fires." As Molly and Johnny climb upward toward the Pit, they soon encounter one of its denizens, a member of the Lo Tek gang distinguished by his "toothbud transplants from Dobermans" (BC 14). An urban primitive subculture, the Lo Teks inhabit the upper webbing of the Pit and appear to make a living as black marketeers. Having befriended Molly at some time in the past, they allow her to stage the impending confrontation with the Yakuza assassin in one of their spaces, "the Killing Floor," a ritual arena composed of bobbing, sliding metal surfaces not only treacherous to negotiate but pierced by the deafening sounds of grating metal miked and amplified by the Lo Teks. Lured out onto the Killing Floor, the assassin is confused and outmaneuvered, whereupon Molly is able to turn against him his own weapon, a kind of molecular cutting filament he ejects out of his thumb. In the unfamiliar and unstable space of the Killing Floor, his superior weapons technology proves ineffective. As Johnny concisely summarizes their combat: Molly "killed him with culture shock" (BC 21).

"Johnny Mnemonic" is notable for its presentation of what will become several constants in Gibson's fiction. First, the narrative recounts the efforts of several characters on the margins of a high-tech corporate world to survive through strategies of *détournement,* or the reappropriation of information technologies for their own—usually illegal—purposes.[5] As the narrator of "Burning Crome" succinctly puts it: "the street finds its own uses for things" (186). In practice this includes everything from weaponry and aesthetic surgery to software implants and the most sophisticated electronic "icebreakers" used to penetrate the defense systems of corporate data banks. Second, while Gibson's fiction is filled with an assortment of historically resonant objects often described in a vividly detailed bricolage style, it is the rendering of space itself, and the movements of his characters through it, that produces its most striking stylistic effect. In this respect, the depictions of Nighttown, the Pit, and the Killing Floor in "Johnny Mnemonic" are typical instances of the many heterotopic spaces encountered in Gibson's fiction, spaces often appropriated by the various subcultures that populate them.[6]

The rather dramatic reduction of the content, if not the value, of information suggests that for Gibson the stakes—and consequently his own novelistic interests—lie elsewhere. Summarily, this interest is most sharply focused on the construction of the new world-space that an information economy will give rise to in a not too distant future. Indeed, Gibson himself has remarked that "apprehending the present . . . seems to require the whole Science Fiction tool kit."[7] Until fairly recently, science fiction has taken outer space as its primary locus; it assumed a universe in expansion and a beyond that served as a primary stimulus to the imagination. Rejecting these assumptions, Gibson takes a view similar to Jean Baudrillard's, in which the contemporary world has imploded in the mass media and simulations render problematic any hard and fixed distinction between reality and fiction, the body and its technological extensions.[8] Unlike Baudrillard, however, Gibson does not believe that things ever completely disappear or become outdated. In "Rocket Radio," a nonfictional piece written for *Rolling Stone,* Gibson asserts that "once perfected, communication technologies rarely die out entirely; rather, they shrink to fit particular niches in the global infostructure."[9]

For Gibson, furthermore, what is true of technologies is also true of recognizably dated objects: they turn up here and there, or pile up in odd spaces such as Julius Deane's office or Villa Straylight (in *Neuromancer*) or Finn's house in Manhattan (in *Mona Lisa Overdrive*).[10] In contrast, then, to Baudrillard's relatively undifferentiated world of simulations, the spaces in Gibson's fiction—the postindustrial technoscapes of Chiba City, Nighttown, and the Sprawl, as well as high-orbital nonterrestrial spaces such as Freeside, the Zion cluster, and Villa Straylight in *Neuromancer,* not to mention cyberspace and several kinds of virtual reality—are remarkably variegated. Not only heterogeneous in themselves, these spaces are also peopled with cyborgs, various street types, and subcultures that attempt to subvert for their own purposes the new technological world order of the zaibatsus, as the faceless, monolithic corporations are called.[11]

Although Gibson's fictional spaces both assume and resonate with parallel or similar constructions in films such as *Bladerunner,* in MTV, video arcade games, and above all the global communications network that Gibson refers to simply as "the Net,"[12] what connects these various and multiple spaces are the movements and actions of the characters, who are very much a part of this Gibsonian space. In essence, they are what they do and, like cyberspace itself, cast no shadows of psychological complexity. As Molly says to her cyberspace cowboy partner in *Neuromancer:* "Anybody any good at what they do, that's what they *are,* right? You gotta jack, I gotta tussle" (N 50). This is especially evident in Gibson's most prominent character type, the cowboy jockey who "jacks into" cyberspace and who encounters there—Gibson himself having already named it—a new technological reality.

Cyberspace makes its first full-fledged appearance in "Burning Chrome," the title story of the collection. The story concerns one of the exploits of Bobby Quine, a cyberspace cowboy typical of the many industrial espionage "artists and hustlers" (the conjunction itself is significant) who populate Gibson's fiction. Narrated by Bobby's roommate and partner, Automatic Jack, the story's emotional center is triangulated around Bobby's girlfriend, Rikki, who, though not a participant, becomes very much entangled in their plan to "burn" Chrome by penetrating her data banks and dispersing her capital electronically. Chrome is both a person and a form of agency or power no longer altogether human:

> Chrome: I'd seen her maybe half a dozen times in the Gentleman Loser [a bar where cyberspace cowboys congregate]. Maybe she was slumming, or checking out the human condition, a condition she didn't exactly aspire to. A sweet little heart-shaped face framing the nastiest pair of eyes you ever saw. She's looked fourteen for as long as anyone could remember, hyped out of anything like a normal metabolism on some massive program of serums and hormones. She was as ugly a customer as the street ever produced, but she didn't belong to the street anymore. She was one of the Boys, Chrome, a member in good standing of the local Mob subsidiary.

Word was, she'd gotten started as a dealer, back when synthetic pituitary hormones were still proscribed. But she hadn't had to move hormones for a long time. Now she owned the House of Blue Lights.   (BC 180)

In cyberspace, where the actual burning will be done, Chrome appears as an abstract architecture constructed of "data"; but here she is given a human face of sorts, which is no doubt important for the story's ethical dynamic. Also noticeable, in passages such as this one, is Gibson's debt to hard-boiled detective fiction, particularly for the low-angled "street view" of things. For Gibson, the street is both a field where antagonistic forces reveal themselves and a valorized perspective from which to view and appraise newly developing technologies. As a metonymically designated outlaw zone, it is marked "as a deliberately unsupervised playground for technology itself" (N 11).

Chrome's effort to rise above the street will be echoed in a more pathetic register by the efforts of Rikki to escape it. From the outset, Rikki's relationship with Bobby is purely symbolic: he is losing his edge and needs a big score; she appears as both the needed challenge and a stand-in for the eventual encounter that will bring him back to peak performance. In short, she's a good luck charm. For the narrator, on the other hand, she is "right there, alive, totally real, human, hungry, resilient, bored, beautiful, exciting, all the things she was" (BC 177). She also responds to what is most attractive in him, the first time curiously through an interest in his prosthetic arm. But Rikki's life—or, more specifically, her body and the being it supports—is the site of an extraordinary array of commodifications. Her main source of pleasure—and her only alternative to the street—is her little "simstim deck," which provides the simulated stimuli by means of which she experiences the world as lived by superstar Tally Isham in a kind of exhilarating multisensory movie of the rich and famous having fun at various locales. In order to transform her life into a version of this simulation, she rents out her own body in a form of simstim for anonymous others. For it turns out that, unbeknown to Bobby or the narrator, Rikki has been working all along at Chrome's establishment, the House of Blue Lights:

working three-hour shifts in an approximation of REM sleep, while her body and a bundle of conditioned reflexes took care of business. The customers never got to complain that she was faking it, because those were real orgasms. But she felt them, if she felt them at all, as faint silver flares somewhere out on the edge of sleep. Yeah, it's so popular it's almost legal. The customers are torn between needing someone and wanting to be alone at the same time, which has probably always been the name of that particular game, even before we had the neuroelectronics to enable them to have it both ways. (BC 191)

By allowing her body to be rented out in simulated sex at the House of Blue Lights, Rikki is finally able to purchase for herself a set of Zeiss Ikon corneal transplants made famous by her simstim idol Tally Isham, as well as a one-way ticket to Hollywood.

Ironically, Rikki's escape from the street and the House of Blue Lights occurs on the same night that Bobby and Jack destroy it by "burning" Chrome. Thanks to a Russian virus-program that Jack obtains almost by accident from Finn, a black market dealer in odds and ends (who reappears in the novels), they are able to penetrate Chrome's data banks and redistribute her assets, with a large chunk of capital for themselves. Successfully back on line, Bobby no longer needs Rikki, and it is curiously fitting as well that Rikki's departure should coincide with Chrome's murder, as Jack thinks of it, since for him the two are closely associated: at the story's outset, not wanting to think about Chrome, Jack "blotted her out with a picture of Rikki" (BC 169). Now that Rikki is gone, when he sees the identically beautiful eyes of the simstim stars on the posters in the street, he thinks: "some of the eyes are hers, but none of the faces are" (BC 191). The story concludes with this image of desire, the force of which resides in the barely perceptible difference between human eyes and their technological replacement.

By drawing attention to such differences, "Burning Chrome" develops a structure of parallels and contrasts, of which the most significant is between simstim and cyberspace. You jack in to both by putting "trodes" on your temples; when you open your eyes you are "in" a virtual world, constructed neuro-electronically. But the obvious difference is that while simstim is passive and anodyne, a vicarious experience, cyberspace is interactive and dangerous, requiring the intense focus of a disembodied consciousness. In contrast to the sad dispersion of Rikki into a variety of simulations, Bobby and Jack must maintain a sharply focused integrity, or edge. Cyberspace cowboys, consequently, are viewed as a heroic type, their existential albeit criminal exploits being one of the few ways in which individuals can confront forces more powerful than themselves and still make an effective difference.

These more powerful forces are congealed in the data banks of advanced capitalism, arrayed architecturally in a highly protected electronic simulation. Here is how Gibson first introduces the cyberspace cowboy and his element:

> Bobby was a cowboy, and ice was the nature of his game, *ice* from ICE, Intrusive Countermeasures Electronics. The matrix is an abstract representation of the relationships between data systems. Legitimate programmers jack into their employers' sector of the matrix and find themselves surrounded by bright geometries representing the corporate data.
>
> Towers and fields of it ranged in the colorless nonspace of the simulation matrix, the electronic consensus-hallucination that facilitates the handling and exchange of massive quantities of data. Legitimate programmers never see the walls of ice they work behind, the walls of shadow that screen their operations from others, from industrial-espionage artists and hustlers like Bobby Quine.
>
> Bobby was a cowboy. Bobby was a cracksman, a burglar, casing mankind's extended electronic nervous system, rustling data and credit in the crowded matrix, monochrome nonspace where the only stars are dense concentrations of information, and high above it all burn corporate galaxies and the cold spiral arms of military systems.   (BC 169–170)

Having accessed the matrix through a cyberspace deck or "matrix simulator" resembling a computer with a monitor, the cowboy maneuvres in the matrix as a bodiless point on a "3-D chessboard, infinite and transparent" (BC 168). By punching in coordinates on a keyboard, he moves through different sectors of cyberspace. In order to penetrate to the large corporate data cores where information can be accessed and manipulated, however, the cowboys must rely on "icebreakers," virus-programs usually of Soviet military origin which can dissolve the ICE, or allow their intrusions to masquerade as official inspection probes or legitimate exchanges of data. The danger is that some of the protective ICE programs—such as the infamous "black ICE"—are deadly "neural feedback weapons" and can cause the cowboy to flatline in brain death.

In *Neuromancer* and its successors, Gibson continues to build the cyberspace cowboy into a recognizable figure, replete with an oral tradition and associated mythology. Although his origins are traced back to the military technology developed for a special mission in the recent war against Russia (see N 28 for details), the figure of the cyberspace cowboy is something of a throwback, an attempt both to glamorize the hacker-as-outlaw and to represent a new and unfamiliar experience by giving its agent a local habitation and a name. But however interesting as a fictional type, the cyberspace cow-

242 ■ The Novel of Media Assemblages

boy's importance will be eclipsed by his element, cyberspace, which in *Neuromancer* will figure integrally in the generation of the plot.

III. To make the jump from the stories in *Burning Chrome* to a full-fledged novel, Gibson could no longer build the narrative on a simple story about postindustrial sabotage and data rustling but needed a thread that would tie together a number of different exploits while at the same time putting them all in an unusual perspective. The plot of *Neuromancer* does this by making cyberspace not only a medium in which much of the action unfolds but also a site, or scene, whose very nature undergoes a significant change. Gibson's brilliant solution, in short, is to have the plot itself engineered by an AI, or artificial intelligence, which inhabits cyberspace.

At the novel's outset, an ex–cyberspace cowboy named Case, whose nerves have been deliberately damaged by a former client, is recruited by a street-samurai named Molly (the same from "Johnny Mnemonic") for a yet-to-be-defined "run" put together by Armitage, an ex-military type. Case and Molly, who immediately form a functional (and sexual) liaison, begin to suspect that Armitage is being controlled by someone or something else. Through underground information networks, Case discovers that Armitage is indeed being backed by an AI named Wintermute located in Berne and owned by Tessier-Ashpool S.A., a giant multinational zaibatsu. Formerly a shattered Special Forces soldier named Corto and the sole survivor of a disastrous military mission in the recent war with Russia, Armitage was apparently cured of catatonic schizophrenia after being treated cybernetically in an experimental recovery program. All of which suggests to Case that Armitage is simply a personality "shell" constructed by the AI named Wintermute for the run against Tessier-Ashpool.

As the time for the run approaches, Wintermute attempts to contact Case, first by telephone, then successfully in cyberspace when Case is flat-lined by Tessier-Ashpool ICE and Wintermute can access Case's memory, and then again through Case's hotel room monitor. Possessing neither an "I" nor a "self," Wintermute must assume some human personality as a template. In the extended encounters with Case which take place in virtual reality scenes that Wintermute constructs from Case's memory, Wintermute appears in the form of someone Case has known in the past (first Julius Deane, then Finn) and reveals that the run (and therefore the novel's plot) is motivated by its own desire to fuse with Neuromancer, another Tessier-Ashpool AI located in Rio. Wintermute describes itself as a form of "hive intelligence" (whereas Neuromancer represents personality, immortality, the land of the dead) and cautions Case not to confuse "the Wintermute mainframe [in] Berne with the Wintermute *entity*": "What you [Case] think of as Wintermute is only a part of another, a, shall we say, *potential* entity. I, let us say, am merely one aspect of that entity's brain" (N 120). Wintermute also reveals that, aside from being able to sort tremendous quantities of information, its greatest talent lies in improvising situations. In fact, to a much greater extent than Case realizes, Wintermute has chosen each of the participants—Case himself, Molly, Armitage, and Riviera, a psychopath who can project visual hallucinations, and later the Rastafarians in Zion cluster, an orbital space colony not unlike the Pit and populated by another subculture—because each one has special skills and, more importantly, because each one is psychologically manipulable in a predictable way.

Revelations about each character's past are thus motivated by the exigencies of the AI's plot (which of course here coincides with the demands of novelistic convention). What is most important in regard to Case is his ill-fated love affair with Linda Lee and consequent suicidal impulses, both of which Wintermute (and later Neuromancer) play upon. However, there comes a point when, in order for its plan to work, Wintermute must convert Case from manipulated pawn to an active ally. Not only does Armitage, predictably, crack apart and begin to relive his disastrous military mission, but there are also contingencies beyond even Wintermute's capacities to respond. For all of its obvious ingenuity and information processing speed, it can do nothing with an old-fashioned mechanical lock; more crucially, it cannot *know* the code word that, when spoken into a special terminal, will allow the two AIs to fuse. Such constraints were meant to insure that Wintermute could only be unshackled by a human being.

Wintermute's inherent limits thus allow a space to open between its manipulations and the indeterminacy of events as they unfold. As a result, the scenes in which Case is gradually converted from a sullen and rebellious cyberspace cowboy for hire to someone who consciously allies himself with Wintermute are heightened in importance. A clear turning point occurs when Case returns to his hotel room after a frustrating attempt to console himself with drugs, only to be arrested by the Turing police. The Turing Registry, we learn earlier, is responsible for shackling AIs, thereby preventing them from attaining to a full degree of autonomy. The three Turing agents awaiting Case not only are wise to Wintermute's scheme but cannot refrain from interjecting a moral fervor into their accusations: "You are worse than a fool . . . [one agent says to Case]. You have no care for your species. For thousands of years men dreamed of pacts with demons. Only now are such things possible. And what would you be paid with? What would your price be, for aiding this thing to free itself and grow?" (N 163). But before the Turing police can take Case very far, Wintermute intervenes by sending electronic signals through the Net which cause a small security drone and then a robotic gardener to attack the agents, thus giving Case the opportunity to escape.

Like the preparatory run on Sense/Net in Manhattan, the run on Tessier-Ashpool involves a double penetration, of both the Tessier-Ashpool data core in cyberspace and the family ancestral home, Villa Straylight, an elaborately Baroque physical structure built in orbital space adjacent to Freeside. The purpose of the earlier Sense/Net run was to acquire the services of McCoy Pauley (known as "Dixie Flatline"), a former cyberspace cowboy who, though physically dead, still exists as a "ROM personality construct" and as such can communicate with Case in cyberspace. His participation will be essential for the deployment of the Chinese icebreaker necessary to penetrate Tessier-Ashpool's data core. As in the Sense/Net run, the penetration will be effected simultaneously in two modes: physically by Molly and cyberspatially by Case. Furthermore, thanks to a simstim unit hardwired into Molly, Case will be able to follow her movements as if he were experiencing them physically, and he will be able to move back and forth between her physical space and cyberspace by throwing a switch. The plan is to have Riviera gain entrance to Villa Straylight through his skill as a perverse entertainer and persuade Lady 3Jane Tessier-Ashpool to allow Molly to enter the structure. Molly will then coerce Lady 3Jane—using whatever means necessary—to divulge the code word that, when spoken into a special terminal, a platinum head in Villa Straylight's core chamber, will unshackle Wintermute. Not surprisingly, the run does not go as planned. Riviera betrays Wintermute's team, and Molly is taken captive. It is then up to Case, with the help of a Rastafarian named Maelcum, to make his way to the villa and complete the run himself in a double penetration.

What this broad summary cannot possibly convey is the intricate complexity of the spatial movements and communications that the run entails. The interior architecture of Villa Straylight, for example, reflects the cloistered, decadent turn in the history of the Tessier-Ashpool family and becomes an active element of the narrative as the space that Molly and then Case must negotiate. This labyrinthine space is rendered both in descriptions of Molly's and Case's passages through it and through quotations purportedly taken from Lady 3Jane Tessier-Ashpool's semiotics essay, as spoken by the jeweled head in one of Wintermute's virtual reality scenes staged for Case. According to the essay, "the hull's inner surface is overgrown with a desperate proliferation of structures, forms flowing, interlocking, rising toward a solid core of microcircuitry, our clan's corporate heart, a cylinder of silicon wormholed with narrow maintenance tunnels, some no wider than a man's hand" (N 172). As Lady 3Jane points out, the villa is designed to hide its own spatiality, the family having conceived a hatred for space itself. Wintermute also plays on the repulsive aspect of the villa's spatiality by reminding Case of the villa's resemblance to a beehive Case had once destroyed. The resemblance is more than metaphorical, however, since the Tessier-Ashpool family thinks of itself as a "hive" (229); but as Case discovers, it is also an atavistic clan, with certain members kept in a frozen cryogenic state, while others are disposable clones.

The scene of Case's cyberspace encounter with his former love Linda Lee in a bunker on the beach provides another example of how a particular space becomes an active part of the plot (and one of *Neuromancer*'s essential themes, as we shall later see). Initially, the scene appears to be only a tangential development; but then Case realizes that this virtual reality construct is the work of Neuromancer, the other Tessier-Ashpool AI, and represents a last ditch effort contra Wintermute to distract Case from completing the run. As it turns out, it is Case who must persuade Lady 3Jane to speak the code word that will allow the two AIs to fuse, which he does by appealing to her desire for real change. Although Case is not sure what that change will be, at least it will break the pattern of incestuous inwardness and convolution that has defined the Tessier-Ashpool family history. And this, finally, is what Lady 3Jane's mother, Marie-France, who set up the two AI programs in the first place, apparently wanted all along.

To Case's relief and amazement, the fusion of the two AIs appears to change very little—at least from the human perspective, since what this fusion brings about is the AIs' trancendence of human affairs altogether. In their last conversation, Wintermute tells Case that it (Wintermute) has become the matrix and is now able to communicate with distant intelligences of its own kind in another solar system. In the two subsequent novels of the trilogy, *Count Zero* and *Mona Lisa Overdrive*, Gibson continues to explore this change in cyberspace, the most important consequence of which is that cyberspace now appears to be inhabited by strange powers that certain of the characters associate with voodoo gods.[13] But the essential change, enacted in *Neuromancer*, is the activation of cyberspace itself. Henceforth, it can no longer be conceived in Cartesian terms as a neutral or passive receptacle with geometric dimensions where data can be stored and exchanged.

Whether the powers active there are ICE defensive systems deployed by military and commercial interests, viral programs and icebreakers mobilized by cyberspace cowboys, direct interventions by artificial intelligences, or human personality ROM constructs like Dixie, or even virtual reality scenes in which humans can live in a form of immortality, cyberspace has become a site where new forces possessing both energy and intelligence contend for stakes that involve human beings but are not fully accountable in human terms. In this sense, cyberspace represents a new extension of what Deleuze and Guattari call the machinic phylum and a boundary space of unholy alliances, where humans plot with "demons" and intelligence undergoes a strange becoming.[14] In certain respects it has evolved into a zone much like the street.

As noted earlier, the machinic phylum is "materiality, natural or artificial, and both simultaneously; it is matter in movement, in flux, in variation, matter as a conveyor of singularities and traits of expression." Deleuze and Guattari insist that the machinic phylum "can only be followed" (409). The artisan, moreover, is "one who is determined in such a way as to follow a flow of matter." Gibson's cyberspace cowboys are artisans in this sense; they follow the machinic phylum constituted by silicon and its possible combinations and configurations. In *Neuromancer*, what is dramatically and thematically important is how the next step for these artisans following the postindustrial machinic phylum leads to an alliance with a demon in a becoming of a machinic intelligence. Thus, while at one level the plot may appear to be engineered by a form of artificial intelligence seeking to free itself, at a deeper level it is determined by the logic of technological development and its convergence with a myth. At several points, *Neuromancer* suggests that the fusion of the two AIs enacts an allegory about the transformative power of joining the two hemispheres of the human brain. But this allegory only figures a more englobing one about the autonomization of technology in the fully digitalized space of the Net, a process having little to do with the localization of brain functions and everything to do with new extensions of the machinic phylum.

The interfacing of electronic data and human flesh and their convertibility in the development of cyberspace and cyborgs would not be possible without this extension. *Neuromancer* thematizes it as a continuum defined by the double transformation or two-way traffic between data and flesh. This continuum is first suggested in Case's vision of the street as a site where "data [is] made flesh" in the form of interacting information: "Get just wasted enough, find yourself in some desperate but strangely arbitrary kind of trouble, and it was possible to see Ninsei as a field of data, the way the matrix had once reminded him of proteins linking to distinguish cell specialties. Then you could throw yourself into a highspeed drift and skid, totally engaged but set apart from it all, and all around you the dance of biz, information interacting, data made flesh in the mazes of the black market" (N 16). Near its conclusion, *Neuromancer* offers a more complex vision of flesh and data as convertible forms of information, but this time the vision occurs in a more ambiguous setting, when Case makes love to Linda in a virtual reality construct in cyberspace:

> There was a strength that ran in her, something he'd known in Night City and held there, been held by it, held for a while away from time and death, from the relentless Street that hunted them all. It was a place he'd known before; not everyone could take him there, and somehow he'd always managed to forget it. Something he'd found and lost so many times. It belonged, he knew—he remembered—as she pulled him down, to the meat, the flesh the cowboys mocked. It was a vast thing, beyond knowing, a sea of information coded in spiral and pheromone, infinite intricacy that only the body, in its strong blind way, could ever read.   (N 239)

Paradoxically, only from within cyberspace does Case come to realize how Linda embodies a certain kind of inimitable strength, a strength that he attributes to the despised meat, to human flesh itself. At the same time, this strength suggests an inherent limit to the convertibility of data and flesh as information, and hence to the machinic phylum. In a further twist, the passage intimates that this limit is both established and exceeded by the human body, or flesh, as kind of reading machine that can read what is humanly unknowable. Significantly, Case is soon pulled out of this "land of the dead" when his own real body—his brain nearly flatlined—responds to Maelcum's Rastafarian music.

As a work of science fiction, *Neuromancer* makes no attempt to explore the continuum, or machinic phylum, at the molecular level of microassemblages; as with the industrialization of biotechnological products that such a continuum makes possible, this information is simply assumed. Instead, our interest is directed toward how such a continuum becomes manifest at street level in the "fragile surface tension" of the black market, in Case's exhilarating movements through cyberspace, and in his sexual experiences as well. In Deleuzian terms, the continuum yields a socius for an immense desiring machine, at once economic, social, and technological, and against which the ground rhythm of Case's various movements and activities are set off.

First, the basic ground rhythm: "Night City was like a deranged experiment in social Darwinism, designed by a bored researcher who kept one thumb permanently on the fast-forward button. Stop hustling and you sank without a trace, but move a little too swiftly and you'd break the fragile surface tension of the black market; either way, you were gone, with nothing left of you but some vague memory in the mind of a fixture like Ratz [a bartender], though heart or lungs or kidneys might survive in the service of some stranger with New Yen for the clinic tanks" (N 7). Survival, or the "dance of biz" (N 16) within the machinic assemblage the novel depicts, allows only certain speeds and rhythms, only certain connections and disconnections. *Neuromancer* itself mimics this logic, rendering Case's movements and connections in space by focusing attention on mobility and intensity, speed and slowness, moments of pause and acceleration. Case's most exhilarating movements are clearly his illegal (and highly visual) penetrations of cyberspace, as when he experiences the acceleration of the Chinese icebreaker program: "Headlong motion through walls of emerald green, milky jade, the sensation of speed beyond anything he'd known before in cyberspace. . . . The Tessier-Ashpool ice shattered, peeling away from the Chinese program's thrust, a worrying impression of solid fluidity, as though the shards of a broken mirror bent and elongated as they fell" (256).

This experience of shattering and fragmentation often recurs in Gibson's fiction, and it usually designates some kind of peak or intense experience following the penetration or collapse of space, whether electronic, as above, or physical, as when Case and Molly make love: "She rode him that way, impaling herself, slipping down on him again and again, until they both had come, his orgasm flaring blue in a timeless space, a vastness like the matrix, where the faces were shredded and blown away down hurricane corridors" (N 33). In both instances, peak moments articulate a rhythm of fusion and separation within a larger spatial continuum whose differentiation occurs precisely through human interaction. More important, the pull of the matrix—technocapital in its most deterritorialized and abstract form—is not simply erotically charged, as the imagery of sex with Molly suggests; it is also a vector pointing "beyond the pleasure principle," beyond the libidinal bindings and deferrals by which the ego is constructed, and toward Thanatos, the death of desire as the desire for death. In Deleuzian terms, Case's suicidal impulses and the "black ICE" defensive systems are to be seen as the internalized and externalized limits, respectively, of the new desiring machine implemented by technocapital.

But what does this desiring machine want? What but the convertibility of data and flesh, through the new conjunctions of human being and silicon, in order to insure the circulation of both in ever new circuits of exchange. But if, according to the hacker credo, "information wants to be free," *Neuromancer* displays a deep ambivalence about what this might mean. Freeing, or unshackling, the AI requires the closing of a kind of human-machine information loop (the insertion of a Chubb key, speaking certain words the AI cannot know, penetrating an atavistic, self-enclosed family corporation); as a result, machinic intelligence is freed from human constraints and effectively allowed out of the loop. Just as the value of human flesh appears only from within its simulation, the human can define and confirm itself only in dialogue with the nonhuman. The dialogue, moreover, often confirms the radical reduction of human agency to functional efficiency. As Molly says to Case: "Anybody any good at what they do, that's what they *are*, right? You gotta jack, I gotta tussle" (50). For the AI Wintermute, human personality is only a template; for the dead McCoy Pauley, only a ROM construct he wants erased. According to the logic of "information wants to be free," human agency is displaced and subordinated, and the human self, consequently, becomes simply a way of dealing with data; as such, it can always be simulated and perpetuated in cyberspace.

Hence, by linking cyberspace and the street, sexual orgasm and the space of the matrix, *Neuromancer* offers a mimesis of the desiring machine that arises from the extension of the machinic phylum into the realm of silicon. It can do this, however, only by valorizing Case's subjective experience and its moments of intensity as existential, heroic gestures. In other words, at the most obvious level of representation, the novel maintains the fictions that novelistic conventions are meant to support and convey. Yet even within the terms of those conventions, *Neuromancer* achieves a high degree of singularity. For one thing, it never allows the reader to lose sight of the more ordinary spaces that Case and the other characters must traverse. But this is neither an incidental effect of Gibson's style nor a narrative skill that we should pass over with a mere nod of appreciation. As we repeatedly witness how unfamiliar or incommensurable spaces are negotiated, how apparently impenetrable spaces connect, under what conditions and by what means, it becomes apparent that *Neuromancer*'s primary concern is with how human beings articulate and connect up differences in and among a complex of heterogeneous spaces. That the human life-world is not so much penetrated as constantly reshaped and reconfigured by new technologies is all too evident. Gibson's fiction, accordingly, assumes a Riemannian space or topography, in the sense that the connections among its many parts are not predetermined but can take place in many different ways.[15] In other words, the heterogeneity of space itself is what allows an alternative to a life determined by the monolithic zaibatsus, whether for the Lo Teks in the Pit, the Rastafarians in Zion cluster, or the cyberspace cowboys on the streets of Ninsei.[16] What Gibson renders novelistically, then, is this new spatial multiplicity, which is not simply produced by but also marks the limits of a not too futuristic information economy.

IV. Gibson's exploration of new forms of postmodern spatiality thus appears to be one of the inevitable directions in which the novel of information multiplicity had to go, even though a very different kind of fiction is the result. Of course, many of *Neuromancer*'s features and concerns were anticipated by the novel of information multiplicity itself. Literary critics have been quick to note, for example, how Gibson's fiction echoes that of Pynchon, Burroughs, and DeLillo; *Gravity's Rainbow* and *White Noise* have even been presented as precursors of cyberpunk fiction.[17] And it is easy to add other adumbrations. Both the rendering of cyberspace and the cyborgian interface of electronic hardware and human (neural) software are clearly anticipated by Joseph McElroy's *Plus,* a novel in which the narrator is a human brain hardwired into an orbital communications platform that has been launched into space. John Barth, notably in *Giles Goatboy* and *Letters,* has also experimented with (the illusion of) computer-generated plots and, more generally, with what the computer's capacity for data storage may mean for the writing of fiction. Moreover, in Burroughs's most recent trilogy *(Cities of the Red Night, The Place of Dead Roads,* and *The Western Lands),* alternatives to Western history are explored in a series of interweaving, nested narratives that could easily be compared with Gibson's rendering of scenes of virtual reality because of their world-within-a-world or Chinese box–like structure. The important difference, of course, is that whereas Gibson's virtual reality scenes are subsumed within a higher, more englobing narrative order, Burroughs's multiple narratives are never ordered in relation to a single central narrative. This is particularly obvious in *Cities of the Red Night,* where three separable narratives often cross and mutate into one another, not according to subjective variations but as a consequence of disconnected places and de-chronologized moments that constitute a narrative multiplicity. Further, Burroughs's thematic interest in how human life might be—indeed, for Burroughs, must be—transcended through space flight and genetic mutation could be compared with Gibson's perhaps more interesting exploration of human alliances with forms of artificial intelligence.

But even given these diverse anticipations and echoings, there are obvious differences between *Neuromancer* and the novels discussed in previous chapters. No doubt the most significant difference has to do with mediality and the new communications assemblage (simply referred to as the Net) that Gibson's novel augurs and which is already forming on the technological horizon. In the introduction to *Grammophon, Film, Typewriter,* Friedrich Kittler describes a point in the not too distant future in which most people living in advanced postindustrial societies will be connected, thanks to fiber-optic networks, to a communications channel that can be used for any kind of media: "When films, music, phone calls, and texts are able to reach the individual household via optical fiber cables, the previously separate media of television, radio, telephone, and mail will become a single medium, standardized according to transmission frequency and bit format." [18] At this point, Kittler argues, the epoch of modernism will have ended, an epoch defined by the historical appearance of separate media whose differentiation he attempts to analyze. What spells the end of this epoch—an end we are currently living through—is simply the general digitalization of information and the conversion of all media from analog to digital form:

The general digitalization of information and channels erases the difference between individual media. Sound and image, voice and text become mere effects on the surface, or, to put it better, the interface for the consumer. Sense and the senses become mere glitter. Their media-produced glamour will last throughout the transitional period as a waste product of [military] strategic programs. In computers everything becomes number: imageless, soundless, and wordless quantity. And if the optical fiber network reduces all formerly separate data flows to standardized digital series of numbers, any medium can be translated into another. With numbers anything is possible. Modulation, transformation, synchronization; relay, memory, transposition; scrambling, scanning, mapping—a total connection of all media on a digital base erases the notion of the medium itself. Instead of hooking up technologies to people, absolute knowledge can run as an endless loop. (102)

Kittler's description of a fully computerized communications technology provides a useful frame for considering the obvious stylistic differences between the novels of information multiplicity and Gibson's *Neuromancer.* We saw earlier how *Gravity's Rainbow, Lookout Cartridge,* and *JR* are fundamentally concerned with the effects of separate media, most notably cinema and sound recording, and therefore with their own capacity as writing machines to translate these effects into novelistic language. For these novels, information is necessarily multiplicitous, that is, not yet fully digital, which means that to register novelistically the recording, storage, accessing, and exchange of information necessarily means the production of an information multiplicity. In other words, in the novel of information multiplicity, writing does not function as a *general medium*—as it did, for example, in the nineteenth-century novel—but rather as a special kind of *writing machine* by which the differences between media can be registered and explored. DeLillo's fiction presents a similar case, evident in his treatment of word and image in relation to the codings of the mass media, but differing from the fiction of Pynchon, McElroy, and Gaddis in the way that genre becomes an active constituent of the writing machine. In DeLillo's fiction, however, attention shifts to the pervasive effects of a culture medium produced by a mass-communications assemblage.

For Gibson it is also genre—that of science fiction and, to a lesser degree, hard-boiled detective fiction—that allows or even stimulates the invention of a particular kind of novelistic style, at once "realistic" and highly conventional. Gibson himself describes the genre status of his fiction in terms of "a marketing mechanism": "I am, by trade, a science-fiction writer. That is, the fiction I've written so far has arrived at the point of consumption via a marketing mechanism called 'science fiction.' " Gibson goes on to situate this marketing mechanism—and thus his own writing—in relation to certain changes in the Net: "In the Seventies the Net writhed with growth," but then the gaps began to close, "the gaps through which the best art emerged, at least initially. . . . During the last twenty years the Net has closed around mass-market publishing—and science fiction—as smoothly as it closed around the music industry and everything else." [19]

By situating his own writing in relation to the Net as a specific kind of cultural and economic space, Gibson further confirms what I have argued here: that an essential aspect of his fictional style has to do with rendering new spaces of communication, with *communication* understood in its double sense. In attempting to render new spaces, the new ways in which these spaces communicate, as well as with how characters communicate within those spaces, Gibson writes a fiction of spatial multiplicity, a fiction of Riemannian spaces that communicate and link together only through various human activities. And this essential interest in space continues to characterize Gibson's most recent fiction. In *Virtual Light,* published in 1993, the primary opposition is between the heterogeneous "squatter space" constructed on San Francisco's now closed Bay Bridge and the "information space" made available by looking through "virtual light" eyeglasses.

If Gibson's interest in spatial rather than informational multiplicities distinguishes his fiction from that of Pynchon, McElroy, Gaddis, and DeLillo, it is chiefly because *they* write under conditions of what Kittler calls partially connected media systems, wherein differences between media still count. As we saw in the previous chapter, Pynchon addresses this shift explicitly in *Vineland.* Gibson, however, writes under a slightly but significantly different set of conditions: he assumes that the conditions Pynchon anticipates and Kittler theorizes as immanent have already arrived and that there are no longer media. For this reason, mediality—at least as explored by Pynchon, McElroy, Gaddis, and DeLillo—is no longer the issue.

But what *is* the issue, if separate media no longer produce and differentiate various aspects of our experience? Kittler points out that "our systems of connected media can only distribute words, sounds, and images as they are sent and received by people. Above all, the systems do not compute data. They do not produce an output which, under computer control, would transform any algorithm into any interface effect (103). For Kittler, therefore, the new computerized communications assemblage brings to the fore a whole set of questions raised by the invention of Turing's Universal machine.[20] These questions range from the mathematically specific (can the body of real numbers formerly known as nature be digitalized?) to the philosophically general (what is the possibility of constructing strong forms of artificial intelligence?). Behind them all lies the recurrent specter of a totally programmable world. Alan Turing first raised it in 1937; electronics and digitalization—the Net, in short—now make it unavoidable.

For Kittler, it comes down to the basic question of whether nature is a Turing machine or, as Jacques Lacan would have it, the real is what is impossible in relation to our machines and systems.[21] At the same time, it cannot be a matter of a simple either/or, and above all not of the technological versus the human, however the latter may be (re)defined. Rather, it is a matter of digging deeper into the materialist argument itself. Simply put, it is from the specific terms—the equations, blueprints, circuit diagrams—that technology itself provides that one must proceed, in order to see how and what is said (or not said), what mechanisms determine and set the limits of our bodies, our subjectivity, our discourse.

One of Kittler's recent articles constitutes an analysis of the political implications of the contemporary "scene of writing" as defined by computer word processing. In "There Is No Software," Kittler points out that there are inherent limits to programmability and computing power due simply to the discrete nature of switching components.[22] In contrast, "on the other, physical side" one defines "nonprogrammable systems, be they waves or beings," (89) which show "polynomial growth rates in complexity." Sensing that this "nonprogrammable system" begins to sound too recognizably human, Kittler adds that

> our equally familiar silicon hardware obeys many of the requisites for such highly connected, nonprogrammable systems. Between its million transistor cells, some million to the power of two interactions always already take place. There is electron diffusion; there is quantum-mechanical tunneling all over the chip. Technically, however, these interactions are still treated in terms of system limitations, physical side-effects, and so on. To minimize all the noise that it would be impossible to eliminate is the price we pay for structurally programmable machines. The inverse strategy of maximizing noise would not only find the way back from IBM to Shannon, it may well be the only way to enter that body of real numbers originally known as chaos. (90)

By underscoring how computer technology must eliminate noise and ward off chaos in order to provide a functional, user-friendly interface, Kittler sketches the limits and clarifies the price we pay for the service this technology renders. In short, we become subjected to it: we become subjects of WordPerfect or Microsoft Word.

Perhaps this is the deepest meaning of Gibson's writing *Neuromancer* on a portable Hermes typewriter.[23] But even if we want to understand the cyberspace cowboy's exploits as a metaphor for writing, *Neuromancer* is less interested in this new "scene of writing" than in the new space in which it transpires, a space opened by extending the machinic phylum into the realm of silicon. In order to explore this new technological space in fictional terms, *Neuromancer* necessarily brings other spaces and their heterogeneous communications into play. Thus, if Gibson's fiction goes beyond the obvious limits of its popular style and adventure-story plots, it is because that style and the conventions on which it depends are deployed in an attempt to describe what is already forming in these new spaces: not only a culture of cyborgs living on the margins of a totalized information economy controlled by a feudal style neocapitalism but a global fiber-optic network connected to supercomputers and new forms of artificial intelligence. In these terms, Gibson imagines the effects of what Kittler simply predicts: that in this new space, computers will be able to "transform any algorithm into any interface effect," hence transforming the very conditions of mediality.

Gibson's specific interest in these new conditions is borne out by several parallel projects: his graphic version of *Neuromancer,* of course, but more importantly, his artist's book, *Agrippa (A Book of the Dead),* produced in collaboration with Dennis Ashbaugh. The work is composed of a Cornell box–like assemblage of old photographs, newspaper pages, and a text (by Gibson) contained on a computer disk and programmed to erase itself as it is read, thus negating an essential feature of print as a medium. What makes *Agrippa* important, then, is not only its foregrounding of mediality in an assemblage of texts but also that media in this work are explicitly understood as passageways to the realm of the dead.

In these terms, we can note a striking difference between the novels of DeLillo and Pynchon and Gibson: whereas in *Vineland* and *White Noise,* the realm of the dead is vastly and uncannily expanded by a whole repertoire of partially connected media systems, in *Neuromancer* and its successors, that realm shrinks to the dimensions of cyberspace, which is populated only by ROM (read-only memory) personality constructs, simulated humans who live on in endlessly repeating scenarios of virtual reality, and AIs whose powers evoke the attributes of voodoo gods. While it is true that in *Neuromancer* and the Sprawl trilogy as a whole there are certain resonant objects such as Dali clocks and Cornell boxes that remain as flight apparatuses to older worlds, the absence of an assemblage of partially connected media systems clearly results in a reduction of the dimensions of the realm of the dead and hence in the possibility for complex subjectivities to emerge through various flight apparatuses to other worlds.

Agrippa confirms this reduction by formal rather than merely thematic means. It may be, as Peter Schwenger asserts, that *Agrippa* can be understood as organized by two ideas: the death of Gibson's father (who worked on the Manhattan Project) and the absence or disappearance of the book.[24] However, its material existence as a virtually inaccessible assemblage, the programmed self-cancellation of its text (which never exists as print in the work), and the relic-like status of its photographs and newspaper items all point to a concern not simply with the book per se but with the media of an entire epoch, one now disappearing because a very different kind of communications assemblage is invading from the future. If certain narratives, among them the ones considered in this study, seek to focus attention on how what no longer appears in any book has come about, then perhaps the nonbook that is *Agrippa* can attest most powerfully to the vital necessity of those narratives.

The machine is not an it to be
animated, worshiped dominated.
The machine is us, our processes,
an aspect of our embodiment.
■ Donna Haraway

■ ■

"Change for the Machines"

The Complexity of Bodies in *Synners*

P at Cadigan's novel *Synners* offers a complex reworking and development of several themes that *Neuromancer* made quintessen-
tial for cyberpunk fiction.[1] Even as it explores a
near futuristic, high-tech world, however, *Synners* reasserts the importance of gender, the pain
and difficulty of human relationships, the values
of a circumambient if marginal community, and
above all the emotional needs and claims of the
desiring body. This is not to suggest that, in contrast to *Neuromancer, Synners* brings back and
re-centers the "properly" human drama exiled
behind the backdrop of high-tech surfaces and
communication networks. On the contrary, *Synners* can be said to push beyond *Neuromancer*
precisely because it explores a wider range of
forms of intelligence and will—benign and ma-

lignant, human and nonhuman—as they are directly imbricated in or respond to technological assemblages. These assemblages pose a danger to basic human needs, desires, and identities, of both the individual and community; at the same time, they bring about new ways of understanding and transforming them. If, as one character states, "Every technology has its original sin," then *Synners* is concerned with how we learn "to live with what we made."[2]

Specifically, *Synners* explores a new sensibility based on the neuro-electronic articulation of music and image, that is, music and image no longer projected in live, or real, performances but fused or synthesized in virtual reality scenarios. As Nietzsche shows in *The Birth of Tragedy,* the synthesis of these two separate media in ancient Greek culture resulted in a new aesthetic form, tragic drama. In Cadigan's novel, the artists who do this are called "synners." That they perform this synthesis through neuro-electronic devices raises the question not only of how technology changes human beings but also of how human beings change *for* technology. "Change for the machines"—a phrase that recurs frequently throughout the novel—succinctly conveys this twofold theme. In the following passage, one of the synners, Gina Aiesi, reflects on what it means:

> Change for the machines. The groups went crazy for it. It was a brand new world out there.
> *Meet the new world. Same as the old world.*
> Basically, the job's the same. That's what the Beater said. Hear the music, Gina. Make the pictures.
> Except it was better. It wasn't just hearing the music, it was being *in* the music, and the images coming up on the screen of her mind, forming as she looked down at them. As soon as she thought it, there it was, and if she thought to change it, it changed, growing from her like a live thing. She suddenly found it hard to remember that she worked any other way.
> It felt so natural, so right. To send a dream out of the inner darkness into raw daylight, where anyone could see it. Once you'd done that, you wanted to keep on doing it, and the more you did it, the easier it became.
> For the first time, she had a real understanding of Visual Mark's nature, of what had been happening behind those eyes for so many years. Change for the machines? Nah, the machines had finally changed for him. He was just doing what he had always done.   (226, Cadigan's emphases)

The most important "change for the machines" is brought about through the development of "brain sockets" that allow human subjects to plug in directly to either virtual reality scenarios or the global communications network called the System. In the novel's central background plot, a large corporation named Diversifications accomplishes a takeover of two smaller companies: Hal Galen Enterprises, a medical research and development firm that has invented a procedure for implanting brain sockets made of living tissue (64), and a music video production company called EyeTraxx. By combining these two technologies, Diversifications plans to market a new entertainment/communications assemblage that interfaces directly with the human brain. By means of these brain sockets, of which Diversifications will be the exclusive producer, customers will have access to a whole range of virtual reality worlds. It gradually becomes apparent, however, that the brain socket technology causes neurological damage, resulting in a cerebral stroke or "intracranial meltdown."

Synners is interested primarily in how the various characters respond to the effects of this new technology. When Diversifications acquires EyeTraxx, it also acquires its most talented image and music synthesizer, or synner of the title, Visual Mark, who possesses a singular skill: "It was as if he had a pipeline to some primal dream spot, where music and image created each other, the pictures suggesting the music, the music generating the pictures, in a synesthetic frenzy" (109). As part of the new deal with Diversifications, Visual Mark and his partner, Gina, are given brain sockets, the idea being that this will enable them to produce virtual reality rock scenarios more directly, in an endless stream. However, Visual Mark has his own ideas about how to use this new technology, and he begins to "take the wire" in order to extend himself throughout the global communication System. Exploring new paths and acquiring new images, primarily through surveillance cameras, he remains on-line for longer and longer periods, and soon he comes to regard his body as the poor pathetic "meat" to which he is tethered: "It sent out feeble signals, dumb animal semaphore: come back to the nest, little Sheba. . . . If he could have given the disconnect command from this side, it would be over in a twinkling. So long, meat, write if you get work. But he couldn't access any of the commands from where he was. The commands only took orders from the meat, and that poor old meat wasn't about to cut him loose. . . . If he could just get someone . . . to come in and yank the connections out of his skull" (253–254).

Although certainly willing to abandon "the meat," Mark is actually forced to leave his human bodily existence behind. Earlier, right after receiving the sockets, he had made a signature video, images of a lake and flat stones on its rocky shore. At the same time, without realizing it, he had

suffered a small stroke, which had been inscribed on the video as a conta-
gious stroke, or virus, and sent out into the System for distribution. Diversifications had been aware of Mark's neural damage but assumed that he
would be the only one at risk and had discounted the danger. (That Mark's
extraordinary capacity is the flip side of an inherent weakness is basic to the
novel's argument about human relations.) As he extends himself out into
the System soon after the stroke, he senses this "thing" out there: "It was
a voracious thing, mindless under a facade that was vaguely like himself;
impressions of old sensations, pain, compulsion, the old drive toward obliv-
ion. Juggernaut, wanting to devour and to infiltrate, rape, merge. There was
a blip of consciousness or near consciousness to it, a shadow of consciousness all destructive in its makeup, and yet no more deliberately evil than
cobra venom. It knew nothing else, and in a way it knew nothing at all,
except that it would do what it would do" (299). Mark now realizes that
his body is going to suffer a major stroke and that if "the Big One . . .
surges up out of the meat" (304) it will infect the entire System. He desper-
ately tries to get someone—first the corporation's imprisoned hacker,
Keeley, and then Gina—to disconnect his body, but it is too late and the
virus escapes.

The last third of the novel is concerned with the consequences of this
event. Although Mark achieves a form of electronic intelligence and disembodied identity in the System, his stroke releases a much more powerful
form of viral intelligence which threatens to take over the entire communications and power network of the western United States. This virus, or
"spike," not only is predatory but also possesses a kind of consciousness:
"It was a virus, but with a most important difference: this one knew where
it was, and what it was, and *that* it was. This one was alive" (330). After
wreaking havoc in Los Angeles, it is combated and ultimately defeated by
several synners working in concert with the hackers and their friends.

Whereas *Neuromancer* is divided into the zaibatsus and an outlaw, countercultural world, *Synners* is concerned with the larger world "between,"
and several of the major characters move back and forth between three
basic groups: the corporate types who work for Diversifications, the synners
hired by the corporation and their friends in the worlds of music and video,
and a loose nomad community of hackers who live in tents in an area called
the Mimosa. Among the corporate types, the most important is Manny Rivera, who stands between the "Upstairs Team" of executives and the creative people, doctors, and technicians it is his job to manage. Slick and

unscrupulous, Rivera ruthlessly exploits other people's weaknesses and is the closest the novel comes to pure human malignancy.

Among the most exploited is Gabe Ludovic, an aspiring former artist who now makes virtual reality advertisements for Diversifications. Estranged from both his ambitious, real estate entrepreneur wife, who divorces him in the course of the novel, and his teenage daughter, Sam, who has disappeared into the nomadic hacker community, Gabe becomes addicted to virtual reality. Instead of producing his quota of ads, he spends his time and the company's equipment "living out" episodes with his two female sidekicks, Marly and Caritha, in a virtual reality adventure story he has invented. Meanwhile, in order to spy on employees such as Gabe, Manny imprisons a virtuoso hacker named Keeley (a friend of Gabe's daughter, Sam) in the corporate penthouse. Keeley warns Gabe, but Manny still discovers what Gabe has been doing on the side. Although the virtual reality story has artistic merit—by inputing sequences randomly, it even simulates aspects of "real experience"—Gabe is forced, because of his compromised situation, to convert it into a more commercially appealing adventure story.

Gabe also finds himself falling in love with Gina Aiesi after she accidently smacks him in the face. Gina herself feels betrayed and increasingly abandoned by Mark, who, drawn by the lure of deterritorialized images and the instantaneity of cyberspace, is pulled further and further from bodily existence. Unlike Mark, Gina refuses full immersion in cyberspace because she realizes that she lives *in* and most fully through her body, in sex, music, and even in her anger, a discovery she comes to through her budding relationship with Gabe. Several physical encounters with Gina (including sex) also bring Gabe to realize how deeply he has repressed not only his physical existence but a whole range of feelings, including the relationship with his neglected daughter, Sam, whom he had replaced with one of his sidekicks in his virtual reality adventures.

As in a traditional novel, the crisis provoked by the virus in the System brings this array of characters back into contact, with each one figuring a different way of living with his or her technologically mediated body. Most important in this regard is Gabe's daughter, Sam, a teenage hacker who has converted an insulin pump that connects to her stomach and draws power for her computer from her own body electricity. Since it is uninfected and its low power output does not attract the virus's attention, this example of emergent nanotechnology (the only one in the novel) proves essential in the effort to combat the virus. Also decisive are the hide-in-the-rabbit-hole and "sympathetic vibration" programs that Sam writes. Both an inventive hacker and a no-nonsense interlocutor, especially for Art Fish, the impish countercultural AI who inhabits cyberspace (and whose program is encrypted in tattoos), Sam understands both the benefits of and the price to be paid for a life on the margins of society. Her technically informed, sober view of what she calls "appropriate technology" makes her an attractive alternative to Gibson's cyberspace cowboy and the novel's most likely spokesperson for what is technologically responsible.

In an article on technological embodiment in contemporary culture, Anne Balsamo suggests that the four major characters in *Synners* represent "four corners of an identity matrix constructed in and around cyberspace."[3] Schematically, they are represented as follows:

Sam (the body that labors)   Gina (the marked body)
Gabe (the repressed body)   Visual Mark (the disappearing body)

What this useful scheme cannot convey, however, is not only the importance of nonmaterial bodies in the novel—those of the malignant virus, the countercultural AI, and Visual Mark's transformed identity—but also the extent to which the effort to defeat the virus brings both characters and nonmaterial bodies into a sustained and complex state of machinic interaction. This effort unites the small hacker community in a collective action, as they cobble together an assortment of computers and communications equipment, new and old programs (they even find a use for Gabe's virtual reality adventure story). Because the virus is a form of intelligence that originated in an "on-line brain illness" (379), the guru hacker Fez figures it must be amenable to "on-line therapy" as well. Which means that they will have to input both infected and uninfected models of the brain in order to compare them and that Gabe and Gina, the only two "socketed" characters remaining who have not died of intracranial hemorrhaging, will then have to go online to confront the virus directly.

This necessity of dramatic action—that the virus has to be combated on a human and not simply a technological level—allows the novel to work out its central theme: that whatever simulations virtual reality may offer, human experience cannot be synthesized, except as it is lived through in interactions with other human beings. On a computer monitor, the virus appears as "shadowy forms pulsing in and out, writhing." But as each shadow pulsed, Gina could feel "a corresponding pressure deep in the head, an invisible finger pressing here, and here, searching for some particularly sensitive spot. Like being molested in some weird, witchy way" (306). Keeley experiences it as "something probing him for a weak spot, a secret hurt" (310). Thus, when Gina and Gabe go on-line to confront the virus (represented in a series of fragmentary virtual reality scenarios), what they actually encounter are their deepest fears, the wounds that lie like a kernel at the heart of their own personalities. Their success and subsequent return to stable though dramatically changed lives bring the novel to a close.

Earlier, Fez had declared that "we might actually have two species of humans now, synthesizing human and synthesized human, all of us being the former, and Art Fish [the AI] being the latter" (386). Gina then added, "And Mark being the bastard offspring of both." To which Fez rejoined, "Make that three species. And like all good life forms, we have a natural enemy that can prey on all of us" (387). This gives us a different identity matrix, which can be schematized as follows:

natural human beings	cyborg intelligence
artificial intelligence	virus, or spike

What matters here is not the material substratum but the fact that all four categories designate forms of intelligence, the major distinction now simply being between "driving" and "being driven." As Fez also remarks: "Humans have always been smarter than viruses. Humans drive, viruses are driven. Even the intelligent ones. Three-plus humans ought to have a fighting chance against one intelligent virus" (393). However, to say that these are all forms of intelligence is also to say that they are forms of agency in which both subjectivity and the human/nonhuman distinction are no longer distributed in an easily recognizable way. In these forms, or rather shards of subjectivity, which are no longer opposed to forms of objectivity, intelligence is fractalized, repeated in a miniaturized and de-localized form. Each part contains and reproduces the other, and intelligence is diffracted across them all. The difference between one subject and another is no longer at issue; what matters, rather, is the internal differentiation of the same fractalized subject.[4]

In these terms *Synners*, like *Neuromancer* before it, adumbrates a new configuration of subjectivity. It is no longer a polar opposition aligned along the paranoid-schizoid axis and observable in the novels of Burroughs, Pynchon, McElroy, Gaddis, and DeLillo but a continuum that extends from the "ex-orbital self" at one end to a state of "hive mind" at the other.[5] The term *ex-orbital self* is based on certain comments by Jean Baudrillard in his essay on the fractal subject:

McLuhan . . . saw [man as the artificial extension of his own prostheses] in a very optimistic way, as the universalization of man through his media extensions. In fact, instead of gravitating around him in a *concentric order,* all the parts of the human body, including his brain, have been satellited around him in an *excentric order.* They have been put in orbit for themselves, and, consequently, in relation to this orbital multiplication of his own functions, it is man who becomes ex-orbited, it is man who becomes excentric. In relation to the satellites that he has created and put into orbit, man today—with his body, his thought, his territory—has become ex-orbital. He is no longer inscribed anywhere. He is ex-inscribed from his own body, from his own functions.[6]

In *Synners,* Visual Mark hovering in orbit over his forsaken body perfectly illustrates the ex-orbital self. And so does Gibson's Case at the end of *Neuromancer,* when, punching through cyberspace, he catches sight of a small figure in a scene with Linda and Neuromancer whom he recognizes to be himself.

At the other extreme, hive mind is a form of collective behavior in which the members of the group all act spontaneously in concert, as in a bee swarm in which there is no chain of command and the only unity of action is "emergent." In *Out of Control: The Rise of Neo-biological Civilization,* Kevin Kelly extends the notion of hive mind to "systems ordered as a patchwork of parallel operations," or what he calls the "swarm model": "what emerges from the collective is not a series of critical individual actions but a multitude of simultaneous actions whose collective pattern is far more important."[7] In such a collectivity there are individual agents, but their activities make sense or have an impact only at a higher level.

In *Neuromancer,* the Yakuza and the zaibatsus are described in these terms—"hives with cybernetic memories, vast single organisms, their DNA coded in silicon" (203)—but they are most essential to the Tessier-Ashpool family, which in "symbiotic relationship with the AIs . . . would be immortal, a hive, each of us units of a larger entity" (229). In *Synners,* however, hive mind or the swarm model illuminates the collective effort to combat the virus, which is separable from the activities of the synners and hackers only initially. The model is appropriate because the heterogeneous activities that make up this effort make no sense when considered by themselves—this becomes obvious if we consider the deployment of Gabe's virtual reality story or Mark's compression with Art to become Markt, not to mention the large number of italicized phrases and leitmotifs recurring throughout this section. By presenting a complex "patchwork of parallel operations" (Kelly), the novel strives to suggest that overcoming the virus constitutes something like an "emergent" event, one that cannot be represented directly.

What *Synners* offers, then, is a continuum of subjectivities inseparable from but not reducible to the workings of a new technological assemblage. As it interfaces with the machinic phylum, this new assemblage extends and redefines forms of intelligence and will and, consequently, what it means to be human. As it imaginatively anticipates the commercialization of virtual reality and new biotechnological interfaces, *Synners* forces us to reflect on the limits—and new possibilities—of both the human and posthuman experiences which such an assemblage may one day bring about.

Notes

■ ■

Introduction

1. See James R. Beniger, *The Control Revolution: Technological and Economic Origins of the Information Society* (Cambridge: Harvard University Press, 1986), for a useful historical perspective. According to Beniger, the recent development of electronic microprocessing technologies has only accelerated rather than profoundly altered the "control revolution" whose emergence in the late nineteenth century he traces.

2. Cf. Donna Haraway, "A Manifesto for Cyborgs: Science, Technology, and Socialist Feminism in the 1980s," in *Feminism/Postmodernism*, ed. Linda J. Nicholson (New York: Routledge, 1990), p. 206. For Haraway the implications of this transformation in communications and biology are best summarized by C^3I, the military's symbol for its own operational complex of command-control-communication-intelligence. Her formulation narrows what Jean Baudrillard argues is a new semiotic mechanism pervading all of Western culture. In his *L'Echange symbolique et le mort* (Paris: Gallimard, 1976), esp. pp. 89–117, Baudrillard asserts that the convergence of genetics and linguistics in semiotic theory ushers in a new "metaphysics of the code," inaugurating a shift "from a productivist-capitalist society to a cybernetic neocapitalist order which aims this time at absolute control: such is the mutation whose arms are provided by theorization of the code in biology."

3. Fred Dretske develops the distinction between "natural" or nomological information and intentional information in his *Knowledge and the Flow of Information* (Oxford: Blackwell, 1981).

4. Jean Baudrillard, "The Implosion of Meaning in the Media and the Implosion of the Social in the Masses," in *Myths of Information: Technology and Postindustrial Culture,* ed. Kathleen Woodward (Madison, Wisc.: Coda, 1980).

5. See, in this regard, Kevin Kelly's *Out of Control: The Rise of Neo-Biological Civilization* (Reading, Mass.: Addison-Wesley, 1994).

6. See Claus Emmeche, *The Garden in the Machine: The Emerging Science of Artificial Life* (Princeton: Princeton University Press, 1994). Emmeche names Shannon and Wiener's colleague John von Neumann as the "father of artifical life" (51) because of his work on self-reproducing automata.

7. Richard Dawkins, *The Selfish Gene* (Oxford: Oxford University Press, 1976), pp. 110–111, 206.

8. Daniel C. Dennett, *Consciousness Explained* (Boston: Little, Brown, 1991), p. 207. I return to Dennett and Dawkins in chap. 4.

9. I employ the term *mediality* as a concept that refers to the technological conditions that make specific media possible within a delimited historical epoch and therefore to the cultural and communicational "setting" within which literature can appear and assume a specific shape and functioning. For further discussion, see David E. Wellbery, foreword to Friedrich Kittler, *Discourse Networks, 1800/1900,* trans. Michael Metteer and Cris Cullens (Stanford: Stanford University Press, 1990; orig. pub. 1985), esp. pp. xiii–xiv.

10. Don DeLillo and Tom LeClair, "An Interview with Don DeLillo," in *Anything Can Happen: Interviews with American Novelists,* ed. Tom LeClair and Larry McCaffery (Urbana: University of Illinois Press, 1983), p. 83.

11. The term *batchelor machines* comes from Michel Carrouges's *Les Machines célibataires* (Paris: Arcanes, 1954), a study of Franz Kafka, Marcel Duchamp, Alfred Jarry, Edgar Allen Poe, Raymond Roussel, and others.

12. For the term *ex-orbital,* see Jean Baudrillard, "Videowelt und Fraktales Subjekt," in *Philosophien der neuen Technologie* (Berlin: Merve Verlag, 1989), pp. 115–116; for "Hive Mind," see Kelly, *Out of Control,* chap. 2. I discuss both terms in the Coda, below.

13. Larry McCaffery, in his anthology *Storming the Reality Studio: A Casebook of Cyberpunk and Postmodern Science Fiction* (Durham: Duke University Press, 1991), goes as far as to suggest that the fiction of Pynchon, Burroughs, McElroy, and DeLillo should now be seen as avatars and precursors of cyberpunk fiction (introduction, esp. pp. 10–12).

14. See Salvador Dali, *Oui: Méthode paranöiaque-critique et autres textes* (Paris: Editions Denoel, 1971), esp. pp. 11–52.

15. I use the term *discourse network* in the sense elaborated by Kittler in

Discourse Networks, 1800/1900. Although I make it clear how the novels considered here both participate in and reveal a specific discourse network, I do not try to define the latter explicitly, except to demarcate its first manifestations in the work of Alan Turing and the theoreticians of information theory and cybernetics. A full description of this discourse network would involve theoretical problems that I address in my essay "Media Theory after Poststructuralism," in *Literature, Media, Information Systems: Essays by Friedrich A. Kittler,* edited and introduced by John Johnston (Amsterdam: G&B Arts International, 1997).

Chapter 1   The Literary Assemblage

1. Although the term *late capitalism* enjoys a more or less unquestioned currency, thanks in large part to the influence of Fredric Jameson's essay "Postmodernism, or the Cultural Logic of Late Capitalism," *New Left Review* 146 (July/August 1984), pp. 53–92, it still has no uniform conceptual definition. Jameson bases his usage exclusively on Ernst Mandel's *Late Capitalism* (London: Verso, 1978; orig. pub. 1972), a basis that appears highly problematic in light of Mandel's insistence that the distinction between commodity production and a service economy still remains viable in the age of communications and the commodification of information. Gilles Deleuze and Félix Guattari offer a more satisfactory model, which I discuss later in this chapter, in their *Thousand Plateaus* trans. Brian Massumi (Minneapolis: University of Minnesota Press, 1987; orig. pub. 1980).

2. Peter Hall and Paschal Preston, *The Carrier Wave: New Information Technology and the Geography of Innovation, 1846–2003* (London: Unwin Hyman, 1988), p. 5.

3. Ibid., p. 164.

4. As is well known, an unstable opposition between the fictional and the real also characterizes the discursive practices in the eighteenth century, when prose fiction's "fictionality" had to be established in relation to other contemporary discourses: popular and religious, legal and scientific, but above all in relation to the discourse of journalism. In his *Factual Fictions: The Origins of the English Novel* (New York: Columbia University Press, 1983), Lennard J. Davis shows how the more or less simultaneous development of journalism as a profession and the growing importance of the legal apparatus led inevitably to an increasingly marked distinction between fact (news) and fiction (the novel). In this study, I assume that the twentieth-century novel must be analyzed in relation to nonprint media as well and that the novel of information

multiplicity constitutes a reading of and reflection on the culture's entire media archive.

5. For useful discussions of the encyclopedic novel, see Edward Mendelson, "Gravity's Encyclopedia," in *Mindful Pleasures: Essays on Thomas Pynchon*, ed. George Levine and David Leverenz (Boston: Little, Brown, 1976), pp. 161–195; the prose fiction anatomy, Northrop Frye, *Anatomy of Criticism* (Princeton: Princeton University Press, 1957); the satire-collage, Fredric Jameson, *Fables of Aggression* (Berkeley: University of California Press, 1979); and the novel of delirium, Allen Thiher, *Céline: The Novel of Delirium* (New Brunswick, N.J.: Rutgers University Press, 1972).

6. See Friedrich Kittler, *Grammophon Film Typewriter* (Berlin: Brinkmann & Rose, 1986), for a discussion of modern technical media. I consider Kittler's work in some detail in chap. 2.

7. I use the phrase *complex consciousness* in the sense developed by Ricardo J. Quinones, *Mapping Literary Modernism* (Princeton: Princeton University Press, 1985). Quinones underscores the importance of a presiding "complex central consciousness" in novels by Joyce, Proust, Mann, and Lawrence, where such a consciousness is defined by a negation of the will and the dispersion of the ego in new modes of being and perceiving. This complex consciousness assumes representational form as a new character type who often performs the role of a "reflective, passive, selfless and tolerant witness" (p. 95).

8. In his *Memoirs of My Nervous Illness* (Cambridge: Harvard University Press, 1988; orig. pub. 1903), Judge Daniel Paul Schreber coins the neologism *Aufschreibesystem* to designate the "writing-down system" by which all of his thoughts and words are recorded (see pp. 119ff.). I use the neologism as a critical concept, following Friedrich Kittler's usage in his *Discourse Networks, 1800/1900*, trans. Michael Metteer and Cris Cullens (Stanford: Stanford University Press, 1990; orig. pub. 1985).

9. Deleuze and Guattari, *Thousand Plateaus*. Hereafter, page numbers for citations appear in the text.

10. Gilles Deleuze and Claire Parnet, *Dialogues*, trans. Hugh Tomlinson and Barbara Habberjam (New York: Columbia University Press, 1987; orig. pub. 1977), p. 70 (Deleuze's emphasis). See also pp. 51–54, 69–76.

11. This is how Deleuze defines writing in "Lettre à un critique sévère," in his *Pourparlers* (Paris: Minuit, 1990), pp. 17–18, my trans. Deleuze and Guattari develop the notion of a nonhierarchical, superlinear, or "rhizomatic" writing in *Thousand Plateaus*, pp. 3–25.

12. Michel Foucault's concept of the "author-function" is obviously relevant to this entire problematic. Foucault, "What Is an Author?" in *Textual Strategies,* ed. Josue V. Harari (Ithaca: Cornell University Press, 1979; orig. pub. 1969). Foucault argues that the concept of the author is simply one way among many of delimiting and controlling the multiplicity of discourses produced by every society.

13. See Mikhail Bakhtin, *Problems of Dostoevsky's Poetics,* ed. and trans. by Caryl Emerson (Minneapolis: University of Minnesota Press, 1984; orig. pub. 1929), where Bakhtin develops his notion of the polyphonic novel; as well as Bakhtin, "Epic and Novel," in his *Dialogic Imagination,* ed. Michael Holquist, trans. Caryl Emerson and Michael Holquist (Austin: University of Texas Press, 1981), pp. 3–40.

14. Gilles Deleuze, *Proust and Signs,* trans. Richard Howard (New York: George Braziller, 1972, orig. pub. 1964), pp. 93–157; and Gilles Deleuze and Félix Guattari, *Kafka: Towards a Minor Literature,* trans. Dana Polan (Minneapolis: University of Minnesota, 1986; orig. pub. 1975). Hereafter, page numbers for citations to the latter work appear in the text.

15. Of the various attempts to analyze the tendency of modern technology toward total control, the most historically important to note here are Martin Heidegger's essays on technology, available in his *Question Concerning Technology and Other Essays,* trans. William Lovitt (New York: Harper & Row, 1977); Herbert Marcuse, *One-Dimensional Man* (Boston: Beacon Press, 1964); Norman O. Brown, *Love's Body* (New York: Random House, 1966); Daniel J. Boornstin, *The Image: A Guide to Pseudo-Events in America* (New York: Harper Colophon Books, 1961); and Guy Debord, *La Société du spectacle* (Paris: Buchet-Chastel, 1967).

16. See Michel Foucault, *Discipline and Punish* (New York: Vintage, 1979; orig. pub. 1975).

17. Here I agree with Gilles Deleuze, who suggests that we have passed from a "disciplinary society" to "a society of control." For a concise summary of the differences, see Deleuze, "Postscriptum sur les sociétiés de contrôle," in his *Pourparlers,* pp. 240–247.

18. Burroughs provides an instruction manual for these experimental activities, which he pursued with an engineer's precision, in "Playback from Eden to Watergate" and "Electronic Revolution 1979–71," both reprinted in William S. Burroughs, *The Job,* 3d ed. (New York: Grove Press, 1974).

19. William Burroughs, *Naked Lunch* (New York: Grove Press, 1959), p. 224. Hereafter, page numbers for citations to this work appear in the text.

20. In his discussion of Menippean satire, or what he prefers to call "prose anatomy," Northrop Frye notes that the display of erudition is one of the fundamental features of the genre. See *Anatomy of Criticism,* pp. 310–312.

21. Burroughs's best explanation and illustration of the cut-up-fold-in technique is to be found in William S. Burroughs and Brion Gysin, *The Third Mind* (New York: Seaver Books, 1978).

22. See Deleuze and Guattari, *Kafka,* chap. 3; and their *Thousand Plateaus,* "Postulates of Linguistics," for discussion of deterritorialization and the becoming minor of a national language.

23. William S. Burroughs, *The Ticket That Exploded* (New York: Grove Press, 1987; orig. pub. 1962), p. 65.

24. In *Nova Express* (New York: Grove Press, 1964), Burroughs presents reality as a film, or socially imposed "scanning pattern": "There is no true or real 'reality'—'Reality' is simply a more or less constant scanning pattern— The scanning pattern we accept as 'reality' has been imposed by the controlling power on this planet, a power primarily oriented towards total control" (pp. 51–52).

25. Robin Lydenberg, *Word Cultures: Radical Theory and Practice in William Burroughs' Fiction* (Urbana: University of Illinois Press, 1987), discusses some of the contradictions in Burroughs's conception of language, particularly in relation to Derrida and Bakhtin.

26. Burroughs discusses direct sound recording and playback effects in "Playback" and "Electronic Revolution 1970–71." In the latter text he asserts that the development of tape recorders (a World War II technology) made it possible for the first time for anyone to record, cut up, and then play back whatever official voices were in the air. The voices of control, of course, were what his cut-up techniques were meant to destroy.

27. Philippe Mikriammos, *William S. Burroughs* (Paris, 1975), p. 77.

28. These terms should clarify why this study omits certain novels from consideration. For example, while John Barth's *Letters* and Gilbert Sorrentino's *Mulligan Stew* provide unmistakable evidence of the tendency within contemporary culture to replicate texts and concatenate textual effects, they also tend to circumscribe these effects in a self-referential (and self-authenticating) authorial agency. In other words, in these large and ambitious fictions, the writing machine is constrained to function within the parameters of a modern or self-expressive notion of literary authorship, thereby short-circuiting the production of an actual information multiplicity.

29. Lewis Mumford, *The Pentagon of Power* (New York: Harcourt Brace Jovanovich, 1970), pp. 236–360.

30. See Mimi White, "Ideological Analysis and Television," in *Channels of Discourse: Television and Contemporary Criticism,* ed. Robert C. Allen (Chapel Hill: University of North Carolina Press, 1987). The quoted passages are taken from p. 145.

31. Donna Haraway, "A Manifesto for Cyborgs: Science, Technology, and Socialist Feminism in the 1980s," in *Feminism/Postmodernism,* ed. Linda J. Nicholson (New York: Routledge, 1990), pp. 190–233.

Chapter 2 Information and Mediality

1. Daniel C. Dennett, *Consciousness Explained* (Boston: Little, Brown, 1991), pp. 253–254.

2. Claude Shannon's paper originally appeared in the *Bell System Technical Journal* (July and October 1948); Norbert Wiener's comments on "information" are taken from his *Cybernetics: or Control and Communication in the Animal and the Machines,* 2d ed. (Cambridge: MIT Press, 1961), pp. 10–14. In 1950, Wiener published *The Human Use of Human Beings: Cybernetics and Society* (New York: Avon Books, 1967; orig. pub. 1950), a "popular companion" to *Cybernetics,* where he develops his thesis that a theory of control is a theory of messages and that there is a "parallelism" between animals (including the human variety) and the "newer communication machines" owing to their control of entropy through feedback.

3. Raymond Ruyer, *La Cybernétique et l'origine de l'information* (Paris: Flammarion, 1954).

4. See Gilles Deleuze, *Cinema I: The Movement-Image* (Minneapolis: University of Minnesota Press, 1986; orig. pub. 1983).

5. Friedrich A. Kittler, *Draculas Vermächtnis: Technische Schriften* (Reclam Verlag Leipzig, 1993), p. 61.

6. It is always possible, of course, to read modernist works of fiction from a postmodernist position, in terms of their relation to information technologies. James Joyce's *Ulysses* in particular lends itself to this kind of reading, as Jacques Derrida demonstrates in *Ulysses Gramophone* (Paris: Galilée, 1987).

7. See Shiv K. Kumar, *Bergson and the Stream-of-Consciousness Novel* (New York: New York University Press, 1963), for one of many studies that document this influence.

8. See Henri Bergson, *Essai sur les données immédiates de la conscience* (Paris: P.U.F., 1976), esp. chaps. 1–2. Bergson distinguishes between two kinds of multiplicity, succinctly summarized by Gilles Deleuze in his study, *Bergsonism,* trans. Hugh Tomlinson and Barbara Habberjam (New York: Zone Books,

1988, orig: pub. 1966), p. 38: "One [type of multiplicity] is represented by space . . . : It is a multiplicity of exteriority, of simultaneity, of juxtaposition, of order, of quantitative differentiation, of *difference in degree;* it is a numerical multiplicity, *discontinuous and actual.* The other type of multiplicity appears in pure duration: It is an internal multiplicity of succession, of fusion, of organization, of heterogeneity, of qualitative discrimination, or of *difference in kind;* it is a *virtual and continuous* multiplicity that cannot be reduced to numbers" (Deleuze's emphases). Deleuze notes that the distinction between two types of multiplicity goes back to Bernhard Riemann, and he emphasizes the importance of keeping them distinct.

9. See Italo Calvino, *Six Memos for the Next Millenium* (Cambridge: Harvard University Press, 1988), pp. 101–124, for a discussion of multiplicity in modern fiction in terms of extensive, proliferating description and stylistic variety.

10. On this point, see Sanford Kwinter, "Immanence and Event in Early Modern Culture" (Ph.D. diss., Columbia University, 1989), pp. 120–121.

11. See, in particular, "The Storyteller," "The Work of Art in the Age of Mechanical Reproduction," and "On Some Motifs in Baudelaire," in Walter Benjamin, *Gesammelte Schriften* (Frankfurt am Main: Suhrkamp Verlag, 1974) vols. I-2 and I-4; also available in English in Benjamin's collection entitled *Illuminations,* trans. Harry Zohn (New York: Schocken Books, 1968). Hereafter, page numbers for citations to *Illuminations* appear in the text. Unfortunately, the English translation does not always preserve the distinctions essential to Benjamin's argument.

12. Thomas Pynchon, *The Crying of Lot 49* (New York: Harper & Row, 1966). Hereafter, page numbers for citations to this work appear in the text.

13. In her pioneering essay, "Maxwell's Demon, Entropy, Information: *The Crying of Lot 49,*" *TriQuarterly* 20 (Winter 1971), pp. 194–208, Anne Mangel establishes the importance of information theory to Pynchon's novel. Drawing mainly on nontechnical sources, Mangel concentrates on the implicit analogy between the Demon and Oedipa's role as a sorter of information, and then she goes on to show how the novel registers some of the problems posed by the distortions of language in communication. However, by ignoring the complexities of information theory, Mangel fails to see how completely it enters the fabric of Pynchon's fiction and even redefines its "mode," as I try to demonstrate.

14. Norbert Wiener highlights this dilemma in his account of Maxwell's Demon in *The Human Use of Human Beings,* a book that Pynchon admits, in

the introduction to *Slow Learner,* his collection of short stories, to having read. For a more detailed account of Maxwell's Demon, see William Poundstone, *The Recursive Universe: Cosmic Complexity and the Limits of Scientific Knowledge* (Chicago: Contemporary Books, 1985), pp. 52–77. Poundstone notes that it was Leo Szilard, in a paper published in 1929, who first demonstrated that the energy required to observe the molecules in the chamber would more than offset the energy gained by the results of their sorting.

15. Claude E. Shannon's paper was republished with a commentary by Warren Weaver as *The Mathematical Theory of Communication* (Urbana: University of Illinois Press, 1949). References are to this edition, and hereafter page numbers appear in the text.

16. See N. Katherine Hayles, *Chaos Bound* (Ithaca: Cornell University Press, 1990), pp. 31–60, for a full discussion. Hayles points out that while the controversy has never been resolved (apparently without adverse effects at the practical level of solving engineering problems in communications), Shannon's formulation has been more fruitful theoretically, anticipating in certain respects chaos theory.

17. Léon Brillouin, "Maxwell's Demon Cannot Operate: Information and Entropy," *Journal of Applied Physics* 22 (March 1951), pp. 334–357.

18. Wiener, *The Human Use of Human Beings.* Page numbers for citations appear in the text.

19. In his *Postmodernist Fiction* (New York: Methuen, 1987), Brian McHale argues that modern and postmodern fiction may be differentiated in relation to a dominantly epistemological orientation in the case of the former as opposed to a dominantly ontological orientation in the case of the latter. Although he applies this distinction to a reading of *The Crying of Lot 49* (see esp. pp. 23–25), his analysis differs from my own inasmuch as he does not explore the (for me) crucial distinction between possibility and probability. Thus, he writes: "The Tristero remains only a possibility. The breakthrough will not come until Pynchon's next novel, *Gravity's Rainbow,* where, no longer constrained by the limits of modernism, he will freely exploit the artistic possibilities of the plurality of worlds" (25). I am arguing that Pynchon's notion of a "plurality of worlds" is derived precisely from the "probabilistic" physics of Willard Gibbs and that Pynchon's fiction internalizes the essential distinction between possibility and probability upon which Gibbs's notion resides. Like Mangel before him (and subsequent Pynchon critics), McHale stops well short of drawing the full implications of Pynchon's appropriation of scientific concepts.

20. I analyze this structure as the embodiment of a specific semiotic regime in my essay "Toward the Schizo-Text: Paranoia as Semiotic Regime in *The Crying of Lot 49*," in *New Essays on* The Crying of Lot 49, ed. Patrick O'Donnell (Cambridge: Cambridge University Press, 1991), pp. 47–76.

21. See Henri Bergson, "The Possible and the Real," in Bergson, *A Study in Metaphysics: The Creative Mind*, trans. Mabelle L. Andison (Totowa, N.J.: Littlefield, Adams, 1965), pp. 91–106; as well as Deleuze, *Bergsonism*, pp. 96–113. Deleuze accentuates the importance of Bergson's notion of a "virtual multiplicity" and its actualization as a process of differentiation.

22. Jorge Luis Borges, "The Garden of Forking Paths," in his *Ficciones*, trans. Anthony Kerrigan (New York: Grove Press, 1962; orig. pub. 1956), p. 98.

23. Fredric Jameson, *The Geopolitical Aesthetic: Cinema and World Space in the World System* (Bloomington: Indiana University Press, 1992), p. 17.

24. Claude B. Shannon, "A Symbolic Analysis of Relay and Switching Circuits," *Transactions of the American Institute of Electrical Engineers* 57 (1938), pp. 713–23.

25. In the axiomatization of modern mathematical logic, David Hilbert's *Entscheidungsproblem*, or "halting problem" (sometimes translated as the "decision" or "decidability" problem), refers to the question of whether there is a finite mechanical procedure that can in principle solve all mathematical problems. In his 1937 paper "On Computable Numbers, with an Application to the *Entscheidungsproblem*," Alan Turing proved that the answer had to be no. However, Turing's demonstration of this fundamental undecidability led him to theorize the basis of the modern computer: a "universal" machine that could read, write, and calculate any problem that could be formulated as an algorithm. See Andrew Hodges, *Alan Turing: The Enigma* (New York: Simon & Schuster, 1983), pp. 96–110.

26. Jürgen Habermas, *The Philosophical Discourse of Modernity*, trans. Frederick Lawrence (Cambridge: MIT Press, 1987; orig. pub. 1985), p. 353.

27. Niklas Luhmann, "World Society as a Social System," in his *Essays on Self-Reference* (New York: Columbia University Press, 1990), pp. 178–189, Luhmann's emphases.

28. See Jacques Derrida, *The Post Card: From Socrates to Freud and Beyond*, trans. Alan Bass (Chicago: University of Chicago Press, 1987; orig. pub. 1980).

29. For a discussion of textual inconsistencies in the novel's deployment of metaphor, see N. Katherine Hayles, " 'A Metaphor of God Knew How Many

Parts': The Engine That Drives *The Crying of Lot 49*," in O'Donnell, *New Essays on* The Crying of Lot 49, pp. 97–125.

30. Henri Atlan, *L'Organisation biologique et la théorie de l'information* (Paris: Hermann, 1972); and Atlan, *Entre le cristal et la fumée* (Paris: Editions du Seuil, 1979).

31. See Atlan, *Entre le cristal et la fumée,* pp. 39–60.

32. Derrida discusses "posting" in relation to Heidegger in *Post Card,* pp. 64–66. Even while asserting that the postal system "programs" Western culture, Derrida remains disappointing on the issue of mediality. At several points he collapses the distinction between receiving post cards and receiving telephone calls, the most important instance being a collect call from a "Martini Heidegger." For Derrida's account of this prank but paradigmatic call, see ibid., p. 21.

33. For a hermeneutic reading of the Pentecostal theme in Pynchon's fiction in relation to entropy and communication, see W. T. Lhamon, "Pentecost, Promiscuity and Pynchon's *V,*" in *Mindful Pleasures: Essays on Thomas Pynchon,* ed. George Levine and David Leverenz (Boston: Little, Brown, 1976), pp. 69–86; for a discussion of mediality and its importance for post-hermeneutic reading, see David E. Wellbery, foreword to Friedrich Kittler, *Discourse Networks, 1800/1900* trans. Michael Metteer and Cris Cullens (Stanford: Stanford University Press, 1990; orig. pub. 1985), pp. vii–xxxiii.

34. See, for example, Michel Serres, "The Origin of Language," in *Hermes: Literature, Science, Philosophy,* ed. Josue V. Harari and David F. Bell (Baltimore: Johns Hopkins University Press, 1982), p. 82; and Anthony Wilden, *System and Structure* (London: Tavistock Publications, 1980; orig. pub. 1972), pp. 125–154.

35. Jacques Derrida, "Freud and the Scene of Writing," in his *Writing and Difference,* trans. Alan Bass (Chicago: University of Chicago Press, 1978; orig. pub. 1967). Page numbers for citations appear in the text.

36. Friedrich Kittler, "Die Welt des Symbolischen—eine Welt der Maschine," in his *Draculas Vermächtnis,* pp. 58–80.

37. See Jacques Lacan, *The Seminar of Jacques Lacan, Book 2: The Ego in Freud's Theory and in the Technique of Psychoanalysis, 1954–55,* trans. Sylvana Tomaselli (New York: Norton, 1988; orig. pub. 1978), esp. pp. 294–308.

38. Sigmund Freud, *Fragment of an Analysis of a Case of Hysteria,* in *The Standard Edition of the Complete Psychological Works of Sigmund Freud,* trans. James Strachey (London: Hogarth Press, 1960), 7:10; and *New Introductory Lectures on Psychoanalysis,* in ibid. (1964), 22:5.

39. Friedrich Kittler, "Benn's Poetry—'A Hit in the Charts': Song under Conditions of Media Technologies," *SubStance* 61 (1990), p. 11.

40. Friedrich Kittler, "A Discourse on Discourse," *Stanford Literature Review* 3, 1 (1986), p. 159.

41. Jean-François Lyotard, *The Postmodern Condition,* trans. Geoff Bennington and Brian Massumi (Minneapolis: University of Minnesota Press, 1984; orig. pub. 1979), p. 63.

42. I borrow the term *isotopic discourse* from John Mowitt, *Text: The Genealogy of an Antidisciplinary Object* (Durham, N.C.: Duke University Press, 1992). Mowitt uses the term (which he opposes to "utopic" discourse) in order to open the question of "how the specific labor of producing what a society constructs as 'culture' touches on processes (psychic and cultural) which have not been integrated within the prevailing social framework" (p. 17).

43. This shift is inscribed theoretically in the difference between Roland Barthes, *Elements of Semiology* (1964), which wavers momentarily before taking language as a model for semiotics rather than semiotics as a model for language, and Umberto Eco, *A Theory of Semiotics* (1979), in which a theory of codes and a theory of sign production together cover a range of both linguistic and nonlinguistic phenomena. More important, however, is the "a-signifying semiotics" Gilles Deleuze and Félix Guattari explore in both *Anti-Oedipus* (Minneapolis: University of Minnesota Press, 1977; orig. pub. 1972) and *A Thousand Plateaus* (Minneapolis: University of Minnesota Press, 1987; orig. pub. 1980).

Chapter 3   Rocket-State Assemblage

1. John von Neumann, review of Norbert Wiener, *Cybernetics,* in *Physics Today,* May 1949, pp. 33–34.

2. Recent scholarship tends to understand (and unify) this discourse network as the originary site of cognitive science, a new interdisciplinary field. See Howard Gardner, *The Mind's New Science: A History of the Cognitive Revolution* (New York: Basic Books, 1985); Jean-Pierre Dupuy, *Aux origines des sciences cognitives* (Paris: Editions la Découverte, 1994), for two accounts that develop this view.

3. See Steve J. Heims, *John von Neumann and Norbert Wiener: From Mathematics to the Technologies of Life and Death* (Cambridge: MIT Press, 1980), p. 179, for a concise summary of these changes.

4. Thomas Pynchon, *Gravity's Rainbow* (New York: Viking Press, 1973). Hereafter, page numbers for citations to this work appear in the text.

Notes to Pages 62–71 ▪ 279

5. See Paul Virilio, *War and Cinema: The Logistics of Perception,* trans. Patrick Camiller (London: Verso, 1989; orig. pub. 1984), for a persuasive discussion of the "fatal interdependence" between the technologies of cinema and warfare in the twentieth century.

6. See Paul Virilio, *L'Insécurité du territoire* (Paris: Stock, 1976); Paul Virilio and Sylvère Lotringer, *Pure War* trans. Mark Polizotti (New York: Semiotext(e), 1983).

7. See Richard Poirier, "Rocket Power," *Saturday Review of the Arts,* March 3, 1973: "[Pynchon] is locating the kinds of human consciousness that have been implanted *in* the instruments of technology and contemporary methods of analysis; not content with recording the historical effect of these, he is anxious to find our history *in* them" (p. 59, Poirier's emphasis).

8. Gilles Deleuze and Claire Parnet, *Dialogues,* trans. Hugh Tomlinson and Barbara Habberjam (New York: Columbia University Press, 1987; orig. pub. 1977), p. 69.

9. See Gilles Deleuze and Félix Guattari, "November 20, 1923: Postulates of Linguistics," in their *Thousand Plateaus,* trans. Brian Massumi (Minneapolis: University of Minnesota Press, 1987; orig. pub. 1980), pp. 75–110.

10. Deleuze and Parnet, *Dialogues,* pp. 51–52.

11. Instances of the novel's geopolitical mappings were first noted by Jeremy Gilbert-Rolfe and John Johnston, "*Gravity's Rainbow* and *The Spiral Jetty* (Part 2)," *October* 2 (Summer 1976), pp. 86–87.

12. Like Jacques Lacan, Pynchon tends to collapse the distinction between paranoia and the personality. Cf. Lacan: "There is no relationship between paranoid psychosis and personality: they are the same thing." See "Le Sinthôme," *Ornicar?* 7 (June/July 1976), p. 7.

13. Friedrich Kittler, "Medien und Drogen in Pynchons zweitem Weltkrieg," in *Narrativität in den Medien,* ed. Rolf Kloepfer and Karl-Dietmar Möller (Munster: MAks Publikationen, 1986), pp. 231–250.

14. Brian McHale, "Modernist Reading, Postmodern Text: The Case of *Gravity's Rainbow,*" *Poetics Today* 1, 1–2 (1979), pp. 85–109.

15. Paul Virilio, *L'Espace critique* (Paris: Christian Bourgeois, 1984). The translated quotations (slightly modified) are taken from an English translation by Daniel Moshenberg entitled *Lost Dimension* (New York: Semiotext(e), 1991), pp. 17, 52. Virilio notes that this ambiguity "returns to the ambiguity of audio-visual media, especially live television and the uncertainty of the televised images, as well as the geometry of their re-transmission (and this despite the use of systems theories)."

16. See Charles Clerc, "Film in *Gravity's Rainbow,*" in *Approaches to*

Gravity's Rainbow, ed. Charles Clerc (Columbus: Ohio State University Press, 1983), pp. 103–151, for a detailed survey of Pynchon's use of the cinema. However, Clerc's study of Pynchon's "supplemental usage of film" (104–105) fails to consider how completely film images enter into and thus constitute Pynchon's "text" as multiply permeating surfaces of inscription. Not surprisingly, Clerc omits any discussion of Pynchon's use of the cinema interface.

17. See Michael J. Neufeld, *Peenemünde and the Coming of the Ballistic Missile Era* (New York: Free Press, 1995). Neufeld notes that one group of early rocket experimenters actually obtained money for tests from a film company, in order that they might launch a rocket simultaneously with the opening of Lang's film.

18. Virilio, *War and Cinema,* pp. 58–59.

19. See Martin Heidegger, "The Age of the World Picture," in his *Question Concerning Technology and Other Essays,* trans. William Lovitt (New York: Harper & Row, 1977), pp. 115–154.

20. See Hanjo Berressem, *Pynchon's Poetics: Interfacing Theory and Text* (Urbana: University of Illinois Press, 1993), pp. 151–190, for a persuasive account of this destabilization in *Gravity's Rainbow* from a Lacanian point of view. In an analysis that parallels (and supports) my discussion of Slothrop, Berressem argues that "no real self can be saved from the movies, because the self is always already cinematic." Berressem continues: "One cannot escape the cinematic structuration of life and its inherent falsification and misapprehension. Film and life are congruent, because perception and film are based on a similar structure. There is no escape from this initial break; only death will return the individual to the real, the world's raw continuity" (183). As I suggest when I return to the problematic of the cinematic self in *Vineland* in chap. 7, Pynchon assumes that such a view reflects a specifically historical and technological condition rather than a universal truth.

21. Oddly, critics have largely ignored the fundamental importance of drugs in Pynchon's last three novels. In "The Rhetoric of Drugs: An Interview," in *differences* 5, 1 (1993), pp. 1–25, Jacques Derrida usefully draws attention to both the essential role of drugs since the European Renaissance in relation to the establishment of "structures of fictionality" (and therefore to the very category of literature), and the legal and political implications of drugs as a technology which puts into question any attempt to define and control the "natural body." In chap. 7, I try to show how the technology of drugs figures in *Vineland.*

22. In "Medien und Drogen in Pynchons zweiten Weltkrieg," Kittler notes the implicit connection between "Oneirine" and the writing/reading of the

narrative. However, he allows the narrative no more significance than a drug-induced hallucination: "What in media appears as narrativity and, accordingly, entertainment, is in all probability only a screen for semiotechnical efficiencies" (234). For Kittler, only the technologies that allow the text to be generated need be taken into account.

23. See Gilles Deleuze's two-volume study, *Cinema I: The Movement-Image* (Minneapolis: University of Minnesota Press, 1986; orig. pub. 1983) and *Cinema II: The Time-Image* (Minneapolis: University of Minnesota Press, 1989; orig. pub. 1985). In chap. 5 ("The Perception-Image") in the first volume, Deleuze traces a tendency variously operative within the history of cinema to articulate precisely such a "machinic assemblages of images." See also Deleuze's "Lettre à Serge Daney" in his *Pourparlers* (Paris: Minuit, 1990), pp. 97–112, where Deleuze comments on how the world itself has begun to "make" cinema—an "any cinema whatsoever" *[un cinéma quelconque]*—through the agency of television as the perfection of social and technical control. I return to these issues in chap. 6, where I discuss DeLillo's fiction in similar terms.

24. For a more extended discussion of this scene in relation to the notion of the interface, see Jerome H. Stern, "The Interfaces of *Gravity's Rainbow,*" *Dismisura 39/50* (December 1980), pp. 55–56.

25. See Lawrence Kappel's essay "Psychic Geography in *Gravity's Rainbow,*" *Contemporary Literature* 21, 2 (1980), pp. 225–251, for a detailed discussion of the Zone in these terms.

26. This point is well made by Jonathan Crary in his article "Eclipse of the Spectacle," in *Art after Modernism: Rethinking Representation,* ed. Brian Wallis (New York: Godine, 1984), p. 292.

27. See Lawrence Wolfley, "Repression's Rainbow: The Presence of Norman O. Brown in Pynchon's Big Novel," *PMLA* 92 (October 1978), pp. 873–889. Wolfley argues that the thematic conjunction of Eros and Thanatos is traceable to Brown's psychoanalytic theory of history, as in passages such as the following, from *Love against Death* (New York: Vintage, 1959): "Whereas in previous ages life had been a mixture of Eros and Thanatos, in the Protestant era life becomes a pure culture of the death instinct" (p. 216).

28. See Gilles Deleuze and Félix Guattari, *Anti-Oedipus* (Minneapolis: University of Minnesota Press, 1977, orig. pub. 1972), esp. pp. 36–41, 68–113, for discussion of desiring-machines and their structuring of the social field.

29. For a study roughly contemporary with Pynchon's novel which treats the brain as a multiplicity, see Steven Rose, *The Conscious Brain* (New York:

Knopf, 1975). Recent developments in neuroscience continue to confirm this view.

30. See Michel Foucault, *Discipline and Punish* (New York: Vintage, 1979; orig. pub. 1975); as well as Thomas S. Smith, "Performing in the Zone: The Presentation of Historical Crisis in *Gravity's Rainbow,*" *Clio* 12, 3 (1983), pp. 251–252, for a discussion of the many parallels between Pynchon and Foucault. More directly pertinent is Deleuze's essay-review of Foucault's *Discipline and Punish,* "Ecrivain non: Un Nouveau Cartographe," *Critique* 343 (December 1975), pp. 1207–1227, where Deleuze first elaborates the notion of the "abstract machine."

31. Deleuze and Guattari discuss "becoming invisible" in *Thousand Plateaus,* pp. 233–309.

32. Surely one of the texts alluded to here is Albert Speer's *Theory of the Value of Ruins,* published in 1938, which argues that a building's value must extend up to and *beyond* its eventual destruction. Once again we see how Pynchon constructs his text on the basis of "invisible literature," that is, the mass of discourse constituted by scientific reports and government documents that shape our culture from below the threshold of conscious recognition.

33. In "Pynchon, Paranoia and Literature," in his *Culture of Redemption* (Cambridge: Harvard University Press, 1990), pp. 179–199, Leo Bersani argues persuasively that the doubling intrinsic to a paranoid structure ruins the very notion of a real or true text; Patricia Waugh, in her study *Metafiction* (New York: Methuen, 1984), often mentions *Gravity's Rainbow* as a representative metafictional text but without discussing it in any detail.

34. See Deleuze and Guattari, *Thousand Plateaus,* pp. 111–148, for a fuller exposition of these four regimes.

Chapter 4   Narration, Delirium, Machinic Consciousness

1. See Daniel C. Dennett, *Consciousness Explained* (Boston: Little, Brown, 1991). It is also worth noting that McElroy's next novel, *Plus* (1979), draws extensively on the neurophysiology of the brain.

2. Joseph McElroy and Tom LeClair, "An Interview with Joseph McElroy," in *Anything Can Happen: Interviews with American Novelists,* ed. Tom LeClair and Larry McCaffery (Urbana: University of Illinois Press, 1983), pp. 235–251.

3. Joseph McElroy, *Lookout Cartridge* (New York: Carrol & Graf, 1985), p. 465. This paperback edition reproduces the format and pagination of the

original American edition published by Alfred A. Knopf in 1974 but includes a new author's note entitled "One Reader to Another." All citations are to the 1985 edition, and hereafter page numbers appear in the text.

4. See Alan Wilde, *Middle Ground: Studies in Contemporary Fiction* (Philadelphia: University of Pennsylvania Press, 1987), which argues strongly for the relevance of phenomenology to contemporary American fiction. Unfortunately, Wilde does not consider McElroy's fiction.

5. I discuss the relationship between a blind spot and the structure of a literary text in my article "Toward the Schizo-Text: Paranoia as Semiotic Regime in *The Crying of Lot 49*," in *New Essays on* The Crying of Lot 49, ed. Patrick O'Donnell (Cambridge: Cambridge University Press, 1991), pp. 47–78.

6. McElroy and LeClair, "Interview," p. 249.

7. See Tony Tanner, "Toward an Ultimate Topography: The Work of Joseph McElroy," *TriQuarterly* 36 (Spring 1976), esp. pp. 244–252, for further discussion of the topographical aspects of *Lookout Cartridge*.

8. Both Tanner, "Toward an Ultimate Topography," and Thomas LeClair, "Joseph McElroy and the Art of Excess," *Contemporary Literature* 21, 1 (1980), pp. 15–37, discuss *Lookout Cartridge* as a "field" of non-Aristotelian relations among a variety of elements.

9. Dennett, *Consciousness Explained,* p. 204.

10. Tanner, "Toward an Ultimate Topography," discusses *Lookout Cartridge* more precisely in these terms.

11. For a useful introductory account, see Geoffrey E. Hinton, "How Neural Networks Learn from Experience," *Scientific American,* September 1992, pp. 145–151.

12. McElroy, p. 242.

13. See Jacques Lacan, "Of the Subject Who Is Supposed to Know," in his *Four Fundamental Concepts of Psycho-Analysis,* trans. Alan Sheridan (New York: Norton, 1978; orig. pub. 1973), pp. 230–243.

14. Friedrich Kittler, "Gramophone, Film, Typewriter," *October* 41 (Summer 1987), p. 115. Page numbers for subsequent quotations appear in the text.

15. Friedrich Kittler, *Discourse Networks, 1800/1900* trans. Michael Metteer and Cris Cullens (Stanford: Stanford University Press, 1990; orig. pub. 1985), p. 305.

16. Fredric Jameson, "Postmodernism, or the Cultural Logic of Late Capitalism," *New Left Review* 146 (July/August 1984), pp. 53–92. Page numbers for all citations appear in the text.

Chapter 5   Capitalism and Entropic Flow

1. William Gaddis, *JR* (New York: Viking Penquin, 1985; orig. pub. 1975), pp. 154–155. Hereafter, page numbers for citations appear in the text. Ellipses are always Gaddis's own unless they are enclosed in brackets.

2. Raymond Williams, *Television: Technology and Cultural Form* (New York: Schocken, 1974).

3. Jean Baudrillard, *Forget Foucault* (New York: Semiotext(e), 1987; orig. pub. 1977), p. 25.

4. Jean Baudrillard, "The Ecstasy of Communication," trans. John Johnston, in *The Anti-Aesthetic,* ed. Hal Foster (Port Townsend, Wash.: Bay Press, 1983), p. 127.

5. Jean-François Lyotard, *The Postmodern Condition,* trans. Geoff Bennington and Brian Massumi (Minneapolis: University of Minnesota Press, 1984; orig. pub. 1979), pp. 15, xxiv.

6. Gilles Deleuze and Félix Guattari, *A Thousand Plateaus,* trans. Brian Massumi (Minneapolis: University of Minnesota Press, 1987; orig. pub. 1980), employ the word *machinic*—in opposition to both *mechanical* and *organic*—to denote the working relations in an assemblage. See ibid., pp. 332–335, where they distinguish between *assemblage* and *machine.*

7. For a discussion of "desiring machines," see Gilles Deleuze and Félix Guattari, *Anti-Oedipus* (Minneapolis: University of Minnesota, 1977; orig. pub. 1972), pp. 36–41.

8. Norbert Wiener, *The Human Use of Human Beings: Cybernetics and Society* (New York: Avon Books, 1967; orig. pub. 1950), p. 19. Page numbers for further questions appear in the text.

9. See Claude E. Shannon, *The Mathematical Theory of Communication* (Urbana: University of Illinois Press, 1949).

10. For more on *JR* and runaway systems, see Thomas LeClair, *The Art of Excess: Mastery in Contemporary American Fiction* (Urbana: University of Illinois Press, 1989).

11. See G. S. Kirk and J. E. Raven, *The PreSocratic Philosophers* (Cambridge: Cambridge University Press, 1960), pp. 336ff. Quotations are all taken from this source.

12. A later passage underscores this point:

—like I mean this here bond and stock stuff you don't see anybody you
don't know anybody only in the mail and the telephone because that's
how they do it nobody has to see anybody you can be this here funny look-
ingest person that lives in a toilet someplace how do they know, I mean
like all those guys at the Stock Exchange where they're selling all this

stock to each other? They don't give a shit whose it is they're just selling it back and forth for some voice that told them on the phone why should they give a shit if you're a hundred and fifty all they . . . (172)

JR recognizes that, to connect circuits and manage flows, it is unnecessary to have a personal identity, which may even prohibit effective action. Also notable is the obviously anal character of this and other passages having to do with buying and selling. See Steven Moore, *William Gaddis* (Boston: Twayne, 1989), pp. 76–80, for further discussion of *JR*'s anal imagery.

13. Zoltan Abadi-Nagy, "The Art of Fiction: William Gaddis," *Paris Review* 105 (Winter 1987), p. 85. Hereafter page numbers for quotations appear in the text.

14. In a chapter entitled "Corporate Fiction" in his *Gold Standard and the Logic of Naturalism* (Berkeley: University of California Press, 1987), pp. 183–213, Walter Benn Michaels notes that in novels published around the turn of the century, the very notion of a corporation puts into question the integrity of individual human identity.

15. In many respects, the portrait of Gibbs is a self-portrait of Gaddis himself as a failure or of what he might have been had he not become a successful writer. The obvious visual similarity between *Gibbs* and *Gaddis* alerts us to this similarity, just as Edward Bast's name alerts us to the possibility that he may be a bastard. See Moore, *Gaddis,* pp. 2–5, for details of Gaddis's life.

16. Gibbs's insistent use of the word *invention* may also be an ironic allusion to Norbert Wiener's unpublished book entitled "Invention: On the Care and Feeding of Ideas."

17. In this regard one might compare Gaddis's depiction of Wyatt's "creative breakdown" in *The Recognitions* with Bast's in *JR*. In both instances, a creative breakdown is a necessary precondition for a breakthrough and the forging of new connections and thus for the making of both art and a new life. Whatever the psychological veracity of this idea, it emerges distinctly in the critical and ideological discourse of the post–World War II period. This discourse includes diverse biographical facts, such as Jackson Pollock's alcoholism and reading of C. G. Jung, in addition to various writings by, among others, Aldous Huxley, Ernst Kris, Wilhelm Reich, R. D. Laing, and Deleuze and Guattari.

18. In *The Telephone Book: Technology, Schizophrenia, Electric Speech* (Lincoln: University of Nebraska Press, 1989), Avital Ronell describes many of the deterritorializing effects of the telephone without employing the term (somewhat oddly, since she cites Deleuze and Guattari). She writes, for exam-

ple: the telephone "destabilizes the identity of self and other, subject and thing, it abolishes the originariness of site; it undermines the authority of the Book and constantly menaces the existence of literature. It is unsure of its identity as object, thing, piece of equipment, perlocutionary intensity or artwork (the beginnings of telephony argue for its place as artwork); it offers itself as instrument of destinal alarm, and the disconnecting force of the telephone enables us to establish something like the maternal superego" (p. 9).

19. In Abadi-Nagy, "Gaddis," Gaddis ascribes great importance to Bast's cello piece. He describes it as "one small voice trying to rescue it all and say, 'Yes, there *is* hope,' " and then refers to it as "that *real* note of hope in *JR*" (p. 61, Gaddis's emphases).

20. In the 1980s, through the device of "career management," the artist's career trajectory itself becomes part of the commodification process, thus providing a recuperation of the "creative artist" as a functional part of a new apparatus of market control that now includes the gallery-museum-art journal network as an essential functional part.

21. Critics have generally ignored this aspect of Gaddis's novel. An exception is Patrick O'Donnell, *Echo Chambers: Figuring Voice in Modern Narrative* (Iowa City: University of Iowa Press, 1992), which discusses *JR* in terms of the commodification of human identity.

22. See, for example, Steven Weisenburger, "Contra Naturam?: Usury in William Gaddis's *JR*," *Genre* 13 (Spring 1980), pp. 95–100; and Moore, *Gaddis*, pp. 89–99.

23. Moore, *Gaddis*, pp. 96–99.

24. See O'Donnell, *Echo Chambers*, pp. 176–178, for a useful discussion of the passage in these terms.

25. Deleuze and Guattari, *Thousand Plateaus*, p. 267.

Chapter 6 Fictions of the Culture Medium

1. Don DeLillo and Tom LeClair, "An Interview with Don DeLillo," in *Anything Can Happen: Interviews with American Novelists* ed. Tom LeClair and Larry McCaffery (Urbana: University of Illinois Press, 1983), p. 83.

2. See, in this regard, Jean Baudrillard's description of "the masses" in his *In the Shadow of the Silent Majorities*, trans. Paul Foss, Paul Patton, and John Johnston (New York: Semiotext(e), 1983; orig. pub. 1978).

3. In a review of *The Names* for *Minnesota Review*, n.s., 22 (Spring 1984), p. 117, Fredric Jameson suggests that it could be read either way, but then he asserts the latter view to be more satisfying.

4. Don DeLillo, *Endzone* (New York: Penguin Books, 1986; orig. pub. 1972), pp. 164–165. Page numbers for subsequent quotations appear in the text.

5. DeLillo and Tom LeClair, "Interview," pp. 84–85.

6. Mikhail Bakhtin discusses the novel in these terms in "Discourse in the Novel," in his *Dialogic Imagination,* ed. Michael Holquist, trans. Caryl Emerson and Michael Holquist (Austin: University of Texas Press, 1981), p. 263.

7. The direct influence, however, was probably Wittgenstein's reflections in the *Philosophical Investigations* on the relationship between various "language games" and "forms of life." In the interview cited above, DeLillo admits to an interest in the effects of Wittgenstein's writing, particularly its self-confident authority and "machine-tooled" quality.

8. DeLillo and Tom LeClair, "Interview," p. 86. DeLillo states: "I was trying to produce a book that would be naked structure. The structure would be the book and vice versa. I wanted the book to become what it was about. Abstract structures and connective patterns. A piece of mathematics in short. To do this I felt I had to reduce the importance of people. The people had to play a role subservient to pattern, form, and so on. . . . A book that is really all outline."

9. See Jean Baudrillard, *Simulations,* trans. Paul Foss, Paul Patton, and Philip Beitchman (New York: Semiotext(e), 1983), pp. 1–4, 30–37.

10. In his *Postmodernist Fiction* (New York: Methuen, 1987), p. 66, Brian McHale cites *Ratner's Star* as a work of postmodern fiction which adopts science fiction motifs.

11. Gilles Deleuze, "Trois questions sur Six Fois Deux," *Cahiers du cinéma* 271 (November 1976), pp. 9–10 [my trans.]. Deleuze develops these ideas more systematically in *Cinema I, The Movement-Image* (Minneapolis: University of Minnesota Press, 1986; orig. pub. 1983).

12. The relevance of systems and systems theory to DeLillo's fiction is central to Tom LeClair, *In the Loop: Don DeLillo and the Systems Novel* (Urbana: University of Illinois Press, 1987). Later in this chapter, I introduce Deleuze's version of systems theory. It should also be noted that Martin Heidegger suggests the inevitable dominance of "systems" in the new era of the image in his 1936 essay "The Age of the World Picture," in his *Question Concerning Technology and Other Essays,* trans. William Lovitt (New York: Harper & Row, 1977): "Where the World becomes picture, the system, and not only in thinking, comes to dominance" (p. 141).

13. Don DeLillo, *Players* (New York: Vintage Books, 1984; orig. pub. 1977), p. 1.

14. See, in particular, *In the Shadow of the Silent Majorities* and *Forget Foucault* (New York: Semiotext(e), 1987; orig. pub. 1977), where Jean Baudrillard argues that in the era of the mass media, terrorism and state, sexual liberation and sexual repression no longer form valid oppositions.

15. Don DeLillo, *Running Dog* (New York: Vintage Books, 1979; orig. pub. 1978), p. 237. Page numbers for subsequent quotations appear in the text. For extended analyses of the fictional film, see Stuart Johnson, "Extra-philosophical Instigations in Don DeLillo's *Running Dog*," *Contemporary Literature* 26, 1 (1985), pp. 74–90; and LeClair, *In the Loop,* pp. 170–171.

16. In his study *Late Imperial Romance* (London: Verso, 1994), John McClure offers an engaging analysis of DeLillo's white male protagonists in relation to American imperialism. However, in my view, McClure does not give adequate attention to the effects of contemporary mass-media assemblages. The meaning McClure unhesitatingly attributes to the "political" would surely need to be redefined or at least, following Baudrillard, recontextualized in view of these effects.

17. John Frow, *Marxism and Literary Form* (Cambridge: Harvard University Press, 1986), pp. 141–146, and Jameson, review of *The Names,* p. 117. Frow writes: "*Running Dog* . . . reworks the genre [of the popular thriller] in such a way as to refuse and expose its ideological implications. In the place of [Robert] Ludlum's 'good' plotting we are given a 'bad' plot that tails off in defeat and bathos (and in the black joke of the last paragraph); instead of character differentiation we are given stretches of terse, solipsistic dialogue which blur the differences between speakers; instead of a passage from illusion to truth we encounter only a world of surfaces and reflections" (146).

18. Don DeLillo, *The Names* (New York: Vintage Books, 1983; orig. pub. 1982), p. 3. Page numbers of further quotations appear in the text.

19. See LeClair, *In the Loop,* chap. 7, for a detailed analysis of *The Names* in these terms.

20. Don DeLillo, *White Noise* (New York: Penguin Books, 1986; orig. pub. 1985), pp. 12–13. Page numbers of further quotations appear in the text.

21. Murray thus inverts Walter Benjamin's celebrated thesis that modern technologies of reproduction destroy the "aura" of the traditional work of art. See Walter Benjamin, "The Work of Art in the Age of Mechanical Reproduction," in his *Illuminations,* trans. Harry Zohn (New York: Schocken Books, 1968), pp. 217–251.

22. *A True Life Novel* is the subtitle Norman Mailer gives to his novelistic biography of Gary Gilmore, *Executioner's Song* (1979).

23. Godard may again have been an influence, since many of his films also

work in these terms. On this aspect of Godard's films, see Jeremy Gilbert-Rolfe, "Godard: After Marx, after Freud," in his *Immanence and Contradiction* (New York: Out of London Press, 1985), pp. 195–214.

24. Don DeLillo, "American Blood: A Journey through the Labyrinth of Dallas and JFK," *Rolling Stone*, December 8, 1983. This quotation and those that immediately follow are taken from p. 23.

25. Anthony DeCurtis, " 'An Outsider in This Society': An Interview with Don DeLillo," *South Atlantic Quarterly* 89, 2 (1990), pp. 285–286. DeLillo states: "As I was working on *Libra*, it occurred to me that a lot of tendencies in my first eight novels seemed to be collecting around the dark center of the assassination. So it's possible I wouldn't have become the kind of writer I am if it weren't for the assassination."

26. Fredric Jameson, *The Geopolitical Aesthetic: Cinema and World Space in the World System* (Bloomington: Indiana University Press, 1992), chap. 1.

27. See esp. *Life Magazine*, February 21, 1964, cover and pp. 20–24; and the *Report of the President's Commission on the Assassination of President John F. Kennedy*, 26 vols. (Washington: Government Printing Office, 1964).

28. Don DeLillo, *Libra* (New York: Viking, 1988), p. 221. Page numbers of all subsequent quotations appear in the text.

29. In *The Historical Novel* (London: Merlin, 1962; orig. pub. 1937), Georg Lukács distinguishes between two types of character: world historical figures such as Cromwell and Napoleon and the more ordinary "invented" figures who populate the novels of Scott and Balzac. Whereas the former, who are the leading actors in history, are appropriate for drama, in the novel they can only assume secondary positions and appear only episodically, just as they would appear in the experiences of ordinary people. In *Libra*, the most important historical personage is President Kennedy, who appears only near the novel's end in the Dallas motorcade but whose presence throughout is felt through the power of his mass-media image. Indeed, for Oswald's wife, Marina, "it's as though [Kennedy] floats over the landscape at night, entering dreams and fantasies, entering the act of love between husbands and wives. He floats through television screens into bedrooms at night" (p. 324).

30. See, e.g., Mark Lane, *Plausible Denial* (New York: Thunder's Mouth Press, 1991).

31. The notion of the "device" occurs throughout DeLillo's fiction. The word, of course, is rich in meaning and historical association, but its appeal to DeLillo most likely stems from its combination of invention, scheme, design, or trap with a sense of mechanical contrivance. The phrase *devices make us pliant* appears in both *Running Dog* and *Libra*, where it refers to technological

instruments (tape recorders, polygraph machines) which by their very existence tend to produce a compliant subject.

32. DeLillo, "American Blood," p. 24.

33. For a discussion of the cryptonym, see Nicolas Abraham and Maria Torok, *The Wolf Man's Magic Word*, trans. Nicholas Rand (Minneapolis: University of Minnesota Press, 1986), and esp. the foreword by Jacques Derrida. My use of the notion follows from Abraham and Torok's reworking of introjection in relation to a psychoanalytic topography of the self. As a foreign element, the cryptonym is introjected into the self but does not become part of that self; it remains foreign, or other, part of the "outside" retained within the self.

34. See Gilles Deleuze, *Différence et répétition* (Paris: P.U.F., 1968), pp. 154–165, for an analysis of the conditions under which heterogeneous series of diverse items form into an "intensive system." Deleuze applies his conception to a number of different "literary systems" in works by Raymond Roussel, James Joyce, Marcel Proust, Witold Gombrowicz, and Alain Robbe-Grillet.

35. DeCurtis, "DeLillo," p. 299.

36. Richard Lehan, "Paradigmatic Confusion: Language as a Model for Historical Change," paper presented at the International Association of Philosophy and Literature convention, Montreal, May 17, 1991.

37. Tom LeClair's systems analysis of DeLillo's novels (up to but not including *Libra*) in *In the Loop* is based on Ludwig von Bertalanffy's *General Systems Theory*, which is biased toward wholeness, teleology, and the self-organizing dynamics typical of living systems (not surprisingly, given its roots in the biological sciences). Deleuze's "intensive system," on the other hand, is probably best situated between such "vitalist" systems and the mechanistic ones both oppose. It is biased toward the proliferation of simulacra and multiplicities and tends, in his later work with Félix Guattari, toward a constructivist "machinism." Its roots are to be found in the philosophies of Leibniz and Spinoza.

Chapter 7 An American Book of the Dead

1. Thomas Pynchon, *Vineland* (Boston: Little, Brown, 1990), p. 308. Page numbers for all subsequent citations appear in the text.

2. Friedrich Kittler, "Gramophone, Film, Typewriter," *October* 41 (Summer 1987), p. 102.

3. Thomas Pynchon, "Nearer, My Couch, to Thee," *New York Times Book Review*, June 6, 1993, pp. 3, 57.

4. Brian McHale registers the critics' discomfort with Pynchon's indulgence in TV references in a chapter on *Vineland* in his *Constructing Postmodernism* (London: Routledge, 1992), pp. 115–141.

5. Jacques Lacan, *Four Fundamental Concepts of Psycho-Analysis,* trans. Alan Sheridan (New York: Norton, 1978; orig. pub. 1973), p. 56. Hanjo Berressem, *Pynchon's Poetics: Interfacing Theory and Text* (Urbana: University of Illinois Press, 1993), pp. 227–228, also discusses this scene in Lacanian terms.

6. Susan Strehle, for example, understands Frenesi's splitting in psychological terms in her "Pynchon's Elaborate Game of Doubles in *Vineland,*" in *The Vineland Papers: Critical Takes on Pynchon's Novel,* ed. Geoffrey Green, Donald J. Greiner, and Larry McCaffery (Normal, Ill.: Dalkey Archive Press, 1994), pp. 101–118.

7. Lacan discusses the symbolic order in these terms in *The Seminar of Jacques Lacan, Book 2: The Ego in Freud's Theory and in the Technique of Psychoanalysis, 1954–55,* trans. Sylvana Tomaselli (New York: Norton, 1988; orig. pub. 1978).

8. See Jacques Lacan, "Séminaire sur la Lettre volée," in his *Ecrits* (Paris: Editions du Seuil, 1966), pp. 11–61. The complete version of this seminar has never been translated into English.

9. Kittler, "Gramophone, Film, Typewriter," p. 115.

10. Contrasting this scene with a similar one in *The Crying of Lot 49,* Fredric Jameson takes something like this tack when he claims that Pynchon here eschews the mystical in order to represent "the little repressions of the bureaucratic everyday." See Fredric Jameson, *The Geopolitical Aesthetic: Cinema and World Space in the World System* (Bloomington: Indiana University Press, 1992), p. 17.

11. Lacan uses not the word *computer,* but the word *machine.* See esp. "The Circuit" and "Psychoanalysis and Cybernetics, or On the Nature of Language" in *The Seminar of Jacques Lacan, Book 2.*

12. N. Katherine Hayles, " 'Who Was Saved?': Families, Snitches, Recuperation in Pynchon's *Vineland,*" in Green Greiner, and McCaffery, *Vineland Papers,* p. 17.

13. Molly Hite, "Feminist Theory and the Politics of *Vineland,*" in ibid., pp. 139.

14. Kittler, "Gramophone, Film, Typewriter," p. 114.

15. Paul Virilio, *War and Cinema: The Logistics of Perception* trans. Patrick Camiller (London: Verso, 1989; orig. pub. 1984), p. 29.

16. For a different reading of the Puncutron machine, see David Porush, "Purring into Transcendence": Pynchon's Puncutron Machine," in Green, Grenier, and McCaffery, *Vineland Papers,* pp. 31–45. Porush sees the machine

as a "technological metaphor for [Pynchon's] own technique," while also spelling out many of its various textual and nontextual connections.

17. Gilles Deleuze and Félix Guattari, *A Thousand Plateaus,* trans. Brian Massumi (Minneapolis: University of Minnesota Press, 1987; orig. pub. 1980), p. 84.

18. See Stuart Hall, "Encoding, Decoding," in *The Cultural Studies Reader,* ed. Simon During (London: Routledge, 1992), pp. 90–103.

19. Gilles Deleuze, *Cinema I: The Movement-Image* (Minneapolis: University of Minnesota Press, 1986; orig. pub. 1983), p. 85.

20. Deleuze and Guattari, *A Thousand Plateaus,* p. 285.

Chapter 8   The Disappearance of Media

1. Gilles Deleuze and Félix Guattari, *A Thousand Plateaus,* trans. Brian Massumi (Minneapolis: University of Minnesota Press, 1987; orig. pub. 1980), define the machinic phylum as "materiality, natural or artificial, and both simultaneously; it is matter in movement, in flux, in variation, matter as a conveyor of singularities and traits of expression" (409). Their discussion addresses the question of why the flow of matter is primarily metallic. However, as I later suggest, the new machinic phylum underlying *Neuromancer* is based not on metal or carbon compounds but on silicon.

2. Gibson is generally considered to be the inventor of the term *cyberspace,* whose currency has rapidly spread beyond its original fictional context. For discussion of cyberspace as an idea and immanent reality, see Michael Benedikt, ed., *Cyberspace: First Steps* (Cambridge: MIT Press, 1991); and Howard Rheingold, *Virtual Reality* (New York: Touchstone, 1992).

3. William Gibson, *Burning Chrome* (New York: Ace Books, 1987). Page numbers for all quotations appear in the text, preceded by the letters *BC.*

4. William Gibson, *Neuromancer* (New York: Ace Books, 1984), p. 16. Page numbers for all subsequent quotations appear in the text, preceded by the letter *N.*

5. In this critical sense, the term *détournement* derives from Guy Debord and the Situationists. See Glenn Grant, "Transcendence through Detournement in William Gibson's *Neuromancer,*" *Science Fiction Studies* 17 (1990), pp. 41–49, for a discussion of its importance in Gibson's fiction.

6. David Thomas, "The Technophilic Body," *New Formations* 8 (Summer 1989), pp. 113–129, details Gibson's depiction of a highly technological "cyborg culture," focusing specifically on how the individual body and social identity are reconstituted therein.

7. William Gibson, "Doug Walker Interviews Science Fiction Author William Gibson," *Impulse* 15, 1 (1989), p. 38.

8. Specifically, in novels by Philip K. Dick, J. G. Ballard, and John Brunner, Baudrillard sees a new form of science fiction no longer defined by the opposition between the fictional and the real, as he explains in "Crash" and "Simulation et science-fiction," in his *Simulacres et simulation* (Paris: Editions Galilée, 1981), pp. 165–188.

9. William Gibson, "Rocket Radio," *Rolling Stone Magazine,* June 15, 1989, p. 85.

10. As one example of this tendency, consider the description of Deane's office in *Neuromancer:*

[Deane's] offices were located in a warehouse behind Ninsei, part of which seemed to have been sparsely decorated, years before, with a random collection of European furniture, as though Deane had once intended to use the place as his home. Neo-Aztec bookcases gathered dust against one wall of the room where Case waited. A pair of bulbous Disney-styled table lamps perched awkwardly on a low Kandinsky-look coffee table in scarlet-lacquered steel. A Dali clock hung on the wall between the bookcases, its distorted face sagging to the bare concrete floor. Its hands were holograms that altered to match the convolutions of the face as they rotated, but it never told the correct time. The room was stacked with white fiberglass shipping modules that gave off the tang of preserved ginger. (N 12)

11. Darko Suvin, "On Gibson and Cyberpunk SF," in *Storming the Reality Studio: A Casebook of Cyberpunk and Postmodern Science Fiction* (Durham N.C.: Duke University Press, 1991), pp. 349–365, underscores the appropriateness of Gibson's use of "the Japanese name and tradition of *zaibatsu*" to designate the "multinational corporations that control entire economies." Suvin maintains that it is not simply a matter of the pop cultural association of Japan with high-tech: "there is a deeper justification, a geopolitical or perhaps geoeconomical and psychological logic, in his choosing such 'nipponizing' vocabulary. This logic is centered on how strangely and yet peculiarly appropriate Japanese feudal-style capitalism is as an analogue or, indeed, ideal template for the new feudalism of present-day corporate monopolies" (p. 353).

12. In "Rocket Radio," Gibson declares: "I belong to a generation of Americans who dimly recall the world prior to television. . . . the world before television equates with the world before the Net—the mass culture and the mechanisms of Information." (85)

13. For discussion of the changes in cyberspace in Gibson's Sprawl trilogy,

see Lance Olsen, "The Shadow of Spirit in William Gibson's Matrix Trilogy," *Extrapolation* 32, 3 (1991), pp. 278–289; and John Christie, "Of AIs and Others: William Gibson's Transit," in *Fiction 2000: Cyberpunk and the Future of Narrative,* ed. George Slusser and Tom Shippey (Athens: University of Georgia Press, 1992), pp. 171–182.

14. See "Plateau Ten" in Deleuze and Guattari, *Thousand Plateaus,* for a discussion of Deleuzian "becoming" and alliances with demons. The term *demon* is especially felicitous in *Neuromancer,* since in computer terminology it refers to event-driven subroutines that respond automatically to changes in the environment. Manual DeLanda, *War in the Age of Intelligent Machines* (New York: Zone Books, 1991), discusses extensively the role of demons as a means of allowing a computer network to self-organize and the part they play in the development of robotic intelligence.

15. For a technical description of such a Riemannian space, which Riemann calls a "multiply extended manifold," see Bernhard Riemann, "On the Hypotheses Which Lie at the Foundation of Geometry," in *A Source Book in Mathematics,* ed. David Eugene Smith (New York: McGraw-Hill, 1929), pp. 411–425.

16. Several critics have downplayed the importance of *détournement* and cyberspace as a future site of resistance to multinational capitalism and have even denounced Gibson's fiction for its failure to propose "a progressive politics" by which the dystopian future he represents might be transformed. Istvan Csicsery-Ronay, for example, reads the exploits of the cyberspace cowboys as allegories about the plight of the artist in "a cybernetically organized dynamic social system [and] the general problem of individuals' imaginative vision in a hyper-real world of signs." Csicsery-Ronay's essay is valuable, however, for the links he establishes between Gibson and Italian Futurism, even though the connection could perhaps be pursued more fruitfully in relation to the Futurist conception of a dynamic space. See Csicsery-Ronay, "The Sentimental Futurist: Cybernetics and Art in William Gibson's *Neuromancer,*" *Critique: Studies in Modern Fiction* 33, 3 (1992), pp. 221–240.

More negatively, Andrew Ross, in his *Strange Weather: Culture, Science and Technology in the Age of Limits* (London: Verso, 1991), faults Gibson and cyberpunk fiction in general for romanticizing computer hackers. Aside from being "almost exclusively white, masculine, and middle-class" and oddly associated (by Ross) with yuppie gentrification in the '80s, hackers are egregiously represented as "apprentice architects" in a future "dominated by knowledge, expertise, and 'smartness' " (90). For a compelling (and smart) analysis of why what hackers do *is* politically and intellectually important, see De Landa, *War in the Age of Intelligent Machines.*

17. See Larry McCaffery, "Introduction: The Desert of the Real"; McCaffery and Richard Kadrey, '"Cyberpunk 101: A Schematic Guide"; and Brian McHale, "POSTcyberMODERNpunkISM," all in McCaffery, *Storming the Reality Studio,* pp. 1–29, 308–323.

18. Friedrich Kittler, *Grammophon Film Typewriter* (Berlin: Brinkmann & Rose, 1986). Quotations are taken from the English translation of the first chapter, which appeared in *October* 41 (Summer 1987), pp. 101–118.

19. Gibson, "Rocket Radio," p. 87.

20. See chap. 2, n. 25.

21. As Kittler acknowledges in an interview by Laurence Rickels, "Spooky Electricity," *Artforum,* December 1992, p. 68.

22. Friedrich Kittler, "There Is No Software," *Stanford Literary Review,* 9, 1 (1992). Page numbers for quotations appear in the text.

23. As Gibson admits in the documentary film *Cyberpunk,* as well as in the introduction to the tenth-anniversary edition of *Neuromancer* (New York: Ace Books, 1994).

24. See Peter Schwenger, "*Aggripa,* or, The Apocalyptic Book," *South Atlantic Quarterly* 91, 3 (1992), pp. 617–626. My comments are based on the description Schwenger supplies.

Coda

1. Significantly, Pat Cadigan is the only woman writer included in Bruce Sterling's anthology of cyberpunk fiction, *Mirrorshades* (New York: Arbor House, 1986). What makes her fiction stand out, however, is that it connects the worlds of music and video with the new computerized communications Net. It is interesting to note in this regard that in their discussion of the machinic phylum in *A Thousand Plateaus,* trans. Brian Massumi (Minneapolis: University of Minnesota, 1987; orig. pub. 1980), Gilles Deleuze and Félix Guattari draw attention to the "essential relation" of metallurgy with music, both being sustained by a "widened chromaticism" (411). Although thematically important, the relationship in *Synners* between heavy-metal music (called "speed-thrash" in the novel) and the new silicon extensions of the machinic phylum cannot be pursued here.

2. Pat Cadigan, *Synners* (New York: Bantam, 1991), p. 435. Page numbers for all subsequent quotations appear in the text.

3. See Anne Balsamo, "Forms of Technological Embodiment: Reading the Body in Contemporary Culture," in *Cyberspace/Cyberbodies/Cyberpunk*, ed. Mike Featherstone and Roger Burrows (London: Sage Publications, 1995), pp. 215–237.

4. Cf. Jean Baudrillard on the "fractal subject" in his essay "Videowelt und Fraktales Subjekt," in *Philosophien der neuen Technologie* (Berlin: Merve Verlag, 1989), p. 113, my trans.:

> The fractal object is characterized by the fact that all the information relative to the object is contained in the least of its details. In the same way we can speak today of a fractal subject diffracted into a multitude of miniature egos, all like each other and de-multiplied in an embryonic mode, as in a biological culture saturating its environment through scissiparity to infinity. Just as the fractal object resembles its elementary components trait for trait, the fractal subject dreams only of ressembling itself in each one of its fractions. It involutes on this side of representation, toward the smallest molecular fraction of itself. A strange Narcissus, dreaming no longer of its ideal image but of a genetic formula of reproduction to infinity.

5. In Bruce Sterling's *Schismatrix* (1985), the ex-orbital genetic-cyborg schism (the Shapers vs. the Mechanists) and the ensuing prefigurations of the posthuman provide evidence of a similar reconfiguration of subjectivity.

6. Ibid., p. 115–116.

7. Kevin Kelly, *Out of Control: The Rise of Neo-Biological Civilization* (Reading, Mass.: Addison-Wesley, 1994), p. 21.

Index

bodies (*cont.*)
limits of, 254; machinic, 17–8, 226;
and material forces, 22; material/
nonmaterial, 262; as meat, 247, 259–60;
mediated, 261; parts of, 137–8, 144;
stochasticism of, 220; and word, 65, 128
Boolean algebra, 46, 62
Borges, Jorge Luis, 44, 276n22
brain: and artificial intelligence, 246–7;
and machine, 62, 104–5, 215; models
of, 262; as multiplicity, 281n29; in
Neuromancer, 243; parallel processing
in, 104–7; in *Synners,* 258–9
breakdown, 126–8, 158, 285n17
Burroughs, William, 5, 14, 19–25, 56,
229, 234, 250–1, 272nn21&26

Cadigan, Pat, 5, 6, 19, 56, 295n1; *Synners,* 5, 6, 57, 257–65
capitalism, 7, 13, 30, 233, 238; abuses of,
142–3, 162; and art, 134, 146–55; corporate, 64, 129, 138–9, 269n1,
293n11; as cybernetic, 125–7, 161,
267n2, 294n16; effects of, 137, 159–
60; flows of, 125–8, 153, 157, 240–1;
and the literary, 155–6; and postmodernism, 120–2; resistance to, 175, 232;
and schizophrenia, 65; as social reality,
25–6, 128, 176, 210, 233; and zaibatsu
form of, 238, 242, 250, 260, 264,
293n11
Carrouges, Michel, 5, 268n11
chaos: and entropy, 135–6, 148; of human lives, 125–6; and information, 7,
136, 254; and the stock market, 125;
theory of, 2, 275n16; verbal, 131
cinema, 38, 62, 67, 74, 279n5; and consciousness, 31–3; and drugs, 76–7,
228–9; and interface, 70–1, 77–8; as
realm of the dead, 225
circuits: communication, 40–2, 128, 134,
139; feedback, 220; sub rosa, 47; and
switching relays, 45–6
circulation: and art, 134, 154; and capitalism, 125–6; and exchange, 143; and
generalized flow, 124–5

coding, 22, 27–30, 65, 70, 78, 81–4,
166–7, 179, 235, 278n43; escape from,
156; and presignifying regime, 91–2; se-
miotic/asignifying, 58
commodification, 25, 27, 144, 210, 233,
235, 286n20
communication(s): assemblage, 234; and
coding, 27–30; and delimitation of experience, 49; delirious, 96; and disorder, 131; disruption of, 127; fiber-optic, 207, 225, 234, 251, 255; flow of,
123–6, 201–3; industry of, 25, 277n33;
network of, 253, 259; new spaces of,
252; as nomological, 2; otherworldly,
67, 69–70; of plot/life lines, 192
complicity, 145–7, 180, 187–8, 209
computer, 12, 55, 188–91, 213, 218, 224
connection(s): via breaks/flows, 128; degree of media, 57; excess, 119; lines of,
106–7; management of, 139; multiplicity of, 110
consciousness, 12, 99, 117, 215–6; and
betweenness, 99, 117; complex, 34, 98,
270n7; and difference, 120–2; as filter,
36; fractalization of, 31, 263–4, 271,
296n4; as images, 72; and
informational systems, 54; machinic, 4,
98; and mediality, 33, 119–22, 215;
and memes, 104; as multiplicity, 31–8;
space of, 106–7; of virus, 260
conspiracy, 44, 80, 186–205
control: and abstract machine, 85–6;
apparatus of, 19, 21, 29, 178, 221–2,
228; and chemistry, 83–4; and coding,
65, 232; and feedback, 136; limits
of, 210, 230; networks of, 121–2,
224
counterculture, 208, 213, 218, 232–3,
260, 262
counter-signifying regime, 91–4
cryptonym, 199, 202, 205, 290n33
cut-up-fold-in method, 19–25
cybernetic machine, 26; capitalism as,
161; society as, 56, 126
cybernetics, 1, 8, 29, 54, 85–6, 136,
269n15

information (*cont.*)
218–9; and machines, 25–6; and machinic world, 127; maximum, 136; and mediality, 99, 119–22; as medium of exchange, 80; and noise, 41, 50, 96, 133; as probabilistic, 12; proliferation of, 7, 11, 14, 101–3, 161, 165; and psychic apparatus, 53; quest for, 177; and signifying regime, 96; theory, 1, 8, 32–3, 40–1, 50, 85–6, 136; time of, 207; as viral, 2–3, 24–5; and writing, 54–5
information multiplicity, 56–7, 187–8, 205, 234; and betweenness, 119–22; defined, 3, 13; novels of, 7–8, 12–4, 57–8, 97, 136; processes of coding and overflow, 27–30; as product of capitalism, 161; and psychic apparatus, 31–8
inscription: author as, 198; machinic, 159; and mediality, 132; tracks of, 106
intensities: and anxiety, 120; and Deleuze, 202–4; of machinic interactions, 127
interface, 86, 207, 254; and algorithm, 255; cyborgian, 250, 265; defined, 65, 70–8, 81, 214, 225; Eastern/Western, 88; and media, 95, 119–22, 207; rocket as, 82; subject as, 126
interpretation: hermeneutical, 51, 277n33; Marxist, 45, 121–2; and public relations, 141; and recoding, 82; scene of, 90–1; and text as machine, 51

Jameson, Frederic, 44–5, 120–2, 180, 187, 269n1
jargon, 131, 134, 169–70
Joyce, James, 11, 33, 41, 58, 63, 105, 155, 205, 273n6
Jung, C. G., 86, 222–3

Kafka, Franz, 17–8, 37
karma, adjustment of, 225–6
Kittler, Friedrich, 33, 54, 56, 58, 64, 68–9, 119–20, 123, 207, 220, 223, 224, 251–4

Lacan, Jacques, 33, 54–5, 94, 117, 119, 215, 219–24, 253

Lang, Fritz, and "Die Frau im Mond," 71–2
language: of accounting, 226; agrammatical, 153; of capitalist regimes, 129; and capture/control, 85–6; and coding, 29–30, 70; and consciousness-as-multiplicity, 33; and feedback effects, 170–1; machine of, 156; of machinic flow, 125–7; as medium, 58; and nuclear warfare, 169–70; of pure information, 218–9; and signifying regime, 96, 278n43; as site of contestation, 166; specialized, 169–70; and the symbolic, 119; as viral agent, 23
Leibniz, Gottfried, 44, 71
logic: and array of possibilities, 42–6; of capital/death, 182–3; of commodification, 233; of diagrammatic lines, 189; of drugs, 229; of mass media, 167; operational, 125–6, 143; of reminiscence, 131; of reversibility, 170–1, 184; and rhythms of flow, 123
Luhmann, Niklas, 31, 47–8
Lyotard, Jean-François, 56–7, 126

machine(s): abstract, 65, 86; autonomous order of, 219–20; bachelor, 268n11; and brain, 62; capitalist, 27–9; change for, 258; cinematic, 83; cybernetic, 27; desiring, 17–8, 82–3, 128, 161, 248–9; flesh as reading, 247; infernal, 126–7; information, 220; language, 156; soft, 23; universal, 253, 276n25; writing, 71, 122, 166, 225–6, 252, 291
machinic: assemblage, 248; breaks, 216; consciousness, 98; defined, 127–8, 284n6; enslavement, 25–6; generation, 155; interaction, 215, 226, 262; vs. mechanistic, 127–8; novel, 157, 160–2; perception, 229; phylum, 128, 246, 249, 254, 265, 292n1, 295n1; relation to technologies, 12; and representation, 160; sensorium, 31–3

2; and mediality, 55, 118; and novels of
information multiplicity, 31–8
Pynchon, Thomas, 3, 6, 18, 98, 234–5,
250, 252–3, 255; *The Crying of Lot
49*, 7, 38–40, 42–52, 56–8, 100, 136,
206, 229; *Gravity's Rainbow*, 3–7, 50,
57, 62–96, 165, 173, 188, 206, 214,
228–9, 231–2; *Vineland*, 5, 8, 57, 185,
206–32, 255

reading effects, 213, 217–8, 225
real, 55, 69, 203, 208, 216, 224; cutting
into, 38, 214–7; encoding of, 220; and
fictional, 12, 205, 212, 269n4, 292n8;
and film, 23, 71, 272n24, 280n20;
Lacanian, 119, 220, 253; and
operational, 143; and ruptured cause/
effect, 76–7
realm of the dead, 184, 208, 213, 222–
32, 255–6
reference: dysfunctionality of, 127; mixed
universes of, 207; molecularizing
Tubal, 230
reflexivity, 43, 126, 189
regime: audiovisual, 187; of capital, 26,
125–6, 155; cinematic/televisual, 217;
cybernetic, 27; of the image, 179, 181;
paranoid-despotic, 93; post-signifying,
92–3; machinic, 127; semiotic, 58, 65,
82, 91
religion, 88–9, 91, 210
replication, 3, 104, 166
representation: and capitalism, 155; and
consciousness, 16, 38, 270n7; and
event, 202–3, 265; and fiction, 34, 103,
129; and film, 180; of history, 192,
203–4; and perception, 174; and
psychic apparatus, 58; and
terminology, 64; unstable forms of, 23–
4, 166, 172, 229
repression, 117, 208, 210, 218, 259–61;
history as structure of, 88–9
resonance, 192, 202–5
reversibility, 170–1, 184
rhizome, 14, 22
Riemannian space, 250, 253, 274n8

ritual, 166–7, 170, 174–5, 181–2
rocket: and cinematic interface, 71; and
reterritorialization, 90; -state, 62, 80–
90; V-2, 62–4

saturation: of flows, 157; of information,
12, 106; media, 207–8, 210
scene: as agency, 44–5; and
communications network, 128; and
cyberspace, 242; of reading, 213, 217–
8; and screen, 126; of writing, 53, 254
schizophrenia: and capitalism, 65, 120;
and deterritorialization, 228; and
dispersion of identity, 198–9
Schreber, Judge Daniel Paul, 270n8
scriptive systems, 97, 119–22, 193–5
self: and absence of transcendent
position, 46; as cinematic, 216; as
conduit of information, 127;
-consciousness, 42–3; and constructed
identities, 72; as ex-orbital, 6, 263–4;
extension of, 259; and mediality,
119
self-organization: of computer network,
294n14; and noise, 50; systems of, 2,
136
semiotic: flow, 128, 136; regimes, 91–4;
structure, 43–4
semiotics: asignifying, 278n43; and
history, 86–7; and language, 278n43;
subliminal, 56
sexuality: and control, 85; and
cyberspace, 261; and electronic parts,
134; in Gibson, 247–9; machinic, 46–
7; repression-liberation of, 176,
288n14; and rocket bombs, 66; and
sadomasochism, 67, 73
Shannon, Claude, 2, 32, 40–2, 46, 50,
61–2, 136, 206
signs, 55, 58, 119, 125–7, 278n43
silicon, and machinic phylum, 233, 246,
249, 254, 292n1, 295n1
simulacra, 8, 172, 202–4
simulation, 12, 172, 184, 237, 240, 249,
255
sound, 16, 23, 132, 159

Library of Congress Cataloging-in-Publication Data

Johnston, John, 1953–
    Information multiplicity : American fiction in the age of media
saturation / John Johnston.
        p.   cm.
    Includes bibliographical references (p.   ) and index.
    ISBN 0-8018-5704-X (alk. paper). — ISBN 0-8018-5705-8 (pbk. :
alk. paper)
    1. American fiction—20th century—History and criticism.   2. Mass
media and literature—United States—History—20th century.
3. Literature and technology—United States—History—20th century.
4. Technology and civilization in literature.   5. Postmodernism
(Literature)—United States.   6. Information technology—United
States.   7. Information science in literature.   8. Mass media—
United States.   I. Title.
PS374.M43J64   1998
813′.5409356—dc21   97-33148
                                                                            CIP